Please renew/return this item by the last date shown.

So that your telephone call is charged ~~ rate,
please call th~

HERTFORDSHIRE LIBRARY SERVICE

**Please return this book on or before the last
date shown or ask for it to be renewed**

L32/rev79

D1389781

JUVAT IMPIGROS DEUS

The Borough Arms: an interpretation by L. E. Rothwell

THE STORY OF
Huddersfield

ROY BROOK

With a Foreword by
THE RT. HON. HAROLD WILSON
O.B.E., M.P.

———

Introduction by
ALDERMAN JACK SYKES
Mayor of Huddersfield

MACGIBBON & KEE

FIRST PUBLISHED 1968 BY MACGIBBON AND KEE LTD
3 UPPER JAMES STREET GOLDEN SQUARE LONDON WI
COPYRIGHT © ROY BROOK 1968
PRINTED IN GREAT BRITAIN BY
EBENEZER BAYLIS AND SON LTD
THE TRINITY PRESS
WORCESTER AND LONDON

The drawing of the Market Cross on the title page
is by Noël Spencer

63.R PS

SBN: 261.61983.7

134421.
942.813

FOREWORD

by

The Rt. Hon. Harold Wilson

O.B.E., M.P.

ONE HUNDRED years ago Huddersfield was a group of villages. It still is; but in the meantime, without losing their identity or independence of spirit, these villages have become a great industrial community, bound together by pride and skill.

Huddersfield men and women go for quality in cloth, in engineering, in chemicals, in anything we produce. We expect quality in music, in sport and in the other things we enjoy. Without being arrogant, we are proud of our town and will be prouder still when at last we can abolish the dirt which still prevents the stone of our buildings, the water of our streams and the peat of our surrounding moors from showing their full beauty.

Huddersfield will change in the next hundred years. It will rise to still greater heights. But in the changes two things, I hope, will remain unchanged—the search for quality and the neighbourliness which has grown from our village roots.

HAROLD WILSON

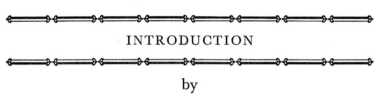

INTRODUCTION

by
Alderman Jack Sykes
Mayor of Huddersfield

THIS BOOK is one of the ways in which the County Borough of Huddersfield celebrates and commemorates one hundred years of Borough status.

The task of writing this book was entrusted to Major Roy Brook, M.A., a native of Huddersfield, who was educated at The College in New North Road. He expressed a desire to do this work, largely as a labour of love; whether he has since regretted undertaking such a heavy commitment, I do not know. But I do know that he has spared neither time nor effort in his determination to produce a book worthy of its subject and of the occasion.

The author was invited to write the story of Huddersfield and its people in such a form that the ordinary folk of every age group would want to read it and would find it interesting. At the same time, it had to be accurate, as far as possible, in fact and detail, to withstand examination by critics, specialists and historians.

Although he started with the advantage of a personal knowledge of Huddersfield, the author had to undertake a great deal of research and has been assiduous in checking his facts with historians and consulting the best authorities he could find on the many facets of life and activity which make up the town and community.

Older readers will enjoy re-living the scenes and activities which were the background to their youth: the younger generation will find the book gives an insight and understanding of the factors of character, geography and climate which have combined to make Huddersfield a town of which its citizens are proud.

CONTENTS

x   *Contents*

ILLUSTRATIONS

ILLUSTRATIONS IN THE TEXT

PREFACE

WHEN I left Huddersfield in October 1946 I little thought that
I was never again to live there permanently. Thus, for over
twenty years my visits have been confined to occasional periods
of university vacation or of leave from the Forces. Each time I
returned I noticed that my circle of friends had decreased with
the passage of time. As a soldier, I am accustomed to setting up
home wherever I happen to be stationed, but for most servicemen there is somewhere in England regarded as 'home'. In my
case I discovered some years ago that I was becoming a stranger
in my own town. Since I began to collect material for this
book this is no longer the case and I now feel that I really
belong to Huddersfield once more.

Living at a distance from the town has, however, had its
advantages. I have been able to return to London after each
visit and then to look at Huddersfield from a distance of both
space and time. My absence over the years and my position of
political neutrality have, I hope, made it possible for me to look
at the town impartially whilst retaining my own deep sense of
regard for Huddersfield and her citizens. Naturally, there are
many things one might criticise; this ought to be true of any
place which really lives and changes over the years.

My travels have taken me to many places in the world but,
on reflection, I can honestly say that the people of Huddersfield
have much of which to be proud and many things for which to
be thankful. Writing this history has been for me very much a
labour of love and each visit very much a sentimental journey.
I have come to regard this task as a privilege and I hope that
some of my readers will discover opportunities of looking
further into the history of their town.

I must pay tribute to some of those who have helped make
the production of this book possible, their names are not
necessarily given in any order of priority.

First I must thank the Prime Minister and the Mayor for

their words of encouragement. The Town Clerk, Mr Bann, and Mr Beverley, the Mayor's Secretary, who have been most helpful at all times, have been my permanent link with the Borough Council. My principal source of local information has been the Huddersfield Public Library, through the kindness of Mr Aldridge, Mr Dibnah and Mrs Kipling. At the *Huddersfield Examiner* Office my contact has been Mr Ford from whom has come information, advice and some of the illustrations. Many of the line drawings and the book jacket have come from the Huddersfield School of Art at the College of Technology through the good offices of Mr Maris. All the heraldic material in the book is the original work of Edward Rothwell and the quality of this will be self-evident to the reader. The index has been prepared by Miss Miller, now in retirement from the Huddersfield Public Library. Two London friends who previously assisted me with a similar project, Peter Harrison and Arthur Boughey, have again been of inestimable help with respectively checking the text and drawing some of the maps. My namesake, Roy Brook of Crosland Moor, has supplied many of the photographs, including one specially taken for this book. I have also had valuable help in checking the proofs from my friend David Pennyfather. My secretary, Mrs Howell, and my typist, Mrs Fenn, have managed to read my writing, coping with most of the book through all its many stages. J. P. W. Mallalieu, M.P. has been of practical assistance and encouragement to the venture from its outset. Philip Ahier, who once taught me at Huddersfield College and now lives in retirement in his native Jersey, has read through every word of the text in its first draft. Much detailed professional advice has been received from Dr T. B. Caldwell of the School of History, the University of Leeds, and from Professor E. M. Cairns-Wilson, now retired from the London School of Economics.

Finally I should like to thank all the members of the Centenary Sub-Committee for inviting me to undertake this task and for the way in which they have supported me at every stage; in particular I should like to mention Alderman Clifford Stephenson whose encouragement and experience have proved invaluable.

Others who have helped are listed at the end of the book and to any I have unintentionally omitted I can only, at this stage, tender my sincere apologies and grateful appreciation.

Eltham s.e.9. August 1967 ROY BROOK

HUDDERSFIELD—AS SEEN BY OTHERS

'In Odersfelt, Godwin had six carucates of land to be taxed . . . but it is waste'. 1086: Extract from *Domesday Book*.

'I rode over the mountains to Huddersfield. A wilder people I never saw in England . . . [they] seemed ready to devour us.' 1757: John Wesley in his diary.

'. . . Huddersfield . . . the handsomest by far of all the factory towns of Yorkshire and Lancashire by reason of . . . its modern architecture.' 1844: Friedrich Engels; *The Condition of the Working Class in England*.

'We know of scarcely another Institute that can compare with it'. [referring to Huddersfield Mechanics' Institute]. 1853: James Hole in his *History and Management of Mechanics' Institutions*.

'London should emulate Glasgow, Liverpool, Dublin, Nottingham and HUDDERSFIELD in a large-scale municipal housing programme.' 1891: a demand made by Sidney Webb in his 'London Programme'.

'Huddersfield is plainly in a dark and pagan condition.' 1930: George Bernard Shaw, after poor support for his play *Back to Methuselah* at the Theatre Royal.

'Of Huddersfield Station: . . . the most splendid station façade in England'. 1964: John Betjeman in an article entitled 'Huddersfield Discovered'.

'The post-war rebuilding of the larger towns in the West Riding is a dismal story . . . relieved only by the example of Huddersfield'. 1968: Derek Linstrum in *The Dalesman*.

These iron moors and unrelenting hills
Do not give up their secrets easily;
What they have seen is carved too deep
Among the embedded rocks for passers-by
To find, for idle wanderers to pluck
Like flowers, haphazard at the wild wayside.

Only those generations that have sucked
At this hard breast can sense the deep-seated heart,
Conjure life-giving warmth and love
From such maternity; but, this achieved,
Nothing except their own default can blight
The rich harvest of their strength and will.

But always, and here above all, there is no finish
To the work without some payment due,
No joy unstained by tears; here above all
Hope stirs the dust of disappointment
As readily as it will crown success;
Here what we have is earned, and proudly earned,
Here we can dare the years to brand our pride as sin.

PETER HARRISON

To the children of Huddersfield
—of all ages

CHAPTER I

Unwritten History

WHEN I was a schoolboy I saw the excavations of 1939 at Castle Hill. The diggers did not open up much of the ground but worked in trenches cut at various parts of the site for no apparent reason to my boy's eye. The work was continued after the war and this opening chapter is based on the results of such excavations and upon geological and botanical evidence, all the fruits of many years' patient endeavour by numerous investigators.

Apart from the works of a few classical authors like Tacitus, our knowledge of the Roman period of English history comes from the finding of objects in the ground, especially coins and pottery which can be dated. Evidence of the post-Roman period up to the Norman Conquest is scanty and consists of an occasional stone cross perhaps bearing a fragmentary inscription, from which legend and outright fiction must first be discounted before anything of value can be deduced. In more recent years it is to the sciences that we have looked for help in our acquisition of knowledge of pre- and ancient history. Even so, our information is still far from complete and much of this chapter is necessarily conjecture. For the same reason few of the dates I quote should be taken as exact. The modern historian takes his facts and from their general trend produces a picture. The older historians often had few facts, and their stories were thus founded on very little evidence; but, for the want of better, they were widely accepted, though frequent copying from each other did little or nothing to widen the understanding.

Let us, then, begin our story before ten thousand years B.C. An icefield then stretched over Lancashire and Cheshire and the Vale of York was occupied by a glacier which reached to the valley of the Dearne. Thus when the Calder was blocked by ice at Horbury, water accumulated and in the valleys of the Colne, Holme, Fenay and Calder all land below 400 feet was submerged. At this period Huddersfield lay below the waters of Lake Calderdale (*see illustration*) but the land above 1,200 feet was not covered by the ice.

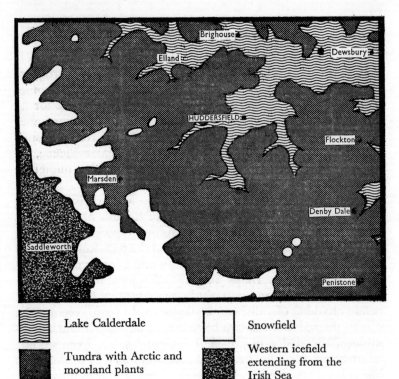

≈≈≈	Lake Calderdale	☐	Snowfield
▓▓▓	Tundra with Arctic and moorland plants	░░░	Western icefield extending from the Irish Sea

By about 7000 B.C. the climate became milder, and forests grew right over the summit of the Pennines and these eventually brought man to our area. This was Mesolithic man, a hunter, and fisherman, who generally lived above 1,000 feet. Flint tools used by these men as scrapers and cutters have been found on March Hill, Windy Hill, Pots and Pans Hill, West Nab and Wessenden Moor. Many are tiny arrowheads which have been named 'microliths'. The occupation of these sites was spasmodic however; perhaps Mesolithic man used the Pennines as a hunting ground where he lived in temporary huts or tents, or the 'microliths' were left by travellers going north.

About 6000 B.C. the climate deteriorated and, with increased rainfall and a lowering of the temperature, began to resemble our own; and the waters of the English Channel began to divide England from the Continent. The rain swelled the rivers and Lake Calderdale, blocked at the eastern end with clay and boulders left behind by the Vale of York glacier, burst its banks. All rivers in our area running into the then fast flowing Calder began to cut deeper channels in the hillsides, while the valley bottoms, silted up with sand and gravel, became swampy. On the tops of the hills the soil became sour, peat accumulated and as the summit forest decayed, so cotton grass began to make more peat as it grew and died each year. Man at this stage occupied the land between about 400 and 1,000 feet, where there was mixed woodland on the lower ground and birch forest with grass higher up.

After 4000 B.C. came Neolithic man. In our area he kept animals and made pottery. The Neolithic people used stone axes to fell the trees and their flint arrowheads reach a perfection of primitive workmanship. Stone axes, known as 'celts', and flint implements have all been found together. Neolithic finds have been made at Castleshaw, High Flatts, Meltham Moor, Windy Hill and Holme Moss; and, more interestingly, items have been found at Moldgreen and Woodsome Hall from which one might possibly assume that these people were beginning to move to lower altitudes.

By about 2000 B.C. the West of England was producing bronze, but Bronze Age finds are scarce. Bronze Age man in our area frequently used flint probably because metal was hard to come by. The most important site for us is at Pule Hill near Marsden, where a Bronze Age burial site containing cups, and food vessels holding burnt human remains has been found.

Around 600 B.C. the Celtic people, who used iron, gradually overtook the Bronze Age folk. As we know, they reached this area and they possibly left some of their names behind, for Calder has been derived from 'Celldwyer', the river of wooded waters. The tribe probably occupying the district at this time was that known as the Brigantes, the 'hill folk', a name derived from the Celtic word 'bryn'. Hardly any Iron Age relics have been found around Huddersfield despite the fact that this period lasted until the first century A.D. and the coming of the Romans.

Although we know the Brigantes had influence at various times from Lincolnshire to North Yorkshire, coins found at Lightcliffe are those of the Coritani, a Midland tribe, thus indicating that the Brigantes were themselves subject to influence from other people. However, Castle Hill was certainly fortified by the Brigantes, and it is hard to imagine this being done with flint tools; they must surely have used iron digging implements. All known settlements of this period are below the maximum altitudes and yet away from the valleys, thus Castle Hill may have been a refuge rather than a place of permanent occupation.

Castle Hill was excavated in August-September 1939, and again from 1947 onwards. The findings have established that, about 200 B.C., a small earthwork was built at the western end of the hill, but this was found to be not prominent enough, so the whole of the hill was enclosed in a series of double banks and ditches with a very elaborate north eastern entrance. By the first century B.C. it must have been decided that mounds and ditches alone were insufficient and the inner walls were rebuilt. Here we meet a very early example of the way warfare speeds up technology; a double dry stone wall was filled with alternate layers of shale and timber; then the whole was fired and this formed in places, a solid clinker core. This was a Gaulish idea and produced a wall of great strength. An alternative theory is that the wall was fired by the Romans at a later date. This inner wall was surrounded by yet another pair of banks and ditches with sloping sides. Sharp stakes driven into the ditches may have served as a defence against a frontal attack by chariots—a kind of early tank trap. This was a likely stronghold of Queen Cartimandua of the Brigantes.

After about 75 B.C. there was a migration of Belgic tribes from the continent to England in the wake of the Romans as they conquered Gaul. The Belgae never infiltrated to the north but they introduced coinage to Southern England, some of which eventually reached our area, as we have seen.

Caesar came to Britain in 55 and 54 B.C. because the Belgae
were helping their friends in Gaul and his commission to
conquer Gaul might have been interpreted as including all the
Belgae wherever they were; also Britain was believed to be rich
and Caesar was short of money.

These expeditions were only of propaganda value, but they
did whet the appetite of future conquerors, and by A.D. 43 the
Emperor Claudius could resist the temptation of England no
longer. He sent Aulus Plautius, a most distinguished commander, with the II, IX, XIV, XX Legions and part of the VIII
Legion. Each Legion had 4,500 regular Roman soldiers, 4,500
auxiliaries (colonial troops) and 1,000 cavalry. Thus about
50,000 men came altogether. Claudius extracted tribute from
some of the British tribal areas, probably including that of the
Brigantes; and, before leaving for Rome as 'Claudius Britan-
nicus', he ordered Aulus Plautius to conquer the rest of the
island.

By A.D. 51 Caratacus, the leader of the defeated Welsh,
sought refuge with Queen Cartimandua, possibly at Castle
Hill. Cartimandua, in a friendly gesture towards the Romans,
handed over her refugee to Ostorius Scapula, the Roman
commander. This betrayal led to a quarrel with her husband
Venutius who began to threaten Cartimandua. The Queen
there appealed to the new Roman Governor, Aulus Didius. A
detachment of the IX Legion arrived in the district, she was
rescued, and a truce was made.

With the arrival of Petilius Cerialis as governor in A.D. 71 an
interest in the north was aroused amongst the Romans. He had
previously commanded the IX Legion at Lincoln and was now
personally responsible for moving that Legion to York. One
result of this move was that a road was made through Doncaster
and Castleford both as a means of supervising the Brigantes and
ultimately of attacking the tribes further north. Some time
about this period the XX Legion was moved to Chester.

The large Roman fortresses at York and Chester were each designed to accommodate a legion but Frontinus, Roman Governor A.D. 74 to 77, who was also a military engineer, intended
that there should be a small fortress at the end of every day's
march along each principal highway. Each fort or *castellum*

should hold one cohort, about five hundred men, and the design should be on lines very similar to the larger fortress or *castra*.

Agricola, who arrived in A.D. 78, turned his attention to the Brigantes, building forts at Slack and Castleshaw on a route over the Pennines. In A.D. 80 he set out for Scotland where he reached the Forth-Clyde valley and sailed his fleet round the north coast to establish that Britain was, in fact, an island. Trajan was Governor from A.D. 98 to 117 and he attempted to rebuild all the *castella* in stone, so as to replace the wooden buildings, with roofs of thatch or tile.

About A.D. 120 the IX Legion at York disappeared, virtually without trace, and as some of its officers were later found serving in Africa, it would appear that the Legion had suffered a major defeat, perhaps through its own fault, and for this reason was not re-formed. Be that as it may, the Emperor Hadrian came over personally in A.D. 121 or 122 to deal with the trouble. The VI Legion went to York, and then Hadrian decided to build the wall, from the Tyne to the Solway Firth, for which he is today chiefly remembered. When the wall was finished in A.D. 127 some 55,000 men were needed to man it; consequently about three quarters of all the soldiers in Britain were sent to the wall. Concentrating most of the troops in one place, represented a large-scale risk which was, on the whole, successful.

At Slack there were the usual five hundred men under a Prefect. Supplies and heavy weapons came from York. There was a *praetorium* or headquarters containing two courtyards, one open and one roofed over. Although it may have been intended to rebuild all four barrack blocks in stone, when the camp was abandoned only one block had been completed, with glass in the windows and tiles on the roof. The garrison consisted of the IV Cohort of the Breuci; this we know from a number of tiles, made in a tile kiln found in Grimscar Woods, and stamped 'COH IIII BRE'.

Slack was a regular square-shaped camp, with its corners at the four cardinal points and there was much activity outside its walls. There were built the '*canabae*', huts containing settlers or camp followers, local people and Romanised Britons who traded with the soldiers and supplied them with comforts; indeed outside a large camp a whole town sometimes grew. Also outside lay the bath house, with hot rooms, cold room and lounge. The baths, that traditional Roman amenity, became a kind of social club, and gaming counters have been found there. The impression left by all this, is that the Romans at Slack were never hemmed in by hostile tribesmen. Few weapons were ever found there and the whole area around Outlane appears to have been peaceful and prosperous under the Roman occupation.

At Castleshaw two forts have been found, one inside the other. The outer fort was probably built about A.D. 80 and was slightly smaller than Slack; but it was abandoned, probably about A.D. 90, and in 104 a much smaller fort was built capable of housing no more than two hundred soldiers. Castleshaw was abandoned around 120 and the Romans left Slack in 140—or possibly a little later.

The reason generally accepted for the abandonment of both forts was the building of a much better road, properly metalled, over Blackstone Edge. This road ran through Ripponden and Greetland to the Calder.

A Roman altar found at Longwood is dedicated both to the God of the Brigantes and to the Emperor, showing an intermingling of cultures. Thus Romanisation did develop in this area despite the isolation of the people in their small villages. The nearest villas, sure signs of Roman culture, were in Airedale.

As a consequence of the milking of the garrisons to man Hadrian's Wall the Brigantes rose again in A.D. 155; but to no avail, and Roman victory coins were struck to commemorate the end of the rising. At the close of the second century, however, Roman influence was on the wane though it persisted for another two hundred years. About the year A.D. 300, people in our area began to hoard coins, indicating a general feeling of insecurity; and from 350 there began the long struggle against the attacks of the Picts. In 383 some Roman armies were taken from Britain to fight in Europe, and by about 410 they had all gone from our shores, never to return.

To the local inhabitants of our area, the Romans were known

only as soldiers and there were no lasting conditions likely to encourage the spread of Roman civilisation. The *canabae* around the fort at Slack might have become a town but there is no evidence that these dwellings were occupied after the soldiers left; the Romans had traded with the natives and that was about all. As for place names, not one Roman name survives in our area. Further, within a few years of the departure of the Romans, Yorkshire itself was almost depopulated. The Britons, however Romanised, never learned to unite in self-defence, having always relied on the Legions; but East Yorkshire was certainly worth plundering, so the people, before they finally disappeared, suffered at the hands of the Saxons from over the North Sea, the Picts from Scotland and the Scots from Ireland.

About A.D. 500 the Anglo-Saxons came from northern Europe and settled in eastern England, intermarrying with such of the native population as remained. Thus, while the Saxons went to Essex, Sussex, and Middlesex, Yorkshire became the Anglian kingdom of Deira. Ida, King of Bernicia (Northumberland) conquered Deira and eventually by 635 the whole of Northumbria comprising Bernicia and Deira was one kingdom under Oswald. The kingdom remained intact until the Danes came in 867.

The Angles confining their attention to eastern Yorkshire had left the West Riding alone, and we find the kingdom of Loidis and Elmet existing as an independent British territory under King Cerdic whose daughter Hilda (614–680) became Abbess of Whitby. Cerdic died in 616, Elmet joined Deira under King Eadwine and in 627 Eadwine and Hilda were baptised in York by Paulinus who later established monasteries at York and Doncaster. Paulinus is alleged to have come to Dewsbury although his mission was to the pagan Angles and not to the Christian Britons of Loidis and Elmet.

A concentrated attack by the Britons of North Wales and the Angles of Mercia in 633 laid Deira waste; the King was killed but the Queen, the mother of Hilda, and Paulinus managed to escape. Only after Oswald had reconquered the whole of Northumbria was Anglian settlement possible in the Huddersfield area, and the extent of this settlement can be seen in the

8

origin of our place names. The Angles settled extensively to the east of Huddersfield and their place names include, besides Huddersfield, Edgerton, Lindley, Bradley and Birkby, a preponderance of villages in the area of Shepley, Shelley, Emley, Cawthorne and Clayton. They appear to have penetrated the Holme Valley as far as Honley but not to have left any trace in the Colne Valley. We believe the Angles formed isolated farming communities and probably penetrated very slowly westwards.

The centre of Anglian Christianity for much of the area we now know as the West Riding was Dewsbury and the original parish included Mirfield, Thornhill, Kirkheaton, Kirkburton, Bradford, Almondbury, Huddersfield and Halifax, stretching towards the Pennines as far as the settlements went. If we believe the old legend of his visit to preach and celebrate the Holy Communion, the Anglian parish was probably centred on an Abbey at Dewsbury founded by Paulinus.

These Anglian settlements flourished during the eighth century, but declined in the ninth when the Danes came. The Anglian Abbey system finally died in the tenth century and was replaced by the separate parishes of Huddersfield, Halifax, Almondbury, Kirkheaton and Kirkburton, each probably centred on a tenth century chapel. The Huddersfield area was late in being settled by the Danes and not many of their names have survived. They appear to have lived peaceably with the Angles from some time after 867. A number of pieces from stone crosses found at Dewsbury demonstrate the beautiful work of the Anglian masons, while a cross found at Kirkheaton shows Danish influence of the late tenth century. In the place-names of the period, the ending 'thorpe' is of Danish origin as in Northorpe, and Skelmanthorpe. The word 'Denby' may imply 'the dwelling of the Danes'.

From 930 to 940 the Norsemen drove in from the North West, through the Craven Gap. This may seem surprising until we learn that they came, in fact, from Scotland and Ireland through Cumberland, and not directly from Scandinavia at this time. They came as isolated families of sheep farmers, who were content to take land unfit for corn, and they tended to settle higher up the valleys, as their place names show. Golcar, Fixby,

Crosland and Greetland are Norse in origin, as are Quarmby and Stainland.

Some new settlers who were also of Norse extraction, came over from Lancashire and Westmorland after the Norman Conquest and from them are dated Linthwaite, Slaithwaite, Lingards, Scammonden and Scholes. Also at this time we find roads called 'gates', woods become 'storthes', fields are 'carr' or 'holme' and hills are called 'nab', 'scout' or 'scar'. Dialect survives nowhere more strongly than in rural areas, and in early medieval times there was in our area a body of people who spoke Norse up to the middle of the twelfth century, when the local dialect of English finally prevailed.

With the arrival of the Normans and the completion of Domesday Book, historical evidence comes to be largely based on the written word. Archaeology has provided the background for most of this chapter but we may never know the whole truth. It is interesting however to find that when new discoveries are made in early history, they tend to confirm the order of events which we now have, and it is merely dates and details which are sometimes altered.

CHAPTER II

From Domesday Book to the Coming of the Ramsden Family

As I write this, in 1966, Englishmen celebrate or regret the Battle of Hastings. The overall effect of the Norman Conquest on the country cannot be dealt with here, but there are some aspects of the Conquest which affected our district and these must be mentioned.

William not only took over the Anglo-Saxon kingship but also the aura of Christian justification which had been built up around it since before the days of Alfred the Great. He used the Church to support the crown by the appointment of Norman bishops and in particular by making the Bishopric of Durham into a palatinate or semi-independent state. By this move the English were protected from the Scots by a bishop who was not hereditary. Similar arrangements were made as a defence against the Welsh.

In the rest of the country, crown ownership of lands increased and William's followers were rewarded with shares of what was left over. Their estates were divided into small areas so arranged that they were scattered, and interspersed with each other and by those of the crown. Thus it was extremely difficult for a Norman Landlord to become an 'overmighty subject' and indeed there was to be no organised, large-scale, baronial opposition until the fourteenth century. William thus arranged that when Ilbert de Laci was given land in Huddersfield, his rival the Earl of Warren received land in Halifax and Holmfirth.

In local government, the Normans took over the Anglo-Saxon machinery as they found it. Each Saxon shire was divided into hundreds or, in Yorkshire, wapentakes. These were very

THE ANCIENT PARISHES OF
HUDDERSFIELD AND ALMONDBURY

ancient divisions which probably stemmed from tribal group-
ings or areas each capable of raising one hundred warriors at
one time; the word 'wapentake' (a 'holding' of weapons)
conveys this general idea. The hundred moot, or court of
ordinary jurisdiction of the Anglo-Saxons, developed in the
hundreds, and after the Conquest the freemen of the hundred
were bound to attend this court and to sit in judgment there.
The wapentake that concerns us is that of Agbrigg which
comprises the lower and middle valley of the Calder and the
land south of Huddersfield and over the Pennines to Saddleworth (*see map facing p.* 300). Within it there are many townships, of which Huddersfield was one and Almondbury another.

The village or township remained unchanged in form after
the Conquest. The term 'manor', however, is used frequently

in surveys of our area for Domesday Book although the Normans never define it. Thus not all the manors mentioned in this chapter are synonymous with the townships on the map. We know, of course, that the manor was an estate controlled by a lord and managed as an economic entity, and that in a single township or village there might be several manors though sometimes manor and township coincided. Englishmen traditionally regarded themselves as belonging to a village rather than to a manor.

In 1086 the Conqueror had completed 'Domesday Book', the great inventory of all the manors of England. The returns disclose the value of the land, particulars of its arable, woodland, pastures and plough teams together with details of who owned the land before and after the Conquest; and under Huddersfield we find:

'In Odersfelt Godwin had six carucates of land for geld where eight ploughs can be. Now the same has it of Ilbert but it is waste. Wood pasture one league long and one wide. In the time of King Edward (The Confessor) its value was 100 shillings.'

The entries for some West Riding manors are set out in tabular form. Huddersfield was, of course, only one of several villages each of which had its own manorial jurisdiction. Looking at the names mentioned before the Conquest, more than half were Anglian, the rest Norse or Danish. Huddersfield under Edward had been assessed the richest manor in the district and was worth £5 when Almondbury was worth £3 and Lindley only £1 (*see Appendix I*).

In 1069 William, with characteristic singlemindedness, had set out to crush the North as a reprisal for rebellion. The total value of this district was, by 1086, a few pounds; of this, the area of the present County Borough of Huddersfield was worth merely ten shillings and this was all at Dalton. We must not however directly attribute this loss of value to the ravages of the Norman soldiers since it is most likely that they never came to the Huddersfield area. Moreover from 1069 to 1086 is a long time for arable land not to have recovered. When Domesday

Book refers to Huddersfield as 'waste' it probably means that there were no people about; they may well have migrated to the richer lands further east where we know the ~~Romans~~ did great damage in 1069.   *Normans*

  We now meet Ilbert de Laci, a prominent supporter of William the Conqueror who received, as the reward for his part in the adventure, a number of estates in this area, and some 204 manors in Yorkshire, the whole forming the Honour or Barony of Pontefract. Besides Huddersfield, Ilbert held Bradford and Leeds while his greatest rival the Earl of Warren and Surrey

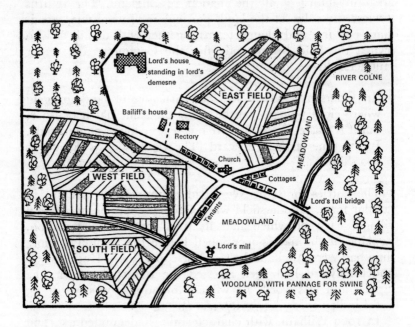

held the Honour of Wakefield, which included Halifax, Brighouse, Elland and Holmfirth. Thus the Conqueror put a wedge of hostile territory between parts of Ilbert's lands. Whether the Godwin who held Huddersfield before and after the Conquest was the same person we cannot tell. The Honour was ruled as a single unit by the Norman lord through his own council, exchequer and court; a mirror of that of his own lord, the king, who held the Honour of All England.

We cannot be certain what the Manor of Huddersfield was like in the twelfth century as there is no contemporary evidence. The three-field system of mediaeval agriculture which was common in the South of England was not practised to the north or west of our area. Moreover, such a system could have only existed in Huddersfield on the low-lying land near the River Colne. A map of 1634, described in Chapter III, affords us possible evidence of strip cultivation in the adjacent Manor of Almondbury. A map of the Ramsden Estate in Huddersfield in 1716 shows signs of strip cultivation titled 'Town Ings' in an area later known as 'Newtown'. Thus it is just possible that the Mediaeval Manor of Huddersfield bore some resemblance to the artist's drawing opposite.

There were certainly exceptions to any three-field system in the Huddersfield area when men began to push outwards into the hills and to cultivate lands which had never previously been occupied; but more of this later.

Domesday Book has no mention of a church in Huddersfield. Small churches there were at Thornhill, Cawthorne, and Batley, while Dewsbury was recognised as the mother church to which Huddersfield and Almondbury still pay tribute each year. The de Laci family, who came from Lassi in Normandy, followed the Norman tradition of endowing religious buildings on their estates, and they founded Kirkstall and Nostell Priories and the Parish Churches of Huddersfield and probably Almondbury. Walter de Laci is traditionally said to have fallen into a swamp whilst riding between Huddersfield and Halifax and to have vowed that, should he escape, he would build a church on his father's manor. This he is alleged to have done sometime between 1090 and 1100. In 1122 a Robert de Laci was dispossessed of his lands by Henry I who granted them to Hugh de Laval. This Hugh de Laval then granted the right of appointing the Vicar of Huddersfield to the Prior and Monks of Nostell. The Priory thus became the owners of the lands and other income of the church, appointed a vicar from among themselves,[1] and duly made a profit. All the vicar received

---

[1] The first recorded Vicar of Huddersfield was Michael de Wakefield, appointed in 1216.

were the baptismal, marriage and burial fees while the prior drew tithes from the whole of the parish. From the eleventh to the nineteenth century this parish covered the northern bank of the Colne from Marsden to Bradley and out to Scammonden and Edgerton (*see map on page* 12).

In 1288 Pope Nicholas IV ordered a survey of church property in order to raise money by tithes to enable Edward I to campaign in the Holy Land. Huddersfield Parish Church was valued at £9. 6s. 8d. and the vicarage at £6. 13s. 4d. Almondbury was valued at £40 while Halifax Parish Church was worth £93. 6s. 8d.

The origins of Almondbury Parish Church are obscure and it is impossible to say with certainty when or by whom it was built. Taking for granted the de Lacis' reputation as church builders, and if we associate the church with the building of Almondbury Castle in the days of King Stephen (1135–1154), then we arrive at a time somewhere in the first half of the twelfth century; the earliest recorded event is the institution of William de Notyland[1] as 'Rector of Almannebrie', on 23rd March 1230. The original church was probably on the site of the present chancel and was replaced by a larger building at the close of the fifteenth century.

A study of the early rectors provides an interesting picture of the state of the Church during the Middle Ages. Most of the rectors were absentees; one was so 'afflicted with old age and blindness that he neither exercised the cure of souls in his parish nor even governed himself'. Another, Boniface de Saluzzo, was appointed at the age of twelve, at twenty he held two other livings, and by 1313 he was tried by the Archbishop of York; his parishes were taken away from him and he was excommunicated. Yet another Rector of Almondbury was not even ordained, while one William St Aubyn who held office for over thirty years was invariably absent studying elsewhere.

It is fairly safe to assume that the de Lacis built the Norman castle which once stood on Castle Hill. They had built Pontefract Castle as their chief seat and another at Halton in Cheshire. Almondbury, a naturally commanding site, lying midway

[1] Probably 'Notynham'.

between the other two, would afford a useful place from which to control the de Laci manors around Huddersfield. The likelihood is that Henry de Laci built Almondbury Castle during Stephen's reign, at a time when the barons were able to do very much as they pleased. Many castles were built at this time without the King's permission and they were destroyed by Henry II when he was strong enough to do so. Henry de Laci, a loyal supporter of Stephen, obtained his licence to crenellate and Almondbury Castle was completed. Later, in 1154, he made his peace with Henry II and was present at the Council of Northampton.

Modern excavation seems to indicate that the castle on the hill was not one of those grim stone fortresses traditionally associated with the Normans. All that Henry de Laci seems to have done was to dig a great ditch, at the west end, near the present hotel, and then build a high bank of shale. His men lived at the south-westerly end, after sinking a crude building into the earlier embankments. Here men and animals perhaps lived together; there was also that essential feature of military architecture, a well. It is thought that Henry de Laci only ever visited Castle Hill, he never lived there.

In 1310 or 1311 Alice de Laci, heiress of Henry Laci, Earl of Lincoln, married Thomas, Earl of Lancaster, the most powerful nobleman in England, cousin of Edward II and leader of the baronial opposition to the weak king and his favourites. But Lancaster had troubles of his own as his wife eloped with his rival, John de Warenne (1286–1347), Lord of Wakefield— an incident which originated what became known as the 'Elland Feud' between the families. Thomas divorced Alice about 1318.

The quarrel between the Earl and the King culminated in the battle of Boroughbridge in 1322, and the defeat of Lancaster. A chronicler of the times[1] reported that 'Thomas, Earl of Lancaster, whose generosity and wealth made others cling to him as though he were immortal, was condemned to be hanged by a sentence passed on the sixth day after the King's triumph. The King's mercy did not allow his kinsman to be spared the

[1] Geoffrey the Baker.

death penalty, but mercifully changed the treason sentence to decapitation.' The Earl was executed at Pontefract on 22nd March 1322 and it is reasonable to expect that Almondbury Castle was demolished or left to decay when his estates were confiscated.

In 1359 Blanche, granddaughter of Thomas, Earl of Lancaster, married, as his first wife, John of Gaunt, fourth son of Edward III. John of Gaunt was created Duke of Lancaster in 1362 and he was also Lord of Pontefract and of the manors of Bradford, Almondbury and Huddersfield; it was his son who became Henry IV in 1399, thus making all his possessions Crown property. The Manor of Huddersfield was a Crown estate when Elizabeth I sold it to William Ramsden in 1599; the Manor of Almondbury was leased[1] to his son John Ramsden in 1627 but the actual freehold of Almondbury passed from the Royal Family at a later date. This explains why it was that when Almondbury Grammar School received its Royal Charter, in 1608, the grant of land came out of the royal domain of 'King James in Almondbury'.

In 1318 a certain John del Cloughes was the Lord of the Manor which he held in fee from Lancaster. He wrote: 'Know present and to come that I — have given, granted and by this present charter confirmed to Richard de Byron, Knight, and his heirs all my messuage and all my lands with their appurtenances which I had in the town of Hodresfeld and Gledholt and their territories.' The Byrons held Huddersfield until 2nd March 1573 when John Byron mortgaged it to Gilbert Gerrard, the Queen's Attorney-General, for £700. A document of 1580 mentions that Gerrard had purchased Huddersfield from John Byron; however, when the manor changed hands again in 1599 it was the Queen, not Gerrard, who sold it. Either the Queen had acquired the estate personally from Gerrard, and we do not have any record of this transaction, or Gerrard was acting for the Queen when he acquired Huddersfield from Byron; after all he was her Attorney-General.

Queen Elizabeth made a profit since the document of sale runs:

[1] In consideration of £467. 11s. 1¾d. paid to the Crown, and an annual rent of £20. 11s. 0½d.

18

'Elizabeth by the grace of God, etc.—Know ye that we in consideration of the sum of NINE HUNDRED AND SEVENTY-FIVE POUNDS AND NINEPENCE have granted to William Ramsden, his heirs and assigns ALL THAT our Manor of Huddersfield, etc. and all our capital messuage or tenement called Bay Hall, in Huddersfield aforesaid, now or lately in the tenure or occupation of John Brooke, and all our several messuages, lands, etc.—which Manor and premises were lately part and parcel of the land and possessions late of Gilbert Gerrard, our Attorney-General and of one John Sankey, or of the one of them, with us recently exchanged, and to a certain Thomas Norris for or under the yearly rent of £23. 19s. 9d. granted for a term of 21 years'.

This, incidentally, is one of the earliest recorded references to Bay Hall and scholars are still uncertain of the origin of its peculiar name. It has been said that Bay Hall at Birkby was built in the mid-sixteenth century at the cost of the Lord of the Manor, to be his agent's residence. From thence the resident agent looked after his lord's estate and the house became an office or a public building—never a private residence like Longley Hall or Fixby. I think it likely that the name derives from the magnificent Tudor gable which can still be seen. There is also a 'Bay Hall' in Colchester which had to do with the sale of 'bays', a type of woollen material; but this use of a building as a cloth market would be most unlikely in sixteenth century Huddersfield when markets at Almondbury were patronised from much further afield than Birkby. It was in its function of estate headquarters that Bay Hall was referred to in the deed as a 'Capital Messuage'.

The William Ramsden of 1558–1623 thus became first of a long line of Ramsdens who were Lords of the Manor of Huddersfield. His uncle, also William Ramsden, had acted as agent when the lands of the priory at Kirklees were sold in 1545. It was this William Ramsden, the uncle, who laid the foundations of much of the Ramsden fortune in land; although it was his dealings in land, particularly as agent for others, that led him into prison, as a debtor in 1557.

There were Woods or 'Wodes' at Longley as early as 1342

and Thomas de la Wode is recorded as living there in 1354. In 1523 a taxation roll of Henry VIII assessed John Wode de Longley at £10 which made him the richest man in Almondbury. In 1531 his daughter Johanna Wode married William Ramsden (1513–1580) described in 1547 as 'William Ramsden of Longley, Yorkshire, gent. alias late of Almondbury, yeoman, alias of Elland, yeoman, alias of London esquire'. Longley Hall[1] eventually went to the Savile Family by the marriage of Cecile Wode, and William Ramsden bought it from them.[2] The Ramsdens, who came from Elland, were, in the space of less than a century, to acquire almost all of Huddersfield[3] central area and much of the east and south parts of the County Borough — about 4,000 acres in all.

---

[1] The old hall at Lowerhouses. This was the only part of the Ramsden Estate in Huddersfield to be retained by the Ramsden Family when the estate was sold to Huddersfield Corporation on 29th September 1920.

[2] See the Ramsden Pedigree facing page 28.

[3] See p. 27.

CHAPTER III

From the Break-up of Feudalism in Almondbury to the Huddersfield Market of 1671

THE TUDOR monarchs were most careful to account for their possessions and in 1584 Queen Elizabeth I in typical fashion ordered a comprehensive survey of Almondbury.

The first task was to establish the boundaries of the manor, and the report said: 'The ring and uttermost boundaries of the said manor and lordship of Almondbury are as followeth, that is to wit:— First from the Ravensknowle Hill as one hedge divideth to John North's house and so eastward upon the height to the Smithy Dyke, from thence up to the vale southwards joining Mr Harrup's land, and so southward by the water unto the Fenay Bridge on the east part, from thence up a little river called the Birk Brook—to Lumhead into the New Hey Yate—to the Parke Pitt on the west and—following the water of the Colne as it descendeth to the Queen's Majesty's Mills named in the records Huddersfield Mills, and from the said mills eastward—to tayle goit and southward by the head of a meadow called Long Inge—and so—eastward along the bottom to the Netherwood Inge and so by the south side of two little pig hills called the Lime Pighills—until against one house called Hole Bottom—so far as the waste ground [which] was lately ploughed by the tenants of the said Manor. Thence to the north end of one close called North Royd—being the said Ravensknowle Hill where the said boundary first began.'

The manor was bounded by Woodsome on the south, the Manor or Lordship of Honley on the west, the manors of North and South Crosland on the north-west and north, across the

River Colne, the Manor of Huddersfield, the Manor of Dalton on the north-east and Lepton on the east.

The Court Leet at Almondbury was attended twice a year by the constables and men of Huddersfield, Honley, Meltham, South Crosland, Slaithwaite and Quick (Saddleworth). At these meetings new constables were sworn in, and cases were heard of 'affrays, bloods and other common annoyances' which had been committed within all the townships.

Twenty-three freeholders are mentioned in the report by name including John Ramsden, gentleman. Their duties included repairing the Queen's Mill when necessary, with the aid of villeins, using timber from the estate; also to use the Lord's Mill for all the corn and grain grown within the manor; to collect Her Majesty's rents and to attend the Lord's Court when required, and on death the new freeholder had to pay an estate duty equal to a year's rent. John Ramsden and John Kaye are together bound to repair the mill wheel.

There were nineteen copyholders with conditions similar to those of the freeholders. A certain Giles Kaye 'held burgage[1] upon top of Castle Hill' for a penny a year.

Three little fairs were recorded in Almondbury, on St Martin's Day, in winter, on Easter Monday and on Whit Monday. Two small fairs in Huddersfield on St Helen's and St Peter's days were also mentioned.

The Manor Mill of Almondbury, which is mentioned in the 1584 survey, stood on the River Colne, the boundary[2] with Huddersfield. It was frequently called 'Huddersfield Mill', originally the 'Lords Mill', and later the 'King's Mill', when the manor passed to the Crown. It was probably built about 1100 by the de Lacis and stood in what is still King's Mill Lane. The tenants were obliged to grind their corn there. The income from this would be considerable, and the benefits did not finish there, for the tenants were also under obligation to help the lord keep the mill in good repair. The survey records that there was a corn mill belonging to the Queen, and that the fulling mill in the tail goit had fallen into decay; moreover a second fulling

---

[1] Tenancy

[2] On the site later stood a large textile mill, seriously damaged by fire in 1967.

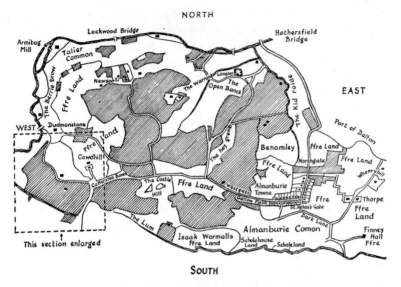

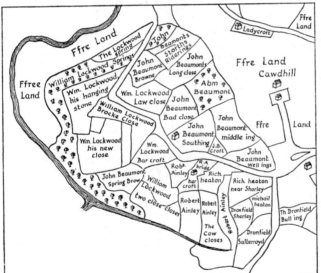

The Manor of Almondbury in 1634

These maps first appeared in Taylor Dyson's *History of Huddersfield*, drawn by N. L. Houslop: they are here re-drawn by A. Boughey.

23

mill nearby had recently been built by William Ramsden but this also was in some decay. Fulling is a process in woollen cloth finishing and more will be said about this later.[1] The point here is that the Ramsdens had the privilege of 'farming' the mill; they paid the Queen a fixed sum and received the right to collect fees from those using the mill, making what profit they could.

There is an interesting map of Almondbury, dated 1634, and a study of this reveals many trends which were to become important later. The township then included Berry Brow, Taylor Hill, part of Lockwood and Newsome, and stretched from Somerset Bridge to Fenay Bridge and Dalton, all of which area is now included in the County Borough of Huddersfield. Most travel tended ultimately to go towards Huddersfield so that, when the main routes eventually by-passed the steep Almondbury Bank, the town of Almondbury became a dead end. These changes were to occur in the nineteenth century, but if we examine Jefferys' map of 1772, Almondbury appears on the through route south from Halifax via Elland, Fixby, Halifax Old Road, Almondbury Bank, and Kirkburton to Barnsley. At Almondbury there was a main road leading off to the east via Fenay Bridge to Lepton, Horbury and Wakefield.

The 1634 map of Almondbury shows all Manorial land of the Ramsdens shaded, while the large unshaded areas are free land,[2] or common land. The village roads are few in number. Northgate[3] runs through the 'towne', down Almondbury Bank[4] then branches right towards Dalton, and then left to what is now Somerset Bridge. Westgate follows a direct line towards Castle Hill. St Helen's Gate leads to Dark Lane which divides into two branches. One branch goes through Thorpe to Dalton while the other leads to Fenay Hall and Fenay Bridge.

If we examine the enlarged section of this map, it will be seen that the communal system of agriculture had almost disappeared by 1634, although there was still plenty of woodland

[1] See p. 41.
[2] 'Free land' here means freeholdings belonging to persons other than the Ramsdens.
[3] Gate = Road.
[4] Somerset Road was not constructed until the nineteenth century.

and common land used for pasture. The significant fact is that, by this time, the arable land was privately occupied and each tenant's holdings was in blocks of fields, as compact as possible. This can only mean that if the three-field system had ever existed in Almondbury, it had broken down in all but name. John Beaumont, for example, held several pieces of land but each one comprised many strips adjacent to each other; thus perhaps, by interchange of strips, the Beaumont lands had been consolidated into permanent holdings. The same applied to many of the other tenants and their names are still common in the district—Armitage, Kay, Shaw, Blackburn, Woodhead, Hirst, Haigh, Heaton, Sikes and Brook.

In addition to the fairs previously mentioned there was a weekly market at Almondbury. Edward I had granted to Henry de Laci a charter, dated 6th June 1294, which allowed him to hold a market every Monday. We know little about this market and one can but speculate as to what it was like. Throughout the Middle Ages there was almost certainly no market in Huddersfield. Any produce for sale in the two parishes would be taken on foot, by pack mule or on horseback to Almondbury.

Huddersfield Market received its Royal Charter in 1671 and this caused the Almondbury market to lapse. Huddersfield and Almondbury markets, the one on a Tuesday and the other on a Monday, could have existed side by side, but since it would undoubtedly have been easier to travel downhill to Huddersfield than to toil up the hill to Almondbury, Almondbury Market probably dwindled gradually as Huddersfield grew rapidly in size during the eighteenth century. Moreover, the King's mill on the Colne was in fact closer to the centre of Huddersfield than it was to Almondbury. Therefore business activity probably tended to gravitate towards Huddersfield before 1671.

Little is known of the selling of cloth which apparently took place in Huddersfield Parish churchyard, before the building of the Cloth Hall in 1766, but this may well have been a result of the general market charter granted by Charles II to John Ramsden in 1671. Tradition has it that the clothiers were at first permitted to sell their wares on the churchyard wall and nowhere else. However, as trade increased and more manufacturers used this facility, the very tombstones began to serve as shop counters giving rise to local indignation and protest. This may have led to the Cloth Hall being built in order to put a stop to this practice.

The year 1671 found John Ramsden Sheriff of the West Riding. His grandfather had fought for the King, and had been taken prisoner by the Parliamentarians at Selby in 1644. The Ramsden family were Stuart supporters by tradition, and Charles II was no doubt pleased to reward their loyalty with this document:

I, the King to whom these presents shall come, send greeting.—
Whereas by a certain inquisition taken by our command at Huddersfield in Ye County of York on Ye 12th day of September last past before the date of these presents, and returned in due form and now to be found remaining on record, it now appears to us that it will not be to the damage or prejudice of us or any others if we do grant unto John Ramsden Esq., that he and his heirs may have and hold one market in ye town of Huddersfield, on Tuesday in every week for ever, for ye buying and selling of all manner of goods and merchandise, and receive ye tolls profits and advantages from thence coming and arising for him and his heirs for ever.—
And may have, hold and enjoy the aforesaid tolls, profits and other premises aforesaid unto the said John Ramsden, his heirs and assigns to his and their own proper use and uses for ever without anything to us, our heirs and successors to be paid or performed. And we do by these presents finally command that ye said John Ramsden, his heirs and assigns, shall freely, lawfully and wholly have, hold and enjoy ye aforesaid market and ye tolls and profits to ye same belonging or from thence from time to time coming and arising according to ye tenor and true meaning of these our Letters Patent, without molestation, hindrance or denials of us, our heirs or successors or of our sheriffs, bailiffs, officers or ministers or any other persons whatsoever.
Dated ye first day of November, in ye twenty-third year of our reign (1671)

(Charles II dates his reign from 1649, the execution of his father, Charles I. Thus the twenty-third year is 1671, not 1672.)

This document is, of course, only one instance of the extent to which the fortunes of the Ramsdens are bound up with the history of our town, and it will perhaps be as well to study the family in some detail at this stage.[1]

As with so many old families there were recurring christian names in the male line, and the Ramsdens ran true to form with a succession of Johns and Williams. For our purposes we can start with Robert Ramsyden of Elland who made a marriage settlement with John Wode of Longley in respect of Johanna Wode and his eldest son William Ramsden. They were married in 1531, and William speculated in monastic lands. His youngest brother John built a new Longley Hall. The building[2] was completed in 1577. Prior to this, John had rented accommodation from his brother William in Longley Hall, the former home of the Wodes. William died in 1580 without issue. John's son, William Ramsden of Longley Hall (1558–1623), purchased Huddersfield from the Queen in 1599 and was an original governor of Almondbury Grammar School. John Ramsden of Longley Hall and Byram (near Ferrybridge) (1594–1646) was knighted in 1619, M.P. for Pontefract in 1627, sheriff in 1636, fought for the King in the Civil War and died in Newark Castle. He married the daughter of Sir Peter Frecheville.

His son William Ramsden (1625–79) of Longley Hall and Byram, was succeeded by Sir John Ramsden of Longley and Byram (1648–90) who obtained the Huddersfield Market Charter in 1671, was created a baronet in 1689 as part of the policy of William of Orange to conciliate those whose families had loyally supported the Crown.

The second Baronet was Sir William Ramsden (1672–1736), and it was his son, Sir John Ramsden (3rd Baronet) (1698–1769) who built the Cloth Hall in 1766.

He was succeeded by another Sir John Ramsden (4th Baronet) (1755–1839) who enlarged the Cloth Hall in 1780. He outlived his son John Charles Ramsden and the estates passed

---

[1] See the Ramsden Pedigree facing page 28.

[2] Now the 'Old Longley Hall', in Longley village at the top of Wood Lane.

to his grandson, Sir John William Ramsden (5th Baronet) (1831–1914), who was M.P. for the West Riding 1859–65. John William Street was named after him.

He was succeeded by Sir John Frecheville Ramsden (1877–1958) (6th Baronet) who sold the family estates in Huddersfield to the Corporation in 1920.

Sometime shortly after 1671 the Ramsden family erected a market cross. The shields on the cap illustrate various marriages[1] of the Ramsdens. On the south side is represented the marriage of William Ramsden and Rosamund Pilkington of Bradley in 1589; on the east, that of Sir John Ramsden and Margaret Frecheville in 1624; on the north, that of William Ramsden and Elizabeth Palmes about 1648; and on the west, the marriage of Sir John Ramsden and Sarah Butler in 1670. As the arms show no sign of the baronetcy which Sir John Ramsden received on 30th November 1689, the cross was apparently designed before this date.

In 1852 the market cross is said to have been removed from Longley Hall back to the Market Place and re-erected on three steps, but we have no evidence as to when it was taken from the centre of the town. An engraving of between 1780 and 1800 shows the cross still standing in the Market Place but it was seen at Longley Hall about 1825. During the riots of 1820 the cross may well have been removed to a place of safety. After its return to the Market Place the condition of the cross seems to have deteriorated until by 1906 when its position was shifted for the building of public conveniences in the Market Place. The cross was again moved in 1927. The centre piece of the column was renewed and, in an attempt to disguise the new section, the stone was soaked in beer for a fortnight. Following this restoration the column was placed on two steps. The shields were almost unrecognisable. It is very appropriate that they are now restored to their original splendour as we celebrate our Centenary.

---

[1] Full details of these marriages are contained in an article by L. E. Rothwell in the *Huddersfield Examiner* for 18th January 1967.

CHAPTER IV

The Origins of the Cloth Industry

THIS CHAPTER is perhaps the most important in the whole book. The very origins of Huddersfield germinated in the rich soil of textile development long before the coming of the machines, and events prior to the eighteenth century foreshadowed what was to follow. More specifically, if the cottage-based clothiers had not been rugged individualists, determined to triumph over difficulties, the industry could have stagnated before the machinery arrived, and the necessary financial resources might never have been available when the time was ripe for expansion.

Huddersfield is today a town of many industries, most, as will be seen, owing their origins to wool textiles. It is not generally appreciated, however, just how important wool was to the economy of the country as a whole before the Industrial Revolution. This is perhaps because the subsequent dramatic growth of other industries elsewhere in the country has tended to crowd the picture.

But there were those who were conscious of wool's place in their own time. Camden writing in 1607 mentioned English cloth as 'one of the pillars of State'. Bacon referred to wool as 'the great wheel of the realm', while a seventeenth century writer's comment on the Woolsack was that it was there to remind the House of Lords of the need to preserve and advance the trade of wool. Defoe, ever ready with the masterly compression, said in 1724, 'Be their country hot or cold, the English woollen manufacturer clothes them all;' and in 1668 two thirds of English exports were of woollen cloth. A contemporary wit remarked that the world was England's servant because all other countries wore England's livery!

English foreign policy, and many geographical voyages of

29

discovery were inspired by a need to capture new markets for our cloth. When we remark that once nearly every cottage woman in the land spun, it is hardly surprising that our language has become enriched by such expressions as: 'to spin a yarn', 'a tangled skein' or 'the thread of an argument'. Single women are still known as 'spinsters'.

Of course rivalry between textiles and agriculture has been traditional in our economic history. As long ago as 1614 it was claimed that textiles diverted labour from the land and so created an unstable economy; and later in that century the commercial interests did succeed in obtaining a free trade in the import of new wool. In the nineteenth century the same interests obtained a free trade in the import of food.

We may perhaps begin in 1331 when Edward III issued a general invitation to foreign clothworkers to come to England. Only a few immigrants are known to have reached Yorkshire but we hear of a Simon Fleming in Almondbury in 1379. In general, they appear to have gone to the textile producing areas of East Anglia and the West Country.

Fostered by royal ordinances, and with little assistance from any immigrants, the native industry of Yorkshire expanded rapidly during the fourteenth century. Increasing quantities of raw wool were consumed and in 1337 restrictions were placed on the export of wool from England to the Continent. This measure had the result of reducing the King's revenues because there had been a tax levied upon every sack of wool leaving the country. To compensate for this loss of income to the Exchequer, a tax of fourpence was placed on each piece of cloth made and sold at home, and an official called the ulnager was appointed to collect the new taxes in return for a commission of a half-penny per piece.

As each piece of cloth was measured, and found to be of the correct size, an official seal was affixed to it. Back in 1197, standard width had been defined as 'two ells' (2½ yards) between the 'lists' or strips of waste which ran down each side of the piece and which were used for 'tentering'. In 1354, the standard size of broad cloth was laid down as from 26 to 28 yards by 6 to 6½ quarter-yards (about 4ft. 10½ins.). When it was later found that the 'Kersey', one quarter the size of the standard piece and frequently manufactured in our area, was escaping all payment of ulnage, it was decided in 1393 that it should bear the proportional duty of one penny. This tax lasted for about three hundred years.

During the fifteenth century, the ulnagers' returns and other evidence point to an even more substantial increase in cloth production in Yorkshire. Although recent research has shown the ulnage statistics to be unreliable, those for the West Riding are thought to be more accurate than for some other parts of England. However, the rapid expansion of Yorkshire cloth production is not fully reflected in them; West Riding cloth was of inferior quality, and much of what was made was sold and used locally and was not marketed openly. There was, at this period, a wider market developing, and by 1470 Yorkshire was the third largest producer of woollen cloth in England, after Suffolk and Somerset. What is important for us is that this increased output came not from the ancient gilds of York and Beverley, but from the whole of the West Riding, including our own area.

Geographically, the scene to which the textile industry came so long ago in the West Riding was one of inhospitable but well-watered moorland. To the north and south of our area the Pennines are formed of limestone which yields good grass for long haired sheep but there are few springs and the water is harsh. Below the Aire Gap the Pennines are of Millstone Grit covered with peat and clay. The land supports few animals but the coarse grass is suitable for the short haired sheep. Springs on the hillsides are thrown up by the impervious shales beneath the surface and wells are easily made. The rock outcrops in many places, consequently stone for building is available. The streams have cut deep narrow valleys through which water still tumbles, and as the 'becks' reach the lower slopes the valleys become wooded. The key to the development of Yorkshire woollens was the abundance of soft water, which is a characteristic of our moorland streams.

The grit country was never ideally suitable for the three field system and whereas the manors of Huddersfield and Almondbury were satisfactory units in themselves, the fact that their parishes stretched into the barren wasteland encouraged the enterprising to press outwards into the moorland in search of a livelihood.

From the earliest times rough woollen material was pounded in water or 'fulled' to make it thicken and 'felt' the fibres together. This process was originally carried out by trampling on the cloth.[1] Early records refer to a certain Roger the Fuller of Holme in 1274, there is also a John the Dyer of Almondbury in 1297. The earliest textile workers were probably making cloth for themselves only, but the founding of the Almondbury Market in 1294 suggests that a regular cloth trade was beginning. Between 1473 and 1475 we know that 427 pieces were sold at Almondbury. This represents 1,708 kerseys, since a kersey was a quarter of a complete piece of broad cloth. Allowing for two years' production 1473-4 and 1474-5 this amounted to 854 kerseys per year. If we assume each weaver produced a kersey each week on forty weeks out of the year, then twenty-one weavers supplied this market. All this has been deduced from the returns of contemporary ulnagers, as they levied their tax and then sealed each piece of cloth.

At Almondbury there was a fulling mill towards the end of Edward I's reign and a survey of 1340 mentions a water mill for corn, a fulling mill and a dye house, but does not say where they were. It may be that they were on the Colne, probably the King's Mills which had expanded since they were first established. Taxation returns of 1379 show Almondbury with some 100 inhabitants and Huddersfield about 200.

The weaver's gild at York had received its charter in 1164, and for three centuries York led the woollen industry of the county, striving all the time to keep its share of trade. Beverley was also a woollen centre but by the sixteenth century Leland remarked that her trade was 'much decayed'. Ulnagers' rolls for 1393 show York as paying three times as much as the West Riding, but by 1475 it was paying only half as much. Wakefield had developed 'her coarse drapery' and by 1561 York complained that cloth making had gone to Halifax, Leeds and Wakefield, where they had the advantage of water mills, and where rye and fuel were cheaper than in the city. The rising

[1] See Appendix V under 'Walker'.

areas of production around Huddersfield were outside the restrictions of the gilds and when the Tudors tried to insist that cloth making should be done only by apprentice-trained workers in the ancient cities, the attempt failed. It appears that even in those far off days West Riding folk were intolerant of outside authority. In this attitude they were not then alone but local characteristics have survived longer here than in many other areas.[1] Meanwhile the making of cloth on the Millstone Grit around Huddersfield made a living possible for increasing numbers of hardworking folk enabling them to supplement their meagre agricultural earnings from cloth working.

During the sixteenth century Huddersfield and other York-shire towns began to straggle outwards from their Parish Churches. What was left of feudalism did not hinder trade, and many villeins wove or spun as a side line, and so their lords' mills increased in activity. Almost anyone could be a clothier; some had been farmers, others fullers, others weavers—but no man had to forswear an existing trade in order to 'drape the cloth'. The name could apply to anyone who sold cloth at Almondbury market; and most of them wove their own stuff.

In 1563 a clothier was defined as one who 'puts cloth to making for sale.' Many carried out most textile processes themselves; they bought the wool, wove the cloth and then sold it. Some employed others to prepare the wool for weaving and it was estimated that to make a kersey in a week took the labour of one weaver and five others who spun and carded the wool. The clothier was in a small way of business because there was little profit to be made from the inhospitable countryside and little capital available for development. Nevertheless these men ran the cloth trade of the West Riding in the sixteenth century.

Throughout this period there was a general scramble for land on which to graze sheep in order to produce more wool, for it was claimed, 'The foot of the sheep turns sand into gold'. In the South and in East Anglia waste lands were enclosed for this purpose, and much church land from dissolved monasteries shared the same fate. Enclosure of the waste land marked the beginning of the end of the three field system, especially in the

[1] See Appendix VI.

South of England; and where the villeins and the freemen thus lost their own grazing rights to the lord of the manor, it was claimed that the sheep were 'devouring' the men. In our own area where much of the large scale enclosure dates from the eighteenth century, the independent clothier who lived on the edge of the moors merely extended his holding by 'intaking' or taking over, more of the otherwise useless land beyond what he already held. Numerous pieces of land are labelled 'Intak' on the old maps of Huddersfield. As more profits were made so more land could be taken over and scattered pieces joined together into sizeable holdings.

The Yorkshire manufacturing system by which the clothier worked his own looms with his own material and depended upon a very little capital was unique in England. Like everyone else, however, he required a regular market to keep himself going. In some places weaving was subsidiary to farming while elsewhere farming might not even pay the rent. Under this system of work for all, it was seldom necessary to apply for charity or poor relief. Thus, independent enterprise was to engender a spirit of self-sufficiency which was later seen in many fields of human endeavour in Huddersfield.

Although many clothiers worked alone, assisted by their families, there were some who came to employ other labour. Journeymen and journeywomen, in theory hired by the day, were seldom dismissed; so there grew a sense of solidarity and loyalty between master and men. The thrifty, enterprising journeyman was able to become his own master when he had made his own loom and acquired some capital on the basis of his own good name. Indeed, it was not unusual for neighbours to guarantee a newly independent journeyman against his creditors. It became an article of faith that every worker had, as of right, the opportunity to gain his independence, albeit some of those who had struggled to obtain this freedom were to find it very hard when they had to lose it. We, in Huddersfield, have sometimes been described as 'an independent lot', and surely this attitude is deeply rooted in our basic industry.

Throughout the sixteenth century, there were complaints that many clothworkers had not served an apprenticeship. By an Act of 1563, an attempt was made to make compulsory a seven years period of indenture; it was also laid down that for every three apprentices there was to be one journeyman. However, this legislation was not stringently enforced in the West Riding. In 1725, new legislation stipulated that all workers in broad cloth were to have served an apprenticeship; thus, presumably, the narrow-cloth makers in the Huddersfield area escaped notice, and when the Huddersfield Cloth Hall was opened, there were no regulations regarding apprenticeship. When the apprenticeship laws were finally repealed in 1813, they appear to have become a dead letter. It is therefore surprising to find that in 1806 it was reported that apprenticeship had survived longer than elsewhere. Apprenticeship certainly existed in Huddersfield throughout this period but the rules by which it was enforced were not always rigidly applied by the clothiers or by the Justices of the Peace.

In 1603 J.P.'s were ordered to regulate the wages of out-workers and of those employed by the larger manufacturers, but here also there was little stringent application of the Law. Textile wages were generally lower than those in agriculture, therefore it paid the local people to carry out some part-time farm work. In the seventeenth century, a weaver earned about sixpence a day while the spinner received about half this amount. During this century prices doubled, consequently the poor became very poor indeed. Not until the eighteenth century was Arthur Young able to report that weavers were earning from seven to nine shilling a week.

Of course, as long as the work was done at home, and un-supervised, no regulation of working hours was possible. We read of a Wiltshire weaver working for fourteen hours a day in winter and seventeen in the summer. Children worked every-where, and some could even weave by the time they were twelve. It has been alleged, though there must have been exceptions, that the handloom weavers' children worked longer hours for less wages than they afterwards did in the factories. Of course, child labour was not introduced by the factory system; but factory organisation, when it came, did make possible its eventual abolition by legislation as a result of public outcry.

In the Middle Ages it was an offence to buy and sell except at a market. Merchants who bought their pieces from the market sold them to the local shops, or to the clothing trade as far afield as London; or they exported the pieces via Hull to the Continent. It must have been a dangerous life, leading a string of pack horses over the bad roads, sometimes mere tracks, for long distances over the moors.

As the industry grew, some of the merchants themselves began to supply raw wool to the clothiers; but the idea of buying and selling at home was officially discouraged in an Act of 1552, which attempted to abolish the middlemen and wool-drivers and stipulated that the clothiers must purchase their own wool, presumably from markets and fairs. In fact some of the larger clothiers spent much time travelling to markets at Ripon, Doncaster, Wakefield and even down to the Midlands in search of wool.[1]

The local sheep provided wool suitable only for the coarsest cloth. Better quality wool was brought from Lincolnshire and Leicestershire. The local men had to sell their produce for cash immediately it was made. Thus the new Act threatened their independence and they were in danger of losing their supply of wool. The 'wooldriver' bought wool from the farmer, graded and stored it, and it was estimated that £1,000 was necessary in order to set up in such a business. The 'wooldriver' was accused of profiteering, he was blamed for rising prices over which he had no control and the State regarded him as a parasite.

The small men in our area could only live from week to week, in comparative poverty. When each kersey was sold at Almond-bury market the money received bought a few stones of wool for the next piece. A storm of protest arose as a result of the 1552 Act, which led to the passing of the Halifax Act of 1555 giving full permission for the retention of the 'wooldriver'. This Act is interesting:

'For as much as the Parish of Halifax and other places thereto adjoining, being planted in the great waste and moors where the fertility of the ground is not apt to bring forth any corn or good grass but in rare places and by exceeding great industry of the inhabitants; and the same

---

[1] An early member of the Brooke family of Armitage Bridge kept records of how he travelled as far as Norfolk buying wool 'on the hoof'.

inhabitants altogether do live by cloth making and the greater part of them neither getteth corn nor (are) able to keep a horse to carry wool, nor yet to buy much wool at once but hath ever used only to repair to the town of Halifax and some others, nigh-there-unto and there to buy from the wooldriver some a stone, some two and some three or four according to their ability, and to carry the same to their houses, some three, four and six miles off, upon their heads and backs and so to make and convert the same either into yarn or cloth, and to sell the same and so to buy more wool of the wooldriver. By means of which industry the barren ground in those parts be now much inhabited and above 500 households there newly increased within these forty years past'.

It should be remembered that the seventeenth century was, at first, a time of depression. The export of cloth from York and Hull declined and for this, foreign competition, high taxation, fraudulent manufacture and profiteering were all blamed. Trade suffered, especially in Leeds and Bradford, as plague and pestilence were followed by the Civil War in which Yorkshiremen fought on both sides.

Evidence of 1638 shows that, besides the small clothier and the yeoman farmer, there were a few larger men at work in the cloth industry and they employed numbers of spinners, weavers and apprentices. At the cloth markets, not every piece was sold in the open; some traders were tending to order goods in advance from the clothier. Middlemen appear at this period who were employed to make purchases on behalf of the large merchants and Defoe mentions one who spent £60,000 at Halifax Market in a year buying kerseys for export to Holland and Germany. This century saw an increased use of credit and so the wooldriver and the merchant's middleman assume even greater importance and, as the wool was more carefully sorted, there are signs that the quality of our cloth began to improve.

Huddersfield never had a gild, and the State appointed ulnagers and searchers to detect fraudulent work in places outside the ancient gild towns. As the searcher was often a clothier himself he was not usually very diligent. Indeed, by the end of the seventeenth century, ulnage was merely a device for collecting revenue and many local clothiers appear to have been buying the leaden seals in bulk and affixing them to their own pieces. Ulnage finally lapsed in 1724.

In 1688 the large Yorkshire overseas trading companies were deprived of their monopolies consequently anyone could become an exporter of woollen goods. At the same time foreign traders were permitted to come to Yorkshire. There, they bought some goods very cheaply and were accused of not always settling their accounts much to the disgust of: 'Divers cloth buyers, Clothiers and Clothworkers and others concern'd in ye woollen manufacture in Hotherfield and places adjacent'.[1]

Throughout the eighteenth century a powerful cloth industry was well established in the West Riding. The export of raw wool had been expressly forbidden in the interests of home industry and when the American War of Independence led to a trade recession, the Lincolnshire wool growers tried to obtain permission to export some of their accumulated stock. As a result of protest meetings held in Leeds, Halifax, Huddersfield, and elsewhere, the manufacturers successfully prevailed upon the Government to continue the ban on wool exporting.

The eighteenth century saw built up a substantial export of cloth pieces to America, Portugal and North West Europe while naval power was able to reduce piracy from which earlier trade had always suffered. Gentry and clothiers joined in support of road improvements[2] and these were to the great advantage of the clothing industry. As the population increased so did the home market for woollens. Water power, one of the most important natural advantages of our area, provided a basis for the expansion of the industry long before the arrival of steam.

The small hillside cottages with a few acres of land were to be seen everywhere. However, there were a few employers who had larger labour forces and in 1806 Law Atkinson of Bradley Mills had seventeen handlooms in one room and there were many others at work for him in their own homes; he was probably controlling about a hundred workpeople.

The processes involved in the hand and cottage industry

[1] Cookson MSS in Thoresby Society Library.
[2] See Chapter VI.

changed little from the fourteenth to the eighteenth century. Arriving home with a few stones of wool from the market, the clothier and his family opened out the bundles and spread the wool on hurdles or on the floor. The wool was then beaten and tossed with sticks to open out the fibres and any pieces of twig or dirt were picked out by hand. Sometimes the wool was dyed in a vat which stood outside in the yard, or it was left in the natural state to be 'dyed in the piece' after weaving. Then the wool was oiled or greased to make the fibres cling together and, as oil had to be bought in Huddersfield, home-made substitutes including butter, were sometimes used. When the oil had been well mixed into the wool, the fibres were again beaten with sticks, a process known as 'willeying'.

The wool was now ready for carding, that is, 'teasing'. This was done by hand cards of bent wire teeth set in leather and which looked like a very coarse hair brush. This making of cards with iron pins was a subsidiary trade in the Brighouse area, the raw material supplied no doubt by the iron masters at Low Moor, near Bradford. The average size of a wool card was twelve inches by five. After the wool was passed between a pair of cards, worked with a circular motion to produce a sheet of interlaced fibres, the fine 'sliver' or film of fibres thus produced, was wound into a roll known as a 'rolag'.

Carding was usually done by the children while the women did the spinning. Thus, as long as the men wove, there was work for all. A document quoted by Crump and Ghorbal[1] runs 'The pore and needy shal be releeved by spynninge, oyeling, dressinge of wooll and other easie laboure belonginge to the trade, which yeildeth employment to the eldest, yongest, strongest and weakest persons.' The larger clothiers employed women outside the family to spin at home, and until the invention of the 'Spinning Jenny' there was frequently a shortage of yarn for the weavers, a shortage always worst at harvest time when the women were required on the land. Spinning was always poorly paid, at a copper or two for a day's output, consequently some weavers were known to walk miles in order to find yarn with which to work. The primitive distaff was, in

[1] *History of the Huddersfield Woollen Industry*, p. 35.

act, replaced by the spinning wheel by the end of the Tudor period but this had no effect on the organisation of the woollen industry as the wheel found a place in most households. The big wheel was turned by hand and spun only one thread at a time, a laborious process. When the rolag had been drawn out into a long twisted thread, the resulting 'yarn' was wound onto a bobbin.

The long threads of the warp in the loom required strengthening to guard against breaking as the piece was woven; they were therefore dipped in size and hung outside on sticks to dry. The threads of the weft which went across the loom needed to have the 'snarl' or springiness taken out. The bobbins of weft were therefore dipped in water, and the surplus water extruded by whirling the bobbins round and round in a basket on the end of a rope tied to a stick with its end pivoted in a hole in the outside wall—a device which was a forerunner of spin-drying!

The actual weaving by hand consisted of three actions. Alternate threads of the warp were divided by means of treadles. The shuttle was then thrown by hand through the gap and finally each strand of weft was driven home by pressing a wooden batten against it. Weaving was a tiring occupation which made the shoulders and back ache and depressed the chest. The kersey could be woven by one man, but broad cloth required two. Kay's flying shuttle, invented in 1733 made possible a saving of labour here, as it enabled one man to operate a broad loom. The basis of the invention was the 'picking peg' operated by alternate hands, sending the shuttle flying across the warp, while the free hand pressed the batten immediately afterwards. The flying shuttle was taken into general use in the 1760's.

When the piece was taken out of the loom, it was necessary to get rid of the oil, size and oily dirt which the greasy wool had attracted to itself. This cleansing process was the 'scouring' of the cloth. In later times a solution of ammonia was used for dissolving the grease, but before the nineteenth century, stale urine was applied to the cloth in the homestead. The urine was collected, often in a tub standing by the cottage door, and used for 'lecking' the pieces, which were then taken down to the fulling mill, by the river, for scouring. Here stocks driven by water power beat the cloth and forced it round in the water until it was clean. Then the cloth was taken back to the house when it was dried, burled and mended; that is to say each piece was examined for extraneous particles and the defects were made good.

The piece of cloth was then returned to the fulling mill where it was, in fact, 'fulled' in stocks which pounded it in soapy water until it became felted. This process greatly strengthened the cloth as the fibres became entangled together. The spaces between the threads of a coarsely woven piece were filled in and the piece took on a more 'solid' and uniform, though rough, appearance.

Once more the clothier took his piece home where it was dried and stretched on tenter hooks set in a frame, out of doors. Because of the climate, this was a slow process. Many old maps, as on page 48, show the existence of 'tenter crofts'. Complaints were sometimes made that cloths were over tentered or over stretched to increase their size. The cloth later shrank, and one man remarked that if a certain gentleman made a livery of his cloth for any man, in the first shower of rain, 'it may fit his page for bigness!'[1] Tentering was the subject of various Acts passed in Tudor and Stuart Times. In Henry VIII's reign, fifty-five weavers at Almondbury and forty at Huddersfield were accused of using flocks and waste as weft in an inferior quality kersey—a different kind of sharp practice.

Tentering marked the end of the clothier's work and on the Monday following, the pieces were taken to Almondbury, or in later years to Huddersfield Market on a Tuesday. There they were sold to a merchant who could have them 'finished' as he wished. The exception to this was when the larger clothiers did their own finishing.

The merchant took the piece to be finished in a cropping shop, at first at the fulling mills, but later many specialised cropping shops appeared near the town and not far from the market notably John Wood's at Longroyd Bridge, later to become very famous in local legend.[2]

---

[1] *The True Estate of Clothing in the Realm:* J. May (1613).
[2] See Chapter VII.

Inside a Cropping Shop: from a drawing by Leslie Taylor

In the cropping shop, the cloth nap was at first raised by teasels set in a frame and drawn over the surface of the piece. This was known as 'rowing' the cloth. Later, 'cards' set with wire teeth were used in place of, or in addition to, the teasels. For this process the cloth was wound from one roller to another on a 'nelly' as in the illustration on the opposite page.

The raised nap was then cropped with heavy shears which rested on a curved board, across which the piece was drawn. The size of the shears and the strength of the huge spring which connected them necessitated the addition of a wooden lever to the upper blade which the cropper pulled towards himself.

In an engraving[1] of John Wood's cropping shop one can see a man with a watering can. Apparently it was necessary to 'leck' the cloth between some of the finishing processes which culminated when the piece was 'perched', that is drawn over a pole or perch by hand in order to inspect it. The piece was finally brushed and pressed between hot plates.

The merchant collected his cloth and then sold it either at the local markets or sent it to the weekly London market at Blackwell Hall or to the annual St Bartholomew Fair, where agents sold the textile pieces on commission.

Some of the wealthier clothiers had stalls in London, for in 1562 a certain John Crossley of Huddersfield bequeathed 'To my eldest son William . . . one standing or booth in the cloth fair called St Bartholomew's near West Smithfield in London.' Alternatively the merchant took or sent the goods to Hull or York for export by the Merchant Adventurers or the Eastland Company.

At this stage we must take a detailed look at the fulling mills and their owners within our area. In the sixteenth century, so-called 'new men', as distinct from the nobility, bought the old abbey lands and extended their holdings where they could. The new men in our area were local since the southerner seldom ventured north, and the successful local clothier with some capital had little other than land in which to invest his money. A source of water power was particularly attractive and so it was that Arthur Kaye, who inherited the manors of Farnley and

---

[1] Crump & Ghorbal, p. 97.

Slaithwaite in 1506, extended his lands and built two fulling mills at Slaithwaite. His son John Kaye, bought the corn mill and the 'fulling mill' in Honley. The William Ramsden who married Johanna Wode of Longley Hall bought so much monastic land that it was forbidden to sell him any more. He had a number of outstanding debts including one of £800 due to the Crown and because of his failure to pay, the Crown took possession of his lands in 1554. The Ramsdens were yeoman clothiers in Elland, and William, before his death in 1580, had rebuilt the fulling mill next to the corn mills on the Colne. There were three fulling mills on the Fenay Beck and by 1630 the Ramsdens had bought them all. A John Armitage, clothier, of Farnley Tyas acquired the monastic lands at Kirklees in 1565 where his descendants have lived ever since. The family were involved in a law suit regarding the fulling mill at Brighouse. The Brooke family of Armitage Bridge are today directly descended from a line of clothiers and fullers first recorded in the sixteenth century.

These families encouraged the growth of textiles by their provision of fulling mills and, by the early eighteenth century, there were seventeen mills on the Colne, Holme and Fenay. Some had grown from the old manorial corn mills, which meant that the tenants were obliged both to full cloth and grind corn there. Some of the mills were 'farmed' to a miller who paid a rent and made what profit he could from the mill. The mills worked for about half the year only. In mid-winter the rivers froze and in summer they often ran almost dry. An account of the Slaithwaite fulling mills appears in Crump and Ghorbal as:

For half year ending Whitsuntide, 1684

Receipts			Expenditure		
			Milners Commission		
1164 kerseys fulled @ 6d.	£29 2 0		1435 kerseys @ 1¼d.	£7 9 5¾	
271 kerseys @ 5d.	5 12 11		Bonus: 4 men @ 12d.	4 0	
(Total kerseys 1435)			Repairs	4 6 4	
			Profit	22 15 1¼	
Total	£34 14 11			£34 14 11	

The 5d kerseys came from strangers not obliged to full at this mill, the penny cut in price was to encourage an expansion of the business. The 'four men at twelve pence' indicates the gratuities paid to apprentices who were otherwise unpaid. The commission of £7. 9s. 5¾d. divided between two millers for the half year works out at about three shillings each per week. As the profit went to the lord, these men were not the 'farmers' of the mill.

Although the fulling mill on the river later became the nucleus of the factory, the clothier usually lived and worked on the higher ground, often because of the intake of new land from the waste which was there. Furthermore the light was better on the hills and the plentiful water made it possible to work anywhere in the district. The cottage itself was usually two storeys high with a long row of mullioned windows upstairs. It was in the upper storey that the weaving was done. Below was the living room and kitchen which contained the meal ark where the oatmeal was stored for making porridge and oatcake. Adjoining the cottage there would be a farm building comprising barn, stable, and mistal for one or two animals. These buildings were the minimum, but as the clothier prospered, a tall warehouse building would appear and there might be a dyehouse also, and exceptionally, a cropping shop. Local agriculture never improved. It was traditional, with a little oats and larger quantities of potatoes.

One clothier, who died in 1712, left an inventory which gives us a useful guide to his work and circumstances. He had one old cow, a heifer, a stirk and a calf, eight sheep, some bees, one little horse with pack saddle, farm implements, a cheese press, two looms, cards, a pair of tenters, a dye vat, and a weigh beam.

The late seventeenth century saw in Yorkshire the start of worsted manufacture as a means of using the yarn previously sent to Norwich for manufacture. Labour was cheap, and by 1727 Defoe noted that shalloons of worsted, broad and narrow woollens were the three main products of the West Riding. Worsted was at first a novelty, but the keenness of the early manufacturers to imitate their Norfolk competitors led to its manufacture in quantity in the area of Halifax and Bradford.

During the eighteenth century, five towns were pre-eminent

in wool textiles: Leeds, Bradford, Halifax, Huddersfield and Wakefield. In the late Middle Ages, Halifax had been second only to York as a clothing town and since they were alleged to behead cloth stealers there, the Beggars' Litany ran 'From Hull, Hell and Halifax Good Lord deliver us!' Bradford, noted for allegedly fraudulent work, was mentioned in an early Methodist hymn—'On Bradford, likewise look Thou down, where Satan keeps his seat!' (William Darney 1751).

As this chapter ends at the middle of the eighteenth century and before the start of the Industrial Revolution, Defoe's description of the West Riding in 1727 is appropriate.

'The land being divided into small enclosures, from two to seven acres each, seldom more, every three or four pieces of land have a house belonging to them.

'Such has been the bounty of nature to this country that two things essential to the clothing trade are found here—I mean coals and running water upon the tops of the highest hills—neither indeed could one fifth of the inhabitants be supported without them for the land could not maintain them—hardly a house standing out of a speaking distance from another—at almost every house was a tenter and on almost every tenter a piece of cloth—among the manufacturers' houses are likewise scattered an infinite number of small dwellings in which dwell the workmen—the women and children all of whom are always busy carding, spinning, etc., so that no hands being unemployed, all can gain their bread.'

CHAPTER V

Huddersfield in the Days of John Wesley and Henry Venn

AT FIRST GLANCE, the map of 1778 shows Huddersfield to have been a poor straggling town, with the Parish Church, George Inn and Cloth Hall the only large buildings to be seen. Buxton Road Methodist Chapel (1775) and Highfield Congregational (1771), not being in the town centre as it then was, are therefore off the map.

To bring this picture into focus, it would be as well, before going further, to take a brief look at the county as a whole. By mid-century, for example, Methodism had arrived. The lack of Anglican clergymen of quality outside London had virtually opened the door to Nonconformity.[1] Nonconformists, eventually well received, were at first despised; while Roman Catholics, of whom there were many in Yorkshire, were generally mistrusted.

There was almost no social life outside York itself and newspapers were rare. The *Leeds Mercury* (1718), and the *Leeds Intelligencer* (1754), which became the *Yorkshire Post* (1866), had small circulations by modern standards. Even as late as the end of the century, the *Mercury* sold only 3,000 copies a day.

Only two M.P.s sat for the county but there were members for York, Hull and twelve other ancient boroughs. Polling for the county was at York and lasted fifteen days. No member represented Leeds, Bradford, Halifax, Sheffield, Wakefield or Huddersfield. Of course, this was an era when it was generally agreed that society existed for the preservation of property and

---

[1] Methodism in fact remained a movement within the Church of England until 1784 and has never been correctly described as 'Nonconformity' or 'Dissent'.

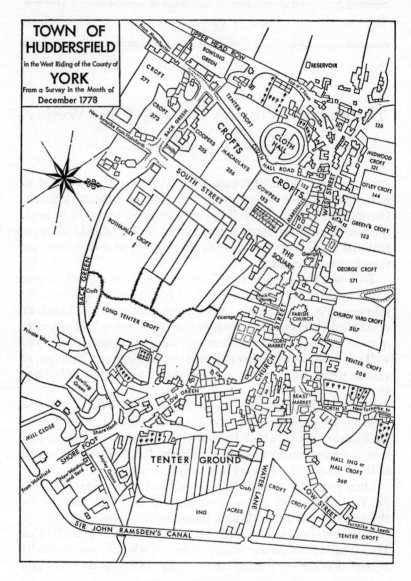

The Town of Huddersfield in 1778

the poor, who had nothing, were regarded as a nuisance. The penal system, designed to deal with any who threatened property or society, was extremely harsh.

There appears to have been a pall of mental and spiritual darkness over Huddersfield and other similar towns, which only her own people were likely to lift, for few travellers ventured north in those days. A few notable exceptions to this will be met in this chapter.

Returning to our map of Huddersfield, it is clear that the centre of the town was the Market Square. At one side of the square was the 'George Inn'—removed[1] in 1850 in order to make John William Street—from the upper windows of which political speeches were made. John Wesley, as we shall see later, preached from the Market Cross. Some of the upper storeys of the buildings in New Street have changed surprisingly little since the late eighteenth century and it was in the square that a general market was held every Tuesday, even after the textiles were removed to the Cloth Hall in 1766. This market stretched to the open space on our map and filled that area of King Street where the Market Hall was to be built in 1880. From the picture (on page 50) it would also appear that some of the carting services, traditionally associated with the Pack Horse Yard, left from the Market-Square. In fact transport of all kinds was based on the Kirkgate or 'Church Street' area, including stage coaches—a form of transport which proved so popular that in 1747 the Government found it profitable to tax them.

From the Market-Square and turning left at the George, the traveller entered West Street, which eventually became a footpath to the new chapel at Highfield. A left turn from West Street led either along Cloth Hall Road or to 'Top o't' Town' and Upperhead Row. Both roads ended at Outcote Bank and the road to Manchester. The right-hand side of South Street (later New Street) going towards Back Green, was almost devoid of buildings. Back Green (later Ramsden Street) ran from South Street curving round through the fields to Shore Head, where there was more property down by the river, around

---

[1] The building was re-erected in St Peter's Street but the name and its licence went to new premises in St Georges Square.

The Market Square, Huddersfield, c. 1800. From a drawing by
Leslie Taylor

Low Green and up to the Parish Church. More property still ran along the left-hand side of Low Street (Lowerhead Row) towards Leeds, and along North Street towards Halifax and Bradford. The plan shows two centres of population, one by the river and the other by the Cloth Hall; the Parish Church and Market-Square stand, as it were, connecting the two.

The little town in those days had no police force. There was a constable appointed by the Parish Vestry to detect thieves, apprehend all vagrants, examine hawkers and pedlars for stolen goods, and to visit all ale houses. Sometimes he had an assistant. A story runs that the constable was knocked up in the small hours with the news that there was a fight in the Beast Market.

'How long have they been at it?'

'They've only just started.'

'Well then, let them fight for another half an hour and I'll be down. Then we might manage 'em. They'll be all the better to deal with, then.'

By the time the officer appeared all had gone, so, duty done, back he went to bed! (*See note on page 68.*)

The turnpike roads in our area frequently ran on the tops of the hills and avoided the valleys used by the present major routes. The valleys tended to be enclosed land in private ownership, while much of the population lived in the hills where there was work and water. It was because most of the people lived in scattered textile communities that the actual town of Huddersfield was quite small in the eighteenth century. The turnpike trust movement was devised as a means whereby road making and repairs could be paid for by the users, who paid tolls. The tariff in 1820, from the Shore in Huddersfield to Austerlands, over Standedge, was:

For every horse, mule or other beast drawing any coach, chariot, chaise, waggon or cart .. .. 4*d.*
For every horse, mule or ass laden, or unladen and not drawing .. .. 1*d.*
Cattle or oxen .. .. per score 10*d.*
Calves, sheep or swine .. .. .. per score 5*d.*

This particular road[1] was completed in 1759 and ran from

[1] See Jefferys' map facing p. 52.

Wakefield to Horbury, Almondbury, Huddersfield, over Crosland Hill to Marsden, thus avoiding the bottom of the Colne Valley. The Halifax road was made by 'Blind Jack' Metcalf in 1777, from Clough House, near Norman Park, and it still runs through Grimscar Woods. It is still known as Halifax Old Road. The still older route to Halifax over Cowcliffe was never turnpiked. In 1765 however, a new route was cut across the open fields from Huddersfield to Cooper Bridge, and equally important in 1768 the 'Huddersfield to Woodhead and Enterclough Bridge Turnpike' was made; this road went through Lockwood over Taylor Hill, avoiding the Holme Valley to Honley and thence over Holme Moss to Woodhead.

The Turnpike Acts were the results of private enterprise. A large number of gentry and manufacturers were given permission to borrow money to pay for the road making, but the collection of tolls was let annually to the highest bidder and, whereas the collectors made a profit out of the roads, the original trustees seldom recovered the whole of their investment.

The success of the Huddersfield Tuesday Market showed that Almondbury was eclipsed as a trading centre by the early eighteenth century and, when Sir John Ramsden built his well-known circular brick arcade in 1766, cloth halls had been successfully erected in Halifax, Wakefield and Leeds. The Cloth Hall was enlarged in 1780 by the addition of an upper storey, and further extended in 1848. The main entrance was in Sergeantson Street and soon all manner of warehouses and offices grew up in Fox Street, Upperhead Row and Dundas Street. Architecturally the place was ugly with few windows on the outside, all the light coming from windows looking on to the inner circular courtyard. Inside there were corridors flanked by small rooms and the goods were displayed within them on benches so that one one could walk round and compare the price and quality before making a purchase. The central hall was not divided and the roof was supported by round stone pillars on a stone floor.

An account of 1822 runs: 'The hall is divided into streets, and the benches or stalls are generally filled up with cloths lying close together on edge for inspection. Here in brisk times an immense quantity of work is done in a few hours. The doors are opened early in the morning of the market-day, which is Tuesday, and closed at half past twelve o'clock at noon. They are again opened at three o'clock for the removal of cloth. Above the door is a handsome cupola in which a clock and bell are placed for the purpose of regulating the time of commencing and terminating the business of the day.' The width of the passages in the Cloth Hall was the subject of a deputation of clothiers to Sir John Ramsden in 1765 at his house at Byram Hall near Pontefract. The ideal width was reckoned as twice that taken by a man carrying a piece of cloth on his back.

When there were 150 stands in the Cloth Hall over 500 clothiers dealt there, 130 of them from Golcar alone, though some came from as far as Saddleworth. Buyers came from Halifax, Manchester, Leeds and even London.

The clothiers usually went to their inns for a meal at 12.30 and in time some preferred to do their business at the inn in privacy. This was particularly so when, later on, design became important. When all were selling simple plain kerseys or broadcloths there was little to hide but when fancy patterns came into vogue secrecy was necessary. Much of the cloth sold in the early days was unwashed and unmilled. The purchaser took the pieces from the Cloth Hall to finishing shops in or near the town, whence they were delivered to the purchaser's inn, or despatched to the customer by canal, pack-horse or coach.

If we compare the map of 1778 with that of 1826, a number of new 'intended' roads will be seen; these and many other roads not on the maps came as a result of the Enclosure Act of 1789.

By the 'enclosure movement' is generally meant that process by which the large fields, divided into strips, and the waste or common land around them were converted into compact permanent holdings. In the south of England the effects of the break-up of the open field system were far more serious than in our area, where the intaking of waste had taken place gradually over the years. The most serious loss to the small-holder was that of grazing rights on the common; the most important gain was that in a compact holding of arable and pasture land agriculture could be greatly improved and made more efficient.

The Huddersfield Act did more than reallocate land, it provided for new roads, footpaths, public wells and watering places and quarries for stone. Land was shared out between many individuals but the lord of the manor received the lion's share. In return for the surrender of some of his ancient rights of mining, quarrying and tithes he received much common land. Grants were made as follows in 1789:

	Acres	Rods	Poles
Sir John Ramsden	286	2	26
The Vicar of Huddersfield	8	1	8
Thomas Thornhill, Esq.	7	0	36
Allotted for quarries	2	0	0
J. Armitage of Bay Hall	0	0	12
Rev. Samuel Brook	0	0	16
Joseph Bradley and others	0	0	3
Bramhall Dyson, gentleman	1	0	20
William Fenton, gentleman	0	3	20
John and Thomas Haigh	0	0	16
Thomas Holroyd	1	0	1
Henry Hirst	0	0	1
Sarah Nicholls, Thomas and Ann Macaulay	9	2	4
John Whitacre	5	3	35
B. Walker and R. Collingwood at Bay Hall	0	0	36
Joseph Walker, Bay Hall	0	1	32

The new roads made towards the end of the century played an important part in the development of the town and the immediate suburbs. They included: the Paddock Road, the Halifax Road over King Cliffe, Cowcliffe Hill, Woodhouse Hill over to Deighton, Ashbrow Road, Birkby Road from Halifax Road to Blacker Lane and other roads near Bay Hall, Lindley Road from Blacker Lane over 'Marsh Common', Luck Lane from Marsh to Paddock, Gledholt Bank, and there were many other minor roads made to connect these and provide alternative and cross routes on the outskirts of the town. As a result of these developments, Birkby, Fartown, Sheepridge,

Marsh, Lindley and Paddock began to take on their now familiar aspect.

The Huddersfield Act also established public wells at Gledholt, Birkby and Sheepridge, and animal watering places at Bay Hall and Cowcliffe. Quarries for road-repairing materials were opened at Paddock, Cowcliffe and Sheepridge.

Later Enclosure Acts covered Lindley in 1798, Kirkheaton in 1799, Old Lindley (Stainland) in 1810, Dalton in 1811, Golcar in 1823 and Longwood in 1825.

It is easy to criticise these Acts which legalised the appropriation of much public land by a few private individuals. It should be said however, that they helped the town to develop a long time before anything like a local authority was able to take corporate action for the common good.

Mention of wells and watering places brings us to the question of how the town obtained its water supply in the eighteenth century. In manorial days there was no need for the Courts Leet of the Lord of the Manors of Huddersfield and Almondbury to interest themselves in water supplies. By 1743, however, Sir John Ramsden found it necessary to construct the first Huddersfield waterworks. The River Colne supplied the water and the power to drive a pump at Folly Hall. The pumping site became known as Engine Bridge, and from there the water was pumped through wooden pipes to a reservoir at the bottom of George Street, shown on the 1778 map just above the Cloth Hall. The Folly Hall pump was driven by a water wheel and the main pipes were large tree trunks with a three-and-a-half-inch hole bored right through them; one end of each trunk was tapered to fit into the next one. The pipes ran under the canal and then to the top of Outcote Bank and along Upperhead Row to the reservoir. On one occasion when the supply of water failed, a large trout was found inside one of the pipes! The water available was only sufficient for part of the town at any one time, so an old woman named Betty Earnshaw was employed to regulate the supply. She carried a large turn-key on her shoulder for turning the mains on and off in various parts of the town. This system lasted until 1828, but by that time water supplies, although supplemented by the Bradley Spout near the present railway station, had become completely inadequate.

The development which perhaps most affected the people's lives in the eighteenth century was the spread of Nonconformity, but in order to understand what happened it is necessary to go back to the Reformation and the Elizabethan Settlement of 1559.

Elizabeth I had enforced a compromise which satisfied neither the extreme Roman Catholic nor the ultra-Protestant or Puritan point of view. As we all know, the latter enjoined a strict mode of life and extreme simplicity of worship which gradually took root in England and Scotland. By 1660, at the Restoration of Charles II, there were indeed many sects of Brownists, Presbyterians and Baptists though their numbers were very small. Some, like the Pilgrim Fathers, emigrated: others ran the risk of persecution until the Commonwealth period filled the Anglican pulpits with Puritan divines. By 1660 a very complex religious situation had developed. The new King was inclined to be pro-Catholic, and he had to establish his authority. The Cavalier Parliament expressed its opposition to the Dissenters by enthusiastically supporting the Church of England and bishops were re-admitted to the House of Lords. When the Prayer Book of 1662 was enforced by law, a fifth of the Anglican clergy left the Church. Then the Conventicle Act of 1664 forbade the dispossessed clergymen to hold services, and led to many being imprisoned. Only a few clergymen in our area resigned from the Church of England in 1662, including David Drury, Curate of Honley, John Hide, Curate of Slaithwaite, and Christopher Heaton, Vicar of Kirkheaton.

When, under the Toleration Act of 1689, Dissenters were permitted to meet, Nonconformity, previously practised in secret, came into the open. A Scottish family named Morton had settled near Salendine Nook as potters and we find recorded:

This may certify the court that the house of Michael Morton where he now liveth in Quarmby is intended and by use the adherers thereunto agreed upon to be a public meeting place for Protestant Dissenters having no other design than to glorify God and edify one another, and promote the public interest of both Church and State in due subjection to the law now established in our nation. God save Their Majesties.

Michael Morton

8th October, 1689   desires a licence

This document has been regarded as marking the origins of Salendine Nook Baptist Chapel. Indeed, itinerant preachers, using private houses as meeting-places, kept alive the spirit of dissent in this area from mid-seventeenth to mid-eighteenth century. Henry Clayton preached at Salendine Nook from 1731 to 1776 walking or riding from his farm near Halifax each week-end; by 1743 Mr Clayton's tiny flock had built their own church with a membership of eleven. The spirit of these pioneers was well captured by Percy Stock in his book *Foundations*, where he describes a meeting in the autumn of 1689.

'The October evening wind flows coldly over the moorland. The houses are few and widely scattered. Lights shine here and there but one is more brilliant than the rest. Men and women are excitedly approaching the light. They are just plain folk, the women with shawls on their heads and clogs on their feet. The scene is in an ancient barn. The door opens and two men come through, one is old, the other of middle age. The old man rises and the service begins as he reads Isaiah Chapter 40 . . . Comfort Ye My people . . . The sermon has as its text "Watchman, what of the night? The morning cometh" and the speaker recounts the difficulties under which his followers have laboured. At this point he shows them a piece of paper—their licence, and dwells on what this means. The blessed morning has come; the big barn doors are open for public worship and, please God, the open door shall never be taken away again. Finally he commends them for keeping alight the flame of the blessed Gospel in that place.

The meeting ended with the singing of the 124th Psalm—not very well rendered for this was the first time they had ever dared to sing aloud together . . .'

Most Nonconformist denominations probably had this kind of start. One of the greatest influences in the Free Churches of the seventeenth century was Rev. Oliver Heywood who founded

Lydgate Presbyterian Church, Holmfirth in 1694—the first Nonconformist chapel building in our area.

An interesting view of the times is given by the Rev. Robert Meeke, who was curate of the chapel at Slaithwaite, within the Parish of Huddersfield from 1685 to 1724, and from whose diary the following extracts are taken:

November 24th 1689: 'Arose in health in the morning. I went towards Holmfirth and he to Lydgate (George Moorhouse one of the leaders of Protestant Dissent in Holmfirth). Lord, grant in Thine own time take away all differences amongst Thy people and grant that we may be willing to meet in one place and join in one way of worship.'

November 25th 1690: 'Though I can submit to many things which others cannot; yet would I not have able and worthy men to be cast out of the Church because they cannot. Lord grant to England's rulers a spirit of wisdom to mend and heal our distempers and unite their hearts to make up our breaches.'

August 30th 1694: 'Went to see a new chapel which is built for a nonconformist—we all preach the same doctrine, pray for the same things; all the difference consists in garments, gestures and words; and yet that difference breedeth heats, dissension, strangeness and coldness of charity and christian affection among friends . . . Lord take away all matters of contention.'

Here was a kindly and well-informed man filled with sadness by the changes which were taking place all around him; yet he retained the friendship of many who had left the Church of England to follow other denominations, mostly in opposition to his own.

In 1743, John Herring, then Archbishop of York, sent a questionnaire round his see, and for an immediate and vivid picture of the Church of England in our area we cannot do better than read the answers relating to the parishes of Huddersfield and Almondbury:

Huddersfield in the Days of John Wesley and Henry Venn

	Huddersfield	Almondbury
1. How many famililies are there in your Parish? of these how many are dissenters? of what sort are they?	1,100. 100 anabaptists. Quakers and Methodists [this shows that Methodism had taken root very early in Huddersfield some 14 years before Wesley came here].	1,300. 4 or 5 families of Quakers. Independents.
2. Have you any licensed or other Meeting House in your Parish? How many? of what sort?	One for anabaptists Believed not licensed [Salendine Nook?] meets fortnightly for about 30 hearers. Others meet in families.	None.
3. Is there a public or charity school?	One charity school. 20 children taught free.	Two schools.
4. Are there any alms houses or other charities?	None.	Yes Nettleton's Charity.
5. Do you personally live in the parish?	Yes.	Yes.
6. Have you a resident curate?	Yes I have a resident curate, not licensed. Allowed £15 a year, the rest depends upon collections.	None.
7. Do you know of any not baptised who come to Church?	All baptised who attend. All confirmed in due course.	All except one Quaker to whom baptism was refused.

59

	Huddersfield	Almondbury
8. How often is the public service read? Is it performed twice every Lord's Day?	Four times a week, twice on Sundays, once on Wednesday and Friday also all feasts at festivals.	Twice on Sunday, Wednesdays and Fridays in Lent also on Holy Days —oftener than we can get a congregation.
9. How often and at what times do you Catechise in your Church?	Catechising begins about Midsummer and continues six or seven Sundays.	On Wednesdays and Fridays in Lent. This is of late years as I am now aged.
10. How often is the Sacrament of the Lord's Supper administered? How many usually receive it? How many communicated last Easter?	On the first Sunday of each month besides Palm Sunday, Good Friday and Easter Day. 50 come each time 400 came last Easter.	On the first Sunday of the month also at Easter. How many come each time is uncertain but 1,343 came last Easter. I administer in four chapels besides at the Parish Church.
11. Do you give timely warning of the Sacrament? Have you refused the Sacrament to anyone?	Open and timely warning is given. I have never refused the Sacrament to anyone.	I have never refused the Sacrament to anyone. Some there are who walk seven miles for it.
12. Have you met with any difficulties, abuses or corruptions? Have you any proposals to make?	I have observed no defects or abuses.	Nothing to report.

Signed
Claudius Daubuz
Vicar

Signed
Edward Rishton
Vicar

From these answers the complacency of the Church of England in the eighteenth century, and the fact that its doctrines were not reaching the mass of the people, appear very clearly. In Huddersfield some 400 individuals came for Easter Communion out of 1,100 families—less than a quarter of the adult population of the town. The Vicar of Almondbury says there are no dissenters at all in his parish, probably because he was too old and infirm to find out the real picture. It should be said in his defence, however, that the Parish of Almondbury was too large for one man, although there were chapelries at Marsden, Honley and Meltham. The mention of some walking seven miles to church is interesting, though many walked much further than this on market-day. The answers to the last question show the two incumbents as being completely devoid of ideas, constructive or otherwise. It is therefore not surprising that the Methodists had made an impact on the town long before Wesley arrived in person. *(See parish map on page 12.)*

When John Wesley finally came, on 9th June 1757, he wrote: 'I rode over the mountains to Huddersfield. A wilder people I never saw in England. The men, women and children filled the streets and seemed just ready to devour us. How intolerable a thing is the Gospel of Christ to them that are resolved to serve the devil!' Perhaps it was at Huddersfield that he fully realised the size of his problem in the North.

Towards the end of April 1759, Wesley returned to Yorkshire and afterwards wrote: 'Preached near Huddersfield to the wildest congregation I have seen in Yorkshire. Yet they were restrained by an unseen hand, and I believed some felt the sharpness of His word.'

It seems that Wesley had made an impression, however slight, on the 'wild men' of Huddersfield. But within a few years the picture was to change out of all recognition, and this was due almost entirely to the ministry of Henry Venn who arrived as Vicar of Huddersfield on 15th April 1759.

Henry Venn 'discovered, from a child, such activity and energy of mind, such decision and zeal in whatever he undertook, that all who observed him expected he would one day become an extraordinary character'. As a young man he was one of the best cricketers at Cambridge. A few days before being ordained he played for Surrey against All England and when the game was over he threw down his bat for the last time saying, 'Because I am to be ordained on Sunday . . . I will never have it said of me "Well struck, Parson!" '

As curate at Clapham, Venn became acquainted with many views on religion and his own experiences widened considerably, but he did not meet with the success he was seeking there, and welcomed the offer of the living of Huddersfield from Sir John Ramsden (1698–1769) to whom Venn had been commended by the Earl of Dartmouth. When he saw his new parish he accepted the post immediately in spite of the fact that the income was less than £100 a year and he already had a wife and two children to support.

> 'As soon as he began to preach in Huddersfield, the Church became crowded, to such an extent that many were not able to gain admission. Numbers became deeply impressed with concern about their immortal souls; persons flocked from distant hamlets inquiring what they must do to be saved. He found them in general utterly ignorant of . . . the redemption that is in Christ Jesus . . . He was never satisfied with his labours among them though they were continued to a degree ruinous to his health. On the Sunday he would often address the congregation from the desk, briefly explaining and enforcing the Psalms and the Lessons. [The people must have been very ignorant and the vicar very zealous for such a situation to arise in that a service was interrupted while he explained to them what was being sung or read.] He would frequently begin the service with a solemn address exhorting them to consider themselves in the presence of God . . . whose eye was upon them . . . in His own house. His whole soul was engaged in preaching and . . . as he only used short notes in the pulpit, ample room was left for the feeling of compassion and love with which his heart overflowed towards his people. In the week he visited the different hamlets in his extensive parish; and, collecting some of the inhabitants at a private house, he addressed them with a kindness and earnestness which moved every heart.'

John Starkey of Cowcliffe, when an old man, said, 'I

esteemed Mr Venn too much for a man; I almost forgot that he was only a creature . . . I was very wild and careless when a lad and would not go to church . . . I heard one sermon which made me begin to think. The text was "God is no respecter of persons"; and he showed me that it was neither money nor learning nor anything else of that kind which could make us happy; but that without holiness we were under God's frown and curse. I then saw something of my real state. I don't think anything would have kept me from him. He was a wonderful preacher. I have often wept at his sermons, I could have stood to hear him till morning.'

This account, redolent of truth, shows why it was that the Parish Church, previously not well attended, was full to overflowing in the days of Henry Venn.

In 1763 Venn published his book *The Complete Duty of Man* as the exposition of his evangelical views. His opinions did, however, change over the years; and, whereas when he arrived in Huddersfield he believed that God bestows His grace on all who repent and believe (Wesley's own view), later he turned to Calvinism with its credo of the frailty and inevitable corruption of man who could be saved by God's grace alone and not by his own efforts. Nevertheless, Venn did not make a point of forcing his views on other people, and he never broke with the Arminians.[1] He did, however, become a friend of the Countess of Huntingdon, and of the movement she started whose members became known as the 'Calvinistic Methodists'.

From all this, one would have thought that relations between Wesley and Venn would have been extremely cordial, and so they were for a time. The vicar allowed Wesley the use of his pulpit, which was quite exceptional, for in many parishes the latter met with a hostile reception from the Anglican clergy. Indeed Venn went so far as to attend a Methodist conference in 1756 with some forty or fifty of Wesley's itinerant preachers.

In 1761 Venn asked Wesley to withdraw his itinerant preachers from Huddersfield since they and he preached the same doctrine. When the local Methodists objected to this,

---

[1] Followers of Arminius of Leyden (1560–1609) who taught that salvation was dependent upon the free will of those willing to accept God's grace.

Wesley and Venn agreed that the preachers should not come more than once a month. Wesley then stopped them for a year, but this failed to placate the vicar; and by 1765 the Methodists were preaching in public on their own initiative. Venn sent his curate round telling the people not to listen, but to no avail. Wesley wrote:

> 'Instead of coming nearer to me, you got farther off . . . we have only one faith, one hope, one Lord . . . come then ye that love Him to the help of the Lord'. (22nd June 1765).

Wesley did, however, agree to suspend itinerant preaching for another year and he preached at the Parish Church in the August of 1765 and 1766.

> 'Friday, I rode over to Huddersfield. The Church, though large, was exceedingly hot through the multitude of people on which I enjoined St. Paul's words "God forbid that I should glory save in the Cross of our Lord Jesus Christ".'

In the meantime Venn had become very friendly with George Whitefield, understandable as both shared Calvinistic views. In a letter of 2nd October 1767 Venn, inviting Whitefield to come to Huddersfield, wrote, 'Have compassion on my people . . . come and lift up your voice in my church on Tuesday. It is our Market Day. I can give notice on the Sabbath day; you will have thousands to hear you.' Whitefield came, stayed in the vicarage in what is now Venn Street, and preached what was to be his last sermon in Yorkshire.

Wesley and Venn eventually agreed to differ in their views. By 1770 Henry Venn, whose work was wearing him out, became so ill that he had to resign. He preached his last sermon on 30th March 1771 and went to a quieter parish at Yelling in Huntingdonshire. He had been regarded as their spiritual father by thousands, many of whom waited for his return to his flock.

Venn was tolerant when the new vicar, the Rev. Holcar Brook, was appointed, Mr Riland the curate having been passed over. But the new man was not of the old stamp. Salendine Nook had had difficulty in keeping going so long as 'T'owd Trumpet' had preached his sermons in town, and at least thirteen of Venn's followers became Independent ministers.

Henry Venn may be regarded as the father of Nonconformity on a large scale in the town. The Anglicans let slip the opportunity of pre-eminence in the evangelical revival in Huddersfield, and the opportunity never again presented itself. Rev. Holcar Brook at once put a stop to outdoor preaching, laying down that all must conform to the customs of the Established Church. He lost half of Henry Venn's hard-won congregation in no time at all.

Henry Clayton at Salendine Nook proceeded to increase his membership to sixty-nine and from then onwards the Baptist Church spread to Pole Moor in 1790. John Wesley continued to visit Yorkshire and Huddersfield, now preaching out of doors once again. On one such visit at the age of eighty-five, he preached at five in the morning at Longwood,[1] by nine o'clock he was at Shelley, and at night he was in Wakefield, still preaching in the open air. On 26th April 1779 he wrote, 'I preached at Huddersfield where there is a great revival of the work of God. Many have found peace with God.' Henry Venn's work had not been in vain.

The Methodists in Huddersfield built Old Bank Chapel, Buxton Road in 1775 but, almost as long as John Wesley lived, the movement remained within the Church of England. In 1795, however, Rev. Alexander Kilham (1762–98) published a pamphlet, *The Progress of Liberty,* in which he challenged the views of the Methodist Conference. He advocated the right of the laity to have a say in how Church affairs were organised and he felt that the Lord's Supper should be held in Methodist chapels and not exclusively in Anglican churches. When Kilham was expelled by Conference in 1796 he and William Thom formulated a new body to be known as the 'Methodist New Connexion'; and it was in Huddersfield at the house of David Taylor in what is now Trinity Street that their ideas were drawn up. By August 1797 Conference had definitely refused to permit any change in Methodist church government, therefore Thom and Kilham declared themselves President and

[1] Longwood House was near Netheroyd Hill: see Jefferys' map.

Secretary, respectively, of the new movement. Alexander Kilham took charge of the Sheffield area while William Thom included Old Bank Chapel in his circuit. In 1798 Kilham died through overwork. His scheme had incurred the displeasure of the Fathers of Methodism because, in the days of the French Revolution, such ideas were naturally viewed with suspicion. The New Connexion which had challenged established

Queen Street Mission: from a drawing by Noël Spencer

Methodist order laid down by Wesley was nicknamed the 'Tom Paine' Church for they were the 'Jacobins' of the Methodist Movement.

Also in 1798, William Thom encountered opposition at Old Bank from Rev. George Highfield and John Drake who had both remained loyal to the Methodist Conferences. On many occasions the preacher who arrived first in the pulpit took charge of the service until Highfield and Drake were successfully evicted. It was not until 1814 that Old Bank returned to the fold of the Wesleyans, by which time preliminary arrangements had been made for a new Wesleyan chapel in Queen Street, to be opened in 1819 as the largest building of its kind in the world.

66

In the meantime, the followers of the New Connexion moved to temporary premises at the top of Princess Street, while Joseph Haigh on their behalf went to Byram House to ask for land on which to start afresh. He was granted a site in High Street and the new chapel was opened in 1815, later rebuilt in 1867.

The largest number of those who left the Parish Church in 1771 went to found Highfield Congregational Chapel where they hoped to be united under a pastor of their own choice. Venn approved of the scheme and although Holcar Brook died in 1773 and was replaced by Joseph Trotter, a man more in sympathy with Henry Venn, the congregation did not return to the Parish Church in any great numbers. Sir John Ramsden, patron of the living of Huddersfield, understandably refused to permit the breakaway congregation to build anywhere on his land.[1] They therefore had to go outside the town and this explains why Highfield Chapel is off our town map of 1778. They built it on land bought from a Mr Bradley long before New North Road was contemplated. Henry Venn not only subscribed towards the new chapel but also recommended the first minister, Rev. W. Moorhouse, one of his own followers. It is believed to have been Venn's hope that the Anglican Liturgy would one day be used in the new chapel but this was not to be. Mr Moorhouse remained as minister for the next fifty years and almost lived to see the building of Ramsden Street Congregational Chapel, the story of which is told in Chapter VIII.

Henry Venn revisited Huddersfield in 1780 when he preached in the Parish Church twice on the one Sunday. The building was so overcrowded that the gallery almost gave way and had to be propped up. This was an isolated event and from now onwards the Anglican Church experienced keen competition from the Nonconformists. The smart new chapels at Highfield, Old Bank, and later, Queen Street, Ramsden Street and High Street absorbed all the religious fervour generated by Wesley and Venn, and it was not until 1836 that the Parish Church saw a revival of Anglicanism.

Nonconformity with its direct approach to the people, its

---

[1] In view of this it is surprising that the New Connexion were permitted to build in High Street some forty years later.

simple services and its music, obviously appealed to the hard-working Huddersfield folk. Furthermore these people, who were by tradition independent in spirit, now had a free choice of where to worship. They valued this free choice and were prepared to dig deeply into their pockets to pay for its continuance. The reaction against the Parish Church was a natural rebellion against any suggestion of being compelled to attend the Church of the Establishment, to which many felt they definitely did not belong. If a generalisation can be made, it might be said that clothiers who prospered and became manufacturers tended to become Liberal in their politics because they felt that Conservatism, rooted in the land, was not for them; and they remained loyal to their Nonconformity as a matter of independent principle.

NOTES

The Parish Vestry Constable, on page 51, should not be confused with the Chief Constable appointed by the Court Leet, under the Lord of the Manor. He was the ancient 'head man' of the town who convened any public meetings.

Old Bank Chapel, referred to correctly as being in Buxton Road, stood on the left-hand side going down Chapel Hill. The Chapel, later known as 'Buxton Road Methodist Church', was pulled down in 1955–6. See also page 126.

CHAPTER VI

Rapid Changes in Industry
and Transport

THE HAND LOOM weavers were accustomed to working long
hours at home in their cottages in the hills. Some were self-
educated; many were shrewd and speculative—a class now lost
to society, upon whom depended the wool textile industry.
During the early eighteenth century many were driven to look
for yarn because the spinners could seldom keep pace with the
weavers' demand, a situation further aggravated by the
invention, already mentioned,[1] of John Kay's flying shuttle.

In 1764 James Hargreaves is said to have seen a spinning
wheel overturned and still revolving on the floor, and the story
goes that this gave him the idea of turning several spindles
together. By 1767, however, the spinning 'jenny', so called
because it did a woman's work, was introduced. Like most
other textile inventions, the jenny was devised for cotton but its
use spread quickly to wool. Indeed most of the Lancashire
inventions came to the West Riding, via Saddleworth and the
Huddersfield Market. The Cloth Hall was regularly patronised by wool clothiers from Saddleworth and district, and the
division between wool and cotton to the east and west of the
Pennines was not then clearly defined. There were indeed
cotton mills[2] in Huddersfield and the Colne Valley, while the
so-called 'Manchester Goods' were in fact a mixture of wool
and cotton fibres. There was certainly wool in Burnley, the
Rossendale Valley and Rochdale, and the card makers of
Brighouse supplied the manufacturers of both wool and cotton
yarns. It was therefore not surprising that some inventions in

[1] See p. 40.   [2] See p. 334.

cotton should, with suitable modification, quickly become used for wool.

By 1776 the spinning jenny had reached Holmfirth and, because it could be worked at home, its use spread rapidly. On the first machines sixteen threads could be spun simultaneously, but soon the number had reached forty. The spinners' wages improved and eventually one jenny could supply two looms with all the yarn they needed. The initial result of this situation was that the clothier could take several pieces to market each week and use the profit from increased output to employ more weavers.

Spinning on an even larger scale was eventually achieved by Richard Arkwright (1732–1792). His original spinning frame was driven by a horse[1] but when, in 1769, water power was used it became known as the 'Water Frame'. Water frame yarn was hard and firm, ideal for the warp while the softer thread from the jenny was preferable for the weft.

The water frame was later adapted for the production of 'rovings', that is, a continuous run of fibres, loosely twisted and able to be wound on to bobbins, ready for spinning. Arkwright's 'Lantern Frame' was a further development of the water frame and was designed specifically for the production of rovings. In the same period the 'Slubbing Billy', working on similar lines to the jenny, produced rovings for spinning into yarn on the jenny itself.

The clothiers at first retained jenny spinning in their own homes but slubbing was a process which went to the scribbling mills. When the need for power to drive the water frame led to some spinning migrating to the river, the cottage spinning industry was threatened with extinction, and when steam power arrived to drive the larger spinning frames the threat became even greater. After 1800, Samuel Crompton's 'mule' began to challenge the frame and jenny for it produced an even finer thread for both warp and weft. The steam-powered spinning frame was found preferable for worsteds and became known as the 'Throstle'. Whereas the jenny had supplied yarn sufficient for two weavers, the mule and throstle could each supply ten.

---

[1] *Wool Research*, vol. 6, p. 21.

Machine-spun yarn was reliable, there were fewer breaks and less necessity for the thread to be sized to give it strength. There was thus no need for the weavers to go in search of farm work in the summer nor did they need to look for yarn; there began to be a shortage of weavers.

Another Lancashire invention was Arkwright's carding machine of 1775 by which a wheel and a comb produced a continuous sliver of material. Before 1780 this machine was in the Huddersfield area and was being used for scribbling or blending various types of raw wool. The machine was first worked by hand, then by horse power, later by water when scribbling and carding joined the fulling mill. Children, previously familiar with carding by hand could now feed the wool onto huge 'card-covered' wooden rollers. Moreover, the fuller could now oversee scribbling, carding and slubbing, scouring and fulling, under one roof. Such multi-purpose mills grew in number in the Colne Valley, from 54 in the 1770's to over 100 by 1800. One such mill was at Ottiwells, Marsden. A notice in the *Leeds Mercury* of 26th January 1779 read:

> 'A complete scribbling machine, with new rollers, carrying 46 pairs of cards with iron-geer in good condition; together with an upright shaft, swimming wheel (water wheel?) and nutt (capable of carrying four machines) with the tumbling shaft and nutt.
>
> Also a smaller machine of seven barrels or rollers with cards in good condition.
>
> Likewise a teazing mill (or 'willy'[1]) on a new construction with the geer thereto belonging, to go by water.
>
> Particulars may be had by applying to J. Kenworthy of Huddersfield, the owner.'

Carding and scribbling by machinery had spread rapidly by 1800 although domestic industry was dislocated by it. In effect another process had simply been added to those already carried out at the Fuller's mill and a practical result was that there was now another reason for adopting steam as a source of power.

---

[1] The teazer opened out and mixed the previously oiled wool.

Many of the inventors of the new machinery, mostly of humble origin, and in their enterprise and application offering a sharp contrast to the gentry for whom change was anathema, lived unhappily for they provoked the wrath of the workpeople. Richard Arkwright's mill at Chorley was destroyed in 1779; many refused to buy his yarn, and he was obliged to flee to Derbyshire. In 1785 Edmund Cartwright invented a power loom which performed the three simple movements of the weaver. Its success led the handloom workers to burn down his factory in 1791. Again, the introduction of the shearing frame, which mechanised cropping, was a main cause of the Luddite disturbances, to be considered in the next chapter.

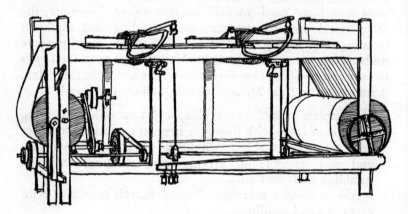

Harmar's shearing frame of 1794

This shearing frame was a carriage to hold and actuate several sets of cropping shears, and was invented between 1787 and 1794 in Sheffield. The handles of the shears were pulled by a fast revolving crank. No original machine of this kind has survived, but a working model of Harmar's shearing frame of 1794 has been made at the Ravensknowle Museum.[1] It was said that one such machine could do the work of three or more croppers and I have drawn attention to this shearing

---

[1] From details contained in *Rees' Cyclopaedia* (1820), illustrated in vol. IV, pl. iii, and described in vol. XXXVIII under 'Woollen Manufacture'.

frame, because of its social repercussions locally. In fact, much greater efficiency was achieved, a little later, by the Lewis cross-cut machine which had a rapid action, similar to a lawn-mower except that the cloth travelled under the cutter instead of the cutter moving over the material.

Of all the inventions, however, it was that of the steam engine which produced the most far-reaching effects. In 1650 Savery's pumping engine was a working reality; Newcomen improved upon it for use in the mines, and by 1764 James Watt had invented the separate condenser, patented by Boulton in 1769. By 1790, steam engines were being widely used in Yorkshire collieries, and in 1795 they were manufactured at Holbeck, near Leeds. They were also made locally in the next century.

Water power had always been uncertain although the droughts of summer were not necessarily inconvenient to a community where haymaking and harvesting occupied all available labour for some part of the year. When more machinery began to be used at the fulling mill, and more yarn was available, it became increasingly important that the mills should be fully worked all the year round—an early recognition of the principle of maximum utilisation of capital invested. At first, reservoirs were built to save water for use in the dry season, as at Wessenden and Merrydale for example, but as soon as steam power became available, it was used at first only to supplement the water power. The picture is not one of sudden change. A new mill near High Burton built in 1815 used steam from the start, whereas the scribbling mills at Slaithwaite, developed in 1787, were still using water power in 1828. By 1834, Golcar and Longwood were said to have twelve water wheels of 170 total horse power, but only three steam engines totalling 57 horse power. If one can generalise at all, it might be said that the smaller valleys, the soonest to dry up, began to use steam during the 1790s; the Colne Valley, which had reservoirs, was later changing over; but that new mills built at this time used steam from the beginning. The boilers were always more profitable when fully utilised and the even running of the new engines produced a finer quality product than did the water mills.

Between the time when water provided the power to drive the first simple textile machinery and today's almost universal electrification of industry, steam was King and the driving force in every factory. First came the days when every mill had its church-high window behind which flashed the rocking beam and the thrusting rods of monster beam engines driving their huge fly wheels two and more storeys in diameter. In grooves across the rim face of the flywheel a row of arm-thick ropes transferred the power of steam to shafts and gears throughout the mill. Each machine room had its maze of flapping belts connecting machines to overhead shafts. Belts frequently needed the attention of the 'strap man' to repair and adjust them. One of the not uncommon occupational hazards of such men was to be 'taken round the shaft' with resulting death or serious injury at least.

The high priest of the engine room was the 'engine tenter', in his hands an oil can and a wad of waste, on his head a greasy cap. His ear was sensitive to the slightest change in note or tempo of his beloved engine; his fingers as delicate thermometers, tested the temperature of each bearing. On him, with no book learning but with patiently acquired knowledge of the ways of his engine, the mill and its workers depended.

The beam engine gave way to the horizontal engine, 'simple' at first, then compounded for better utilisation of higher pressure steam. The making of such engines involved much hard hand work by engineer craftsmen and they were possibly the peak achievement of a hand craft of which the main tools were a hammer, chisel, file and scraper, used with superb skill.

The arrival of the steam engine ended man's dependence on the streams, and coal became the decisive factor in industrial progress. The valleys of the Holme and Fenay were adjacent to the coalfield while the construction of the canal in the Colne Valley facilitated the transport of coal to areas which were not. Even the Millstone Grit areas had some coal and in the early days of supplementary steam power, this coal was taken from shallow pits. Coal mining for domestic use had been in existence long before the arrival of steam and Defoe had seen coal used for the heating of dye vats. He had noticed the pits on the hilltops, 'because the horses which fetch the coals go light up the

Above : Pack horse bridge near Marsden. *Photo : Huddersfield Examiner. Below :* Cross Church Street. This picture, discovered in the Department of Estate and Property Management, probably shows the return of Oastler in February 1844. The banner with the slogan 'Lindley Welcome' might appropriately belong to Lindley Band as there is indeed a brass band heading the procession. The accuracy of the artist can be checked by comparing the buildings at the corner of King Street with photographs taken later in the nineteenth century.

View of Huddersfield in 1830: from a print by G. D. Tomlinson in the Huddersfield Public Library.

hills and come loaden down.' The first steam engines were often supplied with coal found on the spot, as at High Burton where local coal was conveyed straight to the boiler house. At the beginning of the nineteenth century there were tiny coal mines all over our area and as many as twenty were once counted between Huddersfield and Holmfirth, much of the land adjoining Leeds Road, and at Taylor Hill and Primrose Hill was worked for coal. When these small undertakings ran out or became unprofitable, the industry moved eastwards to the Middle Coal Measures, which it works today. Textiles however showed no tendency to follow the coal to its source because the railways had by then made the location of industry far less dependent on geographical factors.

Between Bradley and Bradford there are shales containing ironstone. The monks of Fountains Abbey once had a forge in Bradley Wood mining their ironstone at Colne Bridge. Bridges at Cooper Bridge and Colne Bridge owe their origin to those monks. Iron was being forged and rolled into plates here long before the Low Moor ironworks came into prominence at the end of the eighteenth century. Carding by machinery led to an expansion of the card-making industry—although it still remained near to Low Moor or Colne Bridge—at Cleckheaton, Mirfield, Brighouse and later at Lindley. Because the extensive use of iron for machinery did not come until the second quarter of the nineteenth century, the early machines were extremely crude. Not only the frames but most of the moving parts were of wood.

Seventeen-fifty-five marked the beginning of the extensive use of canals when waterways were authorised by Acts of Parliament and financed by private enterprise. The canal opened in 1761, built by Brindley for the Duke of Bridgewater, brought coal to Manchester and stimulated great interest in the possibilities of water transport. The canal boom lasted thirty years as an increasing number of communities saw the advantages of being served by cheap water transport.

In Yorkshire, many towns had been fortunate in being on navigable rivers and improvements to them had been made towards the close of the seventeenth century. The 'Aire and Calder' navigation system dates from 1698.

Sir John Ramsden conceived the idea of linking Huddersfield with the Calder at Cooper Bridge and on 9th March 1774 an Act of Parliament authorised the digging of a canal fed by the Colne at King's Mill and joining the Calder some three and three quarter miles away. The work took six years and cost nearly £12,000. A toll of 1s. 6d. per ton was levied on all merchandise and in due course warehouses were built at Aspley, where there was a wharf.

By the Huddersfield Narrow Canal Act of 4th April 1794, the Huddersfield Canal Company was empowered to connect Sir John Ramsden's canal with Lancashire. By 1798 this waterway, a narrow canal, had been completed as far as Marsden but there were to be financial and engineering difficulties in making the three-mile tunnel. Further Acts were therefore necessary in 1800 and 1806 to empower the Canal Company to raise more capital. On the 4th April 1811, the work was completed and a large party navigated the new tunnel. Propulsion through the Pennines was by 'legging', the boatmen lying on their backs and pushing with their feet against the tunnel roof.

The junction of the Narrow Canal and the Ramsden Canal was made by a new lock at Aspley and Sir John took out shares in the new enterprise. Huddersfield thus became a centre for east-west traffic, and this helped considerably in the growth and development of the town in the nineteenth century. The Colne Valley was now a through route and the potential of these canals can best be realised when we consider that each barge carried as much as six hundred pack horses. Slaithwaite, in the valley, had never been on the main road; this ran over Crosland Hill. By 1804 docks and wharves had been established there.

In 1830 the Huddersfield Shipping Company advertised 'sloops direct to and from London; fly boats daily to Saddleworth, Stalybridge, Ashton-under-Lyne, Oldham, Stockport and Manchester, whence goods are forwarded to Liverpool, Chester, and to all parts of the South of England; also to Wakefield, Leeds, York, Hull and all parts of the North of England and Scotland'.

Thus Huddersfield became connected to a comprehensive

Canal scene at Aspley: from a drawing by Leslie Taylor

system of waterways. The canals made possible the transport of coal, large loads of textiles, building materials and machinery. Transport was slow by modern standards but reliable. Further, canal water could be used for raising steam, so the mill was no longer dependent on the river, though the choice of site was restricted to the banks of the canal. Thus two ribbons of industry developed side by side up the Colne Valley, alongside river and canal.

In spite of the rapid introduction of new machinery during

this period, there appears to have been little actual machine-making in our area. In Huddersfield, Benjamin Carter had a brass foundry in Quay Street and in 1830 we hear of engineers at Longroyd Bridge. There were Enoch and James Taylor of Marsden who had turned their smithy into a foundry and millwright's shop and who became a target for the Luddites, and Low Moor Ironworks made some castings for frame machinery. All the new work done in the West Riding however was insignificant when compared with the machinery eventually produced by Platt's of Dobcross near Saddleworth; and the basic reason for this was that cotton provided a market for machinery initially far greater than did wool. Worsted was later to provide yet more incentive for the genius of the inventor. Most basic innovations in machinery came first to cotton and was adapted for wool, after allowing for the difference in the properties of the fibres.

CHAPTER VII

The Age of Defiance

ON 19TH June 1833 a certain Doctor Chalmers visited the town. He stayed at the 'George Inn', in the Market Place, and found occasion to record the following impression of what he saw:

'On entering Huddersfield I found that before my window there was a prodigious assembly of people at a market. The crowd was further augmented by a political meeting in the open air, and the whole of the spacious Market Place was filled with the multitude. Mr. Oastler held forth on the sufferings of the factory children, and was enthusiastically cheered. Then followed to me an original scene: the burning of the Factory Commissioners, Captain Fenton, one of the obnoxious members of Parliament, and another unpopular master manufacturer in effigy. The figures were fearfully like men; and it now being dark, the conflagration lighted up the whole square, and revealed the faces of the yelling myriads so as to give the aspect and character of Pandemonium to the scene. The burning figures were tossed ferociously in the air, and to renew their combustion were dashed into a bonfire from time to time. The spectacle, I am sure, is a degrading one, and fitted to prepare the actors for burning the originals instead of the copies.'

This was a change indeed from the peaceful days of the eighteenth century! Huddersfield in 1833 had its own M.P., unpopular master manufacturers, and Richard Oastler fighting both over the question of conditions in factories; and protest meetings, of the sort described by Chalmers, were to be repeated in the Market Place and in other places around the town from the days of the Luddites around 1812 to the Plug Riots and the

The Story of Huddersfield

collapse of Chartism towards the middle of the century. It is too easy to attribute all this unrest to the rapid growth of the factory system and its coincidence with the Napoleonic wars, or to the emergence of a class of hard-hearted employers bent on riding rough-shod over a working class impoverished by the new machinery. Recent research shows that this is by no means the whole story. The various risings up and down country had, however, a common background which it would be as well to examine at this stage. The first half of the nineteenth century is of particular importance to our story since it was during this period that the basic elements of modern Huddersfield were formed. After 1850 the industrial and social character of the town hardly changed at all.

John Wesley had been a traditionalist at heart, loyal to the King and to the Church of England. He left behind, however, an organisation of experienced itinerant preachers, educated and able men, joined in a society which levied subscriptions similar to those of the trades unions. Some of the local preachers, the amateurs, believed in egalitarianism and this philosophy was a considerable embarrassment to the Countess of Huntingdon's Methodist friends. Education for the masses was firmly based on pulpit, Sunday School, *Pilgrim's Progress* and the Old Testament—with special reference to the captivity of the Israelites.

Like its leader, Methodism in the provinces tended at first to support the Establishment. Many of the largest employers, though Dissenters, had had their appetite for civil liberty much reduced by events in France. Local preachers of political sermons were expelled, and the doctrine of an all-seeing God was insisted upon. Wesley encouraged industry and frugality; labour and sorrow became acceptable as the natural lot of man and, added to all this there was a fear of being outside the Methodist Society. The preachers who were prominent during civil disturbances were exceptional: mass religious hysteria was fairly common, with whole villages declaring for salvation— perhaps their shouts of praise were a substitute for revolutionary activity.

In Halifax there were bread riots in 1783 when in righteous anger a crowd stormed the Market Place to intimidate the corn

80

merchants into reducing their prices. In the manner of the time, their leader Thomas Spencer was arrested and executed, but his funeral brought a demonstration of public mourning for the great injustice that had been done. This was a time of mob activity and rioting throughout the country; the many as usual led by the few. At the Gordon Riots in 1780, Defoe commented that many who shouted 'No Popery' did not know whether 'Popery' was a man or a horse. London could always raise a mob, and in 1795 a carriage window broken by a pebble caused the King to open Parliament with the remark 'My Lords, I-I-I've been shot at!' In 1795, an Act directed against anti-monarchism and a Bill forbidding meetings of over fifty people, raised a storm of indignation and 4,000 clothiers rode to York to protest to their County Member of Parliament.

The patriotism evoked by the Napoleonic invasion scare revived the spirit of the Glorious Revolution of 1688, and there was prevalent an idea that, while the French were slaves, the English were 'free born'. Englishmen in the North resented the press gang and the standing army, with its barracks in the towns.[1] If every free man had the right to bear arms there was no need for a professional army of slaves at sixpence a day. Even an organised police force was greatly resented especially when spies were used by the Government to glean information from the people. Local rights and customs were everywhere cherished and Oastler's Tory-Radicalism was perfectly acceptable to his followers regardless of their diverse social backgrounds.

Tom Paine said that there was no skill required in order to be a King and only France and the United States had acceptable governments based on the brotherhood of man. In Leeds, copies of *The Rights of Man* were said to be in the hands of all journeymen cloth dressers, while Sheffield had a Reform Society of 2,000 members in 1792; the Halifax Constitutional Society came into the open in 1794 and its open-air gatherings were attended by contingents from Huddersfield.

Philosophies and systems abounded. In 1795, for example, Francis Place—in anticipation of Oastler—proposed that the

---

[1] In spite of requests from the magistrates to the Home Secretary, barracks were never built in Huddersfield.

working classes should support the aristocrat most likely to improve their lot as the workers could not possibly achieve anything by direct action.

However, by 1797 an Act had been passed prohibiting unlawful oaths and any attempts to suborn the loyalty of the Forces. These were to be used against the Luddites and the Tolpuddle Martyrs. In 1812 Scott wrote to Southey, 'Pitt has driven the miners below ground,' and Jacobin ideas multiplied with every rising price and every hardship. Every workshop became a political debating chamber which no magistrate was able to silence, and it was from the small workshop in particular that Luddism came, for the large factories did not employ the main body of the working class in Huddersfield until the middle of the nineteenth century. The economic misfortunes of the early nineteenth century were, in fact, mainly due to trade depressions and banking difficulties; and historians today regard the enclosure movement, condemned over the years, as a means of feeding rather than of depressing the poor.

It is wrong to assume that all the poor from the countryside flocked suddenly into the town, having lost their common land-rights. The young workers certainly came, but their parents stayed behind, clinging to their homesteads and what was left of the cottage industry, where, until the 1830's, they still outnumbered the factory workers. The Irish, however who came over in large numbers after 1798, flocked into the towns, and after 1834 it was said that the New Poor Law purposely stimulated this movement in order to offset the growing influence of the trade unions. In 1812 and 1814 the Regulations governing apprenticeship were repealed and only the croppers and other strongly organised trades could defend themselves against the consequences of this. In 1834 came the Tolpuddle episode when six Dorset labourers were transported for swearing an illegal oath, and after this the trade union movement was at a low ebb. Except for the skilled engineers, few tradesmen were able to maintain their high standards in the face of exploitation, with the handloom weavers forming a large pool of superfluous labour which could be used at any time to depress the general standard of wages. Paupers went handloom-weaving to avoid the workhouse and, when machinery could be operated by women and children, the men soon lost what little work there was to be had. From 1800 almost every working man felt insecure, and pined for the 'independence' of the 'good old days'. In such an atmosphere the New Poor Law with its evil offspring, the larger workhouse, and centralised control was never likely to be acceptable to the people and Huddersfield became notorious for its opposition to the new regime.

At the same time indirect taxation reached further and further for its revenues, and before long included bricks, hops, vinegar, oranges, dogs, windows, soap, sugar, tea and coffee. In 1833 the revenue from a single family's use of such items was estimated at half the man's wage. Being taxed to pay for the Army's interference was in Huddersfield a very sore point, a tax on the new power looms would have seemed more appropriate.[1]

Factories had been thought of as places for pauper children ever since Peel's Act of 1802 had regulated their apprenticeship, and for those who worked in the new factories, working to a time, the lack of holidays and the monotony were all complained against. To the hillside weaver, factory work was an indignity to be avoided for as long as possible. In fact, there was little work available for men in factories since it was cheaper to employ women and children; only a few able-bodied men were required for moving pieces of cloth about. Further, there was as yet no mechanisation in the mines, the gasworks, in building work, or on the canals, and here again only the fit and strong were required and the Irish took many of the heavy jobs.

In 1812 England was near to commercial ruin. The Napoleonic wars had reached their climax, the country was on the brink of war with the United States, and these factors had shut off a third of the country's textile export market. The Poor Law which cost four million pounds in 1800 was costing six in 1812, and prices were half as much again what they had been in 1789—a quartern loaf in 1812 cost 1s. 8d.

There was no professional police force; this would have been regarded as 'continental'. The Home Office relied for information upon informers, paid in secret, and the military had to deal

---

[1] A view shared by some Tories and Radicals.

with all disorders, however small. As most towns like Huddersfield had no elected local government, it is to be wondered at that the outbreaks of violence were so infrequent. The Lord Lieutenant's office dates from Tudor times and at the period with which we are dealing, the Lieutenant of the West Riding was the Earl Fitzwilliam. It was he who embodied the Militia and the Yeomanry. The Justices of the Peace, persons of standing holding freehold land worth at least £100 a year, were the real administrators and were empowered to read the Riot Act, summon the Militia, enrol special constables in an emergency, and to call on the Regular Army for assistance locally. Because of the land qualification, manufacturers were generally ineligible for the office.[1] In 1812 there were more soldiers in the North than the Duke of Wellington had in the Peninsular Campaign, though Lord Liverpool, the new Prime Minister, maintained that law and order was a local matter. He said that property must protect itself—'The Government must give the impulse to the execution of the Law' by supporting the magistrates whatever happened.

The Militia on foot and the Yeomanry on horseback constituted a citizen army of volunteers for local defence only. As a fighting force they were held in contempt by the regulars, and a certain officer is alleged to have said 'If all you gentlemen were just to go back and leave us to fight it out alone it would be a devilish good thing. We don't want your help I can tell you. Mind I don't want to say anything rude—but that's a fact.'[2]

The Huddersfield Corps of Fusilier Volunteers was formed in 1794 after a meeting at the George Inn under the chairmanship of Sir George Armytage of Kirklees. He subscribed £100 and became the first Major-Commandant; William Horsfall of Ottiwells subscribed £20 and was duly gazetted first lieutenant. The volunteers wore a cocked hat, red cut-away coat and white breeches. When on duty the major received 14s. 1d. a day, the rank and file, precisely one shilling each. The Corps held a

---

[1] Although the successful manufacturer could easily acquire land, there tended to be a social bar to the magisterial bench which was not easy to surmount until he gave up manufacturing.

[2] Blackwood's *Edinburgh Magazine*, May 1871.

review at Dryclough, Crosland Moor, in 1797 on land known afterwards as 'Volunteer Field'.

In 1798 another meeting at the George led to the formation of the Huddersfield Armed Association to assist the magistrates should the Volunteers be called to another town. The 'Armed Associates' received no pay and supplied their own arms. The Parish Constables made a return of all men aged from fifteen to sixty together with details of any horses, carts, boats and weapons which they might have, also of their willingness to undergo training in order to ward off a French invasion, and from it we learn that 'James Sykes is determined to kill a Frenchman!' while 'Joel Hoyle, clothier, will be a labourer, he hath no implements but will work hard!'

Following the Defence Act of 1803, and yet another meeting at the George, headed by Joseph Radcliffe, J.P., the Upper Agbrigg Volunteers were formed. The aim was to enrol six times as many men as had served in the old Volunteers. Fourteen hundred came forward including Lewis Fenton[1] who received a captain's commission from Earl Fitzwilliam. These volunteers survived a change of name in 1808 but all units were finally disbanded in 1816. The magistrates did consider calling them out against the Luddites, in 1812, but this was decided against in view of the popular feeling which supported the rebels.

Although the anti-revolutionary Acts of 1795 had suppressed public meetings, the next fifteen years was a period of secret meetings and of rumours. In Luddism the underground activities reached their climax for the movement was quite impervious to the efforts of the Home Office informers. The only information the authorities ever acquired came from prisoners and much of what we know today about the Luddites only came to light in the late 1870s when the few survivors were quite beyond any satisfactory action at law.[2]

[1] The first Member of Parliament for Huddersfield, in 1832.

[2] See the works of D. F. E. Sykes in the bibliography. Daniel Frederick Edward Sykes (1856–1920) was the son of Edwin Sykes, solicitor. He was educated at Huddersfield College, where he was a brilliant scholar, and the University of London, where he gained his LL.B. D. F. E. Sykes became a solicitor in partnership with his father, and from 1880 to 1883 he was a member of the Borough Council.

See also Frank Peel, *The Risings of the Luddites* published in 1880.

We do know, however, that the Combination Act of 1799 put republicans and trades unionists in the same camp. In the West Riding the best organised union was that of the croppers and the authorities appear to have tacitly condoned their activities. In 1802, we know they paid a penny a week and when the croppers at Gott's, the largest mill in Leeds, went on strike in 1802–3 they won their case and the magistrates actually assisted in the negotiations. The croppers were the élite of the woollen workers, their 'Institution' with its horrendous oath-taking ceremonies, attained a hitherto unknown degree of secrecy and solidarity.

A body so exclusive—for no unskilled worker was allowed to join—could exert a direct influence on production. A cropper's normal wage was five per cent of the finished value of the piece and this would obviously vary, to a great extent, according to the standard of his work.

The gig mill, which raised the nap by means of teasel rollers, had already been demonstrated against though it affected only a fraction of the croppers' work. During the 1790s however, more than one gig mill in Leeds was destroyed; and in 1802 a posse of workmen in a Huddersfield factory prevented one from being operated.

The croppers and their sympathisers raised over £10,000 as a fighting fund to underwrite legal proceedings for the enforcement of the old industrial legislation—covering apprenticeships, the prohibition of gig mills and limiting the number of looms a master could operate. Parliament not only ignored the croppers but by 1809 had actually repealed much of the old protective legislation. Moreover a really serious challenge to their craftsmanship had appeared on the scene in the shape of the new shearing frame, as illustrated on page 72.

Of course, the legislators thought that opposition to machines would fade away. What they did not realise was that they were not only killing the domestic system of manufacture, but also making Luddism and industrial civil war inevitable.

The name of Ned Ludd has passed into English history as a symbol of revolt against the imposition of a new order. If such a man ever existed, though some historians identify him as a young clerk, he soon ceased to have any personal significance, but his name was adopted as the rallying cry of a whole class, and echoes down the corridors of time to this day.

In the early 1800's, however, for a period of little more than a year the name of Ludd was to be as much a symbol of right to textile workers as was the cross to the crusaders; and the pitch of feeling reached by the Luddites is well illustrated by this manifesto:

> 'We will never lay down our arms till the House of Commons passes an Act to put down all machinery hurtful to the communality—
> But we, we petition no more.
> That won't do,—fighting must.
> Signed by the General of the Army of Redressers.
> Ned Ludd, Clerk.
> Redressers for ever: Amen'

Ned Ludd's particular interest for us is that the croppers also chose his banner under which to campaign for their ancient rights. Once the hosiery workers of Nottingham had 'fired the first shot'—against employers who paid in truck rather than in honest cash—by smashing their stocking frames to emphasise their argument, and once their fire had been returned in the form of legislation, passed in February 1812, making machine breaking a capital offence, the war was on.

Economists have explained Luddism as being caused by war and bad harvests and this is true. However, the croppers' leaders in 1812 saw, in their plight, the end of protective legislation for themselves and the beginning of *laissez faire,* or freedom, for the manufacturers. Industry, said the croppers, existed to provide traditional employment while even the Shearmen's Coat of Arms came, in its conception, from the old gilds of craftsmen. Ned Ludd faced a two-headed dragon, the established order, however reluctantly enforced by the gentry, and the new progressive employers of labour. In Huddersfield, for some time the headquarters of the movement, the Luddites could count on the solid support of the general public and of the small manufacturers. It was only the larger employers who were unpopular, if only because the little men of the Colne Valley had seen how the tall chimneys, as in Lancashire, could ruin them. Richard Oastler's father had sold up his business in 1800 rather than use machinery which he believed would further impoverish the poor. General Grey, who commanded some of the troops in the West Riding, was dismayed when he discovered just how much support the Luddites were receiving from what he called 'respectable' people.

The year 1812 has been regarded as a watershed in time, with Luddism looking forward to the ideal situation where motivation arising out of human needs would triumph over that of profit. Luddism also harked back to the State regulation of Tudor industry, and the ten-hour movement might be said to be derived from the same attitude; the movement was also revolutionary in so far as attacks in Nottingham and Leicestershire showed evidence of planning, discipline, method and good communications. When the movement spread to Yorkshire, via Sheffield, the same good discipline and sound tactics were in evidence.

In the Luddite 'Command' for the Huddersfield area there were said to be 2,782 sworn heroes who had made an oath on these lines:

'I—do solemnly swear that I will never reveal to any persons under the canopy of heaven the names of the persons who compose this secret committee—under the penalty of being sent out of the world by the first brother who shall meet me—and I further swear that I will use my best endeavours to punish by death any traitor or traitors— So help me God and bless me to keep this my oath inviolable.'

Many small manufacturers were said to have capitulated for fear of attack from a well drilled army, which on at least one recorded occasion consisted of musket men ten abreast, followed by men with hatchets, men with pistols, then pikemen, with an unarmed gang bringing up the rear.

The spirit of such men is reflected in their song which ran:

> Come cropper lads of high renown
> Who love to drink good ale that's brown
> And strike each haughty tyrant down,
> With hatchet, pike and gun!

Chorus   Oh, the cropper lads for me,
Who with lusty stroke
The shear frames broke
The cropper lads for me

What though the specials still advance,
And soldiers nightly round us prance
The cropper lads still lead the dance
With hatchet, pike and gun!

And night by night when all is still
And the moon is tied behind the hill
We forward march to do our will
With hatchet, pike and gun!

Great Enoch still shall lead the van,
Stop him who dare! Stop him who can!
Press forward every gallant man
With hatchet, pike and gun!

'Enoch'[1] was the great hammer the croppers used for attacking the obnoxious machinery. It was called after Enoch Taylor the Marsden machine maker and one of the Luddites' intended victims. The croppers jokingly said that as Enoch had made them 'Enoch' should break them.

At first the Luddites had everything their own way. On 19th of January 1812 they fired a mill near Leeds; next they attacked a mill at Rawdon causing damage to cloth estimated at £500; then they entered some dressing shops near Leeds where they cut a large quantity of cloth to shreds, and finally destroyed all the machinery at Foster's Mill at Horbury on 9th of April.

Flushed with these successes, the Luddites felt themselves ready to face William Horsfall of Ottiwells and William Cartwright of Cleckheaton, the two local manufacturers most determined to use the new machinery. The anti-Luddite obsessions of Horsfall were such that even the children used to chant after him 'I'm General Ludd!' He had publicly declared his intention to use the new frames at all costs, and, although careless of his personal safety, took care that his mill near

[1] Now preserved in Ravensknowle Museum.

Marsden was defended by armed men and a cannon. In addition, infantry and cavalry were billeted in Marsden for patrolling the area. Cartwright was a quieter man though equally determined. His mill at Rawfolds was also guarded by armed men and soldiers.

The headquarters of the Huddersfield Luddite 'Command' was at John Wood's cropping shop, Longroyd Bridge, across the river from Starkey's Mill. Wood's son-in-law was George Mellor, a bright, fair-haired young man of twenty-two. He was 'King Ludd' of the district. Thomas Smith, Benjamin Walker (Ben o' Buck's) and William Thorpe were Mellor's associates, Walker being the eldest and he was only twenty-five. A meeting was held, lots were cast as to which target was to be attacked next, and Rawfolds was chosen.

At ten o'clock on the night of Saturday, 11th of April 1812, more than a hundred men met Mellor at the Dumb Steeple, Kirklees. They marched off in military style over Hartshead to within sixty yards of Rawfolds Mill where they formed into order for the attack. At about half past midnight, Cartwright came down from his bed and opened the mill door to see who was there. He was met by a hail of musket fire and a crashing of glass as the ground floor windows were smashed. His men inside replied with a steady stream of bullets, and firing was kept up by both sides for about twenty minutes. When he found it impossible to break into the mill, but not before two men had been killed and five seriously wounded, Mellor decided to call off the attack. Reinforcements from other towns had failed to arrive, and he was left a bitterly disappointed man.

This incident showed the lengths to which both Luddites and their chosen enemies were prepared to go. To the manufacturers, however, Cartwright was a hero who had stood his ground, and they subscribed £3,000 to make good any damage he might have suffered. A feeling of anxiety swept through the Luddite camp after Rawfolds, so Mellor decided that some drastic action must be taken to encourage his supporters.

We can turn to the Radcliffe Papers for an indication of the action Mellor chose, and how drastic it was. The manuscripts of this period show Joseph Radcliffe writing urgent requests for military aid, complaining of threatening letters,

The Shooting of William Horsfall: from a drawing by Leslie Taylor

reporting that offers of 100 guineas for the Prince Regent's head were being posted on doors, mentioning an attack on a Mr Vickerman of Taylor Hill, and pleading for, 'one or two Bow Street Runners' in default of anyone else.

There is also a letter from 'General Ludd's Solicitor' citing a declaration of 'Ludd's Court at Nottingham' that unless Radcliffe remains neutral in the present disturbances, his house and life will be forfeited. This passage is followed by two warnings, one from 'Mr Love Good', who claims to know the Luddites' secrets and another from 'A.B.' promising civil war unless the new machinery stops and predicting the death of William Horsfall.

On Tuesday, the 28th of April 1812, Horsfall, who had sworn that he would ride up to his saddle girths in Luddite blood, was due to ride home from Huddersfield Market. This was the day Mellor had chosen for his 'drastic action', and he, Walker, Smith and Thorpe concealed themselves in Radcliffe's Plantation on Crosland Moor, to lie in waiting. At about a quarter to six, the unsuspecting victim rode up to the Warren House Inn, which was then situated just above Park Road in what is now Blackmoorfoot Road and, without dismounting, stopped for a drink before riding on. Mellor, from behind a low plantation wall, near the present Dryclough Road,[1] gave a whistle to indicate the arrival of the victim; he and Thorpe then fired at Horsfall hitting him in the stomach and thigh and severing an artery. Covered in blood he fell from his horse, his feet still fast in the stirrups. The assailants made off into Dungeon Wood, now partly Beaumont Park, where Walker and Smith hid their pistols in an ant-hill, Mellor and Thorpe hiding theirs at the house of a relative near by. Horsfall was taken back to the Warren House where he died the following day.

A letter was sent from 'Peter Plush, Secretary to General Ludd' to 'General Ludd Junior, the Market Place, Huddersfield. It expressed sorrow for those who had lost their lives at Rawfolds, made no mention of Horsfall, but went on, 'as long as that blackguard and drunken fellow called Prince Regent and his servants have anything to do with the Government,

---

[1] Site commemorated by William Horsfall Street.

nothing but miseries will befall us, their footstools. I am further desired to say that it is expected that you will remember that you are of the same stuff as George Guelph Junior and that corn and wine are sent for you as well as for him.'

The death of Horsfall caused less revulsion of feeling than might have been expected and, in spite of a reward of £2,000, no one came forward to offer any information to help the authorities. Joseph Radcliffe, the magistrate, persisted however and eventually, to save his own skin, Walker turned King's evidence. The other three, accused of the murder of William Horsfall, and fifteen other Luddites, were tried at York in January 1813. Altogether some sixty-six men, were tried and six transported for seven years. Luddism, but not the period of general unrest, was over.

[handwritten marginal note: 17 executed. inc. Mellor Thorpe Smith]

However explosive their impact on the localities they chose for their operations, the Luddites were in reality simply the focus for the tension felt everywhere during the economic crises of 1811 and 1812, especially among those who believed that trade difficulties had been used as an excuse for introducing the new machinery, raising prices and depressing the people.

The disaffection of scattered village communities had the effect however, of driving magistrate and mill owner into the same camp, partners, as it were, in apprehension and self-interest. The military were totally unable to cope with these disturbances, for in force they made too much noise, and no small detachment would venture into the trouble spots. In these circumstances it was inevitable that concessions would be made by the authorities to the manufacturers.

Benjamin Walker never did receive his £2,000 reward and he ended his life as a vagabond—an outcast in rags. The other informers were simply ostracised for life. As the last of the Luddites swung in their halters, the crowd sang the Methodist hymn, 'Behold, the Saviour of Mankind, nail'd to the shameful tree.' The death of Mellor's cousin, young John Booth, at Rawfolds was followed by a quiet burial; the authorities succeeded in preventing a massive public funeral in the town by altering the time.

Historians have tended to allow Peterloo and Tolpuddle to dwarf the stature of the Luddites, and George Mellor has not been seen as the heroic figure he undoubtedly was. Locally however, the Luddites had all the support they could possibly require. There never was a national plan, neither was there a need for large scale publicity. What finally ended Luddism was not so much the stand taken by men like Cartwright and Radcliffe as the improvement in trade which came afterwards. The political and revolutionary aspects of Luddism appear to have been incidental to the main object, which was to oppose the new machinery, not to overthrow the monarchy or the government of the day.

The political rebels and reformers did succeed in adding to the general unrest and, no doubt, had a hand in the rude letter about the Prince Regent. A Major Cartwright toured the country demanding the reform of Parliament and he reached Huddersfield on 22nd January 1813—a week after the execution of the Luddites in York. His meeting was broken up by the soldiers, and petitions for parliamentary reform were seized. Cartwright and some of his supporters were taken into custody, but he managed to talk his way out of his difficulties and was released. Hampden clubs,[1] where the moderate reformers were heard, took root from 1816 and in them there was no sharp cleavage between the constitutionalists and the conspirators.

A club was formed in Huddersfield, under difficulties because the Secret Societies Act made it illegal to correspond with other branches; but the radical heroes of this period were often the local booksellers, printers like Joshua Hobson—whom we shall meet later—and the local secretaries of Hampden clubs. Radicalism at this period however was not organised, but 1816 is memorable at least for the initial publication of William Cobbett's, 'Twopenny Trash'.

On 8th and 9th June 1817, while another rising was going on at Pentrich, Nottingham, several hundred cloth workers marched at midnight on Huddersfield from the Holme Valley. Their leader said 'Now lads, all England is in arms, our liberties are secure, the rich will be poor, the poor will be rich.' In so far as the signals from the hills to start the rising were reminiscent

---

[1] Named after John Hampden, one of the principal opponents of Charles I in Parliament.

of 1812 and nine of the twenty four afterwards charged were croppers, this, the Folly Hall Fight, was a local resurgance of Luddism. The Holme Valley had always had strong Luddite sympathies.

An old account quoted by Taylor Dyson runs—'The Yeomanry came down valiantly to disperse the rebels. When they reached the bridge at Folly Hall they made a stand to reconnoitre . . . A few pistols went off, whereupon our valiant Bobadils (the local Yeomanry Cavalry) took alarm, turned their horses sharp around and galloped up Chapel Hill as if they were riding a steeplechase.' As it was, the cavalry were hopelessly outnumbered, moreover I would doubt whether they really had much heart in a business which might have resulted in their attacking hundreds of poor local people. Sykes continues the narrative, 'The horse of Mr Alexander, one of the Yeomanry, was shot and the Corps, remembering that discretion is the better part of valour, retired.' Once military reinforcements had been mustered, the rising melted away but, during the following days, twenty four insurgents were arrested and of these, ten were tried at York in May. They were charged with either stealing firearms or firing at David Alexander, but all were acquitted. This verdict they probably owed to a Government spy called Oliver, who was in the habit of drumming up business by deliberately helping to stir up trouble in order to have something on which to report. Oliver had travelled round with tales of how people in other parts of the country were ready to rise in rebellion to overthrow the Government. Two days before the Folly Hall Fight, he had assembled such a meeting at Thornhill Lees, and troops had intervened, capturing Oliver and ten others. Oliver was allowed to escape. Then, at the trial of Jeremiah Brandreth, leader of the Pentrich Revolution, also on 8th and 9th of June, Oliver was left out of the evidence. The Folly Hall gathering may well have been one of Oliver's schemes.

Lord Liverpool confessed in the House of Lords, 'Mr Oliver had been employed by the Government to gain information from the disturbed districts.' When Edward Baines exposed Oliver in the *Leeds Mercury*, public feeling ran high and this is probably the real reason why the jury refused to convict the leaders of the Folly Hall rising. Many already held the view that a despicable character such as Oliver was quite intolerable in England. In July 1817 the *Mercury* report shocked everyone, and the moderate reformers used Oliver to show that the lower classes should support the Whigs.

We are not concerned with the Manchester 'Massacre of Peterloo' (August 1819) in which the Yeomanry killed and wounded some of a large peaceful gathering of workers, after the magistrates had taken fright; but after Peterloo there were rumours of reprisals. Indeed, November 1819 saw a meeting in Huddersfield, attended by a Halifax contingent which marched over the Ainleys with bands and flags, but by the end of 1819 Radicalism had collapsed, its leaders were in gaol, the Six Acts prohibited drilling and meetings, and stamp duty increased the price of cheap periodicals to sixpence. There was, however, one final episode of defiance in Huddersfield at this period.

It was said that there was to be a simultaneous rising on 31st March 1820. Certainly preparations were made on the Almond-bury side of Huddersfield but not in the Colne or Holme Valleys this time. One section of rebels was to gather on Almondbury Bank, one at Kirklees, another at Fixby Park and a fourth on Lindley Moor. At the sign of a beacon on Castle Hill, all were to congregate at the Dumb Steeple near Bradley and from there make an attack upon the town. The military were ready, but no attack ever came.

On Wednesday 11th April, about two hundred men gathered on Grange Moor ostensibly for a march on London, but expected reinforcements never came, and they dispersed before the military arrived. At about five o'clock that morning, word reached Huddersfield of an armed body of men, seen at Flockton, about to attack the town. It is most likely that these were men going to Grange Moor, but magistrates feared the worst. The town prepared to defend itself; shops were closed and barricaded, special constables were enrolled and the Armed Association volunteered for service. The Regulars barricaded themselves in the Market Place and a detachment went out to Grange Moor. The day ended however in complete anti-climax, nothing happened. Later, an informer managed to secure the arrest of twenty-two allegedly treasonable characters.

They were tried at York on 9th September 1829, and all pleaded 'guilty' but their sentence was commuted to transportation for seven years. One of them was Joseph Tyas, arrested near Huddersfield, three days after the rising which never was. In his pocket was a letter addressed to 'Our brethren in Lankaster Shire' which said, 'Our musick in Yorkshire as played twise where yours in Lankashire has never struck at all, is your Musicians sick?'

After this period, the prosperity of the country as a whole improved.[1] Peterloo had shaken the regime, and Peel was convinced that the landed gentry must ally with the new industrial élite. This is the background to the Reform Bill of 1832, the local consequences of which we shall examine in the next chapter. After Peterloo, the Government never again dared to use such brutal force against the working classes and the handling of the Plug Riots of 1842 was cautious.

Eighteen forty-two was a year of widespread distress, particularly in Lancashire, and the Chartists believed that the remedy lay in a complete reform of Parliament, giving the vote to all men. Hobkirk summarises the position neatly when he says that a large number of men from Lancashire marched across the country drawing the plugs from factory boilers. 'On 13th August, the riotous multitude reached Huddersfield where they drew several plugs, and amongst the rest, those of Messrs. Starkey Brothers and Messrs. Armitage and Kaye. They then held a meeting near St Paul's Church to consult what further steps should be taken; but their deliberations were speedily brought to a close by a diversion of the 17th Lancers, which bore down King Street towards them. The Riot Act having been read, the troops were ordered to clear the streets. This they speedily accomplished, and the authorities of the town, keeping a strict watch over the movements of the rioters, in the course of the next few days restored the town to its usual order.'

There remain two other acts of defiance for inclusion in this chapter, the agitation for the Ten Hours Bill and the struggle against the New Poor Law. As both are intimately connected

---

[1] 1829 saw considerable distress around Huddersfield. The results of an enquiry into the causes were reported in the *Leeds Mercury*.

with the career of Richard Oastler, these will be related against the public life of 'King Richard'.

At this stage it is necessary to consider the attitude of the employers. The more obstinate manufacturers felt they were struggling for survival against unscrupulous rivals who would drive them out of business. Most employers felt that the poverty they witnessed would pass away and all would eventually benefit from the new progress in industry. The political economists believed that wages would inevitably be fixed by the laws of supply and demand; if the workers suffered, it would not be the fault of the employers; if the workers interfered with production, everyone would suffer as a result.

Most mill owners worked hard in their pursuit of profit, and were no doubt, in their own eyes at any rate, godly and upright men.[1] Many of them certainly consoled themselves in the knowledge that long hours of toil were good for the souls of their employees, the thriftless, sinful poor! Both Nonconformist and Anglican manufacturers built their chapels and churches in this mood of religious philanthropy; and these buildings, from time to time, heard thanks given to God for a successful and profitable stroke of business!

By the same philosophy trade unions were considered immoral and dangerous—a denial of the workers' liberty; employers had no qualms about requiring employees to sign a 'Document' denying all connection with unionism. Further, they argued that to regulate the hours of children at work was to deny freedom to the parents. Moreover, any limitation of children's work could result in reduced hours (and wages) for all, thus increasing poverty. Only a few employers were genuinely philanthropic and they were often of the second or third generation of factory owners who felt secure and could thus afford to be generous. Such men were more prevalent in Lancashire, where the industrial revolution in cotton had always been ahead of progress in wool textiles in Yorkshire.

There had of course been a Factory Act of 1802, but this applied to pauper children only. A monument in Kirkheaton churchyard speaks for itself:

[1] Described by one cynic as 'Sunday saints but Monday devils'!

98

The Age of Defiance

To commemorate
The dreadful fate of Seventeen Children
Who fell
Unhappy victims to a raging fire,
at
Mr. Atkinson's factory, Colne Bridge,
Feby the 14th 1818
This Monument
was erected by Voluntary Contribution
MDCCCXXI

These children, who worked in a cotton mill, were all girls, their ages ranging from nine to eighteen. The fire occurred in the middle of the night and the girls, cotton yarn spinners, had been locked in the mill and the key mislaid. Unhappy victims indeed, but not in vain for when Peel's Second Act was passed in 1819, Colne Bridge was mentioned in the House. The Act was ultimately amended to cover cotton mills only and directed that children from nine to sixteen should be protected, and permitted to work not more than eleven hours a day; children below nine were not to be employed at all and it was intended that there should be no night work.

And so we come to Richard Oastler.

He was steward to Squire Thomas Thornhill (1780–1844), of Fixby Park, a high Tory but with little interest in local politics or the issues of the day. However, in 1830 he chanced to call on a personal friend, John Wood of Horton Hall, Bradford, a wealthy mill owner who was trying to abate the evils of factory life, and the following conversation is reported:

'Oastler, I wonder you have never turned your attention to the factory system?'

'Why should I? I have nothing to do with factories.'

'That may be, everyone in the country is now very enthusiastic against slavery in the West Indies; and I have long thought of acquainting you with the cruelties practised in our mills on little children, which if you knew, I am sure you would strive to prevent.'

'Cruelties in Mills! I do not understand, you tell me.'

99

Richard Oastler: from a drawing by Leslie Taylor

Wood then described to Oastler some of the evils in factories, including the fact that, even in his own mill, children worked from six in the morning till seven at night with only a short break during the day. Other mills, he said, did not allow for a meal time at all, some worked even longer hours, most children worked in bad conditions and some were cruelly treated.

Wood eventually obtained a promise from Oastler that he would do something to help, and on the following day Oastler wrote this letter—it has been abbreviated in places.

YORKSHIRE SLAVERY

To the Editors of the *Leeds Mercury*,

It is the pride of Britain that a slave cannot exist on her soil—The pious and able champions of negro liberty and colonial rights should have gone further than they did; or perhaps, to speak more correctly, before they had travelled so far as the West Indies, should at least for a few moments,—have directed attention to scenes of misery, acts of oppression, and victims of slavery even on the threshold of our homes.

Let truth speak out—thousands of our fellow-creatures and fellow-subjects, both male and female, the miserable inhabitants of a Yorkshire town are at this moment existing in a state of slavery more horrid than are the victims of that hellish system—'Colonial slavery.'

The very streets are wet with the tears of innocent victims at the accursed shrine of avarice who are compelled—by the thong or strap of the overlooker to hasten, half-dressed, to those magazines of British infantile slavery—the worsted mills in the town and neighbourhood of Bradford!

—Ye are doomed to labour from morning till night for one who cares not how soon your weak and tender frames are stretched to breaking. You are not mercifully valued at so much per head—No, no, your soft and delicate limbs are tired and fagged and jaded at only so much per week, and when your joints can act no longer, your emaciated frames are cast aside, the boards—are instantly supplied with other victims, who in this land of liberty are—hired not sold—as slaves and daily forced to hear that they are free.

Oh!—listen to the sorrowing accents of these poor

Yorkshire little ones.—If I have succeeded in calling attention to the abominable system—I have done some good.
Why should not children be protected by legislative enact-
ments as well as those at work in cotton mills?

Christians should feel and act for those whom Christ so
eminently loved and declared that 'of such is the Kingdom of
Heaven.'

I remain,

Yours etc,

Richard Oastler.

Fixby Hall,
near Huddersfield September 29th 1830.

This was strong medicine. Oastler's accusations were denied
by the millowners, but came as manna to the readers of cheap
political pamphlets. One result was that a number of workmen
formed the Huddersfield Short Time Committee, the first of its
kind in the country; and six of them[1] called on Oastler one
Sunday morning, the only day on which they were not working
in the mills. They persuaded Oastler that all should work
together for the sake of the children, setting aside party politics
and religious differences; and out of this meeting came the
important 'Compact on the Lawn at Fixby House'.

The Committee experienced its first defeat in the rejection of a
House of Commons Bill introduced by Sir John Hobhouse,
Radical M.P. for Westminster. The movement did, however,
gain ground as spinners, weavers and small shopkeepers
attended the informal committee meetings at the Ship Inn.
Other branches came into being, and the Radical *Leeds Patriot*
went as far as to describe Oastler, the ultra Tory, as a friend to
the country's best interests. As he attended the weekly meetings
so he acquired a mass of information on what conditions were
really like in the factories. These activities led Oastler to other
meetings, and Fixby Hall became the centre of the Ten Hours
Movement.

Oastler seldom missed an opportunity of scoring a success.
When ten Huddersfield mill owners petitioned Parliament, he

---

[1] Including Joshua Hobson.

took examples of 'slavery' from inside their ten mills and published them in a letter to the Tory *Leeds Intelligencer*. In 1831-2 Michael Sadler introduced a Ten Hours Bill, but the matter was shelved to a Select Committee and Sadler attempted to collect evidence from all parts of the country, including Huddersfield.

The Tory-Radical Alliance was further seen in the 1832 elections in Leeds, when Sadler, the Tory candidate, and a Methodist, was supported by Oastler and the Radicals against the Whig Macaulay. The Huddersfield Short Time Committee sent a loyal address to Sadler. This period marked the real beginning of 'Tory democracy', which the *Mercury* denounced as 'trickery'.

A mass meeting held in Huddersfield on Boxing Day 1831 attracted over a thousand people, including the Huddersfield men who were to follow Oastler everywhere he appeared in public; they became his personal bodyguard, known everywhere as 'Oastler's Own'. Committees in Leeds and London now began to raise large sums of money. Oastler had his own fund into which all his savings went, but John Wood of Bradford supplied most of the money (£40,000) towards the cost of running the movement.

The most impressive display of the strength of Oastler's following was to be seen in the pilgrimage to York on 24th April 1832, when thousands of men flocked to the Castle Yard from all over the West Riding. Oastler marched all the way with his men and still had stamina enough to hold a public meeting in the Market Place, followed by a dance, immediately after returning to Huddersfield. That night when Oastler undressed, the skin of the soles of his feet peeled off with his stockings—this was four days after the start of the journey. It was at this great demonstration that Oastler was nicknamed 'The Factory King'; and despite the jibes of Edward Baines, editor of the Whig *Leeds Mercury*—had he delusions of grandeur? did he really think he was a king?—the name stuck; Baines was later branded 'The Great Liar of the North'.

Oastler expounded his philosophy in 1832. He believed in the altar, the throne and the cottage. He believed the Whigs had sold the people into slavery while new Toryism stood to benefit everyone. There should be no taxes on the press, no indirect taxation, a direct levy on property and land, the waste to be reclaimed by the unemployed and settled by the poor. He looked forward to a return to domestic industry and spoke of the respectable little clothier who could make a piece of cloth in a week and always keep his family at home.

Eventually, agitation both inside and outside Parliament led to the appointment in April 1833 of a Royal Commission of fifteen 'to collect information in the manufacturing districts with respect to the employment of children . . .' As the Commissioners went round, Oastler's followers staged demonstrations of which the one described by Dr Chalmers was typical.[1]

They interviewed a youth of seventeen who said he had been working since he was seven. He began in a mill where there were fifty others of the same age, who were always sick and poorly. They laboured from 5 a.m. till 8 p.m. and one overlooker used a strap to keep them awake in the afternoons. 'Sometimes—we had but half got our dinners and the overlooker put the clock forward to one, and he rang the bell and we were obliged to run back to work.—There were about a dozen of the children who died.—The children are often sick with the dust and dirt they eat with their meals.—I found that labour very distressing to me, it increased the deformity which came upon me.' He then spoke of fines and beatings for lateness and of his brother who died from the overwork which affected his spine. He described how 'Last Tuesday but one there was a boy brought in about five or six o'clock (to the infirmary) from a mill. He had been catched with the shaft and he had both his thighs broke, and from his knee to his hip the flesh was ripped up the same as it had been cut by a knife, his head was bruised, his eyes nearly torn out and his arms broken. His sister who ran to pull him off, got both her arms broke and her head bruised. The boy died last Thursday night but one, I don't know whether the girl is dead but she is not expected to live.— These accidents usually happen at the latter end of the day. There was a boy who was kneeling down and a strap catched him about his ankles and carried him round the wheel and

[1] See p. 79.

dashed his brains out.—Oh! if I had a thousand pounds I would give them all to have the use of my limbs again.'

Everywhere the Commissioners went, large meetings were held and when they reached Huddersfield in May 1833 they saw from the window of the 'George Inn' a mass of children who sang:

> 'We will have the Ten Hours Bill
> That we will, that we will,
> Or the land shall ne'er be still;
> We will have the Ten Hours Bill,
> For Oastler says we will.'

The Commissioners were watched day and night. But Oastler refused to help them, declaring that their tactics were to delay the inevitable reform.

Sadler, who had lost his seat in the General Election of 1832, handed over his parliamentary efforts to Lord Ashley.

Eventually, in spite of the defeat of a Factory Bill introduced by Ashley in July 1833, in January 1834 Lord Althorp's Act became law. This provided that no child was to be employed under nine, those under thirteen to be conditioned to forty-eight hours a week with school two hours a day; those under eighteen to work sixty hours with no night work; a system of inspection was to be set up and the Act applied to *all* mills except those manufacturing silk.

Oastler was not satisfied and said so.

Oastler next became involved in agitation against the New Poor Law.[1] Under the old system, parish relief, organised by the townships, was given on a scale which was related to the price of bread and the size of the family. The economic theorists argued however, that charity was wasteful, and encouraged idleness; there was a limited amount of money available for wages therefore to strike was a waste of time. Thus relief should be made as unattractive as possible for the able bodied. The workhouse was to be made worse than the worst possible conditions outside. The areas of administration for the New Poor

[1] The Poor Law Amendment Act was passed in 1834 but not implemented in the North until 1837.

Law were to be larger than either the townships or the old parishes because this would be more economical; and the new areas, known as Unions, were to have elected Boards of Guardians, while the central administrators—'The Bashaws of Somerset House'—were to have overriding powers. The new workhouses were to be large in size and there were to be separate places for the insane and the elderly; once inside the workhouse the men and women were to be separated—perhaps the unkindest cut of all. Some of these features already existed in our local workhouses.

The poor rate in the North had been lower than elsewhere in the late eighteenth century. Real hardship in our area had always been temporary, although many were accustomed to living on the verge of poverty. All that was required in the West Riding was a little help to keep men alive until able to work again. It was estimated that three quarters of the handloom weavers occasionally received parish relief—they were too proud to think of entering an institution. The economists had said that poverty existed to rid the world of its surplus population: Oastler replied that this was unchristian, the old autonomy of parish and county was being undermined and he foresaw a revolution if this new Act upset the Constitution[1]—statements regarded by many of Oastler's friends as an incitement to rebellion.

In 1837 the fear of the Poor Law Commission began to dominate the North as the Government turned its attention to Yorkshire. The Parishes of Huddersfield, Almondbury, Kirkheaton and Kirkburton were to be formed into one large Poor Law Union; and, with growing fears of the poor being shut up and never finding work again, rumour spread. It was said that labour was to be moved to the North in order to smash the trade unions and reduce wages. These were times of depression which by 1837 had again become serious; and, since the Commissioners apparently showed no leniency at all, Oastler

[1] By introducing centralised authority from Somerset House, thus he feared weakening the power of traditional local authority. At this period Oastler began to make unguarded statements in moments of emotion and, when he spoke of revolution, his enemies took full advantage to discredit him.

Above : When the Cloth Hall was demolished in 1930, the entrance and the cupola with clock and bell were re-erected in 1931 as a shelter in Ravensknowle Park. *Photo :* Greaves.

Left : Inside the old School Board Offices in Peel Street : this window was destroyed with the demolition of the building in 1967. *Photo : Huddersfield Examiner.*

Above: One of the old Crewe locomotives used by Hillhouse engine shed until the mid-1880s, here shown approaching the aqueduct at Bradley. From a picture by Ian Fraser lent by Neil Fraser. *Below:* A steam tram of *c.* 1890, showing a typical old Wilkinson engine drawing one of the latest saloon bogie cars. From a block lent by Roy Brook (Crosland Moor).

determined to organise the Short Time Committees in order to frustrate the New Poor Law.

On 10th of January 1837 Alfred Power, an Assistant Poor Law Commissioner, came to Huddersfield. It was Market Day and, as he went to the 'George', he was heckled by the crowds. He returned in April, to be again met by a turbulent crowd, and only a threat to read the Riot Act prevented a scene. His meeting with the Board of Guardians was adjourned and no progress was made at all.

But by now Oastler's master, Thornhill, was displeased that his steward was fighting the Government. He was even more displeased when the parishioners of Fixby refused to elect a Guardian for their township, and he firmly instructed them to do so. The Squire, however, knew very well the extent of the Tory support his steward enjoyed, and he would have known it even better had he attended a mass meeting of thousands of people at Hartshead on Whit Monday 1837. That night the sneers of Edward Baines in the *Leeds Mercury* were countered by the burning of his effigy in Huddersfield Market Place. It was at this time that Baines was actually nicknamed 'The Great Liar of the North'. In Heckmondwike they cremated his effigy again but this time outside the house of a prominent Whig chapel deacon. The resistance of Huddersfield to the Poor Law was coming to symbolise the claim to justice of the Nation's poor.

The Guardians attempted to hold a meeting on 5th of June, asking for the Army to police it, but the Magistrates refused for fear of aggravating the situation. As it was, 10,000 people arrived and when the chairman refused to see a delegation, even Oastler was powerless to prevent the angry crowd from attacking the building. Power and his Board thereupon fled to the Albion Hotel and the mob again paraded outside. There were scenes of jubilation when word came that a motion to appoint a Clerk to the Board had been defeated. More effigies were now burned in the Market Place.

Not wishing to admit defeat, the Central Commissioners decreed that any three guardians could appoint the Clerk. Although tempers rose in the town and the cavalry were put in readiness, the Board were afraid to act and adjourned themselves for a further three months. In fact, the local Whigs were becoming apprehensive. Oastler was blamed, and the Guardians resigned. The protagonists of the New Poor Law blamed the Magistrates for siding with Hobson the Radical but, whoever was to blame, by January 1838 the Board had achieved precisely nothing.

Oastler was narrowly defeated in the General Election of 1837—by a mere twenty-two votes, but somehow Huddersfield continued to hold out against the new system and no inn would consider accommodating the notorious Power. At the next Board Meeting at the Court House a Clerk was still not elected, so the Chairman appointed Mr Floyd, a local solicitor. Three weeks later, and for the second time, the Oastlerites forced their way into the room where this unfortunate man was trying to hold a meeting. The Whig members were forced to withdraw, and the anti-Poor Law members reversed all the Board's previous business, drew up a petition for Somerset House, and adjourned themselves for another two months. Six Oastlerites were charged at York with having caused a 'tumultuous assembly'.

In the spring of 1838 Oastler was ill for three weeks. Squire Thornhill at this time came out in support of the New Poor Law and decided that Oastler must go. Ever since 1820 Oastler had been paid £300 a year. The fact that part of this money had been spent on the estate was Oastler's own fault in that he had entertained visitors, done repairs, and given charity in an attempt, however well intentioned, to be Squire himself. Oastler's finances were always haphazard, indeed he had mixed his own money with that of his master until he owed Thornhill £2,700. By 1837 the debt was down to £1,700 but on 28th May Oastler was dismissed for not devoting his full attention to the estate. His supporters worked hard to provide an annuity and a medal was struck in order to raise money but this was not enough. On 28th August, Oastler was escorted from Fixby by 15,000 people and ten bands. At a meeting near St Paul's Church there was an unprecedented display when thousands turned up to support the 'Factory King'. Propaganda spread by Oastler's supporters annoyed Thornhill who, as a reprisal, accused his steward of squandering the estate moneys. Oastler went away for five months taking the account books with him. His master called for a trial in London.

The Age of Defiance

Two years elapsed before Oastler's case was heard in court; and as he waited, the social picture changed. The Six Points of Chartism were put forward in February 1837 and included manhood suffrage, paid M.P.s and a secret ballot, but by July 1839 the bubble had burst when a general strike was called and then abandoned. The Government struck hard and sentenced three hundred Chartist leaders. In March of the same year, the six riotous Huddersfield Guardians had been found guilty and support for them was weakening. A new Board had a Whig majority, and some of its opponents had, by March 1839, found attractive employment working for the Board. At Kirkheaton there was a local riot when a relieving officer went to inspect the workhouse and was driven off 'like a fox'. The collapse of the Chartist National Convention broke what remained of local anti-Poor Law agitation.

The ultimate outcome of this struggle was to make the Central Board realise that the North of England could not be regarded merely as an extension of the South, where conditions were generally quite different. A degree of compromise was therefore exercised in Lancashire and the West Riding and the Guardians were empowered to continue the old form of poor relief. Thus there evolved a dual system. By 1848 there were 300,000 paupers in workhouses in England and Wales but nearly two million receiving some kind of relief remained outside them.

Driver[1] points out that Disraeli was heard in the House of Commons to utter words identical with Oastler's own philosophy when he spoke on 12th July 1839. Disraeli said that 1832 had given power to a class who acknowledged no social duties. He was wrong in this, for the Whigs saw it as their duty to provide a government but one which cost them personally nothing. The trouble was that they did not realise that this could not be achieved without taking away the civil rights of the people.

Oastler was tried on 10th of July 1840. As the charge was not that of fraudulence he did not defend himself. Thornhill refused to accept repayment of Oastler's debts from his future earnings, and he was sent to the Fleet debtors' prison. It seems likely that

[1] H. C. Driver, *Tory Radical*.

Thornhill's friends in the Government intended that Oastler should be put away. Now the North had no leader.

Many visitors came to see their hero in prison while gifts of all kinds enabled his wife to live near by. Oastler Committees raised large sums of money; 'Oastler's own' in Huddersfield held a festival in the Philosophical Hall, Ramsden Street, a tea, concert and dance which raised £23. From prison Oastler produced *The Fleet Papers* every week and when the Fleet closed down in 1842 he was taken to the Queen's Prison.

Oastler's writings restated his beliefs at this time that Toryism was for the good of all. He was against centralisation, saying that the Government should act as a flywheel to regulate the country as a whole. The 'hungry forties' he blamed on the Whigs' usurpation of agricultural self-sufficiency, and he supported the Corn Laws. The Tories, he believed, should use established institutions to create an ordered society to protect the poor. He looked for the social state in which factories were unable to remove their workers from the operation of the Law.

Kelly, Thornhill's lawyer, and many deputations to the Squire tried to free Oastler. By late 1843 large funds had been collected, even Baines the Elder had subscribed £5! and there was much publicity in the press. By the end of January 1844 over £2,000 had been raised but a further £1,200 was still needed to pay off the interest owing. Twelve guarantors raised this sum and on 12th of February 1844, after three years and two months, the 'Ransomed Patriot' was released.

In those days Huddersfield did not yet have a railway station and Oastler was met from the train at Brighouse where he spent the night at the Railway Hotel. The waiting crowds, accompanied by four bands, marched towards Huddersfield and they were joined by three more bands half-way. It was a triumphal march enjoyed without reservation by ten thousand people.[1] Even the *Leeds Mercury* referred to Oastler as 'a gentleman.'

By March 1844 Parliament had declared itself divided on the Ten Hours Bill issue and a massive campaign for its acceptance was launched. During April, Oastler addressed twenty-two

[1] See illustration facing p. 74.

meetings, all were crowded but he was now less of a fighter, and more of a prophet who saw machinery as a blessing to all the people, and labour to be organised so as to give full employment to all. But even the Twelve Hours Act of 1844 did not assuage the old warrior's displeasure, and he remained a Ten Hours man.

From 1844 to 1846 Oastler was at a low ebb. There were further appeals for money but £1,100 was still outstanding and this the twelve guarantors had to cover. The Liberation Committee advised Oastler to retire from public life and to take up a job. He was a disappointed man and even the *Fleet Papers* had ended in a debt which had to be paid by his friends. He lived at Headingley for two years, then Mary Oastler died and he went to work in Fulham.

The narrow defeat of the Ten Hours Bill by ten votes in 1846 led to renewed campaigning and Oastler re-emerged as leader of the West-Riding. On 8th June 1847 the Bill was finally passed. Thus the victory of the Whigs over the repeal of the Corn Laws had led the gentry to retaliate by supporting the cause of the factory children. Economic depression had by this time limited the work of many to ten hours or less and when recovery came there was to be pressure from masters and men in favour of ignoring the Act. This pressure was supported by the Parke Judgment which said that relays of labour were permissible. Therefore the Act was reduced to nothing, and any inspection to a farce, with machinery running all the time and workers starting and finishing at varying times.

Ashley's Act of 1850 was yet another compromise. Oastler was frustrated and, by this time, ill. He was annoyed to see the Tory Party now full of commercial interests and in 1851 brought out *The Home*, a new family paper of Christian Tory Democracy, but it faded in 1855 through lack of support.

Palmerston's Act of 1853 brought factory legislation a step nearer the goal. There was to be a uniform working day from six to six, therefore the men's day could not be stretched by using relays of children. An effective Ten Hours Act was achieved by Disraeli in 1874, an event Oastler did not live to see.

Oastler died on 22nd August 1861 aged seventy-one. Even Edward Baines, the Younger, paid tribute to his courage in fighting for what he believed to be right. At his burial at Kirkstall, the men of the original Fixby Hall Compact were his bearers; and the last great crowd which Oastler drew was in 1869 when 100,000 are said to have gathered in Forster Square Bradford for the unveiling of his statue.

Richard Oastler was undoubtedly the local giant of the 'thirties and 'forties, but he would have been powerless without the massive support he received from Huddersfield. Many supporters followed him everywhere, and all encouraged him when he needed their help. Oastler succeeded in bridging the enormous gap between Tory and Radical just at the time when a bitter class consciousness had taken root in the North.

The people supported Oastler—as they had supported Mellor—to the end. The great features of Luddism were the absolute secrecy and the massive local sympathy which was aroused. But it was as an opponent of the New Poor Law that the town really acquired a reputation for independence, for when Huddersfield defied the Establishment, defiance was unanimous.

For services rendered in upholding the Law and the Constitution, Sir Joseph Radcliffe, Magistrate, of Milnsbridge House, was awarded a Baronetcy in 1813. He and those who followed had an unenviable task in attempting to keep the town in order during the early nineteenth century.

CHAPTER VIII

Town Life in the Early
Nineteenth Century

THE MAP of 1826 shows a town centre much more familiar to us than that in the map of 1778. New Street now has buildings on both sides as far as Ramsden Street, and King Street and Queen Street have partially filled the area between Back Green and the Pack Horse Yard. Within the town, the Parish Church has been joined by All Saints' (later St Paul's), Ramsden Street Chapel, Queen Street Wesleyan Chapel, and Rehoboth Chapel in High Street for the Methodist New Connexion.

The results of enclosures and turnpike trusts can be seen in the new roads; Manchester New Road, Huddersfield and New Hey Road and the Halifax New Road. St John's Road is still marked 'Foot way to Bay Hall', while behind Upperhead Row there are still the green fields of Spring Grove and Green Head, with a reservoir between them and behind, the largest factory in the town, Joshua Lockwood's.

Until 1820 local government was largely in the hands of the Parish Vestry. The Manorial Court Leet had from earliest times appointed a Chief Constable to maintain public order but by Tudor times many a parish also had its constable. So it was that in 1812 we find the Vestry resolved to appoint a Parish Constable. Later in 1816 the same body decided to provide him with an assistant. This must surely have been born of the troubled times described in the previous chapter.

On 20th June 1820 an Act was passed for 'lighting, watching and cleaning the town of Huddersfield'. The Act said 'The Town of Huddersfield is large and populous' [some 13,000 souls] 'and a place of considerable trade, and is also a great thoroughfare for travellers, and some of the streets, lanes and other public passages within the said town are not lighted or watched, and all of them are not properly cleaned, but are subject to various nuisances and it would tend to the safety, convenience and advantage of the inhabitants . . . if the same were properly lighted, watched, cleansed and regulated'. The Act was law only within a radius of 1,200 yards from the spot where the old cross formerly stood in the Market Place. This area was the same as that of the 1848 Improvement Act and is shown on the 1850 map. Fifty-nine commissioners were appointed under the Act of 1820, including Sir John Ramsden and four other members of his family; every commissioner was worth at least a thousand pounds. New members were co-opted, but each one had to be approved by the Lord of the Manor. This might have made it easy for the ground landlord eventually to fill the Commission with his own nominees but there is no evidence to suggest that he did so. Nevertheless the idea that Sir John Ramsden had the new Parliamentary Borough 'in his pocket' was certainly current in 1832. The commissioners were to meet every three weeks at the George and were empowered to light the town with gas and to employ night watchmen with powers to keep the peace. Those who paid less than six pounds a year in rent were exempted from paying rates, but most of those who did pay rates had no say in appointing the commissioners. Local government elected by all the ratepayers had still to come.

Whilst the Commissioners of the 1820 Act were deliberating, and there was also a Board of Highway Surveyors appointed by the Vestry from about 1835, the town was changing out of all recognition. By 1850 it had grown from a large sprawling village into a very thriving and compact urban area.

It is perhaps not realised how elegant a town Huddersfield became before the steam age. That this was so was largely due to a local builder and engineer, Joseph Kaye, who laid out the new town on the sloping ground above the old church. He gave the town wide streets, two-storey houses of clean cut stone, the waterworks offices, the Royal Infirmary (1831) and St Paul's Church (1829). In John Betjeman's words 'he did for Huddersfield what John Nash did for London and we can probably ascribe to Kaye the layout for the streets in the centre of the town in the form of a grid with vistas down Ramsden Street, King Street and Princess Street to the open country and the hills'.[1] The Huddersfield Gas Works Company was formed in 1821 and eventually supplied gas to 650 street lamps provided by the Improvement Commissioners. By 1824 the gas works had been enlarged and householders were being asked to pay thirty shillings a year for gas lighting from dusk till nine o'clock on week-days, and midnight on Saturdays, with the option of paying an additional five shillings for gas on Sundays. All bills were to be paid six months in advance, burners were supplied by the company but householders were to cover the cost of piping from the street to their premises. A discount was offered to factories and large consumers.

The post office was in New Street, and in the 1830s the Postmaster was William Moore, a prominent member of Ramsden Street Chapel. Mail for London and Wakefield left by coach at 5.45 p.m. and for Leeds, Halifax and Manchester the post left at 10.15 a.m. and 6 p.m. Letters from London arrived at 6 p.m. and from Leeds, Halifax and Manchester at 7.15 a.m. and 2.15 p.m. There were postal deliveries on foot to Lockwood, Honley, Holmfirth, Paddock, Marsden, Outlane and other places at similar distances from the town centre, except on Tuesdays when presumably those attending the market collected their own mail from the office. Postal charges were high, a letter from London costing elevenpence. The charge from Manchester was eightpence and there was a surcharge of a penny for delivery to Lindley and places at a similar distance— twopence for Honley and the outer areas.

It was Moore who issued a writ for libel for £1,000 in respect of certain derogatory remarks made by Oastler against the Huddersfield Dissenters. In January 1834 Moore had countered these remarks by accusing Oastler of embezzling the funds of the factory workers, whereupon Oastler replied by claiming that Moore was opening mail addressed to his political opponents. The case was heard in February 1836. Mr Blackburn, K.C., appeared for Moore while Oastler conducted his own case and succeeded in tearing the Postmaster's reputation

[1] *Week-end Telegraph*, 2nd October 1964.

to shreds. Moore was awarded a farthing damages, leaving Oastler technically guilty, but jubilant over what he rightly regarded as a moral victory.

The old waterworks was totally inadequate and a memorial presented to Sir John Ramsden in 1826 requested 'that an abundant and never failing supply of pure water might be obtained and conveyed to the town at a moderate expense'. The petition was signed by seventy-four leading citizens who said 'the inhabitants are compelled to carry water from springs at some distance from the town, particularly from a place called "Bradley Spout" at which during the last summer there have been, on an average at all hours of day and till a late hour at night, upwards of ten persons collected waiting for their turn, and until their cans were filled'. A scheme was envisaged which would bring water to the town from Longwood but in order to achieve this, a special Act of Parliament was necessary.

The Act was dated 14th June 1827 and to carry out its provisions 120 commissioners were appointed and named. They were persons of standing each possessing at least £1,000, and they were empowered to borrow £20,000 to carry out the new works. Risks were to be borne by the commissioners but interest up to five per cent. could be earned on the investment; and not more than four members of the Commission were to be nominees of Sir John Ramsden. Their first project, Longwood Lower Reservoir, was completed in 1829. Waterworks Offices were built in what was appropriately named Water Street. Above the frontage, on an oval tablet, was inscribed:

WATER WORKS
Established by Subscription
MDCCCXXVIII

Behind was the Spring Street tank, paid for out of the same Act. Unfortunately for the planners, the population of the town (13,284 in 1821) had increased to 25,068 by 1841, and water was being rationed in Huddersfield, especially in the summer, before the system had been in operation for twenty years. By 1845, indeed, it was resolved that no further industrial users could be supplied with water.

Although textiles are the subject of the next chapter it must be mentioned here that by this period there were large mills actually in the centre of Huddersfield, notably that of Joshua Lockwood in Upperhead Row—known to all as 'Joss Lockud's', where woollen corduroy material was made. In 1820, to celebrate the coronation of George IV, Mr Lockwood gave a banquet for his workpeople and rode upon a white horse at the head of a procession of 600 weavers, each man carrying a shuttle. In March 1828 Lockwood's six-storey building was burnt out. Although part of the mill was saved, damage was caused which amounted to over £10,000 and this was, in its day, the worst fire Huddersfield had ever seen.

Mention has already been made of the use of inns by the clothiers who attended Huddersfield Market. Baines' Directory for 1822 gives us not only a list of inns but also the names of their customers. The aim of this information was to tell a potential customer where his supplier might be found if he were not in the Cloth Hall.

There were no fewer than thirty-seven inns in the town in 1822, and of these, eight were in Kirkgate, seven in Westgate— and, if we include the 'George' in the Market Place, then there were sixteen of them in the one thoroughfare. Most of the others were in King Street, Cross Church Street and Cloth Hall Street. The clothiers were listed as attending nineteen of these inns so the rest must have been ale-houses and nothing more. By far the most popular place for business was 'The Cherry Tree' in Westgate, while next in order came 'The Saddle', also in Westgate, 'The Green Dragon' in Market Street, and 'The White Swan' in Kirkgate.

Inns also served as termini and stages for the coach traffic. *Pigot's Commercial Directory* for 1819/20 announced that 'The Cornwallis' would stop at 'The George' and 'The Rose and Crown' in Kirkgate; this coach service between Yorkshire and Lancashire left for Manchester and Liverpool daily at nine, and departed at noon for Wakefield and York. The Halifax coach left 'The King's Head', Cloth Hall Street, at nine and five. 'The True Briton' left 'The Ramsden's Arms', Kirkgate, at two for Manchester and at five-thirty for Leeds.

The banks were, as indeed they are still, located near the

Market Place. In 1822 there were Dobson's on the corner of Westgate, Rawson's at the top of King Street, Hirst and Sikes' in Kirkgate, Wentworth Chaloner and Rishworth's in New Street, and Benjamin Wilson's actually in the Market Place.

The eighteenth century was an age of expanding business and stage-coach transport experienced many difficulties when cash was sent to the North. Metal was dear and coins often scarce. The issue of local bank notes was not permitted until 1797 and, such was the need for them that by 1800 over forty independent banks had sprung up in the West Riding; banking became a profession in its own right as bankers ceased to follow other callings. These local banks had slender resources and should one fail, then the others were immediately affected. They all had agents in London and a financial crisis there meant that the little provincial men suffered. The Bank Charter Act of 1826 strengthened the local banks by insisting that they each had at least six partners and forbidding them to issue their own notes for sums below five pounds. The rest of the century saw the small banks amalgamate to form larger units, though it was not until 1928 that the issue of private bank notes ceased in England.

The first banker in Huddersfield was Joseph Brook and in 1797 we find notes signed by Silvester Sikes as his cashier. In 1808, Brook joined Perfect, Seaton & Co. of Leeds and Pontefract and the firm became Seaton, Brook & Co. Up to 1810, this firm were bankers for the Huddersfield Canal Company. They closed on 23rd July 1816 having held out for three weeks during a run on the bank caused by the failure of Inghams, of whom more below.

THE SIKES FAMILY
William Sikes
(1743–1812)

Silvester Sikes
(1776–1811)

Shakespeare Garrick Sikes
(1781–1862)

Sir Charles William Sikes, Bart.
(1818–89)

We now come to the Sikes family, a name which for over a hundred years permeated banking in Huddersfield. The Huddersfield Commercial Bank, originally Silvester Sikes & Co. lasted from 1799 to 1801 when Silvester and his father William Sikes went bankrupt. Benjamin and Joseph Ingham took over the business name, and presumably the premises, of Silvester Sikes; Shakespeare Garrick Sikes, brother of Silvester was Ingham's manager until he left in 1806 to partner his father-in-law to form Hirst & Sikes' Bank. Ingham's London agents, Bruce Simpson & Co., failed in the summer of 1816 when the Government issued an 'extent in aid' seizing property to pay off a loan. On 4th July 1816 we know that John Ikin, Ingham's manager, took a coach to London to find out the cause of the trouble. For the next eleven years Ingham's struggled in vain to pay off Bruce Simpson's creditors and they finally closed in 1827.

Hirst & Sikes' Bank, Kirkgate, suffered a run on them in 1825 when Wentworth, Chaloner and Rishworth failed. Dobson's stopped all payments and there was a run on Rawson's and Wilson's. Shakespeare Garrick Sikes paid his creditors so slowly that he survived initially for three days from 31st January to 2nd February 1826, when Taylors of Gomersal failed; Sikes then posted a notice on the door asking his customers to be patient. At the end of a further fifty days, all had been paid but this and subsequent strains led Shakespeare Garrick Sikes to close down completely in 1832.

The Act of 1826 led to new companies being formed. One of the first was the Huddersfield Banking Company, which commenced business on 7th June 1827 on the corner of New Street and Cloth Hall Street. Sir Charles Sikes worked there all his life and became manager in 1868. In 1860 he had been instrumental in persuading the Government set up the Post Office Savings Bank, and he held Huddersfield Post Office Account Number One, which he opened with £15. The Huddersfield Banking Company was later amalgamated with the Midland Bank.

Benjamin Wilson, who also had a brewery at Bay Hall, in 1832 joined a new joint stock company in the Market Place. This became the Mirfield, Huddersfield & District Banking

Company and, in 1836 the West Riding Union Banking Company. In 1902 they joined the Lancashire & Yorkshire Bank and finally became part of Martins Bank.

Another of the old banks, Rawson's, a Halifax firm, formed the Halifax & Huddersfield Union Banking Company in 1836, at the top of King Street. They later became part of the West Yorkshire Bank and finally joined Lloyds.

The type of bank which came after 1826 was certainly a steadying influence in the town at a time when social life and trade were unstable and representative politics in their infancy.

The Reform Act of 1832 is best seen as part of a gradual transition from an agricultural nation ruled by squires and landowners to an industrial nation dominated by commercial and industrial classes. The Bill itself was devised by the Whigs who gave the vote to the £10 householder but increased the old electorate by only 50 per cent. The Radicals were bitterly disappointed as the Bill carefully preserved the old principle that Parliament represented property rather than persons. Much more significant was the granting of representation to the new industrial towns of which Huddersfield was one.

In Huddersfield the new voters constituted the 'shopocracy' of traders, merchants, professional men and manufacturers. In December 1832 the candidates were Captain Lewis Fenton of Spring Grove (Whig) and Captain Joseph Wood (Radical). Oastler supported Wood and publicly denounced the new Bill as a swindle on the working man. He was particularly incensed when Sir John Ramsden's son wrote to his father asking him to complain to Thornhill about his steward being a Radical supporter. Wood urged the extension of the franchise saying 'the voice of the people is the voice of God. Your franchise is only a trust (from God) then vote for Wood, the man of the people.' Fenton said little except in support of Lord Grey's government—such was his confidence.

The two days of polling were an occasion for mass meetings and outrage. Hardly a window was unbroken at Spring Grove House, the George Inn or the town's public buildings. Only when the Riot Act had been read and the cavalry arrived, did the crowd in the square sullenly disperse.

The Radicals were soundly defeated. Fenton polled 263 votes to Wood's 152, and the event brought forth the usual crop of pamphlets of which one was entitled as follows:

'The Woodites' Forget-me-not'—being a sketch of a new political farce called 'the Whig-tom-foolery' election, and first acted in the Borough of Huddersfield by 415 out of a population of 20,000 when Captain Fenton, the nominee of Byram House (seat of the Ramsden Family) was returned by a nominal majority as their representative in opposition to Captain Wood, the man of the people.

—by an observer

Printed and published by J. Hobson. Swan Yard, Huddersfield 1833.

Spring Grove House, whose windows suffered so much at election time, had its entrance in Outcote Bank and was demolished in 1879 to make way for Spring Grove School, but in 1832 it was the home of Captain Fenton. A fall from one of its windows in 1833 caused his death.

There followed a by-election in January 1834 and the Whigs chose John Blackburn, k.c., to succeed to the Ramsden interest. Blackburn did not endear himself to the masses by describing them as 'bulls', 'tigers' and 'serpents'. He said he was not against unions, but workers would do better to put their money into a bag and save it at home instead of supporting unions which did harm to everybody (groans from the audience); he did however, advocate a secret ballot.

At this time, the local opposition was in confusion since Althorp's Act had split the Radicals from the moderate reformers. It was therefore necessary to find a candidate able to link them together and Joseph Wood, now a Roman Catholic, stood down for Michael Thomas Sadler the factory reformer. Understandably many Irish voters refused to support the evangelical Sadler, who then decided to stand as an Independent. Wood's supporters urged him not to back down, and Oastler's supporters asked their champion himself to stand. In the end, Wood himself came out into the open.

The votes came out thus:

Blackburn (Whig) 234
Sadler (Ind.) 147
Wood (Radical) 103

—and Oastler was furious. He was even more annoyed when he learned that Edward Baines, the Elder, had got in at Leeds by a majority of six! The *Mercury* was indeed jubilant. Oastler was even more furious when a mill owner prosecuted for violating the Althorp Act was let off, while Hobson was imprisoned for printing unstamped journals. Oastler must have felt like yielding to his supporters and standing for Parliament himself, but he did not come forward yet.

In 1835 there was a General Election. Blackburn, who further entrenched himself in the popular heart by declaring that the proletariat ought to await signs of increased intelligence before being given the vote, was this time opposed by a Major-General Johnson whom D. F. E. Sykes wrongly describes as a 'Carpetbagger'. Once again, however, Blackburn triumphed, polling 241 votes against the General's 109, and the Radicals remained in the doldrums.

When Blackburn died in 1837, there was another by-election and the Whig candidate was Edward Ellice, nephew of Lord Grey and son of the M.P. for Coventry, a colourless character who publicly admitted that he knew nothing of the Poor Law. The Tory and Radical interests combined to offer their support to Oastler and when John Whitacre, Tory mill owner, and William Stocks, the Radical Constable of Huddersfield, together made an invitation to Oastler, he agreed to stand. The Tories had been behind Oastler in 1835 when he had exposed 'The peculating John of Canal' for charging excessive dues and Sir John had been obliged to reduce his charges in conformity with the charter of the canal company. The Radicals opposed the 'Bastilles' of the New Poor Law and 10,000 turned up to Oastler's first campaign meeting.

The Whigs accused the Tories of trickery and said the Radicals were being gulled by the 'altar and throne man'. Oastler promised factory reform, household suffrage, the repeal of Catholic Emancipation and of the New Poor Law; 'Ellice for Bastilles' and 'Oastler is the friend of our factory children' read the banners. The Rev. Stephens urged the workers to boycott all shops and public houses where the Whigs were supported, and Ellice's meetings were broken up in chaos. The magistrates feared the approach of polling day so much that sixty special constables were sworn in.

On Saturday 6th of May, as the Justices and the Dragoons stood by, less than 700 inhabitants went to the polls, with the following result:

Ellice (Whig)	340
Oastler (Tory/Radical)	290

The extent to which Oastler's appeal cut across traditional loyalties can be seen from figures taken from the poll books.

20 Woolstaplers
24 Merchants and Manufacturers } voted for Oastler
13 Cloth Dressers

13 Woolstaplers
51 Merchants and Manufacturers } voted for Ellice.
19 Cloth Dressers

Oastler drew some of his support from second generation manufacturers who had less to lose by showing leniency to their employees and who at the same time resented the Ramsden Interest.

Oastler was a poor loser. He blamed the presence of the soldiers for his defeat and declared that John Ramsden had intimidated the electorate. In reply, the Whigs said that Oastler had intimidated the peace-loving tradesfolk of the town. In fact Oastler had polled more than Sadler and Wood combined in 1834, and more than any previously successful candidate.

After Queen Victoria's accession in 1837, there was a General Election in 1838. This time W. R. C. Stansfield, an 'imported' country gentleman, stood for the Whigs—to be greeted with pieces of bread and cheese held out on long poles (a day's workhouse ration), and Richard Oastler once more stood for the Tory-Radical alliance. Twelve Roman Catholics called on him to ask if he would change his mind and thus withdraw his support for the repeal of the Catholic Emancipation Act, but

Oastler refused to compromise although this was no longer a live political issue.

In those days, votes were publicly recorded as they came in and, anticipating trouble, a dozen London policemen had been drafted in. In the afternoon, when Stansfield had gained the lead, an angry situation developed; the police, hemmed in by the crowd drew their cutlasses and two troops of cavalry appeared as two Justices of the Peace read the Riot Act. The soldiers prepared to charge, the mob fell apart and Oastler had lost again, this time by twenty-two votes:

Stansfield	323
Oastler	301

Had those twelve Roman Catholics voted the other way, Oastler would have won. At the next election in 1841, Stansfield was unopposed.

We cannot leave the stormy scene of public controversy without a word about Joshua Hobson (1810–76), publisher of the anti-Wood pamphlet mentioned earlier. He had supported Oastler at a time when newspapers were liable to a stamp duty of fourpence a copy. He therefore built his own wooden press, set it up in the Swan Yard, near the Parish Church, and started his own paper, *The Voice of the West Riding*. It was in the same yard that the Huddersfield Political Union held its meetings. After twelve months of publishing, Somerset House prosecuted Hobson for evading stamp duty and he chose to go to prison rather than pay a fine. Hobson's journey to Wakefield was a triumphal procession accompanied by bands. In prison, Hobson's friends enabled him to employ a servant and to have his own room. In 1834, we find him in Leeds where three years later Feargus O'Connor, the Chartist Leader, engaged him to publish *The Northern Star*, a new Radical paper.

In 1829 John Charles Ramsden[1] laid the foundation stone of the Royal Infirmary. The Huddersfield and Upper Agbrigg Dispensary had been opened in the Pack Horse Yard in 1814, ostensibly to commemorate the Napoleonic Wars, but in fact (we are told) to counteract diseases brought home by the

---

[1] Eldest son of the 4th Baronet. Died 1836. His father died in 1839.

soldiers. But, as the town grew so did its need for amenities and the dispensary was no longer adequate. The infirmary was opened in 1831 and gave the town one of its new and stately buildings. The first resident medical officer received the princely salary of £20 per annum while the matron received a £5 bonus to her salary provided 'she behaved herself'!

The period covered by this chapter witnessed developments in all branches of Church activity such as have never been seen since.

The hostility of the Ramsdens had led to Highfield Chapel being built outside their territory, but by the nineteenth century a more tolerant attitude prevailed. By this time, Highfield had become overcrowded, and the Independents were losing the membership of newcomers to the town. However, no one wished to set up in opposition to old Mr Moorhouse who was left to see out fifty-one years as minister at Highfield. Shortly after Mr Moorhouse died in 1823, following meetings held at the Rose & Crown, Kirkgate, a site was leased for a new chapel at the corner of Mr Lockwood's field in Back Green, amidst the orchards and tenter crofts which ran from New Street to Shore Head. The Back Green area was an open space where political meetings were sometimes held.

J. P. Pritchett of York designed the new chapel, which was built by Joseph Kaye, and opened on 28th December 1825. Known as Ramsden Street Chapel, it stood on the site now occupied by the Public Library. It was the first church to be lit by gas and one of the earliest large buildings in the town. Pritchett also designed Huddersfield College in New North Road, and the new Parish Church.[1]

The secretary to the Ramsden Street Chapel foundation committee was William Willans (1800–63); he and Rev. W. A. Hurndall of Ramsden Street saw the lack of facilities for the education of boys, indeed many fathers sent their sons elsewhere to receive their schooling. In 1838 these two were amongst the first governors of Huddersfield College.

During the 'hungry forties', the chapel still owed £2,000 and we read that tea was dispensed with at a meeting 'because of

[1] See p. 131.

the badness of the times' but by 1845 the debt had been paid and Ramsden Street became a centre in the town for religious and philanthropic enterprise. As new suburbs sprang up in the fifties, the chapel appointed a Town Missionary.

When Rev. Richard Skinner retired in 1877, he was succeeded by his assistant, Rev. J. T. Stannard. Stannard was not universally popular mainly for doctrinal reasons and the ensuing scandal split the Ramsden Street congregation in two. The affair, which became well known far beyond the bounds of Huddersfield, arose because a majority of the trustees believed that Mr Stannard did not comply with the strict conditions of the trust deed in that he did not believe in Original Sin. In January 1881 the case came before the High Court and, after a hearing lasting seven days, Stannard was forbidden to preach in the Ramsden Street pulpit. He gave a farewell address to a crowded chapel on 8th February 1881 and left. His followers remained loyal however and together they founded Milton Church. Mr Stannard remained at Milton until his death in 1889, and in 1907 the two Congregational Churches, Ramsden Street and Milton, became officially reconciled.

The story of the Methodists at this period is one of growth and fragmentation. Old Bank Chapel in Buxton Road[1] was split when the New Connexion was formed in 1797 as we have seen. Eighteen hundred and twelve saw the rise of the Primitive Methodists, a revivalist movement, who later in 1832 met at Spring Street Chapel. This building was pulled down to make way for the Springwood Railway Tunnel so the Primitive Methodists built themselves a new church in Northumberland Street[2] in 1846. Brunswick Street Free Wesleyan Church[3] was built in 1859 as a breakaway from Queen Street.

Like bees swarming to found new colonies, break-away groups formed new congregations and chapels proliferated. Often the break arose over differences in doctrine or organisation which would seem trifling today, but which were matters of conscience or serious principle in the ardent religious fervour

[1] This Chapel gave the name to 'Chapel Hill' and stood on a site now occupied by part of T. W. Broadbent's engineering works.
[2] Now part of the YMCA premises.
[3] Now a furniture depository.

then prevailing. The dissident group of course had no chapel in which to worship and went wherever they could find accommodation. At Crosland Moor, in a cottage on Matlock Street the preacher addressed his flock from the bedroom stairs. This group was long known as the 'Cushionites' because they took with them the cushions from their old chapel as their share of the assets.

A Baptist Church was not permanently established in the town until February 1846. Regular meetings began to be held in Spring Street and most of the original members were transferred there from Lockwood and Salendine Nook Churches. For the first few years Spring Street was looked upon as a missionary endeavour and the premises were quickly outgrown. So it was that rooms in King Street were taken in 1850 and two years later Rev. W. K. Armstrong became the first permanent minister.

In May 1853 Bath Buildings were purchased for £1,200. They were opened as the first Baptist Chapel in Huddersfield in April 1855. The place in Bath Buildings was not large; consequently, when Rev. Charles Haddon Spurgeon came to Huddersfield on 13th February 1861, arrangements were made for him to preach at Brunswick Street.

By 1872 Bath Buildings had become overcrowded and it was resolved to seek a site elsewhere. The foundation-stone of New North Road Baptist Church was laid by Edward Leatham, M.P., and the opening took place in April 1878.

In 1879 an existing small Baptist Mission Church in Blacker Road, Birkby was taken over by New North Road Church; and all eighteen of its members were received into the larger church. The two churches continued to worship separately but shared the pastor and chapel deacons. This arrangement was to continue until 1907 when Birkby Baptist Church became completely independent; the new church building was opened in 1910.

The Irish rebellion of 1798 and the unequal competition between English and Irish trade which followed the Act of Union of 1800 led thousands of Irish to come to England where conditions were better than at home. From 1828, mass evictions of Irishmen brought them to England where they were able to do heavy manual work for which the handloom weavers were quite unsuited. Although they showed little aptitude for highly skilled trades, the willingness of the Irish made them very acceptable in towns like Huddersfield. This influx of Irishmen accompanied by their priests coincided with the English reformers' support for Catholic Emancipation and Huddersfield in 1828 became a Mission in the care of Rev. John Maddocks, with a mission room at the bottom of Kirkgate.

In 1829 the Catholic Emancipation Act was passed restoring civic equality to the Roman Catholics and at about this time, Rev. Thomas Keily arrived in Huddersfield. He immediately set about raising funds for building a church. Money was collected in England and Ireland and the new church opened in 1832. It was dedicated to St Patrick because had it not been for the Irish immigrants, the building would never have been put up. Joseph Kaye built St Patrick's, and when it was opened 'many Protestants of the first respectability' were present and contributed to the large collection. A large number of Protestant businessmen subscribed to the new church because they valued the Irish labour and realised that a fine new church would help keep their new workpeople in Huddersfield. In the nineteenth century when religious bigotry was rampant among many Protestant sects, the general attitude towards Roman Catholics in Huddersfield was friendly. The Irish lived in all parts of the town and so never became separatist in outlook. Even in 1882 at the time of the Phoenix Park murders in Dublin, there was no violence in Huddersfield.

The legacy of John Wesley lasted long after his death, developing into Methodism on the one hand and the Evangelical Revival on the other. This movement back to the Bible deeply affected the Church of England in the early nineteenth century and gave it the life, enthusiasm and discipline it had so sadly lacked in the eighteenth. Missionary enterprise overseas and humanitarian work at home contributed to the new life of the Church which was saddened only by a lack of charity towards offenders and the harsh discipline of Victorian family life, especially on Sundays.

Huddersfield had its links with this Evangelical Movement in that John Venn, son of Henry Venn, was Rector of Clapham from 1792 to 1813, and there was born the Clapham Sect, a group of fervent laymen whose lives were inspired by a diligent study of the Bible. The most famous of the Clapham Sect was William Wilberforce, M.P. for Yorkshire who, in 1807, succeeded in securing the abolition of the slave trade. It was to the Evangelicals that Richard Oastler directed much of his early campaigning when he spoke of 'Yorkshire Slavery'.

Wilberforce was a personal friend of Benjamin Haigh Allen, the founder of Holy Trinity Church, a sincere Christian, who died in 1829 aged only thirty-six. Allen lived at Greenhead Hall,[1] and was one of the founders of the local branch of the Church Missionary Society Association. In 1813 Rev. William Harding, Curate of Huddersfield, wrote to the CMS: 'The state of the Church here is truly painful. We have a population of 8,000 and only one church and every seat in it is private property. The consequence is that the body of Dissenters and Methodists is very great.' In 1816 B. H. Allen proposed the building of a new church. The vicar, Rev. John Coates, agreed and under a Private Act of Parliament a 'Church or Chapel of Ease in the Parish of Huddersfield' was authorised. The preamble to the Act explains that there was no church except the Parish Church within the township. In the parish there were chapels at Deanhead, Slaithwaite and Longwood. The new church was to be called 'Trinity Church' and Mr Allen was empowered to purchase land, erect the building and to become sole patron of the living. At the stone-laying ceremony, Mr Coates said he hoped Mr Allen's example 'will kindle in the breasts of others a desire to promote the honour of God—in the same way'. John Whitacre, Benjamin Haigh Allen's father-in-law, built Christ Church, Woodhouse, in 1824.

In the meantime other steps had been taken. By Act of Parliament in 1818 one million pounds was granted in aid of building churches in populous places in England and this was supplemented by half a million in 1824. The money came, not from taxes, but from a war indemnity paid by Austria after the Battle of Waterloo and the grants were augmented by public

---

[1] The house was pulled down to build Greenhead High School for Girls in 1909, the grounds are now Greenhead Park.

subscriptions. Thus the parishes of Huddersfield and Almondbury were split up gradually and we find smaller parishes were created.

From Huddersfield—
Golcar, Longwood and Lindley, all in 1843; Woodhouse 1844; Holy Trinity 1845; St Paul's 1859; Scammonden 1862; Paddock 1863; Marsden 1868;[1] St Andrew's 1871.
From Almondbury—
South Crosland, Holmbridge, Linthwaite, Lockwood, and Netherton, all in 1843; Milnsbridge 1846; Armitage Bridge 1848; Marsden 1868;[1] Meltham 1874; Honley 1876.

Holy Trinity Church was enlarged in 1825 with a Parliamentary Grant of £1,000. St Paul's, also in the town, was built in 1829 with a grant of £5,500. St John's, Golcar and St Stephen's, Lindley, were also built with grants in 1829. St Mark's at Longwood was enlarged by Parliamentary grant in 1823. All Saints', Paddock, received a grant and was built in 1830. St Thomas's was built in 1859 by the Starkey family in memory of John, Thomas and Joseph Starkey, millowners of Longroyd Bridge, all three of whom died before the church was completed. St John's, Birkby, was built in 1852 with £7,000 from the trustees of Sir John Ramsden. Christ Church, Linthwaite, (1828) and Emanuel Church, Lockwood, (1830) received Parliamentary grants. Marsden Church was augmented by a grant, South Crosland (1829) and Netherton (1830) were built out of grants.

The Parish Church itself had stood since 1506 and by the nineteenth century had become extremely dilapidated. But, as new churches were built in the outlying villages, the feeling grew that they should be exempt from contributing to the Mother Church. Many wealthy families supported the new chapels and raised huge sums to pay for them (Queen Street cost £8,000); but though the Parish Church could call on the Parish Rate, which all householders were supposed to pay, and which stood at a shilling in the pound in 1830, difficulties arose

---

[1] Marsden Parish was taken from parts of Huddersfield and Almondbury Parishes which had been hitherto divided at the River Colne.

when many non-Anglicans refused to contribute. The Ramsdens, themselves generous towards the Parish Church, were absentee landlords and after 1832 their influence in elections made them unpopular with many parishioners. In this plight, the Vestry even sought to subsidise their funds from the Poor Rate.

On 6th November 1830, a local builder wrote, 'I have examined the Parish Church and with respect to the roof there must be a new one. The rafters and principals are quite decayed and rotten and it is certainly surprising to me that there has not been an accident before this time. A new roof together with other things necessary to put the church into repair would cost £780, but it appears to me that it would be almost useless putting a new roof on to the present walls and pillars, they are in such a bad state. There is not a straight plumb wall about the building. I have seen nearly all the foundations both inside and out, and they are really in a very bad way, being generally footed upon loose boulders. Several of the pillars are also not in perpendicular and must be taken down if the church is repaired'.

By 1831, when the roof needed propping up with long poles, J. P. Pritchett the architect was called in, and a building committee headed by the vicar, the Rev. J. C. Franks, was appointed to organise the collection of subscriptions. It was decided to raise the floor some eight feet, and a new tower was deemed necessary not only to give the building increased height but also because it was desirable to raise the tower to enable the new clock to be more easily seen by the citizens of Huddersfield. It had already been decided to rebuild the nave and chancel. Mr Pritchett's scheme included a new vestry, central heating, an illuminated clock, gas lighting and the remaking of all the old pews.

The last service in the old church was held on 27th April 1834 and demolition commenced the following day. The congregation went either to St Paul's or Trinity. By May over £3,000 had been raised by subscriptions and by June £4,000.

On 5th August 1835 a 'Full Cathedral Service' was held at St Paul's and it was announced that 'a collection will be made after the service in aid of the Building Fund'. The text, from the Book of Ezra Chapter V, 'and this work goeth fast on, and

prospereth in their hands' was sufficiently inspiring to raise £85.
A meeting of ratepayers agreed to contribute a rate of 1s. 8d.
in the pound towards the new clock. The old clock was to go
to the new church at Paddock. At the beginning of 1836 the
Committee found they were £1,000 short of their estimated
expenditure and, what was worse, the grant from the Society
for Promoting the Building of Churches was not payable until
the work was completed. Nevertheless, subscriptions did continue to arrive during 1836 and, when the new church had been
opened on Thursday 27th October of that year, by means of
services twice daily on the Thursday, Friday and Sunday, over
£600 was raised. On the Thursday evening it was estimated
that over 3,000 people were present and the anthems were
composed by James Battye, the Parish Clerk and one of the
founders of the Huddersfield Choral Society which was then
but a few months old.

The new church was almost paid for within a year of its
completion. The 1,000 old sittings were restored and in addition
there were 460 new sittings declared to be perpetually free of
charge. The final cost of building the new Parish Church was
almost £10,000.

However fine the building looked when it was completed,
twenty years afterwards the stone was found to be crumbling, a
process which is still continuing. Instead of employing Joseph
Kaye who in 1857 was to build his masterpiece, St John's at
Birkby, an untried man, a Mr W. Exley of York, had been given
the job on the strength of a low tender. He had used all the
second-hand stones he could find from the old church, and
worse than this, he had laid them the wrong way, so that
flaking commenced even before the building was finished.
Although experts commented on the state of the stonework in
1866 and 1884 it was not until 1933 that attention was paid to
the church's exterior; then a chemical process was carried out to
toughen the decaying stones and parts of the south side were
rebuilt.

The Parish Vestry in the early nineteenth century was
approaching the end of its secular power which had included,
for example, the operation of the Elizabethan Poor Law, the
surveying of highways and the appointment of the Parish

Constable for enforcing law and order. In the 1820s Benjamin Haigh Allen, in keeping with his principles, made strenuous efforts to help the Parish Overseers of the Poor find work for the unemployed. In 1827, the Vestry had to deal with the unsound condition of the canal bridge, Buxton Road [now Chapel Hill]. They resolved to contribute towards the repair of the bridge, but the actual work was to be done by the owners, the Canal Company. The new Poor Law Amendment Act, took from the parish the care of the poor, policing was taken over by the Commissioners of 1820, and responsibility of highways was assumed by the Improvement Commissioners in 1848. The disturbances after 1815 had caused the Parish Vestry some anxiety, therefore an assistant constable, George Whitehead, was appointed as we have seen. He had an office in King Street but after 1820 doubts were raised as to who paid his salary. For a time, the Chief Parish Constable was invited by the parish ratepayers to pay the deputy out of his own allowances.

An instance of the declining power of the Vestry occurred in 1847 when they attempted to levy a Church Rate for a proposed new cemetery at Edgerton. Their proposal for a fourpenny rate was amended to one of an eighth of a penny, and when the amendment was carried the vicar regarded this as a refusal to pay and the Vestry was powerless to act. After 1862 the business of the Huddersfield Vestry was entirely ecclesiastical.[1]

In the 1830s Huddersfield still had the atmosphere of a country town. The 'White Hart' fed up to 250 diners every Tuesday and could also provide stabling for their horses; Manchester Street had houses and shops but sheep grazed in the fields behind; King Street had shops on the left-hand side only as one walked down the hill; behind the 'George' was a thirty-acre field which stretched as far as New North Road where the first building to be seen was St Patrick's new church. Behind Upperhead Row and Macaulay Street were gardens and a duck pond, and there were cattle in Greenhead Park. At night, Parish Constables Jim Hurst and Bill Townend

[1] Not until the Local Government Act of 1933 was it in fact laid down that vestries in urban parishes were for deciding Church matters only.

patrolled the gas-lit streets calling out the time every half-hour. If we remember only the striking scenes of unrest, because in their day they made exciting news, we lose sight of the fact that life in Huddersfield before the Railway Age was fairly quiet on the surface, except on a Tuesday when the clothiers made their noisy invasion.

In 1844 Friedrich Engels wrote in his book *The Condition of the Working Class*, 'Huddersfield is the handsomest by far of all the factory towns of Yorkshire and Lancashire, by reason of its charming situation and modern architecture.'

Joe Kaye died on 18th March 1858 and was buried in the parish churchyard, the only important building in Huddersfield he had not built. Over a period of fifty years he had built Holy Trinity Church, St Paul's, St Patrick's, St John's and churches at Paddock, Lindley, Golcar, Linthwaite, South Crosland; Queen Street and Ramsden Street Chapels, the Infirmary, the Railway Station and the new George Hotel in the Square. Had he rebuilt the Parish Church, 'it would not have been the rickety and scabbed looking thing it is', said the *Huddersfield Weekly Chronicle* of 18th March 1858. Kaye was also a merchant, a brewer and owned four mills at Folly Hall. There were fires at the mills in 1844 and 1856 and all were re-erected before he died. All this was achieved by a man who could barely write his own name.

The End of Cottage Industry

SO FAR, we have looked at the new inventions in spinning, carding and finishing and their social consequences. These inventions competed with home industry but did not end it. They caused home weaving to expand, and the early mills did not kill the domestic outwork system. Power weaving, however, took the whole industry with a giant's step into the future.

Even in the 1830s the typical working man was either at home or in a small workshop; and it has already been said that the majority of the early factory hands were women and children whose labour was cheap and whose long hours of work led to so much agitation from Oastler and his friends.

From 1780 to 1820 there was such a shortage of weavers that they could afford to work for whom they pleased. As the Cleckheaton *Guardian* put it in 1884: 'The "Little Makers" of Cleckheaton doffed their caps to no one—neither squire nor parson had any right to meddle with them; their brusqueness might be offensive, those who did better[1] worked harder than ever'. The decline of the Yorkshire handloom weavers was from fifteen to twenty years behind those of Lancashire.

By 1820 weavers' wages were being cut and in 1829 at a time of trade depression it was said that 13,000 out of a population of 29,000 existed on twopence a day. By 1834 large numbers of outworkers were completely depressed, many barely surviving on oatmeal, potatoes and skimmed milk.

Developments seen so far resulted in the concentration of fulling and dyeing in the valleys and cropping near the town, while weaving went on everywhere. As business expanded so there was more capital for development and always there was

[1] Were more successful.

135

the example of the Lancashire cotton mills where weaving by machinery was already successful. By the beginning of the nineteenth century the American market for all textiles had grown, and the progress of the cotton industry and its example led to the use of wool and cotton mixtures and stimulated the development of fine woollens and worsteds.

The classical economists successfully persuaded the Government to adopt a *laissez faire* policy and as old restrictions on labour were abandoned, so also free trade in commerce was advocated; for example in 1813 there was a duty of 6s. 8d. a pound on all imported wool; but by 1819 this had been reduced to sixpence. In 1766 two million pounds of wool were imported, in 1840 fifty million, and by 1850 some forty million pounds came from Australia alone. Without these imports the textile industry could not have expanded to clothe the world in the way that it did.

The *Report on the State of the Woollen Manufacture of England,* published in 1806, shows that the Huddersfield area was then in a state of transition. Law Atkinson of Bradley Mill described how their scribbling mill had enough power to spare some for domestic clothiers. There were seventeen handloom weavers at work in a shed on the premises, principally to prevent the embezzlement of the high grade Spanish wool they used, at the same time some weaving was given to outworkers. Some cloth sold by the firm was bought at the Cloth Hall, some was ordered in advance. Bradley Mill in those days had gig mills, and shearing frames[1] had been introduced in 1800. This establishment was very small compared with Benjamin Gott's at Leeds where there were 144 handlooms and 48 jennies within the factory walls.

The first power looms were used for worsted weaving and were outside our area. They were openly attacked by hand weavers in Bradford in 1822 and 1826 before they captured the industry between 1836 and 1845.

In the woollen industry carding, slubbing and spinning were mechanised between 1790 and 1825. Woollen yarn was not at first strong enough to weave by machinery, there were many

[1] See Chapter VI.

Inside the Cloth Hall: from a drawing by Leslie Taylor

stoppages and the hand weavers were able to compete with the first power looms which did no more than forty picks (shuttle strokes) to the minute in the 1840s. The Great Exhibition of 1851 contained a display of textile machinery and this period really marks the end of the woollen hand loom. Some local firms were weaving by hand in the sixties but all had chabged over to steam power within the next decade. Typical of local firms, Crosland and James Hirst founded theirs about 1860, based on an old established family cloth finishing business and Joseph Hoyle, who set up in 1866, quickly realised the potential of power weaving. One handloom weaver who continued making his weekly piece persisted until 1880 when his supply of wool was cut off. He was offered work in a weaving shed but he refused to accept.

Most factories grew in a haphazard manner and there were two other influences hitherto not mentioned—the growth of the fancy trade and the concentration of worsted manufacture in Yorkshire. A study of the 1822 list of 102 manufacturers who attended Huddersfield Market reveals that the fancy trade occupied a definite area to the south and east of the town, around Kirkheaton, Almondbury, Lepton, Honley and from Kirkburton to Denby Dale. By 1830 newer products and areas of manufacture were recorded; cords and velveteens were made at Deighton, Sheepridge, Lindley and Outlane and these new products together with fine woollens and cotton mixtures had begun to diversify the market. However, this was luxury trade and it suffered badly at times of depression when it was said that the 'fancy stuff-ers' were worse off than ordinary handloom weavers.

The late 1820s saw the introduction of the 'witch' machine designed to weave patterns by raising and lowering the warp according to a pattern, thus making it possible to weave floral designs into the fine waistcoat material. A witch loom was reputed to cost about £7, of which £5 might be paid by the clothier and £2 by the weaver out of his wages. Here is yet another aspect of the transition from home industry to factory working while the weaver retained his independence.

The arrival of the witch loom is a good example of how these things happen in an emergent industry. A loom for pattern

Laying the cornerstone of the Victoria Jubilee Tower on 25 June 1898 : in the picture can be seen R. W. Harper, J. F. Ramsden (standing behind his father), Sir J. A. Brooke, Isaac Hordern (extreme left), E. Brooke, Sir John William Ramsden (front row centre) and Ald. W. H. Jessop, the Mayor. *Photo :* Advertiser Press Ltd.

John William Street *c.* 1930: this picture shows a variety of types of tramcar, also a Huddersfield Corporation motorbus before the formation of the Joint Omnibus Committee with the L.M.S. in 1930. The General Manager and Chief Inspector are to be seen standing in St George's Square. *Photo:* Huddersfield Corporation Passenger Transport Department.

King Street *c.* 1925, showing the Market Hall, a Moldgreen tramcar and the Cloth Hall in the distance. The corner shop on the right is also on the left of the picture facing page 74 of Cross Church Street in 1844. *Photo:* Aerofilms Ltd.

weaving, invented by a Frenchman named Jacquard in 1804 and for which he had received a pension of £60 from his Government, found its way to England after the Napoleonic wars. At this time there were two kinds of pattern weaving, the Drum Witch, taking about forty threads but rather clumsy, and the Engine or Dobby which could weave up to 160. In 1830 a Frenchman came to the George Inn, and there conducted a demonstration of the new loom; mark what follows.

The Huddersfield manufacturers had not been eager to attend the demonstration at the 'George', but one of them, a Mr Gill was favourably impressed and, having decided to use the Jacquard, built a mill near Almondbury. Once in business, the new looms completely eclipsed all competitors with their elaborate designs since no Jacquard loom had less than four hundred threads. In consequence other manufacturers were obliged to adopt the new loom in order to compete, but Gill's fancy waistcoatings had a long lead over the others. Now the designer came into his own as the Jacquard offered what seemed unlimited scope in intricacy of pattern.

The fancy trade from its outset had from time to time concerned itself with the use of unorthodox fibres. Joseph Etchells, who settled in Almondbury in 1796, was a silk weaver of Huguenot descent; thus it is quite likely that he introduced the idea of combining silk with wool into our district. His descendants acquired a reputation as designers of figured silk and woollen fabrics, and Ravensknowle Museum contains some beautiful examples of their work. The mid-Victorian period saw a tremendous expansion in this field and the trade supplied not only waistcoatings but fancy dress materials, soft furnishings of all kinds, shawls and table covers. The wardrobe and drawing-room of a century ago contained ample evidence of the prosperity of our fancy trade, and its quality was acknowledged by numbers of prizes won by local firms in the Great Exhibition of 1851.

At this point it is necessary to deal with the worsted industry in order to complete the picture of textiles as they were in the mid-nineteenth century. As we have seen, woollens have roots in the West Riding going back to before the Middle Ages. Worsteds, on the other hand, arrived here from East Anglia during the eighteenth and nineteenth centuries due to enterprise in Yorkshire and the lack of it elsewhere.

The worsted industry in Yorkshire began about the year 1700, before which time only woollens had been made in our area. Worsted cloth is made from smooth, thin, strong yarn produced by combing out fibres of long length or staple, and twisting them around each other. Since the cloth is not fulled, it is possible to achieve brighter colours which fulling[1] would tend to deaden, therefore pattern and design can be fully exploited. By 1773 Yorkshire was making as much worsted cloth as was made in the whole of East Anglia. In 1803 nine out of ten worsted weavers had gone over to the flying shuttle although the pieces were all of narrow width.

Although the abundance of water for fulling does not explain why worsted weaving became a Yorkshire speciality, the material lent itself to machine processes and water power was used for the first power looms. Yorkshire attracted the plain types of worsted first and the new material was capable of being introduced here and there because the woollen industry worked on very informal lines.

Norwich lost the competition for worsteds because she failed to mechanise and keep abreast of the times. There were many East Anglian vested interests which worked against the introduction of machinery, workers and clothiers alike being strongly organised and in a position to resist change. This attitude was to lead to their downfall. Eventually, West Riding cloth could be produced cheaper on the new machines and although coal and iron could have been brought to Norwich by sea, no one was prepared to take advantage of this. In 1834, a yarn factory was put up in Norfolk but it was too late to compete, by 1845 Norfolk had 428 power looms compared with 31,000 in Yorkshire. By 1850 the worsted industry had virtually left the East Englian area.

A Handloom Commissioner wrote in 1839; 'While the men of Leeds and Huddersfield were constantly in their mills and taking their meals at the same time as their workpeople, the clothiers of Gloucestershire—some of them—were indulging in

---

[1] See p. 41. Fulling is now referred to as 'milling'.

the habits and mingling with the "gentle blood" of the land'. There was coal and water in the West Country, but opposition to the machine was so great that, when it was decided to make a change, it was too late.

The West Riding obtained almost a monopoly of woollen and worsted manufacture, and it was eventually all produced by power machinery. At the same time, Huddersfield enjoyed its own special reputation for fancy goods.

In 1827, John Taylor founded his own business as a woollen manufacturer only to find, in the 1850's, that his sons had successfully begun to turn over to worsteds in his absence. Patrick Martin was converted from woollen cord making to fancy worsteds while John Brooke & Sons began to manufacture worsteds some time after 1875. Eventually, these and many other firms around Huddersfield gave the area a diversification within wool textiles, in the latter half of the nineteenth century, which it has never lost.

Richard Oastler, defending the handloom weavers in 1834, claimed there were three quarters of a million of them but over the following twenty years this labour force declined rapidly. The young and able bodied found employment in limited numbers in the factories, more went to work on the new railways and in other forms of transport, others to building—there was much to do in a growing town. The elderly weavers eventually retired and were kept by their children until they died. Of course, women and children were employed in as large numbers as the Factory Acts would allow and this helped to offset any reduction in earnings by their menfolk. Many men must have seen the trend of events and solved their own problems. I have an ancestor who abandoned his handweaving and smallholding near Marsden to work at Lockwood's Mill as a cord cutter, and he was obliged to live in lodgings in Upperhead Row in the 1840s.

The domestic clothiers had valued their independence. Family life had been maintained and children had been brought up at home. Yet, rather too much stress has been laid on the advantages of the system of working at home.

Factory discipline was resented at first but in many country villages work had been regulated by the blast of a horn at five in the morning and eight o'clock at night. The clothiers' cottage reeked with the smell of oil, wool and dyes and the traditional health of the little textile communities was derived from the country air and the opportunities there were of doing farmwork outside. As for the tasks of weaving and spinning, they were monotonous occupations and the low grade material on which they worked was hardly conducive to a real sense of craftsmanship.

Employers preferred the factory system since supervision of work done was made easy and larger orders could be quickly undertaken. Also there was little time lost between processes. Thus even before the coming of steam, the early factories did offer some advantages in return for an outlay of money and this the merchants and others who acquired some capital were quick to realise.

The decline of the Cloth Hall has been attributed to many causes, one being that when material was in short supply the buyers rode out of the town to meet the pieces coming in, so that only the leftovers went to the market. Another factor was the development of the fancy trade.

The directory for 1822, mentioned in Chapter VIII as listing the inns used by the clothiers, also supplies details of the fancy trade of the period. The fancy goods men frequented the Huddersfield Market only in so far as they had rooms in the yards near the Cloth Hall. They did business from Lumb's Yard and the 'King's Head' Yard in Cloth Hall Street, from Roberts' Court in Market Street, and from many other yards and courts around the Market Place, Westgate and Kirkgate. Originality commanded reward for the fancy manufacturers, thus their patterns had to be unique or unusual. The fancy trade, for reasons of its own, actually encouraged business not to frequent the open market where their trade secrets would be disclosed.

By 1830 the idea of using a warehouse in the town had spread to the woollen manufacturers. Some of them, from Elland and Stainland, had rooms in the 'White Hart' Yard off Market Street; others, from the Colne Valley, used warehouses in Brook's Yard behind Westgate and Market Street; and the Saddleworth clothiers used the 'George Inn' Yard. The inn yards with their stables and outbuildings had always been busy on Tuesdays. The merchant on horseback, the carrier's waggon and the stage coach all used the inn stabling and many a bargain was struck on the way to the Cloth Hall. Eventually the manufacturers rented parts of the inn yards and the rooms above the stables, approached by outside stairs, became warehouses. The 'King's Head' Yard, just below the 'White Hart' in Cloth Hall Street, became a favourite resort for the fancy manufacturers from Almondbury, Lepton and Honley.

Although the Cloth Hall was enlarged both in 1848 and 1864 it was losing its importance in the 1830s. The fancy traders in the twenties seldom used the Hall, but the actual increase of hand weavers at this period ensured its usefulness for a time. The merchant manufacturer, however, working on a larger scale, began to order what he required from the weavers in the light of advance orders from his customers. Once the power loom really came into its own in the 'forties, the Cloth Hall began to lose its overall importance. Nevertheless Isaac Hordern, cashier for the Ramsden Estate wrote in 1864 'Cloth Hall North and South transepts built, and the Western entrance. These improvements I promoted. The cost was nearly £1,300. At this time I could have let more windows for cloth stands'. It would appear that although increasing business was done outside the Cloth Hall, the expansion of trade generally was such that there was still a need for large numbers of dealers to meet there.

In the 1870s buyers were staying at the new George Hotel where the visitors' register was kept open to enable manufacturers to see who was in town. Consequently the manufacturer could contact the buyer, orders would be placed as soon as the purchaser saw samples he liked and, when trade was brisk, there was no need to leave cuttings of material for further consideration. Pattern cards developed from this period and many manufacturers fixed their prices in advance—a development probably made necessary by the growth of the wholesale clothing industry.

Not all buyers, however, came to the warehouses in Huddersfield. The export market often called for a London agent with an office and books of cloth patterns. An extension of this system required overseas representatives and many a family business found it useful to have relatives in America or on the Continent. Overseas orders were also placed in advance of manufacture, based on what the customer saw in the cloth samples he was shown.

In 1881 the ground floor of the Cloth Hall became an Exchange and News Room. There was a council room for the Chamber of Commerce and a reading room for its members. As a centre of actual trade however the Cloth Hall was finished, and as the years went by this valuable site became the object of much speculation. The building was quite unsuitable for any other than its original purpose and, in my opinion, architecturally it was not really worth keeping. Fifty years later in 1930, the Cloth Hall was pulled down, the cupola, clock and bell being re-erected at Ravensknowle. The site was then developed as a cinema. The Cloth Hall Post Office was continued in new buildings near by. (*See photograph facing page* 106.)

The success of our textiles in the nineteenth century was due not only to the craftsmanship of the operatives, originality of design and the energetic business methods of the manufacturers, but also to the successful achievements of the colour chemists. John Nowell (1794–1869) known locally as 'Th' Aumbrey Witch', who lived at Farnley Wood opposite the Grammar School where he had been educated, was a keen student of chemistry and a friend of Dr Dalton, Sir Humphrey Davy and Michael Faraday. He was a founder member of 'The Chemical Society of King James's Free Grammar School in Almondbury'. In 1852 or 1853 he conducted a course of forty lectures at the school where he had been a pupil fifty years before. This introduction of science into a grammar school curriculum is one of the earliest on record. His enthusiasm was imparted to George Jarmain, who then introduced the subject to the Mechanics' Institute, the forerunner of the Technical College, and to the new Huddersfield College. Nowell and Jarmain experimented in colour chemistry and eventually discovered a means of carbonising wool, so destroying the vegetable fibres in the fleece. This made it possible to manufacture better quality cloth from low-grade wool.

To Read Holliday (1809–89) we owe the development of

dyestuffs and, more important, the establishment of chemicals as one of the principal industries of the town. At the age of twenty-one, Read Holliday rented premises in Leeds Road and there began distilling ammonia. He was not a trained chemist, but he knew that the process of wool scouring required a strong alkaline substance to remove the grease and that the liquor produced by the gas works could be so used. In 1839, Holliday moved to Turnbridge close to where the gasworks tipped their tar and this he used as a fuel. By distilling the tar, which he found in abundance, Read Holliday produced his own supply of naphtha, and the creosote oil, which came as a by-product, was used for treating railway sleepers; pitch which was left behind was eventually used for briquets. By 1848 he had patented a naphtha lamp and business was very brisk until the arrival of the paraffin lamp and improved town gas supplies.

In 1850 he went to Paris where he saw the work being done there on benzol dyes. He brought a French chemist back with him to Leeds Road and the firm entered the dyestuffs industry. By 1860, Read Hollidays were distilling coal tar and ammonia, manufacturing nitro-benzol, analine and magenta, and the series of patents which followed gave a range of colours including violet, blue, green, black, red and, finally, yellow. When Read Holliday died in 1889 Huddersfield was at the heart of a thriving chemical industry, and this did much to maintain the town's reputation as a producer of the widest range of wool textiles incorporating all that was best in design and colour.

Cottage industry had relied on the local drysalter and on the use of natural dyes in the small dyehouses near the fulling mills. However, the domestic system could not have supplied markets on a scale sufficient to make new developments in dyestuffs profitable. Once textile production really expanded in the mid-nineteenth century, there were ample incentives for the chemical industry to forge ahead. Read Hollidays were soon joined by others in this field, and the products of Huddersfield's dyeworks were to be sold all over the world.

CHAPTER X

The Huddersfield Improvement Commissioners and the Coming of the Railways

THE PROSPERITY of the waterways mentioned in Chapter VI was soon to receive a serious challenge. 1825 saw the opening of the Stockton and Darlington Railway, and in the same year Manchester businessmen began to agitate for a railway link with Yorkshire. There was even some talk of filling in the Colne Valley Canal and using the tunnel for a new railway; canal warehouses would be useful, and gradients would be slight. In 1830, the opening of the Liverpool and Manchester line led to further proposals for crossing the Pennines by rail, and George Stephenson himself surveyed a route via Todmorden only to be fiercely opposed by the Rochdale Canal interest. On 16th October 1830, a meeting in Huddersfield urged that the Manchester and Leeds line should pass through the town, but nothing came of the proposal.

Then, in 1834 came the opening of the line from Leeds to Selby, and finally, after a meeting in Manchester on 28th January 1836, George Stephenson was appointed engineer of the Manchester and Leeds line. The route from Manchester to Littleborough Tunnel was completed in 1839, followed, a year later, by the line from Hebden Bridge to Normanton.[1] Littleborough Tunnel itself took over a thousand men four years to make and the route, which became the Manchester and Leeds Railway, followed the Calder and passed through Elland, Brighouse and Mirfield. Huddersfield had been by-passed, the idea

[1] Here the line joined the North Midland to either Leeds or York, or south to London via Derby.

of a Standedge Tunnel was shelved and Cooper Bridge was the nearest station to the town. The inhabitants made the best of the situation, and, from October 1840, Ellam's horse buses conveyed passengers from the White Swan in Kirkgate to meet the trains.[1]

By 1842, Huddersfield passengers urged the Manchester and Leeds Railway Company to consider building a branch line to the town. A meeting ensued at which the Company advocated following the level of the river while the passengers proposed that it should run on higher ground so as to make possible a future extension to Lancashire. The company was not prepared to consider the more expensive project and their spokesman declared 'Huddersfield is not worth stopping the engine for!' Understandably the meeting ended in uproar.

A local company was therefore formed to build the high-level line from Heaton Lodge, near Cooper Bridge, to Huddersfield and eventually to link up with the Manchester to Sheffield[2] line at Stalybridge. The Canal Company decided to support the venture and the Huddersfield and Manchester Railway and Canal Company was authorised, by Act of Parliament, to raise the capital and build the line. The *Leeds Mercury* of 3rd May 1845 reflected the enthusiasm and optimism which was current in the town:

'The 26th of April was a memorable day in the history of Huddersfield and the harbinger of a new and important era in a town of first rate importance, which despite many obstacles has advanced in commercial and social enterprise almost beyond any in the United Kingdom and has laboured long for proper facilities of transport. On Saturday last the important news was imparted that the Parliamentary Committee has decided to grant the Bill for a railway from Huddersfield to Ashton-under-Lyne with a continuation to Cooper Bridge and furthermore the Committee have agreed

[1] From 1845 to 1850 coaches also took travellers to Dunford Bridge to join the Manchester and Sheffield line.

[2] Originally the Sheffield, Ashton-under-Lyne and Manchester Railway, afterwards the Manchester, Sheffield and Lincolnshire Railway or 'M.S.L.'— said to stand for 'Money sunk and lost'!

to recommend to Parliament that the line be continued to Dewsbury and Leeds.

'The bells were instantly set in motion and the whole population rose from their slumbers, and music paraded the town. Mutual congratulations and rejoicings which spread to the villages round were the order of the day. Huddersfield has arisen. Posterity will remember this period with proud delight.'

The first sod was cut on 10th October 1845 at Deighton and the line from Heaton Lodge to Huddersfield was completed on 2nd August 1847. This was remarkable progress as the line is almost entirely cutting or embankment, and culminates in a viaduct of forty-five arches. These arches were narrower then than they are today as the line at first consisted of two tracks only. They were widened between 1881 and 1883 and if one examines the bridges over Bradford Road and St John's Road evidence of how this was done can still be seen.

On 9th October 1846 the foundation stone of Huddersfield Station was laid. The bells of the Parish Church rang all day which was a public holiday and an imposing procession marched through the town behind the Yeomanry band to St George's Square. Beneath the stone, laid by the Right Hon. The Earl Fitzwilliam, were placed a bottle containing newspapers and stamps and an engraved plate carrying the names of the directors of the new Railway company. The first train ran between Huddersfield and Heaton Lodge Station on 2nd August 1847 and within a few years Huddersfield was to become not only a through station but also a junction.

On 29th August 1845 the first sod of the line from Penistone to Huddersfield was cut. This was to give a direct link with Sheffield, a colossal task necessitating four viaducts, six tunnels and fifty seven bridges. The line was not opened until 1850 by which time the Huddersfield and Sheffield Junction Railway Company had amalgamated with the Manchester and Leeds and many other lines to form the Lancashire and Yorkshire Railway in 1847. This gave the company a direct interest in Huddersfield, an interest they had previously declined when invited to link the town to the original Manchester to Leeds line.

An Act of 30th June 1845 authorised the line linking Huddersfield, Dewsbury and Leeds to be built and this, the line through Morley, was opened in 1848, by which time it had joined the L and N.W.[1]

It was the London and North Western Railway Company which actually opened Huddersfield Station in 1847 and completed the line to Stalybridge. The London and North Western had been formed in 1846 as a result of a merger of the Liverpool and Manchester, London and Birmingham and the Grand Junction. The company had its headquarters at Euston and was to pioneer the route to Ireland via Holyhead.

The L & NWR now had a much more direct route between Leeds and Manchester, than the L & YR; but the L & Y became the line from Lancashire to Bradford and with its line to Wakefield and Goole had a coast to coast link which the London and North Western never succeeded in acquiring. The Lancashire and Yorkshire grew into a compact system carrying very heavy traffic.

The Standedge Tunnel was publicly opened on 1st August 1849, and on the same day a link to Stockport and the South via the Manchester and Sheffield line was opened. This tunnel, over three miles long, was for some time the world's longest. Its building had been greatly helped by there being a canal tunnel parallel to it through which the earth could be removed by barge. In those pioneering days the safety of trains in the tunnel was guaranteed by having a pilot engine precede every train in either direction, thus it was impossible for there to be two trains in the tunnel approaching each other on the single track. This expensive system of signalling was later replaced by the passing of a staff between drivers as they entered or left the tunnel. A second tunnel, also single track, was bored from 1868 to 1870 and finally the L & NWR itself excavated a double tunnel under Standedge between 1890 and 1894.

On 1st May 1849 the London and North Western and Lancashire and Yorkshire companies reached agreement on the joint use of Huddersfield Station, indeed, the station staff wore

[1] By the LNWR Act of 1847 the Huddersfield and Manchester Railway & Canal Co., the Sir John Ramsden Canal and the Leeds, Dewsbury and Manchester Railway all joined the LNWR.

'H.J.S.' on their caps until 1922, 'Huddersfield Joint Station'. The two companies came near to fusion many times but they did not amalgamate until January 1922, not long before they both become part of the London, Midland and Scottish Railway Company in 1923. L & NWR coaches were painted purple with white upper parts and gilt lining; L & Y, in contrast, had coaches in two shades of brown. The two companies had separate booking offices at the station; Lancashire and Yorkshire at the West end, nearer the tunnel, London and North Western at the East end. The large building in the centre of the station was, in those days, used for accommodation and dining. Water for the locomotives originally came from the L & NWR canal reservoir at Slaithwaite and for this the L & Y drivers had to pay by depositing a 'water ticket' in a box by the water column. Each company had its own goods section near to its own part of the platform, an arrangement that worked very well so long as the coaches and the locomotives were small.

The arrival of bigger locomotives and longer carriages made the old track obsolete and there were many serious accidents. It was decided to build an island platform and a subway to it, and to erect a large roof over the entire station in the 1880s. All this came after more than a decade of public pressure calling for the station to be improved. At this period the viaduct and the tunnels were doubled and a new goods depot was built.

In 1889 there began a through service from Newcastle to Liverpool and also during the eighties through trains from Bradford via Huddersfield and Sheffield began to run to London. The picture of local lines was completed with the opening of branches to Kirkburton by the L & NWR in 1867 and by the L & YR to Holmfirth in 1850 and Meltham in 1868 and Clayton West in 1879; the 'Leeds New Line' via Cleckheaton and Birstall was opened in 1900.

The Midland Railway Company nearly succeeded in breaking the monopoly of the L & NWR and L & YR when an Act of 1899 gave them power to build a line from Mirfield to Newtown, Huddersfield. The line through Woodhouse and over Willow Lane, Birkby was completed in 1910 and opened to goods traffic. The outbreak of war in 1914 prevented the building of a passenger station, and after the war the Midland and the London and North Western Railways joined the L.M.S. By 1937 the scheme had been abandoned.

Another interesting piece of railway speculation which never materialised, was the idea of a line through the Grimscar valley with a tunnel under the Ainleys to Elland. This scheme, was for an extention of the Hull and Barnsley line to reach Halifax. A spur from Grimscar and a tunnel under Marsh would have joined the Huddersfield main line at Longwood.

Huddersfield station was built on a piece of open land at a distance from the Market Place. As the town was growing in the 1840s, and was likely to grow even more with the coming of the railway, it was decided to develop in an orderly fashion the open space between the station and the Parish Church. Several schemes were considered.

The George Inn which had stood on the north side of the Market Place was pulled down and a new hotel to replace it was built near the new station. John William Street was made as a continuation of New Street. The line of the new street can be seen on the map of 1850. The Swan Yard, which had stood to the west of the Parish Church, was eventually demolished in 1879. This was flanked by a long chain of old buildings containing stables and joiners' shops; a way through the yard led to a footpath to Birkby. The land for development was divided up into building lots, including what is now St George's Square, but it was eventually decided that there would, in fact, be an open space in front of the station.

Under a scheme surveyed by James Armitage, Kirk Moor Street was to run above the Parish Church and Byram Street below it, as in the 1850 map. Between John William Street, Kirk Moor Street and St Peter's Street there was to have stood a Town Hall and in order to add dignity to the site, John William Street was to have been as wide as the Market Place, all the way to the Town Hall.

A map dated 1849 and surveyed by Thomas Brook is almost identical with Nixon's map of 1850.[1] Kirk Moor and Byram Streets coincide but in neither map is the Town Hall shown, and it never materialised. When Brook re-drew his plan in 1850 the

[1] Facing p. 152.

names of the streets had been altered to what they are today with Byram Street above the Parish Church and Lord Street, parallel to it, below. With the Town Hall also disappeared the idea of an enlarged Market Place and John William Street was made to its present day width.

John William Street contrasted sharply with the rest of the town. The new buildings were substantial and spaced out to give an added dignity. The new George Hotel became the north side of St George's Square and was faced by Britannia Buildings,[1] built as warehouses; on the east side, in 1853, Samuel Oldfield built the Lion Buildings which contained an arcade of shops. As new tall buildings were erected in Railway Street, Westgate and along Byram Street the appearance of the town became greatly altered and travellers arriving by train could not fail to be impressed by what they saw.

The 1850 map shows that the town centre was almost completely built up. In King Street there was an open space used as a market, and we are told there was occasionally a fair there. The Shambles were actually used as such and contained butchers' shops and abattoirs. At the corner of Bull and Mouth Street and Victoria Street was the prison and the watch house, with the Guildhall, facing them (to the rear of Ramsden Street Chapel), used as a Magistrates' Court. The King Street market was only busy on a Tuesday or a Saturday night but there was usually a fruit stall there and sometimes a fishmonger's.

Huddersfield lacked a Town Hall for public meetings but there were reasonable alternatives in Ramsden Street. Just below the Chapel, on the site of the old Theatre Royal stood the Philosophical Hall where meetings and concerts took place. A few doors below stood the Apollo Gymnasium, later the Gymnasium Hall where John le Blanc (John William White) taught dancing, fencing and 'hygienic exercises'. It was here that a meeting in 1859 to form a volunteer Rifle Corps ended in uproar; the idea was branded as 'a Tory plot to divert the people from their social evils' and since William Stocks, the Chief Constable, could not maintain order, five pounds was later paid for the repair of damage to the furniture. This

---

[1] Now Huddersfield Building Society head office.

building later became Ramsden Street Baths. Still further down Ramsden Street, facing St Paul's Church, stood the Riding School, also known as 'The Armoury' and here the West Riding Volunteers had their headquarters from 1863 until St Paul's Street Drill Hall was completed in 1901. The land behind St Paul's was not built on in the 1850 map.

The map shows the Spring Grove, Spring Wood, Greenhead and Gledholt estates. The carriageway from Outcote Bank to Spring Grove is clearly marked, and Trinity Street takes its present line. New North Road is not shown as such and North Parade becomes Halifax Road just below St Patrick's Church. Portland Street is shown as Dyke End Lane. The Halifax Road of 1850 contains many large houses and it was along this road and from about this period that Edgerton began to develop as the home of the wealthier manufacturers.

The town centre had grown so rapidly that by 1848 the population controlled by the 1820 Commissioners was over 24,000. Application was therefore made for a new Local Government Act and the case was heard by a Select Committee of Parliament in the summer of 1848. It was reported to the Lords that the Highways Board had drained the main roads but there was 'a large portion of Huddersfield that consists of very close population, small houses and courts and small streets' where the drainage was not adequate. Nevertheless the town was clean when compared with her neighbours in spite of the fact that cleansing and drainage were carried out by different bodies. Joshua Hobson gave evidence to the effect that the 1820 Commissioners' efforts had been totally inadequate for the needs of a large population of poor people. He deplored the existence of a manure tip only a mile from the Market Place and he could recognise from which drains the various unpleasant smells came. Every house had water, but supplies were not guaranteed all the year round. Another source of public nuisance was the Beast Market, but opponents of the new Bill saw little cause for complaint in that the cattle fairs were only held there three times a year.

William Townend also gave evidence; he was one of two paid Parish Constables. He agreed that lodging houses were insufficiently supervised and quoted the case of a certain Timothy

Cochrane who had twenty lodgers but only four beds; another house had nineteen inmates and no beds at all! Two men in a house in Swallow Street had been found dead of a fever.

The 1820 Commissioners had a police force of one day man and eight night watchmen (twelve in winter); there was rivalry between the Parish Constables and the watchmen. There was no police headquarters and no system for reporting crime. Yet in 1847 some twenty-six men from Huddersfield appeared at the York Assizes compared with thirteen from Halifax; by 1848 the figures were thirty-eight from Huddersfield and twelve from Halifax.

Hobson complained of typhus, scarlet fever and thoritus. Thomas Heaton, the Relieving Officer, attributed much of the disease to the coming of the Irish, while Thomas Wrigley, a doctor and Member of the 1820 Commissioners said that the mortality rate for Huddersfield was lower than in adjacent towns; he claimed that the fevers were abating. However, Thomas Starkey, mill owner, died of typhus in 1847.

When the Bill reached a Select Committee of the Commissioners, opinion was crystalising in favour of its provisions for public health and safety. The Hamlet of Marsh however opposed the Bill on the grounds that they were going to lose half their income from rates while retaining practically all their road repairing responsibilities. It was found that Marsh had not been adequately maintaining the roads.

'What is the state of repairs?'

'The last time there was a swamp in New Hey Road you might have buried a horse'

'A horse might have left his hind leg in it?'

'Yes'!

It was decided not to compensate Marsh for loss of rates.

On the 14th August 1848, a Board of Improvement Commissioners was authorised. By this Act the government of the town passed to twenty-one commissioners. Sir John Ramsden appointed three and the rest were elected annually by the ratepayers, six to retire each year by rotation. To be eligible for election one had to be rated at £30 or receive not less than £50 a year in rent from property in the town, or hold at least £1,000. Those rated over £50 and below £100 received two votes and so on up to a maximum of six votes for those rated at over £250. Thus the idea of property being represented rather than the individual was preserved, and a householder who paid less than £10 was excluded from the franchise. The first commissioners included William Moore and Thomas Pearson Crosland.

As with the 1820 Act, the authority of the Improvement Act went only 1,200 yards from the Market Place. On the circumference lay many villages and hamlets each with its own local government: Marsh, Deighton, Bradley, Fartown, Lindley, Lockwood, Moldgreen, Almondbury and Newsome.

On his return to Huddersfield in 1846, Joshua Hobson took a small farm near Birkby Brewery and became Surveyor of Highways for the Township of Fartown. He had seen how local government had been improved at Leeds and in 1840 he had seen a Board of Surveyors appointed for paving and draining Huddersfield town centre. Under the New Act of 1848 Hobson was invited to be one of Sir John's nominated commissioners but he refused. Times had indeed changed since he used to run his illegal press in the Swan Yard.

Joshua Hobson became Clerk to the new Board of Works and set up his office at No. 1 South Parade. Here he became involved in the new cemetery at Edgerton. The Parish Vestry had refused to pay for a burial ground out of the Parish Rates. The Nonconformists in particular urged the need for a public burial ground where their own ministers might officiate. The Commissioners duly obtained Parliamentary powers for purchasing and maintaining the cemetery, at an initial cost of £11,500. Typically, Hobson saw to it that there were twin chapels; one for the Anglicans, the other for the Dissenters. The cemetery was opened in 1855.

Hobson was happier when in 1853 he acquired an old warehouse in Chapel Hill and converted it at a cost of nearly £6,000 into a home for the poor. This Model Lodging House[1] eventually accommodated nearly 200 people and it could be said that the Huddersfield Improvement Commissioners had done their best to help house the living and the dead.

[1] Stated at the time to be the only Lodging House in England constructed and supported out of public rates—its use was discontinued in 1957 after a century of providing cheap clean lodgings.

When the stallholders in the Market Place and King Street markets objected to the scale of fees drawn up by the Ramsden Estate Office, the Commissioners took over the payment of an annual sum to Sir John William Ramsden in 1864. They then levied the charges on the traders. Indeed the influence of the Improvement Commissioners was apparent in many aspects of town life at this period; they paved streets and constructed sewers; and, at an enquiry held in 1867, it was reported that they had maintained since 1849 a very effective police force of thirty-one men.

Joshua Hobson resigned from the Board of Works in 1854 and went back to journalism, becoming editor of the *Huddersfield Weekly Chronicle* in the following year. As might have been expected, he pursued an independent line and opposed the Lord of the Manor on the Tenant Right question. When he died in 1876 it was said that he was 'always independent, no one could ever have made him a slave to either a man or a party. He never ceased to hate intolerance or oppression wherever he found it.'

The dispute between Sir John William Ramsden and his tenants came to a head in 1858. Sir John had inherited the estate on the death of his grandfather, in 1839, and we are told of public rejoicings when he attained his majority in September 1852. He was a member of Parliament for the greater part of his life and offices he held included, at various times, those of Secretary for War, Deputy Lieutenant of the West Riding and High Sheriff of Yorkshire (*see note on page* 159).

During the minority of Sir John William much of the land of Huddersfield came to be held in a most informal manner by mere right of tenancy. When matters came to a head in the House of Lords in May 1866 the Lord Chancellor said 'I confess that this case has satisfied me that it was absolutely necessary for the interest of all parties that some mode be adopted of putting an end to it. It was an attempt to create a new and cheap mode of conveyancing, which was certain, sooner or later, to involve in difficulties those who relied on it. The supposed transfers were altogether ineffectual and it is a matter of wonder to me that litigation was not long ago occasioned by it.'

By 1858 about half the land in the town was held by tenant right and the rest by leases generally for sixty years with an agreement for what amounted to perpetual renewal in exchange for periodic payments. On 28th July of that year at a public meeting[1] held in the Philosophical Hall a deputation was appointed to petition Sir John William on behalf of the anxious tenant right holders.

In the 'Memorial of Deputation' the problem was explained. 'The tenant right system has been regulated and managed as follows: When a person desired to erect a building in the Town of Huddersfield he applied to the Agent for the Estate and stated to him the kind of building which he intended to erect, and the Agent thereupon set out an appropriate plot of land and fixed the rent to be paid by the applicant. The applicant's name was thereupon entered in the books of the Huddersfield Estate, the building was erected and thenceforward the agreed rent was paid.' If the property was sold, the new purchaser's name was put in the Estate Book; if a mortgage were taken out the name of the mortgagee was entered alongside that of the owner. Thus a simple scheme had grown up; and, provided that the public had confidence that the Ramsdens were not likely to dispose of the land, nor to alter the conditions of tenancy, all was well and the town prospered. This was to the advantage of all parties and had led to large numbers of Sir John's tenants buying their own houses through a 'money club' (building society)—'When the amount is paid off the name of the club is erased from the books and the house belongs to the man who built it and he has thereby obtained a status which has every tendency to make him a good citizen.' The deputation went on to say that deposits in the Huddersfield Savings Bank were increasing; at the same time 'Sir John William Ramsden as a young Statesman will no doubt feel that it is creditable to a people to endeavour to obtain that stake in their country which induces a desire for stability of its institutions whilst at the same time it has brought into profitable use for building purposes, a large tract of land previously yielding to his family a very small

---

[1] Reported in the *Huddersfield Weekly Chronicle* dated 17th and 31st July 1858.

income and upon which are now erected piles of buildings second to none in any provincial town.' Sir John William's grandfather and his agents had always stressed the absolute security of the system of land tenure, and public confidence had been such that a quarter of a million pounds had been invested by building societies for the purchasing of property leased on the Tenant Right System. Lack of confidence, it was said, had already caused members of the building trade to leave the town and new building schemes to be abandoned— 'The Deputation would assure Sir John William Ramsden that the fear of being disturbed in their holdings is at present causing widespread anxiety.'

The document ended with a request that, should proper leases be granted, Sir John William should consider offering periods longer than ninety-nine years since the buildings in Huddersfield were well built from local stone. The final outcome of this dispute was that Sir John William eventually agreed to grant leases for 999 years. This was what the tenants wanted.[1]

The general rise in the town's population right through this period is evidenced by the inadequacy of the water supplies even when a new reservoir was completed at Longwood in 1848. In September 1865 it was decided to apply for an Act of Parliament to enable new reservoirs at Blackmoorfoot and Deerhill to be constructed.

[1] Strictly speaking the term 'tenant right' has nothing to do with the system of letting adopted by the Ramsden Estate prior to 1858.

Tenant right is a term used to express the right of the tenant of an agricultural tenancy to take crops which he has sown during his tenancy and which he would otherwise lose by the termination of his tenancy.

Sir John William Ramsden obtained a private Act of Parliament (Ramsden's Estate (Leasing) Act 1859) which empowered him to grant leases for terms not exceeding 99 years to persons who before the passing of the Act had 'built thereon at their own expense without being "lessees" thereof . . .' referring, of course, to land.

In 1867 a further Act enabled a lease to be granted in such circumstances for a term of 999 years and the first of the new leases was granted to Isaac Hordern in 1868 for some land in Viaduct Street. It was necessary to get statutory powers of leasing because the Ramsden Estates were settled estates and the life tenant could not have leased for those periods without special powers.

The mills in the Colne Valley obtained a regular water supply by the construction of the first of the Wessenden reservoirs under an Act of 1836. Similar measures for the Holme Valley were undertaken by an Act of 1837 and in consequence the Bilberry Reservoir and two others were constructed. Bilberry Reservoir was commenced in 1838 but its embankment was weakened by a spring discovered during the building of the foundations. Subsequent attempts to remedy this defect proved unsatisfactory and, at one o'clock on the morning of 5th February 1852, the embankment gave way and eighty six million gallons of water were sent down the valley towards Holmfirth. Eighty-one people lost their lives and seven thousand were unemployed as a result.

The Holmfirth railway line had been opened in 1850 and the guard of the first train of the day saw the scene in the early light of the February morning. He said; 'I left Mirfield—in charge of the first train, arriving at Holmfirth about seven o'clock, when I beheld a most heart-rending sight. The village was a complete wreck, mills, shops and houses with their furniture and even graveyards were swept away by the tremendous flood. The roads and fields in the valley were deep in mud and dead bodies could be seen everywhere.'

Relief for the sufferers was organised at once and the unprecedented sum of £70,000 was raised; but the total loss of property alone was initially estimated at £250,000. The Coroner's Jury stated that the Holme Reservoir Commissioners had been guilty of culpable negligence in allowing the reservoir to remain in a dangerous state, and that had they been in the position of a private individual or firm, they could have been charged with manslaughter.

In May 1866 Parliament considered the Huddersfield Waterworks Bill and much concern was experienced for the safety of the local inhabitants should there be a large reservoir at Blackmoorfoot. The bill was rejected.

NOTE

Relations between the town and the Ramsdens further deteriorated in 1859 over the failure to acquire Spring Wood as a public park. Sir John purchased the park for himself in 1861.

CHAPTER XI

The Charter of Incorporation

BEFORE ATTEMPTING to examine the process by which the Charter of Incorporation was obtained in July 1868, we should take stock of nineteenth-century local government and try to ascertain why the charter came when it did.

Considering the country as a whole, local self-government in the eighteenth century—the partial autonomy of the counties and of some boroughs—did not imply democratic self-government. The rule of squire, parson and the closed corporations of burgesses had survived the Tudor monarchy and the civil war, but remained dependent on the existence of a leisured class of people with interest in local affairs. When, during the industrial revolution, a new ruling middle class arose to challenge the traditional ruling classes, central government slowly at first, began to take the initiative in their place. Thus local independence for Huddersfield in 1868 may at first seem to be a step in the wrong direction; yet the second half of the century witnessed a parallel growth of central direction, delegation of power and local enterprise.

The situation in Huddersfield was that the new ruling class which arose consisted of merchants and professional men and it was they who were appointed to the Improvement Commission of 1820. They tended to follow the Ramsden lead and support the Whig, later Liberal, cause. Oastler, who behaved like a country squire was a Tory. The new centralised Poor Law of 1834 was introduced by the Whigs and challenged by Tories and Radicals.

The Reform Act of 1832 has been said to mark the beginning of the end of the rule of the landed gentry in the country. Members elected for Huddersfield were almost always Whigs or Liberals as representing the interest of the town merchant rather than that of the country landowner. The Ramsdens, although Anglican and substantial landowners, realised that their prosperity was linked with the business of the town. This class of people was to lead the town throughout the nineteenth century. Radicalism may have had the support of the working people, but they at first had no say in either parliamentary or local affairs.

The Huddersfield Act of 1820 was typical of many measures which attempted to meet the new industrial conditions by some piece of permissive legislation within the existing general framework. As far back as 1792, for example, Manchester had been empowered to set up its own police force and to levy a local rate to pay for it. Other Acts in 1818 and 1819 permitted Parish Vestries to pay some of their officials properly; but these and other similar measures merely propped up the old system without clarifying the long-term issue of who should run local government. Gradually, however, it became clear that the central government and the local bodies should have their respective spheres of influence.

The Reform Act of 1832 showed that the *ad hoc* piecemeal system of patching things up had really broken down. Parliamentary elections were henceforth to be based on a register of electors. This was an innovation although actual voters were in the minority of the whole population. The years immediately following saw powers being delegated to local bodies from above. The state had intervened, although in the background, and a new impetus was given to local affairs. In 1833 a half empty House of Commons voted £20,000 to be spent on school buildings; 1834 saw the new Poor Law administered from Somerset House; in 1835 came the Municipal Corporations Act; in 1833 came the first Factory Act to impose inspection of premises.

Under the Municipal Corporations Act of 1835, size and population became the real criteria for the award of independence to a borough. Procedures for holding local elections, reducing corruption[1] and the levying of rates were drawn up. Local government in the towns was to be uniform.

[1] Corruption in Parliamentary elections was not completely removed until the Secret Ballot Act of 1872.

The progress towards state control was, however, haphazard and by no means universally desirable. The early measures for highways were regarded as temporary; an Act of 1856 gave the Home Office power to inspect local police for the first time. The General Board of Health in 1848 set up local boards but the appointment of medical officers was not obligatory. If they were hostile to the Central Board the local authorities needed to do very little. The composition of local boards, as of the Huddersfield Improvement Commission of 1848, was restricted by a fairly high property qualification. Opposition to change was widespread and many harked back to the days when property implied social responsibilities; but by mid-nineteenth century the traditional landed classes scarcely existed in the large towns.

Gradually the concept of minimum standards imposed from above began to take root. Local Acts for watching and lighting were originally intended merely to safeguard life, property and trade; but, in time, local bodies were encouraged to take over public utilities in the best interests of all concerned, though even here there was at first no intention to exercise compulsory powers.

The acquisition of the Charter of Incorporation in 1868 was the result of local enterprise, in the face of opposition and in spite of earlier disappointment. For some time after the Act of 1835, there had been in Huddersfield many who had felt that the town should govern its own affairs, and it should be remembered that Huddersfield town centre by 1841 together with Fartown, Marsh, Deighton and Bradley had a population of over 25,000.

Although a Board of Highway Surveyors had been appointed by the Vestry from 1835 to supplement the Commissioners appointed under the 1820 Act, it was clear that the system of local government was inadequate. Accordingly a petition signed by 2,505 inhabitants representing a rateable value of £23,021 was submitted to the Privy Council requesting the grant of a Charter of Incorporation. A counter-petition asking for things to be left as they were was also submitted. This was signed by only 133 persons, but they represented some £18,885 of rateable value—some wealthier citizens were still anxious to prevent any change. Unfortunately for Huddersfield in 1841, the Whig administration of Lord Melbourne was about to fall and, before the charter was actually granted, a Conservative Government led by Sir Robert Peel had taken office; and the new Privy Council rejected the petition for incorporation. Because of the intense frustration this rejection caused, application was now made for increased local powers, which resulted in the Improvement Act of 1848.

The Improvement Commissioners, as we have seen, successfully ran the town for almost twenty years but the increasing size of Huddersfield and the need to plan ahead for public utilities meant that increased local powers were more and more necessary. So long as the town was ringed by local Boards for Marsh, Deighton, Bradley, Fartown, Lindley, Lockwood, Moldgreen, Newsome, Longwood and Almondbury, co-ordination of essential services was almost impossible. These small townships were under their own Boards of Health authorised by an Act of 1858 but their close proximity to each other and to Huddersfield made it desirable that some general scheme for water supplies and drainage should apply to them all. Indeed the Waterworks Commissioners, before incorporation, were planning the construction of new reservoirs at Deerhill and Blackmoorfoot.

In May 1867 the Improvement Commissioners voted for their own extinction by adopting the following resolution: 'That having regard to the position of Huddersfield and adjoining districts, with respect to population, unity of commercial and public interests, and necessity of increased water supply, for which, and for other purposes, a more united system of local government would be advantageous, it is, in the opinion of this Board, desirable that a Charter of Incorporation for Huddersfield and the adjoining districts should be applied for.'

Joseph Batley, Clerk to the Improvement Commissioners, spoke in support of the resolution; 'Each of these (the outlying townships) has separate and independent jurisdiction and it must be manifest that it is impossible under such circumstances to secure that harmony and unity of action on subjects of common importance which the public welfare requires. On questions of sewage, sanitary regulations, water supply and other local interests, diversity of view and action must be expected. Admitting even that no further or new power can be acquired through the charter for the area incorporated, it must be an obvious benefit to have the same powers exercised with uniformity through one governing body instead of two.'

On 29th May 1867 a public meeting of ratepayers was held in the Philosophical Hall which had by then been made into a theatre. Joseph Turner was in the chair and the meeting endorsed the resolution of the Improvement Commissioners, with only five dissentients. Petitions and counter petitions were signed by ratepayers within the proposed area of incorporation, with this result:

	Signatures	Rateable value represented
For incorporation	4,933	£106,782
Against	2,049	£16,750

These figures are of interest as they show that opposition to incorporation came from small property owners, while their wealthier counterparts—including Sir John Ramsden—probably supported the motion unanimously. The opinion of the larger property owners had changed since 1841.

The Privy Council received the petition for incorporation and sent a Captain Donnelly to conduct a public enquiry. This was held at the George Hotel on 18th and 19th December 1867 and evidence for the petitioners was presented by Joseph Batley. The proposed areas under consideration were:

	Population	Rateable value
Huddersfield Improvement Commissioners' jurisdiction:	24,100	£100,108
Remainder of Huddersfield Township —Marsh, Fartown, Deighton and Bradley:	15,725	34,106
Proposed to incorporate—From Parish of Huddersfield—Lindley		
From Parish of Almondbury—Lockwood, Moldgreen and Dalton, Almondbury, Newsome:	32,630	65,263
Total:	72,455	£119,477

From these figures, it is clear that one half the wealth of the future town's property was in the central area; and that almost half the population lived in the Parish of Almondbury—outside the traditional area of Huddersfield.

Although the Lord of the Manor was clearly not opposed to the town being incorporated, he began to have doubts in case the award of a charter should endanger the rights and privileges of his position. Wynne, Ramsden's solicitor, was therefore instructed to contact Donnelly reminding him of the ancient rights of the Ramsden family, bestowed by Elizabeth I and Charles II, and to ask that the Charter contain a clause to the effect that nothing in it was to invalidate or even change Sir John's rights in Huddersfield. Sir John had, in fact, agreed to abandon his right of nominating three of the Improvement Commissioners and this was as far as he was prepared to permit his powers to be decreased.

Joseph Batley was well aware of the Ramsden case and, having obtained the advice of Counsel, a Mr Cleasby, q.c., he wrote to Donnelly on 27th December 1867. From this letter, the Improvement Commissioners showed that they were afraid Sir John might succeed in invalidating the charter, although they had no intention of interfering with any of his rights. In the presence of Captain Donnelly the spokesman for the Ramsden family had confirmed Sir John's wish not to prejudice the charter. Mr Cleasby's comment had been that a charter issued by the Crown could hardly take away from the Ramsdens any rights given to Sir John's ancestors by the Queen's ancestors; the powers which the new Borough Council would inherit from the Improvement Commissioners would not be changed; as regards the market, existing legislation guaranteed the Ramsdens against any infringement of their rights.

On 7th February 1868 Captain Donnelly made his report to the Privy Council. He was in favour of the grant of a charter of incorporation but, in view of the pressures put on him regarding the Ramsden interests, he left open the question of inserting a clause to safeguard Sir John's position. 'The petitioners', Donnelly writes, 'are very anxious to have the thing pushed on; in fact it is of vital importance to them to have a decision taken, otherwise they will lose a whole year in making their application to Parliament for a new Waterworks Bill.' The Report mentioned that the Improvement Act of 1848 contained provisions for its area of operation to be extended but that this had never been applied for. The Township of Huddersfield was the Parliamentary Borough yet, in local government, it had five local authorities including Marsh, Fartown, Deighton and Bradley where no public works of any importance had ever been carried out. At Lockwood, Lindley and Moldgreen, Donnelly reported active Local Boards and some sewage and other public undertakings had been carried out; at Newsome and Almondbury very little had been done. He said there had been no counter petition actually opposing the charter in principle. The town, really one area, had ten local authorities and all except Bradley were in favour of unification. Indeed only by combining could they obtain an improved water supply.

The Report mentioned several anomalies: who was head of of the town? Was it the Chairman of the Improvement Commissioners, or the Constable who had some powers outside the town? Huddersfield had its own police yet the town was obliged to contribute towards the County force which operated in those populous suburbs outside the Improvement Commissioners' area; town and county police each had their own separate headquarters and prison actually in the centre of Huddersfield.

Captain Donnelly then considered a request that Bradley should be excluded from the new Borough. Here was an agricultural area having little in common with the town yet, being the first station on the railway line to the east, Bradley had all the makings of a prosperous suburb. Joseph Batley had commented that it was without parallel to consider a place within the Parliamentary Borough being allowed to remain outside the Municipality. At the enquiry, a Mr Shaw had argued that the inhabitants of Bradley paid rates of 4*d*. in the pound as against 2*s*. 1*d*. in the pound for Huddersfield, and that Bradley, in the most low lying part of our area had no intention of becoming a sewage farm. Captain Donnelly concluded that Bradley could not be left out if one considered the Huddersfield area as a whole. He reacted similarly to the fact that a local enquiry in Almondbury had resulted in a majority vote against joining the Borough. Petitions against incorporation from Marsh and Newsome had been withdrawn.

This Report came out early in February 1868 yet the charter was not actually acquired until July. During March we find Mr Wynne still agitating for a saving clause for the Ramsdens. When a draft charter was considered by the Privy Council in May, the Lord Chancellor objected to the Council holding £10,000 of land outside the Borough. Waterworks matters, he argued, should be the subject of a separate Act of Parliament.

The charter, when issued, contained no reference to the Ramsden interest, neither did it place any limitations on the acquisition of land by the Council. The charter did however make reference to the Municipal Corporations Act of 1835 which contained detailed arrangements for setting up a borough council.

So it was that the charter was not issued from the Home Office until 7th July 1868, and Joseph Batley brought it to Huddersfield on the night of Thursday the 9th. While there had been some rejoicing on 17th February at the promise of a charter, the actual arrival of the document made little local impact. Joseph Batley was the obvious choice for Town Clerk, a post which he held until his death in 1885.

The first Mayor of Huddersfield was Charles Henry Jones, J.P. (1800–84) who since 1853 had been a member of the Improvement Commissioners. He was a man of great tact and firmness and with his good humour he made an excellent Chairman for the new Council. He had a good command of financial matters and was capable of handling the most exacting business involving Acts of Parliament. An austere Nonconformist and a pillar of Ramsden Street Chapel for forty-two years, he was nevertheless kindly in manner. He lived in Upper George Street where a commemorative plaque still stands. The new Council consisted of fourteen Aldermen and forty-two Councillors representing twelve wards. Their early achievements are the subject of Chapter XII.

The period covered by events leading to the charter also contains interesting developments in the representation of the Borough at Westminster. After his second unsuccessful attempt in 1837, Richard Oastler never again stood as a parliamentary candidate, and his opponent W. R. C. Stansfield—unopposed in 1841—did not fight a contest until 1847. The Privy Council in 1839 had set up a Committee to see to it that grants of money were issued 'for the purpose of promoting Public Education'. The Church, inspired by the Oxford Movement sprang into opposition and the quarrel between church and chapel was extended to all parts of the country. Stansfield, a Whig, supported the Church of England's claim to control all education.

The Liberals, opposing the Whigs, were, in Huddersfield, led by prominent Nonconformists including William Willans and Charles Henry Jones. Their candidate, John Cheetham, lost by a narrow majority and his supporters complained bitterly that the Ramsden-Anglican interest had been unfairly used against them. The 1847 result was: W. R. C. Stansfield (Whig) 542; John Cheetham (Liberal) 487. At the next General Election, in 1852, William Willans lost to Stansfield by an even smaller margin: Stansfield 625; Willans 590.

William Willans was father of J. E. Willans, J.P. and grandfather of H. H. Asquith, a future leader of the Liberal Party.

The conduct of the 1852 election led to an official enquiry, which took place from 5th to 15th March 1853. It was decided that William Stansfield was 'by his agent guilty of bribery and treating at the last election.' Evidence was produced that a Joseph Halowell was bribed by receiving, as a condition of his vote, twenty-four gallons of ale; some of this was given away to electors, the rest he sold at a profit. Over sixty public houses were frequented by Stansfield's agents, and there, refreshments were found to have been supplied without limit, at a final cost of over £1,000. The Committee thought that this had been tantamount to exercising an undue influence on the electorate! Among the witnesses were Elizabeth and Thomas Wigney of the George Hotel—the Whig headquarters. Characteristically, the Liberal headquarters were in a temperance hotel, to which a Mr Bottomley said he had supplied soda water; but when asked; 'In addition to the soda water were there any spirits sent to this temperance hotel?'—he could not tell!

A by-election thus followed in April 1853. The Whigs were split, some went to the Liberal camp, others to the Conservatives, who had also absorbed the old Tories. The result of the petition had given strength to the Liberal cause and Joseph Starkey J.P., the mill owner of Longroyd Bridge, lost to Viscount Goderich (later Marquis of Ripon, Viceroy of India.)

Goderich (Liberal)   675

Starkey (Conservative) 593

The Liberal Party, to represent Huddersfield in Parliament for most of the next hundred years, had come to power for the first time.

At the General Election of 1857 the Liberals had a famous candidate in Richard Cobden, the Lancashire manufacturer, leader of the Free Traders, and an experienced politician. Cobden had opposed the Ten Hours Bill, which put him out of favour with the Radicals, and he was a pacifist; this had emerged as a result of his censure of the Government for attacking a Chinese vessel which had fired on the Union Jack. Cobden's censure motion brought down the Government and vested interests became alarmed. He was a brilliant speaker and great crowds thronged St George's Square to hear him. The contesting parties held meetings at opposite ends of the Square while the Returning Officer stood in the middle. Edward Ackroyd appeared as a Whig supported by the Tories and the appeal of patriotism proved too strong for Cobden who never contested Huddersfield again. The voting figures were:

Ackroyd (Whig)   833

Cobden (Liberal) 587

In April 1859 the Whigs and Tories again put up Edward Ackroyd and a week before the election the Liberals were without a candidate. From about this time the Tories adopted the George Hotel as their headquarters while the Liberals used the Queen Hotel. The election date was fixed and the Liberals hastily chose Edward Leatham; 2,300 voting cards were sent out from the Queen Hotel in the last few days before polling. Ten minutes before the close of the day's voting the Liberals were four votes behind; suddenly a small party of twenty-three came round the George Hotel corner to vote for Leatham who was elected with a majority of nineteen:

Leatham (Liberal)   779
Ackroyd (Whig)   760

In 1865, at an extremely rowdy election, Colonel T. P. Crosland of Gledholt Hall defeated Leatham for the 'George Hotel Party'. Thomas Pearson Crosland (1815–68), who was one of the original Improvement Commissioners in 1848, became a J.P. in 1852 and Lieutenant-Colonel of the Huddersfield Volunteers in 1864. He was also a member of the Waterworks Commission, a Director of the Huddersfield Banking Company and President of the Chamber of Commerce in 1863. He contested the election of 1865 as a Liberal-Conservative. 'T.P.' was a humorist who had many friends at Thornton's Coffee House in New Street, his speeches were impromptu, and Leatham, who always prepared what he said, likened 'T.P.'s' appearances to a theatrical performance where, after a loud fanfare of trumpets, in walked the pantomime dwarf!

Towards noon on polling day feeling began to run very high and, by two o'clock, cabs conveying voters were attacked and fighting broke out in John William Street. The police were powerless, the Riot Act was read and George Armitage, Chairman of the Magistrates, telegraphed from Westgate for reinforcements of police and soldiers. By the time the Scots Greys arrived at six, the crowd had quietened down. Enthusiasm was such that some voters are alleged to have been locked up in the George Hotel the previous night to ensure that they would go to the polls! The final result was:

Crosland (Liberal/Conservative)   1,019
Leatham (Liberal)   787

In April 1866 a petition was presented to the House of Commons accusing T. P. Crosland's party of bribing the electorate. The evidence sheds an interesting light on political affairs in Huddersfield shortly before the granting of the Charter. Thomas Dean said he was engaged to persuade people to go to a meeting outside the Lamb Inn at Hillhouse, to shout for Mr Crosland and prevent Mr Joseph Woodhead and the Liberals from speaking. Thomas Pearson Crosland M.P. told the Committee that he had polled 1,019 out of 1,060 votes actually promised. He would have polled more had not the Liberals

Above: Coronation decorations in Ramsden Street in 1937. Except for the Town Hall, all the property on the right-hand side, including the gas lamps, has disappeared along with the Theatre Royal. *Photo:* Ravensknowle Museum.
Below: Buxton Road *c.* 1925, showing the Huddersfield Industrial Society's older premises, rebuilt in 1937, a tramcar en route for Birkby from Dod Lea, and the verandah of the Victoria Hall. *Photo:* Aerofilms Ltd.

New Street c. 1904, showing a Crosland Moor tramcar and the Huddersfield Banking Company's new premises (later the Midland Bank) demolished in 1967. Block lent by Roy Brook (Crosland Moor).

caused riot and disturbance; he denied all intimidation. William Hannen, Sergeant of Police, said that Colonel Crosland was popular among the respectable people, but that the non-electors were 'dead against' him; 500 special constables had been sworn in for polling day. The cabs bringing voters for the rival candidates had obstructed each other. After two and a half hours of deliberation, the Committee declared that Colonel Crosland had been elected. The pattern of the 1853 Enquiry was not repeated.

He died on 8th March 1868 and was honoured by a public funeral and a glowing obituary notice in the *Huddersfield Weekly Chronicle*, the Conservative newspaper. Indeed, T. P. Crosland was the first Conservative Member the town had ever had.

At the resulting by-election W. C. Sleigh, a serjeant-at-law, stood for the Conservatives. For the Liberals, Wright Mellor stood down to enable Leatham to return and the move was successful as Leatham won his largest majority. The figures were:

Leatham (Liberal)	1,111
Sleigh (Conservative)	789

It will be noticed how the number of electors gradually increased over the years. In 1832 there were 415 voters compared with 1,900 in 1868 and all this increase had taken place in Huddersfield while the franchise remained with the £10 householder. It is a sign of the general rise in wages and prices that the number of voters doubled in the country as a whole. In Huddersfield they increased fourfold, evidence of the town's exceptional prosperity a century ago. This, however, is a general comparison which leaves out of the argument the extent to which some electors abstained. In 1832, for instance, there was no Tory candidate at all.

From 1846 to 1859 there had been a series of weak governments. There had been too many parties and a lack of any solid backing for any single leader. The Radicals could offer no leader of national status at this time. The period of the 1867 Reform Act which gave the vote to the lodger also saw the emergence of Gladstone and Disraeli as National Leaders. From then onwards politicians found themselves more obliged to address their constituents in person. Although no one opposed Mr Leatham at the General Election of 1868, the national tendency ever since this date has been for the number of unopposed seats to decline. The first effects of the new electoral register were not seen in Huddersfield until 1874 and in the meantime, the Secret Ballot Act of 1872 had been passed. T. P. Crosland's election in 1865 was destined to be the last of the old type.

The period covered by this chapter also saw the permanent establishment of a local press. Up to 1836 there had been a stamp duty of fourpence on every newspaper sold, 3s. 6d. tax on each advertisement and a heavy duty on paper. In consequence, the cost was about sevenpence a copy, and many were imprisoned for publishing illegal papers which avoided the stamp duty. After 1836 stamp duty was a penny, advertisements 1s. 6d. and papers cost fourpence halfpenny. In 1850 there was renewed agitation and in 1853, 1855 and 1861 duties on advertisements, the number of copies sold and finally the tax on the actual paper used were all successively abolished.

The growth of local feeling at this time led some to see a need for a local newspaper and in 1850 Hans Bush of London wrote to Richard Brook, bookseller and printer, offering to supply him with a half-filled paper of national news with space for the insertion of local information. The Liberals in Huddersfield and Holmfirth, led by Joseph Woodhead, formed a committee and took out shares in the scheme. Henry Roebuck, printer, of King Street, and Richard Brook were sent to London to purchase a printing press. Joseph Woodhead, who was a Holmfirth woollen manufacturer, declined to edit the paper permanently, but he undertook to write all the local leading articles for the first year. There was no salary for this, just £50 expenses.

The first edition of the *Huddersfield and Holmfirth Examiner* came out on Saturday, 6th September 1851 but there were to be difficulties. The hand press frequently broke down and there were problems associated with relying on half a paper from London. When the Holmfirth flood necessitated a special edition, this had to be printed without the London news and stamp duty was paid locally, then supplies of paper were insufficient. The system was unsatisfactory and Mr Bush had to be paid off. All the shareholders' capital was exhausted and a disappointed Mr Woodhead resigned.

However, the Liberals rallied in support, Woodhead agreed to stay on and sufficient promises were received to cover the outstanding debts. By 1853 a good start had been made and comparative sales were:

Huddersfield Examiner	1,255
Bradford Observer (founded in 1834)	1,235
Huddersfield Chronicle (founded in 1850)	943

The *Chronicle* was supported by the Conservatives. The *Examiner* decided to follow an independent Liberal line and called for full representation of the people in Parliament, no state management of education, free trade, no vested interests and promised to befriend all classes. In its day, the *Examiner* attacked Palmerston, followed Cobden, opposed the narrow franchise of the Improvement Commissioners, took the middle path over the Tenant Right question, and condemned the Boer War. In 1855 the *Examiner* was reduced to threepence; in 1857 the price came down to three halfpence; in 1862 the size of the paper was increased while the price remained at three halfpence. Telegraph news came from the Electric Telegraph Company's office at the Station where a clerk was employed to read out the morse as it came in over the wire. Joseph Woodhead (1824–1913)[1] ran the paper until 1885 when he became Member for the new Spen Valley constituency. He was an original member of the Huddersfield Borough Council, Alderman in 1871, Mayor 1876 to 1878, Freeman of the Borough in 1898 and it was he who laid the foundation stone of the Town Hall.

To close this chapter, it would seem most appropriate to examine the book *Huddersfield; its History and Natural History* by Charles Hobkirk[2] of which the second edition came out in

[1] Photograph facing page 235.

[2] Charles P. Hobkirk (1837–1902) was a banker by profession. He was with the West Riding Union Bank from 1852 to 1897. As a young man of twenty-two he wrote *Huddersfield, its History and Natural History*—for which he is today chiefly remembered. This work has been described as 'a treasure house of flora and fauna'. As a botanist Hobkirk made his mark as a student of mosses. Although he left Huddersfield for Dewsbury in 1884, he is buried in Edgerton Cemetery. (See *The Naturalist* for 1903, p. 105.)

1868. This was just before Incorporation and the writer gives an excellent description of the town as it was exactly a hundred years ago.

After remarking that the town lies partly in a valley and partly on a gently sloping declivity to the north-west, Hobkirk goes on to say 'The greater part of it is of modern erection and this combined with the improved taste for ornamental street architecture, and its being built almost entirely of a fine whitish free-stone renders it one of the prettiest and cleanest manufacturing towns in the West Riding.' He is obviously impressed with the new buildings in St George's Square and John William Street, and now that some of them have been cleaned, we can gain some idea of how they looked a century ago. Hobkirk observes that the town was well paved, drained and lighted (by gas) and then goes on to praise the new railway station, 'the largest building in the town', also 'the magnificent colossal figure of Britannia' surmounting the Royal Arms on the Britannia Buildings opposite. By the central portico of the Station is 'a Russian trophy of two large cannons from Sebastopol mounted on wooden carriages resting on a stone platform.' He describes the Cloth Hall and the Infirmary, mentioning a new wing added in 1862 which has raised the total number of beds to sixty.

Hobkirk then takes a walk up New North Road to 'the College, a roomy castellated building' and he observes 'a large number of handsome villa residences in the most varied style of ornamental architecture—Grecian, Gothic, and several others 'presenting a very imposing and elegant appearance.' The Collegiate School at Clare Hill is 'pleasantly situated facing the East and is built in the Gothic style with a small spire above the main entrance.' He then describes the new Cemetery—'about the centre of the grounds are two chapels built in the Gothic style and apparently joined by a wide arch, surmounted by a handsome spire.' The Parish Church receives mention also a beautiful vicarage in Greenhead Lane 'commanding an extensive view of the hills to the south.' Of St John's Church Birkby, Hobkirk writes 'Situated almost in the country, surrounded by pasture land, and backed to the north by Fixby Hills and Grimscar Wood, it presents a very pleasing aspect.'

The more beautiful St Thomas's is, however, buried by factories and houses, the best view of it being from the canal bridge at Folly Hall. He mentions Queen Street Chapel as being surpassed in size only by one at Leeds 'built in such a manner that its inside measurement should just equal the outside measurement of that at Huddersfield.' In 1865 the New Connexion Methodists had pulled down their old chapel in High Street 'and a new one which was opened on 10th January of the present year (1867)—is a decided ornament to the town, and is certainly one of the handsomest buildings we possess.' Brunswick Street Chapel just off New North Road was built by the Free Wesleyans as recently as 1859. Other places of worship recently built include Hillhouse Congregational (1865) and the Unitarian Church in Fitzwilliam Street (1854).'

Hobkirk then describes various institutions and societies of which Huddersfield could boast in 1867. The Mechanics' Institution in Northumberland Street, opened in 1860, '... contains a lecture hall, reading room, library, class rooms and a penny bank' (patronised by 15,000 depositors in the previous year). The Chamber of Commerce, opened in 1853, has 'a reading room supplied with all the best daily papers—and with telegraphic despatches three times a day.' The Literary and Scientific Society (founded 1857) holds meetings in winter and excursions in the summer and has a small museum and reference library. The Naturalist's Society (1848) meets in King Street. The Archaeological and Topographical Association (1863) has recently carried out excavations at Slack and has resolved to compile the history of the County of Yorkshire.

'The Athletic Club was established in 1863 ... It occupies a small but well arranged Gymnasium in Back John William Street—and now numbers 240 members.' About a mile along the Sheffield Road are the Lockwood Spa Baths, a neat one-storey building in the Grecian Style. 'Some few years ago there was a spring here—strongly impregnated with sulphuretted hydrogen, but it has been diverted—and conducted into Rashcliffe for the general supply of the inhabitants there.' (!)

'The late Philosophical Hall was purchased in 1866 by Mr Morton Price and is now used as a theatre; this hall and the gymnasium in Ramsden Street are the only rooms in town for public meetings, concerts etc; indeed the town is sadly in want of a spacious and good Town Hall—and is in this respect far behind all the neighbouring towns.'

Hobkirk was here probably thinking of the splendour of Leeds Town Hall which had been opened with great ceremony by Queen Victoria, in September 1858. Except for the lack of a concert hall, however, the town was well endowed with public buildings many of which had been built within a decade. In the thirty years prior to incorporation, the population of the town centre had almost doubled, and in every field of enterprise, industrial, religious, and social Huddersfield experienced a boom, the extent of which was never to be repeated. The town has continued to increase in population but the actual rate of increase, although considerable, has never since equalled that of the mid-nineteenth century. Huddersfield had about it, in those days, 'a new look' and the hopes of its citizens ran high.

CHAPTER XII

The Early Achievements of the Borough Council

IN 1918, to celebrate the fiftieth anniversary of the Borough, Owen Balmforth[1] compiled a *Jubilee History*. He wrote: 'On the eve of the Charter of Incorporation being granted, the area of the Huddersfield Township was very limited in extent, containing a small population. The water and gas supplies were of a very restricted nature and owned by private companies. There were no tramways, no electric light, no parks, no Town Hall, no Public Library, nor any publicly managed schools wherein to educate the rising generation.' All these complex amenities were obtained for the Borough within its first thirty years of existence; testimony to the truly remarkable enterprise of successive Town Councils at this period.

The first Council, under the chairmanship of Charles Henry Jones, met on 7th September 1868; their proceedings lasted over six hours and, when printed, became a twenty-seven page booklet. On 10th October 1868 the Improvement Commissioners transferred to the Corporation all their rights, powers, estates, property and liabilities.

[1] Owen Balmforth (1855–1922) was the son of a woollen weaver. Educated at St Thomas's School, St Paul's School and the Secular Sunday School, East Parade, he began work at the age of ten as an office boy, then he attended the Mechanics' Institute. In 1897 he was elected to Borough Council. Alderman in 1904, Mayor 1906–7 and 1907–8, became Justice of the Peace in 1906. In 1883 he had been a Member of the Huddersfield School Board. 1906–8 he was Chairman of the Education Committee. In 1909 he took the unusual step of resigning his seat on the Bench of Aldermen in order to accept the paid appointment of Secretary of Education (Chief Education Officer). He was much concerned with Friendly Societies, the Co-operative Movement and charitable institutions.

One of the first tasks attempted by the new Council was to improve the town's water supply, because, after the failure of their Bill in 1866, the Waterworks Commissioners had decided to delay further progress until after incorporation. By 31st July 1868 Mr Batley had written to the Waterworks Board inviting their co-operation in promoting a Bill for increasing the supply of water and transferring the undertaking to the Corporation. The Bill was granted and the old Waterworks Commissioners were wound up in July 1869. Charles Henry Jones himself became Chairman of the first Corporation Waterworks Committee; Councillor Joseph Crosland, ex-Chairman of the old Commissioners became Vice-Chairman of the new Committee. The purchase of the undertaking cost £58,663 at a time when the annual revenue was only £6,500; by 1898 income had increased to £51,632 per annum.

The first reservoir built under the Act of 1869 was at Deerhill, commenced in 1870 and finished five years later. From the same authorisation came Blackmoorfoot Reservoir, this time developed on a larger scale than that proposed by the Commissioners in 1866. Alderman Wright Mellor, who became Mayor in 1871, also succeeded Alderman Charles Henry Jones as Chairman of the Waterworks Committee, an office he filled from 1872 to 1892 during some critical yet most expansive years. Blackmoorfoot Reservoir was constructed between 1871 and 1876.

A second Waterworks Act in 1876 authorised the construction of Wessenden Head Reservoir, and a further Act in 1890 empowered the Corporation to purchase the old Wessenden Reservoir from its Commissioners and to build Butterley Reservoir, completed in 1906. By the turn of the century, water was being supplied to a population of 128,000 including many users living outside the Borough. After many delays, Blakeley Reservoir, commenced in 1896, was completed in 1903. Thus, in the early years of the Council's existence there was seldom a time when a new reservoir was not actually being made.

The old Gasworks, when erected in 1821, occupied only 843 square yards of land and cost £3,400. By 1861 the Company, still a private concern, had been incorporated by Act of Parliament. Ten years later the new Council purchased the gasworks from the Huddersfield Gas Company for £130,336 and followed up this transaction with the acquisition of the Moldgreen Gasworks in 1874 for £17,000. In 1894 the works was remodelled and enlarged to meet the growing demand for gas. Such was the progress made by the Corporation that sales of gas rose from 187 million cubic feet in 1873 to 578 million in 1900. This is a reflection not only of the increasing size of the town but also of the increasing use of gas by industry, notably in engineering processes and, even though electricity was introduced and developed from 1893 onwards, the demand for gas still grew and profits from sales continued.

The gas cooker, although suggested as early as 1851, did not come into use until the 1870s. The first cookers were hired out and were sometimes loaned free of charge in order to overcome a reluctance to purchase through the fear of gas-cooked food being contaminated. The renting of cookers was continued in Huddersfield right up to the nationalisation of the industry. The industry was, at this time, becoming better organised and in 1870 the *Gas Manager's Handbook* appeared containing all kinds of useful information, including the number of meters which could be watered[1] by one man per day. The early gas lights were fish-tail burners but by 1883 the gas mantle had arrived.

In 1883 Huddersfield became the first municipal authority in the British Isles to operate its own tramway system. Horse-drawn omnibuses had been previously operated privately. An advertisement in the *Huddersfield Directory and Year Book for 1873*[2] read:

To Fartown, Coney's, every half hour from the Market Place.
To Lockwood, 	,, 	,, 	,, 	,, 	,, 	,, 	,, 	,,
To Edgerton, Foxton's, every hour from the Market Place.
To Moldgreen, 	,, 	,, 	,, 	,, 	,, 	,, 	,,
To Lindley, Cromack's, seven times a day from the Market
Place.

As the population grew, some form of public transport

---

[1] Early meters measured the gas as it bubbled through water; hence a man went round to keep them topped up.
[2] Published by George Harper, 'Chronicle' Works, Lord Street.

system became increasingly necessary. The fusion of a number of villages into a borough led their inhabitants to look upon the town as their centre for shopping, and they no longer tended to live and work in the same small locality. The coming of the tramways, in fact, speeded up this process of integration, a process begun long before incorporation. The Corporation tramcar was tangible evidence that the Borough was becoming a coherent unit. Later, as the trams pushed outwards beyond the Corporation boundaries, the magnetic effect of the town could be seen upon a still greater area outside.

In 1877 a private concern, the London Tramways Company, promoted a Bill for the construction and operation of tramways in Huddersfield. The Council, when consulted, decided to oppose the measure. They sought to retain control over the actual track and in 1879 successfully initiated their own Bill for building tramways. It was intended to lease to a private firm the actual supply and running of the vehicles upon their track. The Act was passed in 1880 and construction commenced the following year. It was, however, not possible to find anyone willing to undertake the leasing of the tramways, although by November 1882 ten miles of track had been laid. Tramlines had reached Paddock, Lindley, Edgerton, Fartown, Moldgreen and Lockwood, but there were no tramcars.

The Corporation then took the only course open to them and obtained a licence from the Board of Trade to work the system themselves. This was renewable annually and could be revoked if a private firm, able to operate the tramways, was found. Thus, for the first time, a local authority took powers to operate its own tramcars.

Steam was the first motive power used. Steam trams were like trains in that a separate engine pulled the passenger car along behind it.[1] Before being opened for public use, the system was inspected by the Board of Trade, and the *Huddersfield Chronicle* for the 18th November 1882 describes the maiden voyage. 'The first journey was made down Chapel Hill to Lockwood, and the Inspector had the engine stopped several times in order to test the power of the brakes. The journey to the terminus at

---

[1] See illustration facing p. 107.

Dungeon Wood (along the Meltham road) was completed without a hitch as was also the return to Lockwood.—Upon reaching Chapel Hill (1 in 11½ for 300 yards and the steepest tramway gradient in England) the car was loaded with passengers to test the power of the engine, a severe test indeed as it was a foggy day and the rails were, in consequence, very slippery. It ascended the hill at a good pace but when opposite Buxton Road Chapel, the Inspector ordered the engine to be stopped so that he might test its capacity to re-start from that point with a load. Several unsatisfactory attempts were made and, finding that the engine could not be got to move, the car was relieved of twenty-five of its passengers and then it was able to climb the gradient. The Mayor explained that the Corporation would prohibit a stoppage on such a gradient as Chapel Hill. When Buxton Road was reached it was found that the brake had been on the car all the way from Lockwood!'

The remaining routes were inspected in the following order: Paddock, Moldgreen, Fartown, Edgerton and Lindley and the inspection terminated at 4.20 p.m. The Inspector stated that he was highly satisfied with the permanent way. At 5 p.m. the engine and car were tried again on Chapel Hill with a load of forty-four passengers—the engine stopped and re-started without difficulty.

The first public tram commenced running from Lockwood to Fartown Bar on Thursday 11th January 1883, only one engine and car being used. A large wooden shed on Lord Street, now the Wholesale Market site, was used as a Tram Depot. As more vehicles arrived, new routes were opened to Marsh and Lindley in June 1883, Edgerton in January 1884 and Paddock in December 1884.

The Lindley route had been operating only for about three weeks when a serious accident occurred, on 3rd July 1883. A car went out of control down Trinity Street, gained speed as it continued into Westgate, and failed to negotiate the corner into Railway Street where it overturned. Seven were killed and twenty-eight injured; it was ruled afterwards that all cars would stop in Westgate to allow passengers to alight before they went on to the Square to turn round.

It was then decided that the Moldgreen route should run down King Street, but as it was considered dangerous to run steam trams down such a steep, narrow and busy thoroughfare; horse trams were used starting in May 1885.

In 1886 the Lindley and Edgerton routes were linked as a circular service via Holly Bank Road. In that year, the fleet consisted of nine steam and four horse-drawn cars and, as Lord Street was now inadequate, a new depot at Great Northern Street was opened in 1887. In 1888, steam trams took over the Moldgreen route. The horse trams were then used occasionally for football traffic to Fartown until they were sold in 1892.

Further extensions were made to Almondbury (1889), Park Road, Crosland Moor (1890) and to Waterloo also in 1890. In 1892 trams had reached Bradley and this was linked with the Almondbury route. By this time, nearly all the upstairs passengers rode under cover. In the same year extensions were made to Salendine Nook, Berry Brow and Birkby (where there was a gradient of one in twelve at Birkby Hall Road). During the same period (1889–92) the whole system had been relaid to take newer and larger engines and cars. The only rails which were not renewed were those from Lockwood to Dungeon, a line used only at week-ends and holidays for taking visitors to Beaumont Park. The time-table shows that while Lindley, Moldgreen, Lockwood and Birkby had a tram every half hour and Crosland Moor and Paddock a forty-minute service, all other routes ran hourly.

In 1893 trams were fitted with post-boxes which were cleared every two hours as the cars passed through Huddersfield, a most successful service which was continued up to September 1939. The Newsome route, as far as Stile Common Road, opened in 1896 after King's Bridge over the Colne had been specially strengthened.

In 1897 the Corporation obtained absolute power for working the tramways permanently. By now, Leeds and Bradford were operating electric tramways, to be followed by Halifax in 1898. When the Outlane extension was opened in 1899 the new rails were specially joined in readiness for electrification.

As there was yet no tramway along the Colne Valley, Linthwaite Urban District Council built their own track from Milnsbridge, at the Huddersfield boundary, to Slaithwaite. The Corporation, by 1899, were operating as far as Milnsbridge and Huddersfield trams reached Slaithwaite in 1900. In the same year the Paddock line was extended to Quarmby Clough and this took the steam tramways to their greatest extent, some twenty-nine and a half miles, and made this the second largest system in the country.

Steam trams were not a financial success in their early days but from 1896 to 1901 they were independent of the rates. Replacement of track and vehicles, and compensation paid to accident victims had previously taken away the profit. The cars and engines were painted in crimson and white with gold lines. The Borough Arms appeared in the centre of each car, on the side panels, and they were surrounded by a circular garter device inscribed 'Huddersfield Corporation Tramways'.

The tramways were electrified in two stages in 1901 and 1902 by which time the Corporation had begun to supply its own electricity.

In 1888, approaches were made to the Council with a view to the formation of a private company to supply electricity to the town. When the matter was investigated, it was found that other towns were determined to keep the supply of electricity in their own hands. The Corporation therefore decided to allocate some land for a power station on St Andrew's Road near the Gasworks and invited firms to tender for the construction of a generating station. The Brush Electrical Company was awarded the contract, and supply commenced in July 1893 when eighty-three consumers were connected, for lighting only, at a charge of sixpence a unit.

At the inauguration of the supply Mr A. B. Mountain, the first Borough Electrical Engineer said, 'The following consumers have up to the present time arranged to take the supply of electrical energy: The Town Hall, Market Hall, Technical School, Parish Church and Milton Church, two clubs, six banks, four warehouses, thirty-three shops and sixteen residences.' Amongst local firms who worked on the original power station were J. Radcliffe & Sons, Henry Brook & Co., and Messrs Hopkinson.

The scheme, designed to cater for future expansion, and to facilitate repairs without interruption to supplies, was for high-tension alternating current to be supplied to a number of transformer sub-stations in the town, and from these sent out to consumers at only 100 volts. Ironically, until the formation of the Electrical Committee in 1892, the project was pioneered by the Gas Committee! The success of the system was such that outlying districts were being supplied by 1894 at a time when Bradford, using a wholly low-voltage system, could not supply all its suburbs. By 1899 the works were extended, and by 1905 the mains had reached as far as Milnsbridge and Linthwaite.

In those days, before turbines came into use, the charge engineer at the power station used to dread having a large generator break down on a Friday or Saturday night in winter. If this happened, up to three smaller generators would have to be set in motion to replace it, sharing the load. All coal was carted and hand shovelled to the boiler rooms. Life at St Andrew's Road in the 1890s was not, however, lacking in excitement. One engineer, suddenly called to the telephone, returned to find half a hundredweight of debris in the place where he had been sitting. Part of the cylinder and pistons of an engine had gone through the roof and there was glass, twisted metal and steam everywhere. On another occasion an engineer pulled out what he thought to be a dead plug from the switch-board when it was carrying full load at 2,200 volts. Half the town was blacked out and the power station was bathed in a sea of yellow fog, while the unfortunate man, almost blinded, made more mistakes and some blinding flashes before he managed to get the lights on again.

The Improvement Commissioners had entered the field of Markets, as we have seen. In 1876, the Corporation purchased from Sir John Ramsden all his market rights and tolls for £14,453. Plans were immediately drawn up for a covered market, and the Market Hall in King Street was opened in March 1880 on a site which had been purchased for £6,491. While the Market Hall was being erected, traders were able to use the Cloth Hall. A covered wholesale market was built in Brook Street in 1881.

Prior to 1877, cattle were sold on land still known as the Beast Market, and there was a pig market in Victoria Street near the old shambles. In this year the Council bought land in Great Northern Street where they built a slaughter house and opened a new cattle market in 1881. In 1900 a public abattoir and cold storage premises were opened nearby.

In other fields of activity the Borough was quick to seize an opportunity. When the Gymnasium Hall, erected in 1847 in Ramsden Street, was sold in 1888 the Corporation bought it for £2,000 and had it converted into public baths. Huddersfield was one of the first municipalities to take advantage of the Artisans' Dwellings Act of 1875 which enabled local authorities to clear slums and rehouse the occupants. Between 1880 and 1882, 160 houses were built by the Corporation at Turnbridge.[1] They were conceived as being financially self-supporting, the scheme was very successful and attracted the attention of many other authorities.

During its early years, the principal work supervised by the Borough Surveyor's Department was the building of the Town Hall and Municipal Offices. The Borough Surveyor, John Abbey, was responsible for the general design of the Town Hall and he was assisted by Thomas Wood of Huddersfield and Frederick Wild of Bradford. Abbey died during the construction of the Town Hall and a Mr B. Stocks was in charge when the project was completed. The main contractor was Alexander Graham, grandfather of Alderman Douglas Graham. The offices of the Improvement Commissioners had been at No. 1, South Parade, at the corner of Manchester Road, but the Commissioners had actually met in the front portion of the Philosophical Hall in Ramsden Street. The inauguration of the first Borough Council and the installation of the first Mayor took place there, and the Council met there until 1878. The Municipal Offices in Ramsden Street, built at a cost of £19,000, were opened in 1878, but the Town Hall, comprising concert hall and Magistrates' Court, was not opened until 1881. It had cost £57,000. The Town Hall opened with a three-day festival at which Sir Charles Hallé said that the Huddersfield Choral Society was the best choir he had ever conducted.

This period saw, in addition, the acquisition by the Borough of its parks. In 1883 Beaumont Park was opened by the Duke

---

[1] The original swivelling bridge over Sir John Ramsden's Canal was built in 1815. (See 1826 Town Map.) It was replaced by a hoist bridge in 1865, which still exists. See photograph facing page 203.

of Albany who drove over from Whitley Beaumont for the occasion. The land, formerly part of Dungeon Wood, was presented to the Borough by H. F. Beaumont and the park was laid out by Reuben Hirst, Chairman of the Parks Committee. In the following year, Greenhead Park was purchased by the Corporation from Sir John Ramsden for £30,000, towards which he personally donated £5,000. Norman Park at Birkby was opened in 1896.

When considering the public open spaces in and around Huddersfield one must include Castle Hill, commanding unrivalled views of the town. The idea of erecting a 'Victoria Prospect Tower' was first conceived in 1849, when a private company was formed for the purpose. The scheme was for an eighty-foot tower, a museum of antiquities, refreshment rooms, an observation terrace and a private room for subscribers. 'Huddersfield, being without any place of attraction to the visitor, it is hoped that the deficiency will be supplied and that advantage will accrue to the village of Almondbury. At present the school excursions resort to Kirklees.'[1] A considerable number of shares in the project were taken up, but the scheme collapsed when Mr George Lock, Agent to the Ramsden Estate, objected to the building of a 'castle in the air' on top of Castle Hill.

The idea, nevertheless, lingered in the minds of many prominent citizens including Isaac Hordern, Cashier of the Ramsden Estate, and R. W. Harper, the Editor of the *Huddersfield Chronicle*, and the opportunity for realisation arose on the occasion of Queen Victoria's Diamond Jubilee. Isaac Hordern wrote: 'In 1897 I promoted the scheme for building a tower. The Lord of the Manor did not approve but my old friend G. W. Tomlinson took up the matter with the result that he has had the credit of promoting the tower, whereas he had never thought of such a thing until I suggested it.'

Tomlinson wrote to the Mayor and to the *Chronicle* saying, 'I think the fault of our town has been that too little attention has been paid to its ornamentation, I mean, its ornamentation apart from mere utility. Huddersfield with its widely extended

---

[1] Prospectus—Victoria Prospect Tower, 1849.

municipal boundary has a feature within its borders which I believe to be unique. I know of no city or borough in the kingdom with an elevation of 900 feet above sea level such as we have on Castle Hill and I therefore propose that a Tower should be built on the summit of the Hill with a platform on the top, at least 100 feet high, making a total height of 1,000 feet.'

An influential committee was formed to collect subscriptions and the corner-stone was laid by Mr (later Sir) John Frechville Ramsden on 25th June 1898 in the presence of his father, Sir John W. Ramsden, the Mayor and Corporation: (photograph facing page 138). The Tower was officially opened by the Earl of Scarborough on 24th June 1899. On that day Mr J. A. Brooke, Chairman of the Tower Committee said that the question one day might be asked:

'What meaneth the great Tower on top of Castle Hill?'
The father of the children to come will answer,
'The Tower was built in memory of the time when the
Arts and Sciences and the Education of the people progressed
in a manner as they had never progressed before.'

Stone for the Tower came from Crosland Hill and the walls were built four feet thick at the base, tapering to two feet at the turret. In October 1899, Sir John Ramsden leased the land on the hill to the Trustees of the Tower for 999 years.

The Victoria Tower was not built without some opposition from those who thought it a waste of money and who wished for the erection of a more useful building to commemorate the Diamond Jubilee. It was felt that a public library, first mooted in 1859, would have been more fitting.

In October 1880, at a private meeting of influential people, the Free Library Committee had been formed. Thomas Brooke, J.P., took the chair and those present included the Mayor, several aldermen and councillors, and Owen Balmforth, C. P. Hobkirk, D. F. E. Sykes, Sir Charles Sikes, G. W. Tomlinson and Ernest Woodhead. When the poll was held in 1881 on the question of whether to levy a penny rate for a public library, out of 15,000 eligible to vote, only 3,739 did so and of these 2,483 were against the proposal. A similar poll in 1887 produced a similar result.

In spite of persistent efforts to obtain a library, no progress had been made by 1897 when a pamphlet appeared entitled *In Darkest Huddersfield or Why we have no Public Library* (!). The anonymous author wrote: 'Few infirmaries are better than ours. I do not know a lodging house so comfortable as our Model. Where are the poor people so cared for as at Crosland Moor? Our tram service is second to none. . . . Our supply of water is almost unlimited. . . . To give food to a starving man is a virtue but to give food to a starving soul has a far greater effect.'

This and other kinds of agitation met with success before the year was out, for the Diamond Jubilee Celebrations of 1897 did contain a scheme for a public library.

The Corporation quickly established a public library and art gallery in April 1898 in Somerset Buildings, Church Street. The premises, leased from the Ramsden Estate, were soon outgrown and by 1900 two extensions had been made. In a space of twenty years proposals were under consideration for a completely new library as Somerset Buildings were totally inadequate.

In 1871 Gladstone established the Local Government Board to deal with the Poor Law and Public Health. Action in these fields was to be taken partly by local authorities, assisted by Government grants, and partly by the State direct. As a direct result of this Board being set up, Huddersfield appointed its first Medical Officer of Health; and his first report, published in June 1873, reveals the results of the town's rapid and unplanned growth.

Many of the central areas had become mazes of narrow streets and yards occupied by those who had left their hand-looms in the country; but with the arrival of better public transport many left the cramped and sunless back streets for the rapidly growing suburbs. Thus in the town there arose the problem of its slum areas. In the outlying districts modern sanitation, drainage and provision of clean water became necessary as more people moved out there. At the same time, the general increase in population and the gradual awareness of public hygiene led to a fear of epidemics. Thus the development of the town had by the seventies produced its own problems.

A report of 1873 tells of a stream at Fartown, polluted by refuse from farmyard and stable, being used as a source of water supply. This was in spite of the fact that Corporation water mains had in fact been laid down in the district. A bad case of smallpox was reported in Lowerhead Row in a house where contacts with the sufferer had been going about their business in the heart of the town. From this and other evidence, it is clear that smallpox and typhus were by no means uncommon, though the Sanitary Authority had at first no means of knowing of the existence of these and similar dangerous diseases.

In 1876, however, a local Act was obtained requiring doctors, parents and property owners to notify the Medical Officer of Health of any suspected outbreak of an infectious disease. Only in 1889 were similar measures applied to the whole country. This action resulted in the provision of isolated hospital accommodation first at Birkby[1] and then at Mill Hill.

Alderman Benjamin Broadbent (1850–1925) was instrumental in setting up an Infantile Mortality Sub-Committee in 1903. Realising that the likeliest period of infantile mortality occurred at the earliest stages of life and having aroused the interest of the Council in this matter, Benjamin Broadbent did two things. On becoming Mayor in 1904 he gave twenty shillings to every child born in Longwood during his term of office, the presentation to be made when the child reached the age of twelve months. The scheme lasted two years and it was afterwards claimed that child mortality in Huddersfield was less than half the national average. The parents of all children under the scheme were visited by members of a ladies committee who were thus able to use their influence in the best interests of the young babies. Secondly, Alderman Broadbent's influence was behind the Improvement Act of 1906 which secured powers for the prompt registration of all births within the Borough. This measure was applied to the whole country in the following year.

The excitement over the administration of the 1834 Poor Law had, by this time, died down. The Huddersfield Board of

[1] Site of Birkby Primary School. Known as 'T'owd 'oss' (the old hospital).

Guardians were responsible for the largest area of its kind in Yorkshire covering twenty-three townships. Two institutions were founded, one in 1862 at Deanhouse for 300 chronic sick and harmless mental cases, and another at Crosland Moor which catered for 400 poor and sick of every type. As a means of removing some children from the environment of the workhouse, homes were built at Outlane in 1902 and later at Scholes.

In 1868 the old Police Station[1] in Bull and Mouth Street was still being used. Behind the offices lay the yard with cells for males and females, premises which were completely out of date. It was not until 1898, however, that a new Police Station[2] was opened in Peel Street by the Mayor, Alderman W. H. Jessop. On leaving the old headquarters, the Borough Force had grown to 113 men. Prisoners were taken to gaol in a horse-drawn 'Black Maria' as far as the Railway Station, and from there they went by train to Wakefield or Leeds. At this time the police also ran the Fire Brigade, with the Chief Constable as its Captain. They had two hose carts, one horse-drawn fire engine, and a fire escape, the horses were borrowed, when required, from a nearby cab proprietor. The alarm system was that whoever received the notice of there being a fire, blew a fog horn at the Station entrance in Princess Street to summon his colleagues. In 1899 the Brigade obtained its own horses, and a telephone alarm system was set up in the town.

Parliamentary elections from 1859 to 1886 were overshadowed by the dignified figure of Edward Leatham who represented Huddersfield continuously in Parliament except for the short reign of T. P. Crosland. The electorate increased enormously after the Second Reform Act and we find heavy polling in 1874:

Leatham (L)	5,668
Thomas Brooke (C)[3]	4,985

Thus there was a total of 10,653 voters compared with

[1] The Weights and Measures Department Offices up to 1967 but due for demolition in the 'Murrayfield' redevelopment scheme.

[2] Demolished in 1967.

[3] Of Armitage Bridge Mills: photograph facing page 235.

fewer than 2,000 at the previous election in 1868. In spite of this widening of the franchise and a gradual increase in the number of electors, Huddersfield remained firmly Liberal behind Mr Leatham and it was not until 1893 that the Conservatives were able to retake the seat and then only by a very narrow majority. The working men of the town and the small shopkeepers, many newly enfranchised, continued the Liberal tradition for many reasons: the Nonconformists were Liberal because they supported non-sectarian education for all and their chapels were to be seen everywhere throughout the town; the manufacturers still advocated Free Trade in the interests of increased business and their workpeople followed suit; Edward Leatham had been in Parliament almost continuously since 1859 and was felt to be a reliable man and the Huddersfield folk, then, as now, were reluctant to advocate any sweeping change of policy.

From 1846 to 1874 there were only five years of Conservative government. In the mid-nineteenth century Whig, Liberal, Tory and Conservative parties were dominated by the middle classes. Thus, there were many similarities between the parties and often little to choose between them. After the defeat of Chartism in 1848 and until the arrival of the Labour Party, the Radicals directed their efforts towards the trade union and co-operative movements. After the franchise was widened to include the working classes, they tended to support whichever Liberal or Conservative candidate served their own interests best. In Huddersfield, Nonconformity and Free Trade and the Liberal Party were frequently found together.

Edward Leatham was typified by his well-prepared speeches and his reluctance to curry favour by attending petty functions, indeed it was not necessary for him to do so in order to remain in office. He followed his leader, Gladstone, and only when the Prime Minister changed his mind over Irish Home Rule did Leatham differ from him. So Edward Leatham in 1886 resigned, and found that he was too set in his ways even for the local Liberal Party who preferred a Gladstonian Liberal, William Summers, in his place.

In 1880 and in 1885 Leatham had succeeded in defeating the Conservatives:

1880		1885	
Leatham (L)	7,008	Leatham (L)	6,960
W. A. Lindsay (C)	4,486	Joseph Crosland (C)	6,194

The decrease in Leatham's majority in the latter election is indicative of the popularity of the brother of the late T. P. Crosland. Joseph Crosland claimed to be 'Liberal-Conservative' like his brother, a claim which Leatham countered by remarking, 'My opponent reminds me of a Bluecoat schoolboy who when someone remarked on the blueness of his coat replied "Yes, but come with me round the corner and I'll show you my yellow breeches." '

In spite of the Liberal split over Home Rule, Huddersfield followed Gladstone in 1886.

Summers (L)	6,210
Crosland (C)	6,026

Again in 1892 we find:

Summers (L)	7,098
(Now) Sir Joseph Crosland (C)	6,837

The death of Mr Summers necessitated a by-election held in 1893, and the Liberals nominated Joseph Woodhead, the well-known editor of the *Huddersfield Examiner*. He was a brilliant orator and a commanding figure, convinced of the righteousness of his cause; he was also, however, thought to be intolerant of his opponents, and the Liberals said he was misunderstood by the workers. He was defeated by a mere thirty-five votes, thus:

Crosland (C)	7,068
Woodhead (L)	7,033

In 1895 there was, for the first time, a three-cornered fight when Labour contested the seats both in Huddersfield and in the Colne Valley, a constituency set up in 1885. Sir Joseph Crosland was defeated by Sir James Woodhouse, later to become Lord Terrington of Huddersfield. Russell Smart was able to poll only ten per cent. of the votes cast, so Huddersfield was obviously not ready for Socialism. In 1900 the Labour

Party did not contest the seat and, in spite of the Boer War, Huddersfield remained firmly Liberal. The results were:

1895		*1900*	
Woodhouse (L)	6,755	Woodhouse (L)	7,896
Crosland (C)	5,808	Col. Hildred Carlisle (C)	6,831
Smart (Lab)	1,594		

The Borough expanded in the years immediately following Incorporation. In 1868 the Borough covered 10,436 acres comprising the townships of Huddersfield, Marsh with Paddock, Fartown, Dalton, Bradley, Deighton with Sheepridge, Moldgreen, Lockwood, Almondbury, Newsome and Lindley-cum-Quarmby. In 1871 and 1880, 58 acres and 26 acres in South Crosland were added and in 1890 the district of Longwood was included, an additional 1,334 acres.

Under the Local Government Act of 1888[1] the system of local administration assumed the pattern we know today. County Councils were set up and the Third Schedule to the Act named sixty-one towns and cities which were to receive the new status of County Borough thereby becoming autonomous areas fully responsible for their own affairs. Huddersfield was included in the Schedule[2] and thus became one of the first County Boroughs in the country. Each of the towns mentioned was a borough which on the 1st of June 1888 had a population of at least 50,000. By the same Act the three Ridings of Yorkshire became separate administrative counties and London was made a county in its own right.

The Act went into details regarding the setting up of county councils and the settlement of financial arrangements between the county and county borough authorities where responsibilities and services overlapped. Roads and bridges were transferred to the new county boroughs while provision was made for a Local Government Board to consider any future recommendations as to boundary changes between counties and county boroughs.

[1] 51 & 52 Vict., chap. 41.

[2] The other county boroughs in Yorkshire created in 1888 were Bradford, Leeds, Kingston upon Hull, Sheffield, York, Halifax and Middlesborough. Later came Rotherham (1902), Barnsley (1912), Dewsbury (1913), Wakefield (1915) and Doncaster (1926).

For a picture of the town as it was at the turn of the century, we have only to study the bird's eye view facing this page. Compared with the map of 1848, the whole of the town centre has been built up; everywhere can be seen the work of Joseph Kaye and others whose names have been forgotten, the signs of municipal enterprise and clear evidence of thriving industry and local prosperity.

In St George's Square can be seen not only the steam trams and their turning points, but also the statue of Sir Robert Peel[1] which had been unveiled in June 1873. The inscription on the base of the statue from one of Peel's own speeches was very appropriately worded:

'It may be that I shall leave a name sometimes remembered with expressions of goodwill in the abodes of those whose lot it is to labour by the sweat of their brow; when they shall recruit their exhausted strength with abundant and untaxed food, the sweeter because it is no longer leavened with a sense of injustice.'

In Greenhead Park there were two lakes, one of which is now a rose garden. Notice also the four-track railway system, and the locally famous music hall, Rowley's Empire, behind the Lion Building in the Square. Down Ramsden Street on the left the Congregational Chapel and the Theatre Royal stand side by side and in the far distance on the right of the picture proudly stands the new Victoria Tower.[2]

---

[1] Removed in 1949. By which time it was in very poor condition as the stone had deteriorated.

[2] When the Tower was extensively renovated in 1960, the top seven feet were removed. The top of Victoria Tower is now 996·7 feet above sea level.

CHAPTER XIII

Education from its Beginnings to the School Board

BEFORE THE Reformation, a large number of schools in England were associated with the foundation of a chantry. A chantry was a chapel, either in isolation or as part of a church, founded by an individual who had made an endowment to pay for a priest who would continue to pray for the founder's soul after his death. In some cases the chantry priest ran a school as part of his duties. Where the chantries were small, a priest might have care of more than one, and when this was not possible, he may well have put his literacy to good use by founding a school.

We know that Huddersfield Parish Church had two chantries. There was the Chantry of the Blessed Virgin which had in 1534 an annual income of about two pounds, and the Chantry of the Holy Trinity worth about four guineas a year. There was possibly a third chantry. In 1547 an Act was passed suppressing all chantries and confiscating their property to the King. If there had been a chantry school in Huddersfield then it certainly came to an end at this time.

In Almondbury there were three chantries within the Church, one of St Nicholas, one of Our Lady and one of the Rood. There may also have been a Chapel of St Helen on the hillside below the church and it is likely that one priest would look after all four. John Kaye's *Commonplace Book*, commenced in 1583, reveals that his father Arthur Kaye of Woodsome Hall had ancestors who had built the chapel 'in the lone[1] end above ye Butts at St Elynwell.' Of this chapel he writes that in 1547 'He and I dyd shifte yt and by concent of the parishe dyd translate

---

[1] lane

the same into the schole howsse that now is. And I dyd procure one, Mr Smyth, a good scholar to com and teach here.'

Edward VI's Act had suggested that chantry bequests, when suppressed, might be better used for founding grammar schools. Thus it appears that the Kayes pulled down the old chantry and re-erected it further down the hill, and it is most likely that in doing this they were continuing the educational work of the chantry before its dissolution. When such a chantry school would have been founded is not known, but it is fairly certain that the school re-founded at Almondbury was to be the only school in our area for many years to come.

It was a grammar school, where the grammar taught was Latin; and in 1563 we find that one Richard Hurst, schoolmaster at Almondbury, was examined by Richard Barnes, Chancellor at York Minster: He 'read well, showed himself to be well versed in Latin, wrote it and composed modestly; his knowledge of grammar was exact and perfect, therefore having been examined and found to be a fit and qualified person he was licensed by R. Barnes to teach and to catechise younger boys in their mother tongue and also to teach the elementary stages of Latin Grammar.' Richard Hurst also subscribed to the Forty-two Articles of Religion—a condition of employment as a teacher, and the basis of Anglican church doctrine since 1553. Compared with other schools at this time, the standard of work at Almondbury was not of the highest. They did no Greek, and Latin does not appear to have been used for conversation. However, this was the only school in the district and the education the boys received would be adequate for anyone wishing to enter one of the professions in the sixteenth century.

At the turn of the century the school was probably in disrepair. There were no fixed endowments, apart from a legacy from Robert Kaye, and in 1608 a number of local gentlemen appealed to the King. Robert Kaye of Woodsome, William Ramsden of Longley, Richard Appleyard of Over Longley, Nicholas Fenay of Fenay, Robert Nettleton of Almondbury and George Crosland the Vicar petitioned:

'To the Kings most Excellent Matie—your loyall and faithfull subjects, ye tenants and inhabitants of your highness

mannor and towne of Almondbury—that whereas ye said
Towne is Situate in a rude and uncivill Country Remote
from Townes of accompt and Reputation nearby, ye children
and youths—for want of good education and instruction are
destitute of such necessary understanding both in their
religion towards God and in their loyalty and obedience
towards your Matie—It may therefore please your mose
excellent Matie—to grant that there may be now and hereafter within ye saide towne one free gramer schole—(to) be
called the free grama schoole of King James in Almondbury.'

This plea also contained proposals for the appointment of
governors, a master, an usher or assistant master and provision
for its endowment. Thomas Beaumont duly took the letter to
Hampton Court and after several weeks of expensive litigation
returned with the Royal Charter, and debts of £44. 8*s*. 10*d*.
incurred in obtaining it.

The term 'free' has been the subject of some speculation
amongst scholars. The most acceptable view is that the 'free'
school was so termed because it was free from the operation of
the Statute of Mortmain (1279) prohibiting the bestowal of
lands to the 'dead hand' of the Church from which they could
never pass to the Crown for lack of heirs. A condition for the
grant of exemption from Mortmain was that a proportion of
scholars attending should be admitted free of charge. In order to
remain 'free' whilst paying its way, Almondbury Grammar
School was dependent upon endowments from Robert Kaye,
William Ramsden, Sir Richard Beaumont, George Crosland,
Thomas Wilkinson, Isaac Wormall and Robert Nettleton. The
income from these sources was small, as indeed was the school.
The system whereby the Governors were responsible for
running the school lasted from 1608 to 1869, when their powers
were handed over to the Charity Commissioners.

Statutes drawn up about the year 1700 give us an interesting
picture of life at Almondbury school in the eighteenth century.
'No popish, profane or immodest authors' are to be permitted,
the master is to speak nothing but Latin so far as possible—one
of the reasons why such grammar schools later found it difficult to move with the times. Again, 'The Scolemaster shall—

suppress all disorders in the Schole; and shall not at any time suffer any gaming, joyning (conspiring) clubbing or sending for Ale, Wine or other strong liquors into the Schole at Scholetime'; he is also to ensure that no 'Swearing, cursing, lying, strife or any rude, immodest or irreverent behaviour be used.' The question of 'free' education was clearly answered by the stipulation that only those boys whose parents, in regular receipt of charity or through poverty, pay no taxes should be excused school fees. In return for a free place the children of the poor were to help clean the school, light fires and sweep the floor from time to time 'without neglect to their learning.'

As the eighteenth century wore on, other schools were developed in the area. They attempted to give a more popular education than at Almondbury which remained tied exclusively to Latin and Greek. In 1804 Rev. Walter Smith was appointed Schoolmaster at Almondbury. At thirty-nine he had already held curacies at Rastrick, Huddersfield and Slaithwaite where from 1790 to 1796 as master of the Free School he had proved an outstanding teacher; he died in 1821. Smith was a devoted social worker, a pioneer in attempting to educate the poor by opening a Sunday School in his own school; and in 1818, he pioneered the National School in Westgate, Almondbury.

Slaithwaite Free School had been founded in 1719 and firmly established by the will of Rev. Robert Meeke in 1724. This endowment provided free instruction for ten of the poorest boys and girls chosen by the Curate, Churchwardens and the Overseer of the Poor for Slaithwaite. Girls were to be taught to read well and were catechised. If the Master's wife could teach them to sew then it was to be done. Boys received instruction in reading, writing and arithmetic.

Longwood Grammar School was for many years the only school of its kind in the Colne Valley and it only finally closed its doors in 1921 when the West Riding and Huddersfield authorities jointly opened Royds Hall as a grammar school. The Longwood school dated from 1731 when William Walker of Wakefield endowed it with £20 a year.

Fartown Grammar School was the only other establishment of this type in or near Huddersfield before the nineteenth century. Founded in 1770 the school was built by public subscription on land enclosed from the Common. Under Holroyd's Charity four assisted scholarships were tenable at Fartown and the school, under a Mr Binns, became known locally as 'Binns's School'. After struggling for many years, the school closed in 1928.

Thus as the town grew rapidly in the early nineteenth century, there was felt to be a need for a secondary school in Huddersfield where the sons of the woollen magnates and wealthier trades people might be educated. King James's at Almondbury by 1833 had sixteen boys of whom only two paid school fees. The free scholars learned the 'three R's' while the other two studied Latin Grammar. The new *élite,* however, desired a modern curriculum which the grammar school could not provide, furthermore the Nonconformist elements in the town resented the interest of the Established Church in the older schools.

In 1838 Rev. W. A. Hurndall of Ramsden Street Chapel was instrumental in founding the Huddersfield College Company, floated with 300 shares of £20 each, advertised publicly. The school was opened on 21st January 1839 in some cottages in St Paul's Street and later moved to new premises, in the Gothic style, in New North Road, a part of the town very suitable for the type of pupil it was intended to attract. A brochure of 1843 explains that the College 'was established by a propriety of gentlemen entertaining various religious opinions, with the design of providing for the youth of the middle and upper classes a sound Classical, Mathematical and Commercial Education, upon a Scriptural foundation—there are now upwards of two hundred boys in attendance.' The objects of the school were as we would expect from the hard-headed businessmen who founded it 'to cultivate the formation of early habits of industry, prompt attention, obedience and punctuality—and to promote, on all occasions, integrity of conduct, and gentlemanly deportment.'

Mention was also made of new methods of language study, commercial arithmetic, writing, book-keeping and the composition of mercantile letters. College fees were five guineas a year for the Lower School and £10 for the Upper, thus only the wealthy could afford to send their sons there. Boarders, taken from the start, were domiciled with masters of their own denominations. In 1856 the school had forty-nine such boarders.

The annual report for 1848 gives the following table of hours of work per subject in the Upper School each week:

Subject	Class 3	4	5	6
Latin	5	5	5	5
Greek	–	–	–	5
English	6	6	3	1
French	2	2	2	2
History, Geography, Scripture	4	4	4	5
Arithmetic	8	8	6	4
Mensuration	–	–	1	2
Science (Pneumatics, Astronomy)	1	1	1	1
Mathematics	–	–	3	6
Writing & Book-keeping	3	3	4	4

Extras included German, Chemistry and Mechanical Drawing.

The college had moved far from the classical tradition, and even the time given to English declined as the boy reached the end of his school life. The clear aim was a preparation for the cut and thrust of Victorian business life and it should be said that the Taunton Commissioners in 1868 recommended just this kind of curriculum.

After June 1856 the college began to decline due to the arrival of an inefficient headmaster, and dissension, partly religious, between members of the staff. Some of the staff set up rival establishments and the college company, now in debt, was wound up. The school appears to have recovered quickly as a new company was formed, and by 1865 there were 156 boys on the roll. The numbers reached a peak of 226 by 1874.

In 1844 the college had been affiliated to the new University of London and special classes were formed for boys wishing to graduate. In the 1860s boys were entered for the Oxford and Cambridge Local Examinations, with increasing success until in 1871 Huddersfield College sent to Cambridge twice as many boys as any other school in Yorkshire.

Shortly after this period, the school again began to decline as a result of competition from the now reformed grammar schools, the effects of the Elementary Education Act of 1870, and the booms and slumps in trade which affected the middle classes. The Act of 1870 pointed the way towards free primary education for all, while the Endowed School Act of 1869 enabled older foundations, as at Almondbury and Bradford, to change with the times.

In 1885 the college had less than a hundred boys and, when the headmaster resigned that year, the Head of the Collegiate School suggested that the two schools should amalgamate.

Huddersfield Collegiate School in Clare Hill had been built in 1838 as a proprietory[1] school, with an Anglican bias. The headmaster was always a Church of England clergyman, and the Vicar of Huddersfield, Rev. Josiah Bateman, was the first chairman of the school governors. The Collegiate appears to have suffered from a constant change of staff and pupils. It was reported that the masters would not stay because their salaries were inadequate and the boys refused to stay without the masters in whom they had confidence. In 1887, therefore the Collegiate School sold their premises to Mr Alfred Jubb, the printer, for £3,550 and the pupils and staff moved to New North Road to join the new Huddersfield College Company Limited.

After 1887 the School in Clare Hill was, in D. F. E. Sykes' words, 'devoted to lighter arts than seem the groves of Academe' —Sykes was an Old Collegian, who had attended New North Road in the 1860s. In 1891, Mr Jubb erected the Albany Printing Works, in front of the school, which became the Albany Hall, in commemoration of the visit of the Duke of Albany to Huddersfield in 1883. The Hall became associated with the George Hotel and was used for dinners and dances. In 1910 it became a roller skating rink. Then, in 1912, Messrs T. Collinson & Sons took over the lease and used the premises for some of the more distinguished social functions in the town.

The Huddersfield College Company soon ran into difficulties once again and by 1887 the boys in the combined school

[1] Like Huddersfield College, the Collegiate School had its own shareholders or proprietors.

numbered only 103. There were also girls at the school following the amalgamation with the Huddersfield Girls' College.
Competition from free Board schools, improving grammar
schools and good public schools proved too strong for the
college, and the company was wound up in 1893.

We should now examine the reasons for the apparent stability
of King James's Grammar School, Almondbury, at this time.
When Rev. Alfred Easther arrived in 1848 the school had
ceased to follow a grammar school curriculum and was working
to a very low standard. Had there not been an improvement,
the competition from State aided primary schools would
eventually have swept King James's aside. Easther, however,
had the foresight and business sense to make the school appeal
to the middle classes. The curriculum was extended to include
science and modern languages and Easther welcomed the use of
the examinations of the Science and Art Department[1] and the
encouragement given to boys by the Dartmouth Medal and the
Jessup Prize. Easther was fortunate in that the school governors
in 1848 had revised the statutes so as to widen the curriculum
and to restrict the number of free places given to sons of the
poor. He was also fortunate in having the services first of
John Nowell 'th' Aumbrey Witch' and then of George Jarmain, described as 'the outstanding teacher of chemistry in
the north.' Easther was himself very much the new schoolmaster, versatile, humane, informal. He established a sound
boarding system and, in spite of innovations, the closest links
were maintained with the Church. A southerner, Easther did
not always understand the speech of the village boys when he
first arrived; but he made a careful study of the local dialect
and it is his glossary of local terms, many otherwise now lost to
us, which forms the basis of my Appendix VI.

When Easther died in 1876, the Education Act of 1870 was
beginning to take effect and there were many who saw a future
for their children beyond the elementary stage. A rearrange-
ment of the school's income from charities and the provision of
twelve free scholarships were approved in 1881. More boarders

[1] The Science and Art Department of the Board of Trade established in
1853, came under the Education Department of the Committee of Council
when set up in 1856.

St Peter's Gardens were developed in 1952 from the old Parish Church graveyard. On the right can be seen the dignified mid-nineteenth century buildings along Byram Street and an Almondbury trolley bus. From a *Huddersfield Examiner* photograph taken in 1964.

Above: The canal barge horse has slipped quietly out of the local transport scene: here is probably one of the last to use the Ramsden Canal, passing Turnbridge in 1953. *Photo:* W. B. Stocks. *Below:* Buxton Road in 1962, showing property demolished in 1965, and the Marsden trolley bus which last ran in 1963. *Photo:* Roy Brook (Crosland Moor).

arrived so that by 1883 seventy six boys were on the roll at King James's at a time when Huddersfield College was declining. Furthermore, although Almondbury Grammar School continued to teach religious subjects strictly in accordance with the tenets of the Church of England, there was a conscience clause which enabled parents to withdraw their boys from such instruction if they so desired.

The Technical College developed from the Mechanics' Institute which was itself an offshoot of local industry The attitude of employers in the eighteenth century had been that to educate the workers was a course fraught with danger. It was felt that employees would acquire false ideas of their station in life and this view was confirmed by the fate of the aristocracy in the French Revolution. Attitudes were gradually changed by the increasing complexity of factory life as new machinery required more educated workpeople to maintain and operate it, and the employers increasingly supported technical education.

The early nineteenth century saw the gradual rise of educational establishments where working men could improve themselves. The movement spread from Glasgow to London and thence to Manchester, and in Huddersfield, in 1841, a few 'friends to popular education' led by Frederick Schwann a local business man founded a 'Young Men's Mental Improvement Society'. Classes were held in the British School Room at Outcote Bank where numbers grew, in the first year, from 30 to over 100 pupils aged between sixteen and twenty-four. Subjects taught were reading, writing, arithmetic, grammar, geography and drawing. By 1843 there were nearly 200 students; there was a small library, and elocution and singing had been added to the curriculum. Many, remembering the independence of their grandparents before machinery drove them into the factories, must have seen in education an opportunity for advancement. This attitude was clearly reflected in the rapid growth of the Mechanics' Institute, as the Mental Improvement Society was re-named in 1843 when it moved to Nelsons Building in New Street (opposite Marks and Spencers). A year later 400 students thronged the premises, some of whom could scarcely read or write. By 1849 there were 700 students in 52 classes and larger premises were needed again. These were acquired in Wellington Buildings, Queen Street.[1] In 1859, new premises were again specially built, this time in Northumberland Street. When they opened in 1861, there were 780 pupils and a staff of fifty-one teachers of whom only twenty received any payment. The manufacturers, for their part, saw in adult education at this time a means of improving not only their employees but also the products on which they worked. When chemistry was first studied there, in 1843, scope for development in the field of English textiles was quickly noted when comparing the superior quality of dye and colour in the fabrics of our continental competitors with our own.

Although in some parts of the country the Mechanics' Institutes became frequented by middle class students and the working men lost interest in them, this was not so in Yorkshire. In a report for 1859[2] it was stated: 'It is a prevalent opinion that Mechanics' Institutes are so only in name. . . . This is not true of the majority of those in Yorkshire, however it might apply elsewhere. Some of the most flourishing Institutes are composed almost wholly of the labouring class and in most of them they form a considerable majority.' In Huddersfield in 1876, out of 1,000 students, all but 105 were manual workers, and these 105 were clerks and office workers.

From 1861 to 1884 the Northumberland Street Institute developed considerably. Sir Robert Peel contributed to the purchase of books for the library, and a Penny Savings Bank was set up on lines proposed by Sir Charles Sikes. The general standard of work at the Mechanics' Institute was, however, elementary. Large numbers were still having to be taught to read and write.

After 1870, the new Board schools took over the task of educating the masses, and in 1876 the Chamber of Commerce expressed the need for better facilities for technical education.

[1] Still to be seen, facing Queen Street Mission.

[2] Annual Report of the Yorkshire Union of Mechanics' Institutes. Four years previously Richard Dawes, Dean of Hereford, had surveyed the 600 Mechanics' Institutes which existed in 1855. He described the Huddersfield Institute as 'the best in England'.

The Chamber decided against building their own trade school and instead joined with the Institute to establish a technical school. Negotiations were simplified by the fact that Thomas Brooke at one time held the offices of President both of the Chamber and of the Institute. In 1884 classes were transferred from Northumberland Street to the new 'Technical School and Mechanics' Institute' in Queen Street. The name was changed to the Huddersfield Technical College in 1896 and, as the elementary work disappeared with the rising generations who had attended school, science, art and commercial subjects were extended. In 1903 a further extension was carried out to provide additional laboratory and workshop facilities. In the same year the college was taken over by the Corporation and the Governors became a Committee of the Borough Council.

The need for elementary education for adults was also seen by the Society of Friends who had been meeting in Paddock since before 1770. There, in Church Street, they opened an Adult School for men in 1856 and for women in 1862. Many elderly people first learned to read there, from the Bible; and sometimes, laboriously, to write. When we consider the Education Act of 1870 we tend to forget that it applied only to children, and by 1898 the Adult School had outgrown its premises and it was necessary to raise the money for a new extension. A large Sunday School for children was another important aspect of the work of the Quakers at Paddock before the First World War. There is today no school for men but a small remnant of the Women's School still meets.

Elementary schools, the most complicated issue in the nineteenth century educational scene, have been left out of the picture so far. At the time of Incorporation there were thirteen thousand children in Huddersfield. Based on the standards of those days, there were school places in voluntary schools for about eight thousand but the average daily attendance was only four thousand. Thus less than one child in three was receiving a regular education although valuable work was being done by the Sunday Schools. The large numbers of young men attending elementary classes at the Mechanics' Institute require no further explanation.

Education for the working classes had been left almost solely to charitable and religious bodies. The British and Foreign School Society, founded in 1814, developed the ideas of Joseph Lancaster, a Quaker who had successfully run a school for the poor of Southwark. These British Schools were undenominational and in 1811 the Anglicans had formed the National Society for Promoting the Education of the Poor in the Principles of the Established Church. The National Society took over much of the earlier charitable work done by the Society for the Promotion of Christian Knowledge. From the early days of the nineteenth century, therefore, the educational struggle between Church and Chapel showed itself. In Huddersfield, a British School was founded in Outcote Bank and there were National Schools at Seedhill and Northgate.

Highfield Chapel built a Sunday School in 1812—perhaps the first of its kind in our area. Its original intention appears to have been the provision of secular instruction for poor children who received no other form of education. It was stated that no children could be admitted who regularly attended weekday schools and that it would be wrong to 'keep back numbers of poor objects who have no prospect of even being taught to read but at Sunday Schools.' A Huddersfield witness before the House of Commons Committee on the Ten Hours Bill in 1832 quoted a child as saying to him 'Will you get the Ten Hours Bill? We shall have a rare time then; surely somebody will set up a night school; I will learn to write, that I will!' Ramsden Street Chapel set up a most successful night school in 1844. It functioned three evenings a week and over a hundred at a time were taught to read and write by voluntary helpers. Eventually Mr Alfred Jones of the British School was appointed permanent teacher and received payment towards which the scholars were asked to contribute a penny a week. There were at this time many other elementary schools, some of which charged expensive fees and took the sons of the manufacturers, but many other schools were free or nearly so. The success of the National School at Almondbury, opened in 1818, was such that over a hundred children were taken from the outset in spite of a fee of threepence a week.

The Act of 1870 did not give us free, compulsory education; this did not come until 1895. The 1870 measures were a recognition of the fact that the voluntary societies could not adequately educate the whole country. The voluntary bodies were to decide how best to improve their school accommodation and School Boards, with powers to raise money from rates and to build schools, were to fill the gaps left by the old system. The School Boards were empowered to buy land, regulate school fees and, where the Societies could not maintain any schools, the Boards could take over—this encouraged voluntary enterprise. After 1870 the National Society alone provided a million new places in its church schools throughout the country. Religious education was to be undenominational in Board schools and attendance between the ages of five and thirteen was established by local regulations enforced by the School Attendance Officer known locally as the 'Board Man'.

The first School Board for Huddersfield was elected on 6th February 1871. Sykes remarks on the triennial trial of strength between the supporters of sectarian and unsectarian education. 'Up to the present day (1898) the undenominational candidates have always obtained a majority on the Board, the ratepayers being largely tinged with dissent.' The Board met at first in Byram Buildings, Westgate, later in new premises which were opened in Peel Street[1] in 1890 near the Town Hall. (see illustration facing page 106). The Board abolished all fees in its schools in 1891, and following the Act of 1902 the Board came to an end after a most successful career.

The School Board was able to provide ten thousand school places. Several temporary schools were opened in 1872 but the most important period in its history was from 1874 to 1878 when permanent schools were opened at Almondbury, Beaumont Street, Berry Brow, Crosland Moor, Deighton, Hillhouse, Moldgreen, Mount Pleasant, Oakes, and Stile Common: Spring Grove, Paddock and Longwood followed in the next decade. The largest school, Mount Pleasant, had some 1,520 places. By 1895, the annual expenditure on schools had reached £19,000, a rate of almost a shilling in the pound.

St Patrick's Church provided its own Roman Catholic school,

---

[1] Demolished in 1967 for the 'Murrayfield' re-development and New Market Hall.

and a further twenty-two 'Church' schools, one alongside nearly every parish church, were in existence by the end of the century, accommodating another 6,000 children and maintained largely by private subscription. Thus, if it had not been for religious separation, the burden on the School Board would have been far greater.

Before closing this chapter let us return to Huddersfield College and King James's Grammar School. The College ended its career as a private school when it closed its doors in 1893. The School Board purchased the buildings in New North Road for £5,000 and, after spending another £4,000 on internal improvements, the premises were re-opened in 1894 as a Higher Grade School for some 420 boys and girls. The school also served as a pupil teacher centre until 1904 when this function was transferred to the Technical College. The Higher Grade was available as a crown to the elementary school system, but numbers dwindled in the higher classes and, already, Huddersfield had lost its secondary school when the original College had closed. The Bryce Commission of 1895 contained the comment that beyond the Higher Grade School, the day school of the Technical College, and one or two small private schools there was nothing: 'There are three small grammar schools with endowments, just outside the town (Fartown, Longwood and Almondbury) but these are rather too far away to be of much practical use in supplying the wants of the town itself.' The report criticised the town for allowing the College to close in 1893. The reason for the failure of the outlying grammar schools to fulfil the need for secondary education cannot properly be given as distance, for the town was at this period well served by steam trams. Certainly King James's could have taken more pupils, but it was lack of support which produced the series of financial crises there in the 1890s. The conscience clause of 1881 and the appointment of lay headmasters from 1897 might have helped attract the non-Anglicans to the school, but there was a general feeling that education should be free and without solid financial backing this was out of the question at Almondbury—except for the twelve free places authorised in 1881.

In 1902 the Corporation became the Local Education

Authority for all elementary, secondary and technical education within the Borough. Robert Crump, headmaster at King James's, saw in this situation the means of salvation for his school. It seemed to him natural that the new authority should maintain the old grammar school and pay off the mounting overdraft. If, on the other hand, there were to be competition from a rate-aided grammar school in the town, then Almondbury would be forced to close down. The school did survive; but the problems of its survival were not to be solved immediately.

CHAPTER XIV

To the Early Twentieth Century

OUR NARRATIVE so far has taken us up to about the year 1900 in most fields of municipal enterprise. In the story of wool textiles and chemicals we paused somewhat earlier than this. It is now necessary to pick up these threads and to trace the origins of that diversification of industry which has proved such a blessing to the town in the present century.

In the mid-nineteenth century, Huddersfield was almost exclusively a textile town. Today, textiles employ about a third of the labour force. Mechanical and electrical engineering, the second largest manufacturing industry, takes about one sixth, while the chemical industry, the third largest, employs one person in twenty. Below these three in size can be seen almost every type of productive activity ranging from building to bookbinding, food manufacture to furniture making. Consequently, Huddersfield has never suffered unemployment to the same extent as some other areas, where one major industry has employed virtually all the workers.

Within the wool textile industry every type and quality of work has come to our town within the last hundred years. Local firms have benefited from every innovation including the popularity of tweeds and ready-made clothing. Furthermore they responded to the introduction of electric power during the present century. The growth of population and the rise in living standards throughout the country brought increasing prosperity and expansion to the entire textile industry which thus had the necessary resources to clothe most of the Allied armies during the First World War. Evidence of the prosperity of the late Victorian era can still be seen in the homes of the earlier textile magnates at Edgerton, where coats of arms still adorn the doorway of many a mansion built in the Gothic, Roman or

Italianate style. Many of these houses are now divided into flats or have been taken over for public uses, while the descendants of some of the men who built them live today, within sports-car distance of their mills.

Textiles during this period had their share of troubles. In 1883, the weavers struck for nearly three months against a new scale of wages. In 1890, the United States' imposition of the McKinley Tariff caused the total export of cloth to fall by more than two-thirds, a blow from which the textile trade recovered slowly but surely during the early years of the present century. Again, after 1918 following a sudden drop in demand, wool prices fell and so did the price of cloth; by 1921 over half the textile workers in the town were unemployed and it was not until the thirties that the trade slowly began to recover.

Chemicals, as we have seen, had a direct link with the basic textile industry, and in 1889, the year in which Read Holliday died, Joseph Turner became chief chemist at Turnbridge. Turner had started work at Hollidays as a boy of twelve and by his own determination attained this key position in the most important chemical business in the town. Joseph and his brother James Turner took out in 1895 Holliday's first patent in the field of sulphur colours, and at this time the firm began to manufacture their own sulphuric, nitric and hydrochloric acids and to enter the field of dyes for cotton fabrics. When Thomas Holliday died in 1898, Joseph Turner joined the Board of Directors. Meanwhile, the firm expanded in America and Europe. In 1899 a picric acid plant was installed and a large Government contract for lyddite followed. This process in turn led the firm to enter the field of synthetic drugs and by 1901, Joseph Turner was Chairman of the company.

Read Hollidays, still at Turnbridge, were extremely prosperous. They had their own source of coal, their own transport section for bulk tankers and had agents and contracts all over the world. Hollidays, however, were not completely self-sufficient in that they relied on importing certain intermediate materials from Germany, as the Germans could make them cheaper than we could. It had been policy therefore to leave Germany to explore some fields of research and to buy from there what we needed. The outbreak of war in August 1914 changed the picture overnight and a national effort was needed to break the German stranglehold on our chemical industry.

In 1915 with Government encouragement to organise a more effective chemical industry an amalgamation was brought about between Read Hollidays and Levinsteins of Manchester under the name, British Dyes Ltd. with Joseph Turner and Dr Levinstein as joint managing directors. A large expansion at Huddersfield on the site between Dalton and Leeds Road[1] was constructed by Sir Robert McAlpines. It was largely devoted to the production of explosives and their basic materials. British Dyes produced eleven million tons of T.N.T. without the loss of a single life.

At the end of the war further reorganisation resulted in the British Dyestuffs Corporation and with Joseph Turner as its managing director, intended to match the powerful resurgent German dyestuffs industry. The Dyestuffs Act which prohibited the importation of any foreign dye, irrespective of price, which could be matched by a British product, fostered the growth of the Corporation. A further amalgamation in 1926 of the Corporation with Brunner Mond, Nobell Industries and United Alkali, resulted in the giant I.C.I. of today.

At the Peace Conference in 1919, Joseph Turner was employed as technical adviser to the British Government and he also advised the Board of Trade on the importation of dyes and chemicals for the future. For these services to the country he was knighted in 1920. Shortly afterwards Sir Joseph left British Dyestuffs to found his own business. He died in 1939.

In 1914 Major Lionel B. Holliday, grandson of Read Holliday, went to France with his regiment. By the end of the following year he was back in Huddersfield setting up a new plant at Deighton for the urgent manufacture of picric acid. So, between August and December 1915, L. B. Hollidays was built as a mushroom development which in its first year produced up to 100 tons[2] of picric acid per week. The acid was conveyed to the Royal Arsenal at Woolwich every night by special train.

---

[1] The site on Leeds Road had housed the Great Yorkshire Show in 1904.
[2] At the rate of four ounces per shell, Hollidays made enough picric for about a million shells a week.

After the war Hollidays returned to their original field of dye-stuffs, with a large export business.

Chemicals have been shown as originally having close connections with wool textiles. In the case of engineering the link with textiles is not quite so obvious since the makers of machinery in Huddersfield have always been few in number. John Haigh founded his family business in 1835 and, ever since, Priest Royd Ironworks have made machinery for opening and cleaning wool, and carding engines for the manufacture of woollen and worsted yarn. This machinery is substantial, made to last and is supplied by Haighs all over the world. It is a far cry from the hand cards used for the same purpose by the early cottage clothiers. Founded over a century ago, William Whiteleys of Lockwood became world famous especially for the manufacture of spinning mules and tentering machines which stretch and dry cloth. They were 'taken over' and the manufacture of textile machinery ceased in 1962. Sellers and Company make finishing machinery and specialise in cutting machines, the descendants of the shearing frame illustrated on page 72. Worsted machinery which is more akin to that used for cotton is mainly made on the other side of the Pennines. Although only a small proportion of engineers in Huddersfield today work directly on textile machinery, almost all engineering in the town has had some connection with the original staple industry.

Thomas Broadbent commenced business on his own as a millwright in 1864. Six years later, he made his first centrifugal extractor of water from wool. The machine was such a success that all the local mills became interested in its possibilities. In 1875 Broadbent took out a patent for the first hydro-extractor driven by a steam engine and in 1890 these machines were in use not only in textile mills but also in dyehouses, laundries, sugar refineries and chemical works. Although Thomas Broadbent died in 1880 his firm continued to branch out into a number of engineering fields. Large steam engines were built to drive the mill machinery and when a large overhead crane was necessary in 1892, for moving heavy foundry castings, Broadbents made their own and so developed a new line of business which itself led to the production of other pieces of foundry equipment.

The rise and development of Broadbents closely resembled that of Hopkinsons. Joseph Hopkinson started in a small way in 1843, making fittings for steam engines and boilers used in textile mills. His brother William, believed to be resident engineer at Bay Hall Mills, made a study of steam power and its problems and, although we know little about the background of the two men, it would appear that together they had acquired a technical knowledge of this field which was quite exceptional. In the 1840s, mill engines were generally maintained by men who had little or no training and boiler accidents were commonplace. The early days of the Mechanics' Institute were devoted to basic education, and technical training was as yet unheard of. In these circumstances Joseph Hopkinson, a man of enterprise, saw for himself a future in manufacturing boiler mountings designed to be safe, efficient and foolproof and so save human lives and reduce production costs at the same time. Hopkinsons soon converted two cottages off Lockwood Road into a workshop where they earned a reputation for reliable hand-made products. The large mills which were built in the forties and fifties provided Joseph Hopkinson with a ready market. Larger machines required increased power and this increased the possible danger to power-house personnel. By 1853, Hopkinson had patented the compound Safety Valve.[1] Difficult to interfere with, it was an outstanding success in the prevention of boiler explosions. Joseph Hopkinson is perhaps best remembered, in the mechanical engineering world at any rate, for his book, *Hopkinson on the Indicator*. The Hopkinson cylinder pressure indicator for measuring the power and performance of steam engines had appeared in about 1854 and the book, which became the working manual for many engineers, ran into many editions. The firm was continued by the founder's sons John Addy and Joseph Hopkinson. The title page of the seventh edition of the 'Manual' in 1875 runs as follows: 'The engineer's practical guide and the working of the steam engine explained by the use of the indicator. What the stethoscope is to the physician, the indicator is to the skilful engineer revealing the secret working of the inner

[1] A version of this valve is still in use on Lancashire type boilers.

system and detecting minute derangements in parts obscurely situate.' Using the indicator, it was possible for an engine's performance to be reproduced graphically, and Hopkinson's book makes a thorough analysis of these indicator diagrams in the light of the vast experience acquired by the firm in this field. Hopkinson also realised that an efficient engine would lead to fuel economy and his advertisements drew attention to this.

In 1871 the firm moved to a larger works near Viaduct Street. More patents followed, including a safe steam-pressure gauge and, in 1881 came the Hopkinson Parallel-Slide Valve for pipe lines, which was to influence the future design of all similar valves. In 1904 the Britannia Works were opened at Birkby, laid out, under the direction of Robert Addy Hopkinson, the founder's grandson, so as to be capable of further extension. The firm's activities have expanded into electrical valve control and their electrically operated valves have been fitted in power generating stations all over the world, including Russia.

The firm of W. C. Holmes has no obvious link with the textile industry. In 1800 there was an iron foundry at Engine Bridge, Chapel Hill, owned by Holmes and Price, and no doubt some part of their business was the repair of machinery. In the 1830s W. C. Holmes had an ironmonger's shop at 10 Buxton Road. There, orders were taken for kitchen stoves, fireplaces, cast-iron fenders, coal scuttles, fire irons and iron bedsteads. Besides these articles, probably made at Engine Bridge just down the hill, Holmes were agents for the sale of cutlery, tools and nails and screws. Gas manufacture was booming at this period, and about 1845 the Holmes brothers made small gas plants for private houses. In 1853, W. C. Holmes (1827–82), son of the first W. C. Holmes, took out the first of a series of patents for 'Improvement in the Manufacture of gas and apparatus employed therein.' His enterprise was such that he advertised that 'Messrs. W. C. Holmes and Co., are prepared to assist in the establishment of gas works in any town or village, which after inspection, they know will return a fair dividend upon the outlay, by providing a portion of the required capital.' Over 300 installations were carried out over the next twenty-five years. They were made at Holmes' ironworks at Hillhouse on the site of the present railway sidings.

In 1880 the firm moved to Turnbridge where they specialised in larger gas installations. They also built a few iron bridges. Perhaps their most unusual product was the pie dish used at Denby Dale in 1887 which weighed about two and a quarter tons. As the gas industry entered the field of recovering by-products, so Holmes' made the necessary plant and their equipment is in use today all over the world.

Ernest Brook at the turn of the century was working for an electrical firm making D.C. (direct current) machinery. There was little enthusiasm for alternating current although the Huddersfield electricity supply was A.C. He therefore branched out on his own in 1904 with two assistants in a room in Threadneedle Street. There they made single-phase electric motors. Ernest Brook's originality and determination is reflected in his publicity: 'Electricity has come to stay, and the man who tells you that it is still in its infancy perhaps understands stonebreaking but not our trade ... We will place you electrical machinery in firey mines, deep wells, on roofs, walls or any position with or without foundations ... Ask yourself is there any other class of motive power that you can do the same with? We want you to recognise that electric motors have come to stay ... the most efficient power in the world.' Brook's catalogue went on to give details of electric motor sizes for specific tasks; he says: 'Motor driving is our speciality. How does $\frac{1}{4}$ h.p. per loom strike you?' Clearly Ernest Brook saw the possibilities for his products in textile mills from his earliest days. His beliefs were justified, for in 1916 E. Brook Limited built the Empress Works where up to 800 motors per week were produced. By 1933 100,000 motors had been made by the firm. But Ernest Brook looked still further ahead and, by taking the front page of the *Daily Mail* for a series of full-page advertisements in 1936, he obtained the publicity and the markets he sought. In November 1950 the millionth motor came off the production line, an event celebrated by all the 2,000 employees of the company.

David Brown began making wood patterns in partnership with Thomas Broadbent, who ran a foundry, in 1860. These patterns were for the moulds in which Broadbent cast iron gear wheels. The two worked together as 'Brown and Broadbent' until David Brown moved to new premises and Thomas Broadbent in 1864 founded his own business. Brown, determined to make his way in the world, soon began to manufacture his own gears. In 1873 we find him advertising as 'General Patternmaker and Manufacturer of all kinds of Spur, Skew, Bevel and Eccentric Gear.' Brown's business grew, but slowly, and by 1890 he had only ten employees. Then, in 1895, there was a serious fire. But David Brown, now joined by his sons Ernest, Frank and Percy, worked hard for long hours and business began to expand into the field of machine-cut gears. The family moved to Park Cottage near Lockwood and in a far corner of their estate they built a small factory. In 1902 the gear-cutting machinery was moved into Park Works where a new company was formed. The pattern-making side remained at the old works in East Parade. Frank Brown became the driving force behind the new factory where the firm had branched out into making motor-cars for a while. The First World War caused Browns to expand to five times their size in 1914 as gears were needed for shipbuilding.

Sir David Brown,[1] the present Chairman and Managing Director of the David Brown Corporation is the son of Frank Brown. When he entered the firm in 1921 about a thousand men were employed at Park Works. The Corporation ultimately expanded to employ 10,000 workers in fourteen factories in different parts of Britain besides controlling several overseas companies. The first David Brown tractor was shown to the public as recently as July 1939. Production currently runs at about 500 tractors per week. A large proportion are exported, even into the competitive American market.

Sir David, a motoring enthusiast from his youth, acquired the famous Aston Martin and Lagonda car firms and was so successful in their development that his Aston Martin entries won the great Le Mans road race in 1959.

Huddersfield up to 1900 had been a textile town where work was more plentiful for women than for men. The growth of the large engineering firms and the birth of many smaller ones changed the picture. The new enterprises were a bonus to the

[1] Knighted in New Years Honours List 1968.

prosperity of the town and influenced the population growth from 95,000 in 1901 to 108,000 in 1911. There were also smaller industries which added to the diversification and the *Huddersfield Examiner* mentioned them in a commemorative article in 1928. Some of these no longer exist. The list included Wallaces, 'the largest jam factory in Yorkshire'; Benjamin Crooks where a quarter of a million footballs were made in a year; Lockwood Breweries, now no longer in production; a firm of cigar manufacturers; a rope walk; a firm of organ builders; a firework factory at Crosland Hill and a large wholesale clothing industry near the town centre. Several printers and bookbinders completed the picture.

In the field of national politics the Labour Party came into increasing prominence following the election of 1895 at which they put up a candidate in Huddersfield for the first time. In an industrial area such as Huddersfield one might have expected some substantial support for Labour and in January 1906 the Party came second in a three-cornered fight.

If we compare this with the results for 1900,[1] and allowing for the increase in the number of votes cast, it is clear that Labour had taken votes from the other two parties. The following November the picture was similar except that the Liberal majority was again reduced.

January 1906		*November 1906*[2]	
Woodhouse (L)	6,302	Sherwell (L)	5,762
Williams (Lab.)	5,813	Williams (Lab.)	5,422
Fraser (C)	4,391	Fraser (C)	4,844

In 1910 there were two elections, brought about by the Parliamentary crisis of that year. In the country as a whole the Liberal vote was considerably reduced yet in January 1910 Sherwell actually increased his lead and, although the December result showed a slight fall in the Liberal lead, the Labour candidate, Harry Snell, dropped from second to third place:

[1] See p. 193.
[2] By-election caused by appointment of Sir James Woodhouse as Commissioner of Railways.

January 1910		*December 1910*	
Sherwell (L)	7,158	Sherwell (L)	6,458
Snell (Lab.)	5,686	Kaye (C)	5,777
Smith (C)	5,153	Snell (Lab.)	4,988

Joseph Kaye was a strong local candidate and his result shows the effect of this on the Huddersfield electorate. Looking at Harry Snell's election address for January 1910, it would appear that his was a policy far too sweeping for the comparatively prosperous workers of Huddersfield. He mentions the millions on the verge of starvation in the country and then refers to a Parliament full of capitalists, but capitalism was doing very well for the town and providing plenty of work. Snell also said he would support the abolition of the House of Lords—a sentiment one suspects difficult for the citizens of Huddersfield to appreciate—indeed, their knowledge of the Lords would be slight and Westminster was a long way from Huddersfield. Mr Snell was a Free Trader, but so were the Liberals, therefore the town re-elected Mr Sherwell.

After the war there was an immediate General Election with an increased franchise, the vote having been given to women over thirty. Sir Charles Sykes was returned as a Coalition and Lloyd George Liberal; with Conservative support the Coalition Party swept the country and the Asquith Liberals were hopelessly defeated. In Huddersfield the national picture was only weakly reflected; Ernest Woodhead polled a large number of votes and Sir Charles Sykes' victory was hardly a landslide. The electors were not strongly inclined to follow the rest of the country.

December 1918

Sykes (Coalition Liberal)	15,234
Snell (Labour)	12,737
Woodhead (Independent Liberal)	11,256

By 1922 the three parties were almost equal. Although Sir Charles Sykes polled a similar number of votes to those cast in 1918. James Hindle Hudson increased the Labour vote but the Asquith Liberal candidate, Sir Arthur Marshall, was elected by a narrow majority.

1922

Marshall (L)	15,879
Hudson (Lab.)	15,673
Sykes (Nat. Lib.)	15,212

In the following year the Liberal factions united and the Conservative candidate came bottom of the poll. Labour gained fifty seats in the whole country including Huddersfield for the first time ever, but by a majority of only twenty-six. Hudson advocated a programme of work for the unemployed, reduced taxation and measures to abolish wars. The town was counting the cost of the war now that trade had slackened off and the Labour programme therefore had greater popular appeal. For three elections in a row Huddersfield favoured the Labour candidate:

1923		1924	
Hudson (Lab.)	17,430	Hudson (Lab.)	19,010
Marshall (L)	17,404	Hill (C)	16,745
Tinker (C)	12,694	Marshall (L)	16,626

1929

Hudson (Lab.)	25,966
Marshall (L)	21,398
Hill (C)	20,361

The electorate increased substantially under the Act of 1928 giving all women the vote. In Huddersfield nearly 15,000 'Flappers', aged twenty-one to thirty, were added to the electoral roll and there were now more women voters than men.

By 1931 unemployment in Great Britain had reached 21 per cent.[1] and a national crisis was met by the formation of a Coalition Government of all parties. In Huddersfield the Conservative candidate stood down to give William Mabane a big majority.

Mabane (Nat. Lib.)	47,056
Hudson (Lab.)	20,034

In 1935 Mabane was re-elected with a reduced majority as

---

[1] 26 per cent. in Huddersfield in July 1931.

the Labour Party under Clement Attlee made gains throughout the country and these were reflected locally.

| Mabane (Nat. Lib.) | 37,009 |
| William Pickles (Lab.) | 23,844 |

This was to be the last election until 1945 with the result that William Mabane represented Huddersfield for fourteen years.

We return to the activities of the Council. During the present century the Borough was increased in size: in 1913 Lindley Recreation Ground was added and in 1938 a part of South Crosland, but the largest extension came in 1937 when Huddersfield gained 1,317 acres in Golcar, Linthwaite, Kirkheaton, Lepton, Stainland and Fixby.

In 1920 the Corporation purchased the Ramsden Estate thus becoming its own Lord of the Manor and severing the connection between Huddersfield and the Ramsden family which had lasted over 300 years. The actual purchase was one of the largest financial transactions negotiated by a borough council up to that time. When it became known in 1919 that Sir John was considering selling his estate, negotiations were quickly opened on behalf of the Council by the Mayor, Alderman Carmi Smith, Alderman Ernest Woodhead, Chairman of the Finance Committee and Alderman Wilfrid Dawson.

It was necessary to obtain Parliamentary powers to carry out such a transaction and this entailed some delay. In order to overcome this problem, a Mr S. W. Copley, a native of Berry Brow and a London banker, acted as intermediary. He undertook responsibility for the purchase, carried out the deal, and held the estate pending the passing of the necessary Act.

The purchase price was £1,300,000 and the Treasury, through the Goschen Committee, advised the Corporation to raise the money by making an issue of six-per-cent stock to be repaid over the next thirty years. Ernest Woodhead and Wilfrid Dawson, however, thought otherwise, and the money was, in fact, raised by a short-term loan within forty-eight hours. This loan was then replaced by a larger loan on better terms. During the following two years, rates-in-aid were necessary but within three years the income from the Estate met the annual loan charges. The Council thus became its own landlord by a stroke of Alderman Woolven's[1] pen. A transaction of this magnitude did not go through without its moment of drama for, just as the final signature was about to be made by the Mayor, the lights went out; a coal strike had caused a power cut. The deal was completed by candle light and Alderman Woolven was afterwards able to declare that he had borrowed a cool million and a quarter in the dark!

If the acquisition of the Estate was, in its day, the highlight of municipal enterprise, most other activities, though less costly, were more obvious to the citizens as they affected their means of transport, the education of their children and, for many, the provision of a home.

On 25th February 1899 the Tramways Committee decided to electrify their entire system and to build a power station and depot for thirty cars at Longroyd Bridge. The gauge of 4 ft. 8½ in. used for steam trams was to be continued. The only major difficulty was that, later on, it was never possible to link the system with the Halifax or Bradford tramways because each had a different width of track. In Lancashire most trams ran on one gauge and it was possible to travel from Mossley to Liverpool on the one track.

The Huddersfield electric trams were first run to Outlane, Lindley Circular,[2] Slaithwaite, Longwood and Crosland Moor. The new cars were in vermilion and cream and bore the words 'Huddersfield Corporation Electric Tramways'. The first of the new trams ran to Lindley and Outlane on 14th February 1901 and within the following fortnight the other scheduled routes were in use.

Steam cars still served the rest of the town and in fact a new line was opened to Sheepridge in April 1901 with alternative trams via Birkby and Bradford Road. In June of the same year trams were permitted to run on Sundays but they were not allowed to pass the Parish Church during times of public worship; consequently the Almondbury and Waterloo routes used the single track in King Street, for travel in both directions to avoid making a noise in Kirkgate. The drivers of the new

[1] Mayor, 1919–21.
[2] Via Holly Bank Road and Edgerton.

electric trams, being exposed to the public eye, were asked to wear their best suits on Sundays. In August 1901 the line along the Meltham Road to Beaumont Park was taken up and sold for scrap.

The electrification of the remaining steam services was carried out in 1902. The line to Honley was extended from Berry Brow and run by steam temporarily until June of that year. The Birkby route, circular via Bradford Road, opened in the same month. The electrification of the Bradley route in July 1902 completed the scheme, and the steam trams were sold. One tramcar body was used until quite recently as a tennis club shelter at Newsome. With the new system came more frequent services and, for the first time, the use of printed tickets for each route. All the cars carried a telephone handset which could be plugged into boxes, placed every half mile along the routes, in the event of emergency.

Once the system was established, modifications and improvements were carried out. The last of the steam trams had covered-in upper decks but the new electric cars were open topped. Many of them were eventually covered over, though the driver still had to brave the elements. Shortly after its opening, the Birkby route ceased to be a circular and in 1911 the Edgerton circular line was discontinued. The first extension was made in 1904 when Longwood cars were terminated at the 'Rose and Crown', having previously turned round at Quarmby Clough. In September 1904 the tramways began to carry coal from Hillhouse sidings to some of the mills at Oakes and Outlane. Through services were introduced in 1907 for Longwood to Birkby, Outlane and Lindley to Waterloo, Edgerton to Almondbury and Slaithwaite to Bradley. Only the Crosland Moor and Newsome routes then used St George's Square as their terminus. The Crosland Moor line was extended to Dryclough Road in 1907, and the line from Stile Common to Newsome Church was completed in 1911. With the ending of the Edgerton circular came an extension to Birchencliffe in 1911. In 1912 a Huddersfield tram was altered to become one of the very first totally enclosed vehicles in the world. Parliamentary powers were obtained in 1912 for extensions to Brighouse, Elland and Marsden, all of which materialised,

and to Mirfield, Crosland Hill and Kirkheaton, none of which
came to pass. In January 1914 the first tramcar reached Elland
and the line was continued to West Vale to meet, but not join,
the Halifax system later in that year. In October 1914 the
trams reached Marsden completing a ten-mile route from
Bradley. The *Colne Valley Guardian*[1] describes the extent of the
'tramcar mania' which swept the Valley at that time. 'On
Sunday every car was crowded and many had to ... use
Shanks's pony as the cars were insufficient to carry anything like
the number of would-be passengers. One car alone took £18
in spite of the fact that the cars were running every seven
minutes instead of the scheduled time of fifteen minutes, and
at every stopping place many disappointed passengers were left
behind.' The Marsden route was most popular with those who
were to walk up the Wessenden Valley or tramp the moors. It
gave Huddersfield an outlet and, for the children, the penny
'scholar's return' ticket is something I shall always remember
from my own school holidays.

By the end of 1914 the system had almost reached its fullest
extent and in 1915 route numbers appeared—

1 Lindley/Waterloo.	6 Crosland Moor/
2 Newsome/St George's	St George's Square.
Square.	7 West Vale/Almondbury.
3 Outlane/Waterloo.	8 Longwood/Birkby.
4 Marsden/Bradley.	10 Honley/Sheepridge.

Number 5 was said to be reserved for a possible re-opening of
the Edgerton circular while 9 was for a proposed line to
Brighouse. It was at one time hoped that trams would run from
Honley to Holmfirth. However in 1920 the Urban District
Council decided against the project for fear that, once trams ran
through from Huddersfield, the Borough would extend its
boundary and swallow up Holmfirth.

After the war the tramways discontinued the use of their own
power station and purchased electricity from the Corporation
supply. The old generating plant at Longroyd Bridge was finally
demolished in 1936 to extend the tram depot. At this period,
also, the practice of carrying outside advertisements on public

[1] 9th October 1914.

transport was discontinued. In 1920 the Longwood route was extended to Dod Lea and in 1921 Longroyd Bridge became the principal depot for all trams, Great Northern Street being reserved for overhaul and repairs. In 1922 the Corporation Gas Department commenced running its own railway from Newtown Yard to Leeds Road. The line had no connection with the tramways except where the lines crossed, and continued in use up to 1966.

Before the war, the Corporation had promised to build a line to Brighouse and it was originally intended to follow the main Bradford road. Had this been done, however, the village of Rastrick would have been isolated. This raised a problem however in that there were no roads in Fixby suitable for tramway operation—Lightridge Road was too steep and Bradley Road had not then been constructed. This is why a private tram line, running on wooden sleepers like a railway, had to be made through the open country from New Inn to Fixby. The new route, numbered 9, was the last to be opened and the service commenced on 12th March 1923 when all the fares taken on the first day were given to local charities. At Brighouse the narrow-gauge Halifax system was met and by going as far as Bailiff Bridge on this line one could there take a tram to Bradford. Brighouse trams entered Town up Viaduct Street and, turning down Northumberland Street, completed their circle.

New tramcars purchased at this period were of the all-enclosed type and some of the older ones were improved by enclosing the driver's cab. The last word in tramcar design came to Huddersfield when six new models arrived in the summer of 1931; built to the requirements of Mr Blackburn, the General Manager, they were superior to anything previously seen. They compared favourably with the trolley buses which were to replace them and were found to be so fast that they were generally confined to the Marsden–Bradley route. With domed roof and upholstered seating, they were painted light red and cream, and gradually most of the older cars were re-painted to match. The system was now at its height with 140 trams in operation over thirty-nine miles of track. Brighouse had an off-peak frequency of twenty minutes but most other routes had a service every ten minutes—often less.

In the early thirties came proposals for introducing trolley buses. A new housing estate at Lowerhouses seemed to require a new route and possibly a new service. Eventually it was decided to serve the Lowerhouses area using motor buses and, by way of an experiment, to convert the Almondbury tram route to trolley buses. Trolley buses first appeared on the Almondbury route on 4th December 1933, the six new vehicles being all of different types to enable the Committee decide on the best design to meet future requirements. Meanwhile Trinity Street and Westbourne Road were to be widened and reconstructed. It was found cheaper to convert the Lindley and Outlane routes to trolley buses than to replace the entire tram track. The conversion did however result in the end of the transport of coal to mills at Outlane. The Outlane, Lindley–Waterloo trolley buses appeared on 11th November 1934 and the tramway in King Street was abandoned.

The final decision to replace all remaining trams by trolley buses was taken in April 1935. In June 1936 the name 'Huddersfield Corporation Passenger Transport Department' appeared for the first time and in December 1936 there appeared the first trolley bus which was to become the standard vehicle for the town. It was the first vehicle to have the streamlined cream front and had been exhibited at the Motor Show of that year.

From 1937 to 1940 all the remaining tram routes were replaced. The newest tramcars were sold to Sunderland in 1938 and by 1940 there were 140 trolley vehicles on the road. The conversion of the Honley route was not found to be possible owing to the low stone railway arch over Woodhead Road at Lockwood. After considering single-deck trolley buses it was decided to convert the route to motor buses and the last tram ran to Honley in February 1939. The Newsome route was extended to Berry Brow and trolley buses ran there from May 1937, in which year trolley buses reached Birkby and Crosland Moor. In 1938 they reached Bradley, Marsden and Sheepridge; in 1939 the West Vale and Longwood routes were converted, and finally the Brighouse route changed over on 30th June 1940. The last tram from Brighouse left at 11 p.m. on 29th June 1940, in the wartime 'blackout', carrying the Mayor and Corporation officials. Autographed tickets were sold in aid of the Mayor's Comforts Fund for Huddersfield Servicemen and the proceedings ended with refreshments at the tramway offices.

Thus ended an era in the life of the town. The trams were in their day a profitable asset, contributing thousands of pounds to the relief of rates. The service had been cheap and reliable in all kinds of weather, but track maintenance had proved expensive. However, the trams had been essential when the town was growing rapidly and industry developing. Workers in their thousands had to be conveyed to British Dyes, Browns and Hopkinsons from all parts of the town and its surrounding areas. It might be said without exaggeration that without its efficient tramways Huddersfield could not have progressed in the way that it did.

Of the other local enterprises of the early part of this century only a few can be mentioned. Huddersfield's efforts during the First World War were crowned by the provision of a military hospital at Royds Hall. Royds Hall Estate was originally acquired for housing purposes and the mansion was first used in October 1914 for the reception of Belgian war refugees. By the middle of 1915 a voluntary committee had conceived the idea of building an emergency hospital in the grounds. The project was completed within three months and handed over to the Army on 4th October 1915. Accommodation for 600 patients was provided and the nursing staff were housed in the mansion. The scheme cost over £30,000 raised by local subscription and by the end of the war 17,200 soldiers had received treatment there.

In 1919 Legh Tolson presented to the Borough Ravensknowle Hall and six acres of ground in memory of his two sons who had died in the First World War. The Corporation undertook to develop this gift as the Tolson Memorial Museum and it was opened on 14th May 1921. The house and grounds contain features illustrating nearly every aspect of our local history. There is an interesting collection of textile exhibits within, while outside are to be seen part of the Roman camp at Slack, found in 1824, and the bell tower from the old Cloth Hall. The museum has been an invaluable source of material used in the compilation of this book (*see photograph facing page 106*).

The Municipal Library in Church Street had proved too small almost from its inception. In 1929 the Council decided that the site of the Cloth Hall was to be reserved for the new Central Library and in January 1931 negotiations involving the widening of Market Street were commenced but, before the year was out, the Cloth Hall site had been leased for the erection of the Ritz Cinema and the Library project was shelved. Eventually in 1934 Ramsden Street Chapel was sold privately to the Corporation and plans were put in hand for the building of the present library. The premises were completed in 1940 at a cost of over £100,000 but the building was not fully used as a library and art gallery until 1945. The library stands back from the street and is enhanced by a broad flight of steps. There are seated figures on either side of the entrance symbolising Literature and Art listening to the whispering voices of Inspiration; their design was a source of much controversy when first erected but they are now an accepted part of the Huddersfield scene.

In May 1938 the Corporation opened its new Electricity Showrooms and offices in Market Street, visible evidence of the progress and enterprise of the Electricity Department during this century. Extensions to generating plant, in 1913, 1928 and 1938, had increased output five-fold during these twenty-five years. In 1934, an incinerator was installed whereby steam raised by the burning of the town's refuse indirectly generated electricity. At the opening ceremony for the new showrooms it was disclosed that in 1936 four out of every five homes in the Borough were supplied with electricity and the average consumption was nearly one and a half times the national average. Nearly all industrial firms were using electricity by the thirties and in very few places was it obtainable so cheaply as in Huddersfield, yet another reason for the town's comparative prosperity in the period before the last war. Power was so cheap that most firms now found it uneconomical to generate their own.

In tracing the development of education within the Borough, one can see the tremendous activity of the early School Boards followed by a period of comparative standstill which has necessitated a spate of new development within the past thirty years. Progress has been uneven and we must examine the reasons for this.

By the turn of the century, thirty years after the Education Act of 1870, it was clear that there was a need for an expansion of secondary education. This had hitherto been in the hands of ancient foundations as at Almondbury and the more recent proprietary schools. However, Huddersfield College was by then not strictly a secondary school and the children who stayed on in the top classes were few in number. Under the new Act of 1902 the Borough Council replaced the School Board as the local Education Authority and received the power to provide secondary schools, subsidised out of the rates. Fees were charged at the Council's secondary schools but in Huddersfield it was not long before all children entering had to pass a qualifying examination in which those awarded a 'special place' paid a contribution based on the parents' income. This was the beginning of the 'eleven plus' system but it was to the credit of the Huddersfield Authority that no bright child was debarred from attending a secondary school because the parents were poor. In 1902, 'College Higher Grade' appeared listed as an elementary school, thus there was at first no secondary provision in the town centre at all.

The Corporation, therefore, in 1904, invited Professor Michael Sadler to survey secondary education in Huddersfield and to make recommendations. He remarked, 'for many years the Huddersfield College and the Huddersfield Collegiate School did excellent work. Measured by the standards of the time, the former especially was a vigorous and effective institution. During the course of my enquiry I have been led increasingly to regret the unhappy combination of circumstances which led to its disappearance.' When he visited Almondbury Grammar School he wrote: 'It stands on a hillside overlooking a well wooded valley of great natural beauty ... As it stands, the school could easily accommodate 80 to 100 boys of whom 20 might be boarders. . . . Hardly any boys remain beyond their sixteenth year and no connection has yet been established with any place of higher education.' When he had seen the grammar schools at Longwood and Fartown and the Day School of Science at the Technical College, Sadler made his recommendations:

1. The development of Almondbury Grammar School into a first-rate secondary school for boys, open to all boys of promise.

2. To establish a High School for all girls of talent throughout the Borough.

3. When these schools have been well established, and a second higher grade elementary school has been set up, the College Higher Grade should develop naturally from higher grade to secondary. In the meantime, the school should receive better equipment and teaching staff.

Although these ideas were generally approved by the Huddersfield Teachers' Association, there was opposition to the intention of giving the town's ancient grammar school a monopoly of boys' education. Consequently, although Almondbury Grammar School would receive grants from the Local Authority, on 1st August 1907 the Higher Grade School became the College Municipal Secondary School for boys and girls. In 1909 the girls were transferred to the new Municipal High School for girls at Greenhead.

A new higher grade school at Hillhouse was built in 1909 in the playground of the existing elementary school and Mr Montgomery, the headmaster, was transferred there from the College Higher Grade. The Hillhouse Higher Elementary School, for boys and girls, flourished from 1909 to 1924 and there Robert Montgomery, known to everyone as 'Monty', was beloved by all. He kept a fatherly eye on the Hillhouse Old Students' Union and it was they who helped found the Huddersfield Thespians.[1] The College Higher Grade School became once more a secondary school—Huddersfield College—under the headship of Mr Atkins, a quiet and unassuming man, yet an excellent teacher of mathematics who had effective methods of achieving high standards of work and discipline. He retired in 1937—a most respected man.

The ancient schools at Almondbury, Fartown and Longwood faced extinction just after the First World War. They all experienced financial difficulties and were competing with the municipal schools for their students. Fartown and Longwood closed their doors but, after some negotiation, Almondbury

---

[1] See p. 282.

Grammar School asked the Education Committee to take over. Thus, after 300 years of independence Almondbury became a maintained secondary school where Taylor Dyson,[1] headmaster from 1913 to 1945, successfully continued the school's ancient traditions within its new environment.

After the war, the Military Hospital at Royds Hall was wound up and, in the premises, in 1921, the Borough and West Riding Authorities opened there a jointly run co-educational grammar school. The agreement was for thirty years with the option for Huddersfield of acquiring sole use of the school in 1951; this was, in fact, the case and explains why there has been a considerable expansion of secondary education in the Colne Valley in the past twenty years.

In 1920 when the Council purchased the Ramsden Estate, there went with the lands acquired, New Longley Hall.[2] For some years the house remained empty until in 1924 it was decided to convert the premises into a girls' school to relieve the pressure on Hillhouse, where the old Higher Grade had become a 'Central' school. So it was that two central schools were created, Hillhouse for boys, Longley Hall for girls, and they were the forerunners of what would today be termed 'Secondary Technical' schools.

In 1926 there came the Hadow Report on primary education. In Huddersfield at this time, although the provision of school places was perhaps not inadequate, there were very many small schools, extremely parochial in outlook. We have referred to the arrival of public transport as a unifying factor. When it came to the question of children's education, as late as the twenties, the villages, suburbs, and hamlets stood out for their traditional independence. Even today some of the older inhabitants of the suburbs still refer to shopping in town as

[1] Taylor Dyson (1882–1957) was born in Saddleworth and was educated at the Huddersfield Technical College and Owen's College, Victoria University, Manchester. He took B.A. history in 1901 and M.A. in 1908. In addition he took a degree in languages at London in 1907. Outside the school he was very well known for his books. His *History of Huddersfield & District*, based on a series of newspaper articles, was first published in 1932. In addition he wrote *Almondbury and its Ancient School* and *Place Names and Surnames* all of which gave him a considerable reputation as a local historian.

[2] Not the original Longley Hall. See p. 20.

'going to Huddersfield' as though they were going on a journey of many miles. After the setting up of the School Board the Church of England schools and the Board schools existed side by side and were a source of friction between Anglican and Nonconformist interests all over the Borough. Generally speaking the Board schools were large and the Church schools small. The Hadow Committee looked at the problems of the elementary schools and recommended that all pupils should transfer to some kind of post-primary education at the age of eleven. Here was envisaged the idea of the modern school with its emphasis on practical work. However, the agreement of the Diocesan authorities was necessary before Church school pupils could be transferred elsewhere and although George Thornber, the Director of Education, strove to bring about some cohesion, the various bodies could not be brought to agree to implement the Hadow re-organisation. The school-leaving age became fourteen in 1921 with a further extension to fifteen years if empowered by local bye-laws. Mr Thornber publicly reported that it would be a calamity to raise the leaving age to fifteen in Huddersfield without proper facilities including suitable buildings and curricula; there were simply too many schools in the Borough. In 1937 Mr Thornber retired. He was a sick man and there had been little progress towards reorganising the primary schools.

Harold Kay became the new Director of Education and he came from a completely reorganised area. Within six months he had made a survey and his scheme had been approved; it included ten new senior schools, some new junior schools, six new gymnasia, three school swimming baths and the possibility of new buildings for Huddersfield College and extensions for the Technical College. The first school to be built under the new scheme, at Dalton, was not quite finished when the War broke out, therefore Dalton did not have its junior school until after 1945. The rest of the scheme was shelved in September 1939 so that in 1945 Huddersfield schools were still not reorganised.

The Technical College was surveyed by Michael Sadler in 1904 and he said: 'The College is a public educational trust under representative governors . . . Those who established the College were educational pioneers . . . They were in advance of the opinions held on the subject of technical education by many of the inhabitants of the district. By starting the Technical College when it did, Huddersfield played no unimportant part in the movement which has succeeded in making the nation realise the fact that, under modern conditions, scientific methods of thought and training are vitally important factors in industrial and commercial success. . . . I would urge that the authorities of the school and of the Borough ought to relax no effort until the whole of the community heartily believe in the Technical College.' Sadler concluded by urging that the Technical College Committee and the Education Committee should be amalgamated.

Eventually, in June 1921, the Technical College Committee asked the Education Committee to take over its government and this was in fact agreed upon. One of the strong features of the College has been its Department of Chemistry with special reference to colour chemistry. Just before the Second World War, a new building mainly for chemistry, including research facilities partly provided by industrial support, was erected. The outbreak of war prevented its immediate use and Avery Hill Training College from Eltham, London, was evacuated to the building until 1946.

Thus, although the war halted the reorganisation of our schools and the extension of the Technical College, the years after the war saw all these plans and many new projects come to fruition. These developments will be examined in Chapter XVI.

On 18th September 1918 Huddersfield celebrated the Golden Jubilee of the Charter of Incorporation. The highlight of the occasion was a ceremony in the Town Hall at which six gentlemen, 'persons who have rendered eminent services to the Borough', were made Honorary Freemen of the Borough. Hitherto no more than two persons had ever together received this honour. The ceremony was conducted in the manner of a Council Meeting with members on the platform, in full view of the audience. The new freemen were the Mayor (Alderman W. H. Jessop), Alderman Ernest Woodhead, Councillor G. Thomson, Mr B. Broadbent, Mr J. A. Brooke and Mr J. E. Willans; each received an illuminated scroll and later a carved oak casket to contain it.

In further commemoration, four tablets were placed in the Council Chamber commemorating all past Mayors, Town Clerks, members of the original Council and of its counterpart fifty years later, and the names of all Honorary Freemen. Owen Balmforth's *Jubilee History* was published, and £500 per annum was set aside for the institution of Jubilee university scholarships. The *Jubilee History* has been invaluable in the compilation of this book and, as a boy, I often used to read the names of Jubilee Scholarship holders, on the honours boards at Huddersfield College, during school assembly. The schools were given a holiday and each scholar received a specially designed card as a souvenir of the occasion.

The Diamond Jubilee in 1928 was a more modest affair. The Corporation established the site of the new public baths at Cambridge Road, there were improvements made at the electricity generating station and at the sewage works, the bus garage on Leeds Road was opened and some homes for old people were built at Waterloo.

KEY TO TOWN CENTRE MODEL (opposite)

CC	Civic Centre	NM	New Market Hall
CP	Car Park	PC	Parish Church
FS	Fire Station	PH	Park Horse Yard Scheme
GS	St George's Square	S	Railway Station
H	Hammerson Scheme	TC	College of Technology
L	Public Library	TE	Telephone Exchange
M	Old Market Hall	W	Woolworth Building
	WM	Wholesale Market	

The light-coloured buildings are actually in course of construction or to be built, in 1968.

HUDDERSFIELD TOWN CENTRE MODEL

Model of the new Town Centre scheme.

W. Rhodes, G. H. Hirst, S. Haigh and Joseph Woodhead, J.P., at Blake Lee Guest House, Marsden, on 21 October 1905. *Photo :* J. E. Shaw; from a copy loaned by R. G. Haigh, son of Scholfield Haigh.

The changing face of Huddersfield is seen in this picture which shows the cleaning of the Town Hall, the old Police Station (due for demolition), and part of the now completed Murrayfield Scheme (Phase I). *Photo :* Roy Brook (Crosland Moor).

CHAPTER XV

The Second World War and Afterwards

THE SUMMER of 1939 was a long one. Schools were late in re-opening after the holidays and Huddersfield College returned gradually, form after form, as air raid shelter accommodation became available. The shops were still full and trade was brisk as everyone tried to acquire a stock of tinned food, just in case of an emergency. The black-out was a nuisance, but trams and buses managed to run and, once the cinemas had re-opened and there was some sport, the town appeared to be almost itself, at least until the middle of 1940. There was little evacuation of children either to or from Huddersfield and, from most families, only the younger men were called away during those early months. Industry, which in the late 'thirties had gradually recovered from the depression of the inter-war years, continued to prosper and many firms, particularly in textiles, were encouraged to export peace-time products to America to pay for war supplies bought there on a cash-and-carry basis. It was almost as if there was no war at all.

Then, in June 1940, came a sharp reminder of reality as Corporation buses were seen one day taking men, recently evacuated from the Dunkirk beaches, round the suburbs in search of temporary homes. These men, in their ragged uniforms, many of them wounded, all tired and bewildered, had somehow managed to remain cheerful, even optimistic and, as in many other towns up and down the country, the people responded with warmth and hospitality. Doors were opened and the men were taken in. Later, when the men rejoined their units, there were tales not only of temporary kindness, but of associations formed that have lasted over the years. Over the same period came refugees from Jersey, when the Germans occupied the Channel Islands, counterparts of the Belgian exiles who came to Huddersfield in 1914.

I

Also in June 1940, this time on a wet English summer Sunday, there arrived at Kirkburton two train loads of men of the Royal Corps of Signals. There, in an empty mill, was set up a Holding Battalion and Mobilisation Centre which was to remain there until 1945. Other units of the Royal Signals eventually took premises in the town and in the Colne Valley. Anti-aircraft gun sites were positioned at Salendine Nook, Almondbury, Bradley Road and Castle Hill. Thus Huddersfield became a garrison town for the first time in her long history. To see soldiers in town in pre-war days had been exceptional and usually, to find any at all, one had had to go to Halifax Barracks. Soldiers in Huddersfield had traditionally been there only at the request of the Magistrates, to enforce law and order! But, in 1940, things were different and, as the war began to affect us all more and more, there arose a feeling of real comradeship between the townspeople and the men in uniform.

By the end of August 1940, however, it seemed that the war had really arrived when an anti-aircraft searchlight picked out a German raider, *en route* for Liverpool, and several bombs were dropped near Castle Hill. Two days before Christmas, also in 1940, high explosive and incendiary bombs were dropped on Wellington Mills, Oakes, and there was a land mine in the mill dam which mercifully failed to explode. Families were evacuated from the vicinity including some of my own relatives. At the height of the danger my aunt prevailed upon the police to allow her to return home to rescue her Christmas cake which, in the excitement, had been left baking in the oven.

A few incendiaries fell on Berry Brow in March 1941 and, on 12th June of that year, incendiary bombs fell over a wide area from Colne Road to Newsome and Almondbury, and a high, explosive bomb hit the island in the river near King's Mill but did not detonate. The only fatal casualties from the air were in July 1944 when a British aircraft crashed in Central Avenue, Fartown, in broad daylight.

Though Huddersfield escaped from the war with hardly a scratch and it was only after visiting Sheffield, Merseyside and Manchester that one realised just how lucky we had been, there was a fear in case we were 'next' as enemy planes droned overhead by night. It was feared lest the Germans might decide to use Castle Hill as a landmark, find the Colne Valley and eventually attack the I.C.I. works at Leeds Road— but it never happened. It later transpired that there had been a target of outstanding importance at Meltham Mills, where David Brown's were the sole manufacturers of vital gears for the 'Spitfire' fighter plane. Much had indeed depended upon the output of this factory being maintained.

As the war years dragged on, women entered the engineering works as more men left for the Forces and the engineers applied their native craftsmanship to the war effort. They made, besides gears for aircraft, midget submarines, gun barrels, tank and warship components and rocket projectiles. Textile mills turned over to making cloth for the uniforms of the Allied armies; for the 'Home Front', 'utility' cloth was made for sale against a meagre allowance of clothing coupons.

Since the war, Huddersfield has experienced prosperous trading conditions which have been maintained for over twenty years. Of course the country as a whole, despite pockets of recession in certain areas, has enjoyed full employment; indeed, in mid-1966, only eleven per thousand of the country's labour force were out of work. In Yorkshire nine per thousand were unemployed, and in Huddersfield the figure was only four, one of the very lowest rates in the country. Even during the difficult economic conditions which prevailed at the end of 1966 there were more vacancies in Huddersfield than there were applicants to fill them. We should therefore examine briefly why this is so, and then consider the various ways in which local industry is trying to meet this shortage of labour.

At first glance, the textile industry may give to the stranger the impression that it has not moved with the times. Manufacturers tend to be cautious when assessing their achievements or when looking ahead. Yet, this attitude reflects the mood of many Huddersfield folk, for the town is a closely knit business community with many of the mill owners actually related to each other. Moreover, as the town is a centre for high quality worsteds, the highly skilled labour force has few opportunities for similar employment elsewhere and generations of work-people have tended to stay in their traditional occupations.

Many of our mills are old, some are extremely small, too small in fact to benefit from large-scale production methods. Yet all the textile firms have full order books and some are particularly successful in the field of exports. Why is this so?

Over the years the millworkers have evolved special skills, craftsmanship and 'know-how' in every aspect of wool textiles. Every conceivable type of woollen product is to be found within our area from the finest worsteds to coarse rug wools. The 30,000 textile workers produce materials of original design for the leading fashion houses, and, in adapting to modern trends, they have not been slow to blend synthetic fibres with the traditional wool. True, competition is felt from Italy in European and from Japan in American markets, yet the Queen's Award for Industry was in 1966 awarded to a Huddersfield firm of fine worsted manufacturers who had exported well over ninety per cent of their output over a period of three years. A high proportion of Huddersfield's cloth goes overseas to a wide range of countries and I have seen for myself our products on sale in Japan.

Whenever a new country has achieved independence in recent years the aim has been to establish its own dyestuffs and textile industries. Many of our traditional markets have thus gone, yet initiative and research into new products and enterprise abroad have led to continued prosperity in the field of chemicals. For example, Imperial Chemical Industries, now partly engaged in plastics of all kinds, still have at Dalton one of the largest plants in Europe for the manufacture of dyestuffs.

In engineering also there has been keen competition from all over the world, yet nearly all the Huddersfield firms have expanded considerably since 1945, and today it is probably the shortage of labour which most limits further growth.

The way in which firms have faced up to their labour difficulties is of interest. There is clearly no single solution to this problem, for the growth of the town's population, at its present rate, is just not sufficient to enable every business to expand as it would like. The mining area to the south-east of Huddersfield has become a source of female labour, and it is estimated that about a thousand people now (1967) come into the town each day from South Yorkshire to work in the textile mills. Other industries have set up branches in the mining districts and it now appears that all the available labour has been utilised. Engineering has reached out for labour into the Holme Valley and, even with the extensive use of private cars, the limit to which numbers of workpeople can be brought into Huddersfield appears to have been reached. Full employment in most of the United Kingdom has almost ruled out the possibility of any large-scale migration into our area from elsewhere in the country.

For these reasons, immigrants from overseas have found a useful place in local industry, just as, a hundred years ago, the Irish were accepted into our community. Up to 1958, many Central and Eastern Europeans had arrived. Among these there were some skilled textile workers but a number went into the chemical and engineering industries, and there were unusually large numbers of Irish workpeople who had arrived in the late forties and early fifties. After 1958 the character of the new arrivals changed and there came to live in the town centre, Indians, Pakistanis and West Indians. It has never been easy to find lodgings in Huddersfield due to the large numbers of married women who go out to work; consequently, although Indian men arrived singly at first, by 1960 complete families began to move into some of the ageing property in and near the centre of the town—property left by Irish and Continental immigrants who had by then moved out to the more pleasant suburbs. The Indians came mainly from the Punjab, then came the Sikhs, and there were Pakistanis from Lyallpur in West Pakistan. The Asian families brought their own traditions of hard work and family responsibilities, and large numbers entered the textile mills. On the other hand some of the latest arrivals have been West Indians from Jamaica and Grenada, many of them unaccompanied males although their families have eventually joined them. They have found employment in unskilled tasks in engineering and in public transport. The arrival of large numbers of immigrants has created problems of integration; but not before the education,[1] health and welfare authorities were feeling the strain imposed by the newly arrived families, did the Commonwealth Immigration Act of 1962

[1] See p. 256.

reduce the flood of adult migrants, but not the rapid growth of their families.

The long-term solution to some of our labour problems must inevitably lie in increased automation or mechanisation depending on the size of production units involved. During the last War, the Swiss developed many improved types of textile machinery and this, together with new equipment from many other sources at home and abroad, is gradually being introduced. In at least one modern mill, a mere handful of operatives now looks after an entire shed full of the latest machinery which runs cleanly, efficiently and in comparative quiet. In engineering also, many traditional processes are being eliminated by using modern techniques, but in practice only the largest firms can fully benefit from automation. It has been said that the small undertaking, especially in textiles, is out of date, but it should be remembered that it is the admixture of large and small undertakings which has made our industrial pattern so diverse, and thus helped maintain the stability of the town; nor must we ignore the benefits which have accrued from competition between the firms themselves. At present, there is hardly any type of product based on wool which Huddersfield cannot produce.

Since 1945, there has been a revolution in transport with road vehicles taking the places of both railway and canal traffic. This has formed part of a national pattern, but as long ago as 1943, the L.M.S. announced its intention of abandoning the canals it controlled, and the narrow section up the Colne Valley has become derelict. The Broad Canal, constructed by Sir John Ramsden in the eighteenth century, continued to be used up to 1953 when the last load of coal was delivered to Aspley. Today it too lies unused. There is a possibility that Sir John's Canal may be used for fishing, sailing and canoeing. Whatever happens, the canal barge and the railway horse have slipped quietly out of the picture (*see photograph facing page* 203).

Railway branch lines and most of the small stations have disappeared but the story is not entirely one of railway decline. Early in 1958, diesel cars began to run to Wakefield and later, between Leeds and Liverpool. Both services are fast and efficient, and together with improvements to the long-distance passenger services, railways are genuinely competing with road transport for the longer passenger journeys. Whilst writing this book, I was able to travel from London to Huddersfield and back in a day, in complete comfort, spending most of the day in the town. British Rail are working on the design for a new Huddersfield Station, on smaller lines, but it is likely that Kaye and Pritchett's handsome façade will be preserved, and that the building it fronts will serve some useful municipal purpose after purchase by the Corporation to mark the Centenary of the Borough.

Before dealing with local politics, we should briefly consider the Huddersfield Chamber of Commerce and the Trades Council, as representing both sides of local industry.

By the middle of the nineteenth century the textile industry had completed its transition from the homestead to the factory and the industry had begun to buy and sell in the markets of the world. The individual manufacturers therefore felt the need of some organisation to act in their best interests which were understandably closely linked to those of the town. At a meeting on 14th May 1853 nearly eighty firms and individuals agreed to found the Huddersfield Chamber of Commerce, to promote and extend the trade of the town and district, to spread information and to secure commercial advantages beyond what was considered possible by individual effort, and to try to settle disputes without litigation. The following year a news room was set up where the Electric Telegraph Company's apparatus supplied the latest market information daily for corn, wool and money at the London, Liverpool, Leeds and Manchester exchanges. The Chamber became involved in negotiations to limit tariffs, and representatives went abroad to discuss foreign trade. In local affairs they agitated for a Town Hall, criticised the Post Office and banking services, and took an active part in the establishment of the Technical College in 1877. A close liaison with the College followed, and the prizes and scholarships awarded by the Chamber helped the College to flourish and encourage its students to stay in Huddersfield as qualified men. In two World Wars the Chamber has helped firms cope with Government controls and it now plays a full part in the National Wool Export Group—a most important function since so much of the town's prosperity depends on overseas markets.

The Huddersfield and District Trades and Industrial Council, like the Chamber of Commerce has its origins in the textile industry but today both organisations represent all types of industry in the town. The Trades Council developed from the Huddersfield Weavers' Union which was formed in 1881, combining power loom weavers' unions in the outlying districts. After the failure of the great Weavers' Strike of 1883 Allen Gee, Chairman of the combined union, and himself a weaver from Lindley, decided to obtain more support for their cause by forming a 'Free Trades Council'. Gee became its first president and all the original officials were weavers, but representatives from other trades gradually came in. The original policy was to lobby the candidates at Parliamentary elections but there was no thought of setting up a new party to challenge the Liberals and Tories in those days; the main aim was to secure the best possible conditions for the working man. The Friendly and Trades Club was opened in 1886 in premises vacated by the Mechanics' Institute in Northumberland Street. By 1893, twenty-six unions were affiliated and some of the early officials came from the Amalgamated Society of Engineers and the unions of operative cotton spinners, cabinet makers, and painters. In that year Keir Hardie formed the Independent Labour Party and the Trades Council decided to support this new working class movement.

The objects of the Trades Council were declared to be the consideration of all questions of labour, to stand up to public bodies where necessary and to encourage the entry of working men into public life. In 1892 Allen Gee became a Borough Councillor and was elected Alderman in 1904. In 1913 two working men became Borough Justices, while others had joined the Education Committee and the Board of Guardians. In 1900 the Trade Union Congress met in Huddersfield Town Hall; in which year the Trades Council, with eighty-seven affiliated unions, covered the interests of 8,000 workpeople.

The Trades Council supported the suffragettes, called on the Corporation to build houses by direct labour, urged the nationalisation of land and transport and opposed the First World War on the grounds that it was a capitalist war. In 1924

Huddersfield returned its first Labour Member of Parliament, James Hindle Hudson, and Alderman Law Taylor became our first Labour Mayor.

In local politics, considering that Allen Gee had been a Labour Councillor in 1893, the Labour Party with only six councillors in 1928 had progressed very slowly. In 1931, when Hudson lost the Parliamentary seat to Mabane, Labour had only one seat on the Council and by 1938 this figure had risen to only eight. During the whole of the period from 1868 to 1945 the Liberals had an overall majority on the Council with the Conservatives usually a long way behind in second place. In spite of the prominence of the Labour Party and the decline of the Liberals in national politics between the wars, Huddersfield clung to its traditional opinions and this was reflected in the re-election of William Mabane to Parliament in 1935. At a time of economic uncertainty the Huddersfield electorate thought it best not to change their traditional allegiance.

After the last war, the Parliamentary seat was fought by Labour and two Liberals in a three-cornered fight. The country swung to the left in 1945 and J. P. W. Mallalieu polled almost as many votes as his two opponents combined:

J. P. W. Mallalieu (Lab.)	33,362
William Mabane (Nat. Lib.)	24,496
Roy F. Harrod (Lib.)	11,199

On the Borough Council in 1945 the Conservatives and Labour had fifteen seats each so that the Liberals with thirty, for the first time ever no longer held an overall majority.

By the General Election of 1950 the Borough Constituency had been divided and the results showed the continuing presence of Liberal support in the town in spite of the almost total disappearance of the Liberal Party from the House of Commons.

Huddersfield East		*Huddersfield West*	
J. P. W. Mallalieu		Donald W. Wade	
(Lab.)	22,296	(Lib.)	24,456
J. Woods Smith (Con.)	17,063	H. W. Bolt (Lab.)	17,542

The Borough Council of 1950 comprised:

Liberals 32   Conservatives 16   Labour 12

Thus the Liberals had regained complete control which they were to retain only until 1952 since when they have slowly lost ground although they remained the largest single party until 1962. From 1962 to 1966 Labour were the largest single party in the Borough Council.

The Parliamentary Elections of 1951, 1955 and 1959 showed little change at all in the voting habits of Huddersfield as Mr Mallalieu and Mr Wade continued to represent the town right through the fifties.

1951

Huddersfield East		*Huddersfield West*	
J. P. W. Mallalieu (Lab.)	22,368	Donald W. Wade (Lib.)	24,054
J. Woods Smith (Con.)	17,799	H. W. Bolt (Lab.)	17,066

1955

Huddersfield East		*Huddersfield West*	
J. P. W. Mallalieu (Lab.)	22,835	Donald W. Wade (Lib.)	24,345
Douglas Clift (Con.)	18,611	J. F. Drabble (Lab.)	16,418

1959

Huddersfield East		*Huddersfield West*	
J. P. W. Mallalieu (Lab.)	22,474	Donald W. Wade (Lib.)	25,273
P. M. Beard (Con.)	19,389	James Marsden (Lab.)	15,621

In 1964 all three parties contested both seats with the result that Labour won both. Labour's stronger national position was reflected in increased majorities in both seats in 1966, although the Conservatives ran second in Mr (now Lord) Wade's old constituency.

1964

Huddersfield East		*Huddersfield West*	
J. P. W. Mallalieu (Lab.)	20,501	Kenneth Lomas (Lab.)	14,808
J. Fergusson (Con.)	12,232	Donald W. Wade (Lib.)	13,528
B. Jennings (Lib.)	7,494	J. Addey (Con.)	13,054

The Second World War and Afterwards

1966

Huddersfield East		*Huddersfield West*	
J. P. W. Mallalieu		Kenneth Lomas	
(Lab.)	21,960	(Lab.)	17,990
J. Fergusson (Con.)	11,081	J. Marcus Fox (Con.)	13,514
G. M. Lee (Lib.)	6,303	R. H. Hargreaves	
		(Lib.)	9,470

This strengthening of the Conservative position was reflected in local politics and they emerged as the largest single party in the Council as a result of two by-elections in 1966. This was the first time that this had ever happened. The Municipal Elections of 1967 continued this trend but the Liberal representation on the Council was increased as well as that of the Conservatives. After the July by-elections of 1967 when eight seats were contested, as a result of retirements and aldermanic changes, the state of the parties in the concluding year of the first century of the Borough was (with one seat vacant):

Conservative 30   Labour 17   Liberal 12

The Churches have reflected the changing picture of the town centre as more and more inhabitants have left for the pleasanter suburbs. During this century the Anglican churches of St Barnabas, Crosland Moor, St Cuthbert, Birkby and St James at Rawthorpe have been built and new parishes have been carved out of existing ones. In addition, five mission churches have been established including those of Outlane and Fixby. The Parish Church of St Paul has become the Chapel of the College of Technology while the mission churches of St Mark and St Michael have been closed.

The Roman Catholic Church based on St Patrick's felt long ago the need to minister more effectively to the growing town and accordingly the parish was divided in 1913 between St Patrick's and St Joseph's, Commercial Street.[1] In 1916 St Brigid's at Longwood was established, followed by Our Lady of Lourdes at Woodhouse in 1938. Recent years have seen opened, the churches of St James the Great, Oakes (1960) and Our Lady of Czestochowa, Queen of Poland, Fitzwilliam Street (1962).

[1] Now in Somerset Road.

Smaller chapels now serve the areas of Kirkburton and Bradley.

When the Ramsden Street Congregational Chapel closed in 1933 and the site was sold to the Corporation for the new Public Library, the proceeds went towards establishing a new church opened in 1942, to serve the Bracken Hall Estate. The only Presbyterian church in the town, St James', was opened in 1902.

The Baptist Church has opened two new places of worship in recent times, at Longley in 1939 and at Dalton in 1955.

In 1932 all the Methodist and Wesleyan denominations drew together after the dissensions of the last century, in which Huddersfield had played its part. The town centre chapels of Buxton Road and High Street have disappeared completely and Brunswick Street is also closed. Mount Pleasant, Lockwood, Lindley Zion, Hillhouse Free Methodist (known as the 'tea pot' chapel), Marsh Methodist, Crosland Moor (United) Methodist and Paddock Methodist Chapels are now no more. In 1966 Queen Street Mission celebrated its Diamond Jubilee with the announcement that the idea of a new mission in the centre of the town is to become a reality. The scheme is forward looking to the time when, as a result of the rebuilding of Huddersfield's central area, there will be presented to the Church an exciting social and religious challenge. When the Mission was founded in 1906 it was with the object of bringing Christianity to the masses, indeed the Mission Brass Band in its hey day earned the nickname of the 'Queen Street Fusiliers'.

The Parish Church too has seen great changes this century with the departure of many residents, from the town centre. The Schools in Venn Street no longer educate the children of the town but serve instead as 'Parish House' or social centre, while Church congregations are drawn from all over Huddersfield. The actual Parish of Huddersfield is small but the Vicar is Rural Dean of one of the largest Deaneries in England besides being what has been described as 'spiritual mayor' of the town. Of the three immediate predecessors of the present incumbent two are now bishops and one an arch-bishop. As a tribute to all who had previously held the Living of Huddersfield since 1216, on 27th October, 1966, there was celebrated the 750th anniversary of the appointment of the first Vicar, and Huddersfield once more became the large parish of former days as clergy and choirs from the daughter churches joined in the service of thanksgiving as did clergy and representatives from other Christian Churches in the town.

As we have seen, our main local religious differences go back to the eighteenth century and perhaps reached their climax in the confrontation of Anglicans and Non-conformists over the question of education in the last century. Recent years have seen a drawing together of all Protestant denominations following the national pattern. In Huddersfield, the Roman Catholic minority has grown in numbers, swelled by some of the many immigrants to the town. Yet Roman Catholics and Protestants alike have tended to accept their differences as something never to be discussed; and Huddersfield has seen nothing of the bitter strife which has beset some other parts of the country. Today, when many may well feel that the Christian faith is losing its place in our national life, it is well to note an important occasion in January 1967 when all branches of the Church came together for an address by the Roman Catholic Bishop of Leeds in Queen Street Mission. There was seen to be a real desire for a better understanding amongst all Christians in our town which has been for so long a traditional stronghold of the Faith. It is significant that Huddersfield Parish Church has survived the Reformation, Civil War and Industrial Revolution alike and, since 1216, has occupied at least three buildings on the same site.

In its search for Christian unity as in its acceptance of the immigrant, Huddersfield is setting an example of tolerance which can only be for the good of all. Granted, in days of prosperity it is comparatively easy to be tolerant towards others, but beneath an apparently blunt exterior there is, in Huddersfield folk, a wealth of human kindness to which thousands of wartime servicemen and evacuees still bear witness.

CHAPTER XVI

Local Government and the Public Services

IN 1945 the first post-war General Election returned a Labour Government to power under Clement (later Lord) Attlee with a large majority and pledged to the nationalisation of public utilities including the railway companies, electricity and gas undertakings. The latter were, in Huddersfield, owned by the Corporation and had long been operating successfully and profitably.

Under the provisions of the Electricity Act of 1947 the generating side of the Huddersfield Electricity undertaking was vested in the British Electricity Authority, on 1st April 1948; while the distribution and sales side came under the Yorkshire Electricity Board to form part of No. 2 Sub-Area (now the Huddersfield Area) which includes Huddersfield, Halifax and surrounding districts. The Corporation undertaking had been operating as far as Slaithwaite and Golcar, and had supplied nearly all the Borough, except Fixby. It is a remarkable fact that the demand for electricity has nearly doubled every ten years since the thirties; and, from figures supplied by the Corporation and estimates supplied by the Y.E.B., we find that units sold in the area of the Huddersfield undertaking have been:

| 1938 | 93,839,443 | 1960 | 349,300,000 |
| 1948 | 181,297,301 | 1965 | 501,400,000 |

In August 1966, Huddersfield Power Station was awarded the Hinton Cup, the major award of the Central Electricity Generating Board, having been judged the cleanest in the country.

The Gas Act of 1948 transferred the Huddersfield Corporation gas undertaking to the North Eastern Gas Board in 1949.

An important feature of gas manufacture in modern times has been the disappearance of the smaller gasworks. Long before nationalisation, the Corporation had acquired many of the smaller companies including Longwood and Slaithwaite in 1919 and Honley, Holmfirth and New Mill in 1939. In more recent years, however, all the local gasworks have gone out of production, and the gasworks at Huddersfield is one of the few remaining, supplying gas into a partially completed West Riding grid.

As a source of lighting, gas has steadily declined in favour. The last gas lights to survive are the street lamps, and the last few of these will be replaced in the near future. In the twenties the industrial demand for gas grew as engineering works began to use it on a large scale for processes requiring heat. In time, also, advances in communal cooking and commercial baking made increasing use of gas, while today we find a steadily growing demand for gas as a source of central heating. In 1955, it was thought that the consumption of gas in our area had stabilised itself, but it has since risen by more than 25 per cent, and the figure is still rising.

In 1966 it was decided to abandon the Gasworks' own railway which delivered coal from Newtown Yard to Leeds Road; the train was slow as the law required a man to walk in front with a red flag, and the upkeep of the sidings was expensive. Now all coal is carried by road.

In 1948, under the National Health Service Act of 1946, all local authority hospitals were transferred to Regional Hospital Boards; but the Act left Local Authorities as 'Local Health Authorities'. The largest hospital projects have been the rebuilding of St Luke's at Crosland Moor, and the building of a new Royal Infirmary at Lindley which has cost five and a half million pounds. The scheme for the new Infirmary was first announced by the Leeds Regional Hospital Board in 1951, but work only started in 1957 and little progress was made until 1960, in spite of the fact that the old building simply could not meet the needs of the town. The new Royal Infirmary was opened by the Prime Minister, the Right Hon. Harold Wilson, on 27th January 1967.

The Municipal Health Department today also deals with

environmental health services, and has condemned as unfit some 3,300 houses in the past twenty years as the clearing of slums progresses. The Clean Air Act of 1956 is being implemented, and some results are clearly visible although only about a quarter of the town has yet come under the Act. In terms of statistics the smoke pollution of the local atmosphere has been halved since 1962. Since the National Health Act of 1946, the Department has taken over many of the functions previously carried out by voluntary organisations, and there has been a considerable expansion of home nursing, infant welfare and ambulance services. The Mental Health Act of 1959 has led to big changes in this field and an increase in Local Authority responsibilities.

A School Health Service is provided under the Education Committee and the Medical Officer of Health is also Principal School Medical Officer. There has been a change in outlook which has taken the Health Service from the purely routine inspection of children towards a positive approach to all aspects of their health including the care of handicapped pupils. Since the move to the new Civic Centre in 1965 there has been a considerable extension of the school dental services. Indeed the coming together of the various health departments under one roof at the new Centre has been a long-awaited development, of advantage to both staff and public alike. As many of us well remember, a row of old houses in Ramsden Street was not an ideal setting for a schoolchildren's clinic.

The Welfare Department was formed in July 1948 and it represents the present-day successor to the old Poor Law and Board of Guardians. Centres for the blind and the handicapped have been set up and the disabled and elderly are visited periodically in their own homes. Residential accommodation for the elderly and for the needy has been provided and Huddersfield was the second Authority in the country to close its former Poor Law Institution, for which Old Peoples' Homes are a vastly superior replacement.

Although the nationalisation of water undertakings has been mooted on many occasions, Government policy has been to group them together with their control in the hands of a Board or of one of the larger authorities. Huddersfield already supplied the Colne Valley, Mirfield and parts of Kirkburton when the undertakings of Meltham and the Holmfirth Urban District were acquired by the Corporation in 1961 and 1963 respectively. The Digley Reservoir Scheme which was commissioned in 1954 added 740 million gallons to the amount of water available; the project included a treatment works at Holmbridge and a storage tank at Newsome. A new 1,800 million gallon project was started in 1966 in the Deanhead Valley at Scammonden, where there will be a new reservoir with the new Lancashire–Yorkshire motorway running across the embankment; this dual use of an embankment is unique in this country. In addition there will be a tunnel and pipework linking the new reservoir with Butterley Reservoir and the Colne Valley catchment area.

By the time this book is published Huddersfield will most likely have ceased to have a separate police authority, and the Borough Force will have become a part of a much larger organisation including the West Riding Force, as a result of the Police Act of 1964. Naturally there will be advantages for the West Riding as a whole in having a larger unit policing an undivided area[1] but it remains to be seen whether, in the long run, Huddersfield itself will enjoy a better service from these changes.

In the past twenty years, the Borough Force has almost doubled in size although it has been below its authorised strength for the greater part of this century. Since 1945 the number of indictable offences reported has increased threefold yet the percentage of those detected has improved; the ratio of detection to crimes committed is very much higher than the national average. This success has been due in no small measure to the relatively small size of our area, a closely knit unit where the police have made use of their local knowledge and efficiency of communication. It can be shown, for the country as a whole, that the rate of detection is inversely proportional to the size of the force and the area served. The efficiency of the Huddersfield Police Force has been further

[1] There will, in fact, be four forces: Leeds, Bradford, Sheffield & Rotherham, and the new combined force.

increased by the introduction of wireless controlled cars, the Special Constabulary and, lately, police dogs and Traffic Wardens. In recent years there have been introduced daily press conferences, departments of training and crime prevention, and a highly successful Juvenile Liaison Officer Scheme for the prevention of juvenile crime. A most advanced new Police Station was taken into use in 1967, an urgent requirement as the premises in Peel Street, built for a force half the present size had been for many years quite inadequate. The Borough Force takes with it to the new organisation a proud tradition and it is to be hoped that its members, and the town they have served so well, will benefit from the proposed amalgamation.

Public transport, which started with trams, changed over to trolley buses in the thirties and is changing once again. As the lives of the people undergo changes in pattern so the transport services must adapt themselves to new situations. Since 1945 Huddersfield has become a town of private car owners, and this fact in itself has enabled its citizens to live further out of the town than would have been possible many years ago; and new developments in housing have also altered the town's requirements for public transport. The costs of trolley bus operation have risen by leaps and bounds in respect of vehicle replacement, overhead wires and electric power—the latter no longer produced by the Corporation itself. As other towns have moved away from the trolley bus so there has arisen the doubt that vehicles and their parts may not be available indefinitely, while the decline in the demand for trolley vehicles must certainly contribute to their increased cost. These are hard facts for those who, over the years have taken a pride in our smooth, silent and once cheap system of transport by trolley bus. Some indeed have felt with some justification that the 'trolley' was made for hilly districts such as Huddersfield; others have felt all along that the greater flexibility of a vehicle not needing overhead wires made the motor bus inevitable. Economic facts and the need for flexibility of routes in the future have now made it necessary to change over to motor buses, a form of transport better able to serve a population with a steadily declining proportion of people who are completely dependent on public conveyance.

The ultimate in economy of operation is, of course, the one-man-operated bus. In 1952 the first one-man bus was tried out and for this experiment special permission had to be obtained from the Licensing Authority. Since then further buses of this type have been purchased for use where other vehicles would clearly be uneconomical. This scheme also contributes towards solving the shortage of staff which we discussed in Chapter XV.

Following a Council decision to abandon the trolley bus system, motor buses were introduced, on the West Vale route, in 1961. New vehicles were purchased, Leyland seventy-seaters of the forward-entry type, and there have since been further introductions of the motor bus; and trolley buses will disappear from our streets in 1968. When alterations have been carried out at the Great Northern Street Works and the Leeds Road Garage, they will be among the most up-to-date in the country. One advantage of the flexibility achieved by the use of motor buses has already been seen in the introduction of new through services using together the Corporation and the Joint Omnibus Committee buses. This combined service has only become possible now that both systems operate with similar vehicles. We are now seeing transport controlled by radio and television and further economies in manpower will be achieved by more single-handed vehicles during off-peak periods.

In 1953 the Estate Department, which had managed the Ramsden Estate from its purchase in 1920, became the Estate and Property Management Department, responsible for the management and control of all corporation properties including 12,000 houses, some sixty schools and colleges, Town Hall and Civic Centre, Public Baths, nine children's homes, seventeen Welfare homes and four blocks of town centre buildings.

On completion of the Bracken Hall Housing Estate in 1940, no further major schemes were put in hand until after the war. Then, between 1948 and 1961 over 2,000 houses were erected at Almondbury, Deighton and Dalton. The largest scheme undertaken in recent years has been the Bradley Estate which contains over 1,000 houses. The Ramsden Estate lands have been used for municipal housing to the extent of about 450 acres but, in addition, the Corporation has acquired a further 300 acres for housing from other sources. Moreover, since 1945 over 2,250 leases have been granted to private builders for property development within the Borough.

Obviously, Huddersfield is no longer primarily a farming community, indeed, farmland is being used up in order to house an ever-increasing population. However, some forty farms still cover 1,329 acres within the Borough—nearly ten per cent of its area.

During the thirties educational development was slow, and during the war all progress was suspended. In 1944, the Education Act insisted upon the reorganisation between primary and secondary schools which the Hadow Report had recommended in 1926. Up to 1950, however, progress was slow and the appointment of Harold Gray as Chief Education Officer in 1953 coincided with the realisation that Huddersfield had the highest proportion of pupils in unreorganised secondary schools in the country. With the co-operation of the Church Authorities, plans for reorganisation were pushed ahead, without waiting for new buildings, and the scheme was completed by 1958. Almost every school was affected in some way. Some buildings were improved and many small schools were closed. From 1955 onwards, plans for the building of many new schools were implemented, until 1963 by when approximately half the school places were in post-war buildings. For two years, the Government refused to authorise any new major projects.

In 1958, Huddersfield College was amalgamated with Hillhouse Technical School (formerly Hillhouse Central School) when the schools were moved to a new campus at Salendine Nook, to form Huddersfield New College. In the following year the girls of Longley Hall Technical School were also moved to Salendine Nook to become Huddersfield High School.

Under the post-war reorganisation scheme it was originally intended that King James's should be amalgamated with the College at Salendine Nook, but in 1954 these plans were changed. Old boys of the school like to think this was due, in some measure, to their vigorous campaign; be that as it may, the school remained at Almondbury, where it was enlarged and modernised. It was in that year that the original 1608 School Charter of King James I was returned to the school, having been lost as far back as anyone could remember.

In 1965 the Department of Education and Science required all local education authorities to submit plans for the re-organisation of secondary education on comprehensive lines. This move had been anticipated in discussions between the Authority and the teaching profession which began in 1963. The scheme selected for Huddersfield is for ten fully comprehensive schools for pupils aged from eleven to sixteen; and there are envisaged two such schools for each of the four quarters of the town with two Roman Catholic schools serving the whole town and some outlying areas. Pupils aged from sixteen to eighteen are to be served by separate colleges using existing buildings at Greenhead, the New College and King James's, plus the new Ramsden College, while a similar provision for Roman Catholic pupils will be made at Bradley Bar.

The Technical College extensions occupied during the war by Avery Hill Training College were used, in part, after the war for a newly established training college for technical teachers. This college, now the Huddersfield College of Education (Technical), eventually moved to its own newly built premises at Holly Bank Road in the late fifties and it is one of only four such institutions in the entire country.[1]

Considerable extensions to the Technical College were begun following its designation as a 'Regional College' in 1956.[2] The College's retention of this status was dependent upon separating from it the more elementary work. To achieve this, the Ramsden Technical College was established as a separate entity in 1963, and this division of the work of the old Technical College has continued ever since. In 1966 the College of Technology, as it is now called, was included in the first official list of large colleges to be developed as 'Polytechnics' which will concentrate on work of, or near, degree standard. The former Royal Infirmary premises in Portland Street were purchased by the Authority to be adapted for use by the Ramsden College, thus leaving the old buildings in Queensgate to be handed back to the College of Technology, as part of the Polytechnic. Residential accommodation for students has always presented a problem in Huddersfield and the Infirmary site will also

[1] The other colleges are in London, Bolton and Wolverhampton.
[2] A total of twenty-four colleges were so named.

include some hostel provision. The present figure of 1,000 full-time and 'sandwich course' students is expected to double; even now there are 3,000 part-time day students while a further 2,000 attend in the evenings only.

The training of teachers is not limited to the College of Education (Technical). In 1963 the Authority responded to a request from the Department of Education and Science for additional teacher-training facilities by opening the Oastler College of Education. This college occupies a part of the Co-operative Retail Services' premises and it is intended that Oastler College will be incorporated in the new Polytechnic. If education continues to expand, then there must be found more teachers and they must be properly trained. In this objective Huddersfield is playing a worthy part.

This rise and expansion of technological and further education in Huddersfield has been described as phenomenal; it is bound to benefit the town. The growth of the College of Technology has a direct bearing on the industries on which the town depends. At the same time the College has a large Department of Music, successfully linked to the town's undoubted interest in the subject.

One further aspect of education requires mention. The arrival of immigrants has created problems in the training of their children. At Spring Grove School there has been developed a most successful scheme for Indian, Pakistani and West Indian children, made all the more interesting by an appreciation of the cultural differences of East and West. A special department for the integration of immigrants was set up at Spring Grove and the techniques successfully applied there have been passed on to other schools in Huddersfield where there are children from overseas. A most noticeable feature has been the complete absence of any colour prejudice amongst the children themselves.

When we consider the Borough Treasurer's Department, some idea can be gained of what is entailed in running a town the size of ours. The annual income of the Corporation from rates,[1] Government grants and proceeds from services amounts

[1] There are at present about 55,000 ratepayers.

to some thirteen million pounds. Nearly 7,000 persons receive wages or salaries from the Corporation, and in a given year some 14,000 payments are made to the suppliers of goods and services for the Council. New projects are continually going ahead and to pay for these about two and a half million pounds are at present being borrowed annually. That Huddersfield has a very high proportion of road vehicles per head of population is borne out by the fact that about 58,000 licences are issued annually by the Borough Authorities.

All this municipal activity is indeed reminiscent of the vigorous early days of the Borough Council and leads to the question: 'What of the future status of the town?' The natural features of our area, the drainage of the rivers Colne and Holme have led to a natural unity which will have become apparent to readers of this book. During the thirties talks on the expansion of Huddersfield resulted in only a slight increase in the size of the Borough. In 1947, however, when a Local Government Boundary Commission was examining our area, it was intended that the Corporation should put forward a case for taking in the whole or substantial parts of the Colne Valley, Holmfirth, Kirkburton and Meltham and a little of the Denby Dale Urban District. The various Urban Districts, the Borough and West Riding County Councils, were invited to discuss the matter but the scheme was eventually shelved on the grounds of expense. Indeed, many of the smaller authorities have characteristically tended to prefer to preserve their independence.

A Royal Commission on Local Government is now examining this question afresh in a survey of the entire country. In a report submitted to the Royal Commission by the West Riding Authority, a two-tier structure on the lines of the Greater London Council is envisaged. A first tier, or regional, authority would have at least 500,000 inhabitants, and a second tier, or local, authority not less than 150,000.

The regional authority, if set up, will cater for those services which require a large area in which to function efficiently; the combining of water authorities and the proposed police amalgamations are foretastes of this, and other large-scale operations may include main roads and further education. The second tier authorities would then cover housing, health, welfare, children's and educational services. It is quite clear that the independence of smaller areas may disappear but it is always desirable that contact is not lost between the ratepayers and their representative local government. The danger is that the larger areas, the first-tier authorities, may become too remote from the people, and one of the tasks of the second-tier authorities must be to prevent this from happening. As a second-tier local authority 'Greater Huddersfield' might well include the Colne Valley, Denby Dale, Holmfirth, Kirkburton, Meltham, and Saddleworth urban districts—an area with a total population of about 224,300. Thus in local government, the area covered by this book could become unified for the first time in history, while the County Borough of Huddersfield could lose some of its present powers to a larger authority. The fact that a similar system works in London is, I am sure, no reason for assuming that it will necessarily work effectively in Yorkshire, and certainly if local government no longer reflects the needs and aspirations of the electors, it ceases to be representative government, directly and intimately responsible to the people it serves.

CHAPTER XVII

Sport

ALTHOUGH THE Association Football League was founded in 1888 and the support received led to the establishment of the First and Second Divisions in 1892, Huddersfield remained for many years a stronghold of Rugby Union football. With the formation in 1895 of the rebel Northern Union, however, established Rugby clubs lost many supporters; and the country as a whole went increasingly over to the Association game. More will be said about the Northern Union but first we will trace the rise of soccer in Huddersfield.

In 1897 there were sufficient amateur clubs to merit the formation of a Huddersfield and District Football Association. A cup competition was instituted and in 1899 Honley beat the Technical College in the first local cup final. Enthusiasm for the game continued to grow until in 1906 circulars were sent out convening a meeting at the Imperial Hotel where on 7th February 1907 the Huddersfield Town Association Football Club Limited was formed. The new team joined the North Eastern League in 1908 and lost their first game versus South Shields Adelaide by the odd goal in three. Town were not a wealthy team—their first dressing room was an old tramcar—and thus they soon found travelling to Tyneside for away matches too expensive. So it was that Town joined the Midland League in 1909 only to make a loss of £3,698 by July 1910. Amos Brook Hirst, the Chairman, was undismayed and he countered the pessimists by announcing plans for building a covered stand and completely altering the ground at Leeds Road. In February 1910 an England-Wales Amateur International Match was staged there; and in the following year the new stand was opened. In the meantime Huddersfield Town were elected to the Second Division of the Football League for the season of 1910–11.

Town had achieved only moderate success by 1915 when football was abandoned because of the War. The 1913 season, however, saw the first appearance of the familiar blue and white striped shirts which the club were to retain right up to 1966.

The 1919–20 season opened with the club in financial trouble and their chief backer wanting to withdraw his money, whereupon the Football Association gave permission for Town to pack up and remove to Leeds 'lock, stock and barrel'. In those days the Rugby League club at Fartown was doing well, consequently gates at Leeds Road had been poor. The Leeds City Club was in difficulties and their team were up for auction. The F.A.'s attitude was therefore understandable. The Town supporters were furious. Protest meetings were held and money was raised by the sale of £1 shares to all and sundry in 'pubs' and clubs throughout the town in an attempt to save the club.

As so often happens the hour produced the man, for Herbert Chapman became team manager and revolutionised the situation. He had previously managed Leeds City before it became defunct and was well known in Yorkshire football circles. Enthusiasm grew, generated from the terraces and was transmitted to the players who now carried all before them. In the one season they won promotion to the First Division and reached the F.A. Cup Final of 1920 where they lost to Aston Villa—a game Town should have won. Now there was no talk of moving anywhere!

The first team for the 1919–20 season was: Mutch; Wood and Bullock; Slade, Wilson and Watson (father of Willie and Albert Watson); Richardson, Mann, Taylor, Swan and W. H. Smith. Sam Wadsworth, one of the 'great' full backs, arrived to replace Bullock shortly before Chapman actually took over. Herbert Chapman therefore had a good team upon which to build and he acquired full back Roy Goodall and bought Clem Stephenson, who was to become team captain, from Aston Villa. In 1924 George Richardson, after ten years with the club, was replaced on the right wing by Scottish International Alex Jackson.

In June 1920 the club was re-organised and Amos Brook Hirst rejoined the Board he had left in 1911. He was Chairman of the club until October 1941 when he was appointed Chairman of the Football Association.

Herbert Chapman as 'Secretary-Manager' was given a free hand in the selection of the team and he remained with Town until 1925 by which time they had become League Champions. Town's rise to fame was no accident for in 1921 they were seventeenth in the First Division, 1922 fourteenth, 1923 third and 1924—FIRST. This was the season in which Clem Stephenson 'made a remarkable improvement' by scoring thirteen goals at inside left; his partner, on the wing, Billy Smith also scored thirteen.

During this period Town, known as the 'Babes' because of the club's recent arrival in Division I, gained a reputation for 'Firsts'. The Cup Final of 1920 was the first in which extra-time was played. In 1921 Town won the F.A. Cup beating Preston North End at Stamford Bridge[1] by a penalty goal, something that had never happened before. In 1924 Billy Smith became the first League player to score a goal direct from a corner kick, during a game in which Town beat Arsenal four–nil. In 1925 Town not only won the League Championship but were also Central League Champions. In 1926 they became League Champions for the third successive year and topped the Central League for the second time running. The feat of winning the First Division Championship three times in a row is something only equalled once, and that was by Arsenal in 1933 to 1935— under the management of the same Herbert Chapman! In 1925 Town's away record was better than their home record. In the season of 1927–28 Town were tipped for the League and Cup double—a feat only ever achieved by Aston Villa in 1897 and Tottenham Hotspur in 1961—in fact Town were second in the League and runners-up for the Cup in that Season.

In 1930 and 1937 Town were beaten in a Cup Final at Wembley, indeed it was in '37 that Preston gained their revenge by beating Town by a famous penalty goal scored in the last minute of extra time. In February 1932 Leeds Road had its record attendance of 67,037 for a cup tie against Arsenal. Nowadays the capacity of the ground is restricted by the

[1] The first F.A. Cup Final at Wembley was played in 1922.

Police to 55,000 and the biggest gate since the War was one of 55,168 which saw Town meet Burnley in the F.A. Cup series of 1957. Town's highest scores were in 1927 and 1930 when they beat respectively Cardiff City 8–2 and Blackpool by 10–1.

Many players of international class have played for Town but only a representative few can be mentioned here. During the record-breaking days of the twenties Alex Jackson, a dashing opportunist, played on the right wing, while at full-back were Sam Wadsworth and Roy Goodall. Towards the end of the thirties, however, Town had lost much of their former glory and the fact that they were still in the First Division was due very largely to the consistently steady defence of Hesford, Hayes and Mountford; Willingham, Young and Boot—a combination which rarely changed in the days just before the War. Never again were Town to have so many stars as they had in the twenties, but mention must be made of Peter Doherty who arrived in 1946 and took over as captain at a critical time. In 1955 Manager Andy Beattie discovered Denis Law who, at sixteen, became the youngest player ever to wear the blue and white shirt. Five years later, soccer history was made when Law was transferred to Manchester City for a then record fee of £55,000.

In August 1952 Ray Wilson a lad in his teens, joined the ground staff at Leeds Road. Wilson was to make 263 first team appearances with Town and during this time he was capped for England thirty times. In 1964 he was transferred to Everton and was a member of the England team which won the World Cup in 1966.

In 1952 Town were relegated to Division II but after only one season they were back with the seniors. Four years later they were again relegated and they have remained in the Second Division ever since. Thus for the first period of any length since 1920, Huddersfield is without her soccer team appearing in Division One. Town reached bedrock bottom at the end of 1964, when the team had slumped to the foot of the Second Division and gates had dwindled to a record low figure of 3,641, but by the end of the 1964–5 season Huddersfield Town had climbed to eighth from the top of the Second Division and in 1966, they were fourth. In 1967, Town were still amongst the leading clubs of the Second Division, with an eye on promotion to the realms of their hey day, when opponents from Merseyside, Manchester, Sheffield and Leeds might again draw the really big crowds. Leeds Road is one of the best grounds in the country in spite of a disastrous fire in 1950 and, as a result of recent improvements, it is claimed that 40,000 can see the game from under cover, although by the very best standards the ground is lacking in seating accommodation.

The question one might well ask in a local history is whether more local players of talent could not be brought into the team. The fact is that most of Town's men are from the North and North-East and, though there are usually some local products in the first team, one must bear in mind the tremendous gulf which today exists between professional and amateur play. Whilst every possible report of promising local talent is carefully followed up, a player is usually only as good as the opposition allows. A young footballer must be spotted early if he is to be trained up to the first class game, and all too often he is picked out when he is too old for this to happen. Unfortunately, the vision of eleven Huddersfield lads carrying all before them on the green turf of Wembley is likely to remain just a pipe dream. In spite of this there is the example of Jeffrey Taylor who graduated from the local Red Triangle League to the First Division with Town and Fulham.

Another milestone in the sporting history of our town was the founding, in 1864, of the Huddersfield Athletic Club, as a result of a meeting held at the Queen Hotel. Athletic festivals on the Rifle Fields[1] were amongst the earliest events they ran. We know that Rugby was played as a club activity in 1866. In 1875, the Huddersfield Athletic Club built its new headquarters, the gymnasium in St John's Road. This building, relinquished by the Club in 1908, still survives, and it faces the end of Cambridge Road. 1876 saw the amalgamation with St John's Cricket Club, thus forming the Huddersfield Cricket and Athletic Club—the name the Club still officially bears. In those days, the days of Rugby Union, Huddersfield played their first game at Fartown in November 1878 and, two years later,

[1] Near Greenhead Park.

won the Yorkshire Challenge Cup after beating Wakefield Trinity. At this period several county players were from the Huddersfield C and AC team.

Then, on 29th August 1895 there was held, at the George Hotel, Huddersfield, that fateful meeting which led to the formation of the Northern Rugby Football Union, and Huddersfield was amongst the first twenty clubs which broke away from the English Rugby Union.

Rugby had been played by all classes of men; all had been equal on the field whether the sons of mill owners or of factory hands. The poorer men, however, found the game expensive when earnings were lost as a result of absence from work in order to play; and there were some who tried discreetly to cover the expenses of those players who needed the money; depositing a 'sovereign in his boot' was a common method. The Union, however, was quite adamant on the maintenance of strict amateurism in the game, and this stringency made it quite impossible for some of the northern clubs to carry on. Bitterness developed and, after the establishment of the break-away Northern Union, the Rugby Union carried their hostility still further by ostracising any club or player participating in the new section. The outcome was that amateur clubs were distressed when some of their best players turned over to the Northern Union, the Rugby Union feared to alter its rules lest it should abandon its principles, and the split in the game of Rugby became permanent. That this should have happened at a time when the association game was gaining in popularity was fatal, and 'soccer' became the national sport. Neither code of Rugby has succeeded in regularly attracting the masses throughout the country.

Rugby League today still numbers the mill owners amongst its supporters but, ironically, League players are still not fully professional—they are paid by the match and all must have alternative employment. Except for attendances at international fixtures, Rugby League today attracts the larger crowds of the two codes. The Northern Union became the Rugby League in 1922 but, with the exception of Cumberland, the game has not effectively spread in this country beyond Lancashire and Yorkshire, and even there the game has not caught on in all the larger towns and cities. Several attempts to spread the game to South Wales and to London have so far met with failure.

When Huddersfield first joined the Northern Union they fared badly and, when two divisions were formed, they were relegated in 1904. The following year the league was reorganised into a single section and the Fartown team began to do better. This improvement coincided with the arrival in 1906 of Jim Davies, one of the greatest stand-off halves the game has ever seen, W. F. ('Billy') Kitchen and Harold Wagstaff.

The Halifax Club had at first been interested in young Wagstaff, a fifteen-year-old boy from Underbank, Holmfirth. However, their committee are alleged to have said they wanted 'men not boys', and Huddersfield signed him on for a fee of five guineas. He played his first game for Fartown in November 1906 before he was sixteen and, to prove the point, a copy of his birth certificate was printed inside a match programme. At the age of seventeen Harold Wagstaff played for England and later, in 1914 and 1920, he captained his country's team in Australia. From the 1911–12 season onwards he led Huddersfield through their record-breaking run and was known as 'the prince of centres', at the same time being fortunate in having a good team to back up his brilliant centre play. Wagstaff made his final appearance for the first team in March 1925 and died in 1939, a comparatively young man.

To continue the story of the team, 1907 saw the arrival of Edgar Wrigley and 'Clon' Sherwood; in 1909 Rosenfeld arrived —dubbed 'the greatest winger of all time'. By 1911 the all-star team had been strengthened by such names as Tommy Grey, Stanley Moorhouse another local product, J. W. Higson and Ben Gronow. In the 1911–12 season Huddersfield won the Northern Rugby League Cup, the Yorkshire League Cup and the Yorkshire Challenge Cup; and, with the arrival of Chilcott, Gleeson, Johnny Rogers, Arthur Swinden and Fred Longstaffe, they were to prove invincible. In 1912–13 three cups came to Fartown but in the 1914–15 season all four cups were won—a feat only ever equalled by Hunslet in 1908 and Swinton in 1928. Huddersfield came to within an ace of an all-time record in 1919–20—the next full season—when, with three cups won, they were beaten 3–2 by Hull in the Northern Rugby League Championship having finished first in the League table; on that vital day five Fartown players were away on an Australian tour.

Other records achieved at this period include Rosenfeld's eighty tries in the 1913–14 season and in the same year the defeat of Swinton Park 119–2—an all-time record score. Gronow kicked 150 goals and the points for the complete season were 1,222 against 273.

In the twenties the team was not so mighty as it had been. However Huddersfield were Rugby League and Yorkshire League Champions in 1929 and again in 1930. In 1933, 1945 and 1953 Fartown won the Rugby League Challenge Cup; and were League Champions in 1949 and 1962. Thus successes have been less consistent than in the high days of Fartown. The ground at Fartown held 35,136 for a cup semi-final game in April 1947, while the highest attendance for the home team was in March 1950 when there were 32,912 spectators.

In 1909 there were some in Huddersfield who hoped to see again the amateur game of Rugby Union. So it was that in that year they formed the Huddersfield Old Boys' Rugby Union Football Club and when the team was established at Salendine Nook, it provided its share of Yorkshire County Players. During the thirties the club moved to their present ground at Waterloo where a pavilion, grandstand and full facilities for the players are available.

It is a far cry today from the days of last century when every village had its own rugby team; Primrose Hill, Milnsbridge, Crosland Moor and the rest used to be keen rivals on the football field. Nowadays it is to Fartown that the crowds resort, much diminished, but very knowledgeable, generating the kind of enthusiasm seldom met in any other sport. Players and spectators alike come from all walks of life so that in this respect the original object of the Northern Union has been achieved.

Fartown has seen many famous names from overseas, but the chances of good local material achieving fame are greater in Rugby League than in the association game. There is always the chance that there might yet appear another Harold Wagstaff to wear the familiar Claret and Gold.

Also at Fartown, adjacent to the rugby ground, lies the cricket field where St John's Club first played cricket in 1865. On the formation of the Cricket and Athletic Club in 1875 Huddersfield played cricket there, eventually joining the District Cricket League. Some preliminary meetings at the Queen Hotel in February 1891 led to the formation of the League in March of that year when ten clubs decided to join. They were Armitage Bridge, Cliffe End, Huddersfield United, Golcar, Lascelles Hall, Linthwaite, Lockwood, Meltham Mills, Slaithwaite and Holmfirth. The original Huddersfield United club dropped out of the league during the nineties but by 1901 the Fartown club, hitherto in the West Riding Cricket League had joined the local league and won the championship; they were known officially as 'Huddersfield'.

Yorkshire first played at Fartown in 1874 and in the following year a North v South game was played in which W. G. and G. F. Grace took part. Since the 'Sykes' Cup Competition was inaugurated by Sir Charles Sykes, in 1920, Fartown has always provided the venue for the final tie. Yorkshire played their last game at Fartown in 1954.

Nineteen-twenty-eight saw the start of the Inter-League Matches—first played against Bradford and Leeds—and a player who appeared in three matches received a cap bearing the Huddersfield coat of arms. In 1933, Len Hutton of Pudsey St Lawrence Cricket Club played for the Bradford League against the Huddersfield League at Brighouse.

The Huddersfield Cricket League has provided Yorkshire with every type of player with the exception of a wicket-keeper; but by far the greatest number of local county players has come from Lascelles Hall—indeed, in 1874 we are told that the Yorkshire team once contained six men from there. Most of the local clubs have contributed to county sides and when competition for a place in the Yorkshire team has been fierce Huddersfield players have contributed to other county sides. In 1951 it was written of the Primrose Hill Club that 'much is expected of Ken Taylor (younger brother of Jeff Taylor), the fifteen-year-old player who should develop into an all-round player of exceptional ability'. Taylor has not only played for Yorkshire and England as an opening bat, but, from 1953 to '65 he played regularly for Huddersfield Town as centre-half. Willie Watson of Paddock achieved the same distinction besides playing in first class football for England and Huddersfield Town. However, when one looks at the records, four names stand out above all others—George Herbert Hirst, Wilfred Rhodes, Schofield Haigh and Percy Holmes.

In 1932 Percy Holmes of Paddock partnered Herbert Sutcliffe in a record first wicket stand of 555 for Yorkshire—an opening partnership that is also a world record. Few players have ever scored two double centuries in one match yet Holmes achieved this in 1920; he eventually made sixty centuries for Yorkshire and scored over 26,000 for his county; on three occasions he made over 2,000 runs in a season.

Hirst and Rhodes of Kirkheaton, Schofield Haigh of Armitage Bridge and Joseph Woodhead, J.P., founder of the *Huddersfield Examiner*, are shown in a unique photograph facing page 235. The picture was taken at Blake Lee near Marsden at a time when Yorkshire had won the championship for the seventh time in twelve years. George Hirst had been a member of the championship team of 1893 when Yorkshire topped the table for the first time. He was such a good all-rounder that in the national averages for 1903 he came third for batting and sixth for bowling. Hirst's feat of scoring 1,000 runs and taking 100 wickets in fourteen consecutive seasons was only ever beaten by Wilfred Rhodes who did it sixteen times making him statistically, as well as in the estimation of many judges of the game, the greatest player of all time. Hirst scored two centuries in one match against Somerset in 1906 when he also had bowling figures of six for 70 and five for 36. In all he scored 32,231 runs for Yorkshire and, like Percy Holmes, he scored over 2,000 runs in three seasons. In 1905 George Hirst made 341 runs, the highest individual score ever made, for Yorkshire; and in 1906 he scored 2,000 runs and took 200 wickets, a feat no one has ever equalled. The now legendary Test Match of 1902 against Australia cannot escape mention. Hirst, with fifteen runs needed for victory, was joined by young Wilfred Rhodes, the last man in. It was then that the great man made perhaps the most famous whisper in cricket 'Wilf, we'll get 'em in singles'—and they did: England was on that day saved by Kirkheaton!

Sport

Wilfred Rhodes in thirty-four years of county cricket took 4,188 wickets—an all-time record. Having begun to bat at number eleven for England, by dint of perseverance he became England's opener and, like Hirst, he scored for Yorkshire over 30,000 runs including two centuries in one match. In 1900 Rhodes took the record number of 261 wickets in one Yorkshire season. He is the only player ever to score 1,000 runs and take 100 wickets in test matches against Australia. When Wilfred Rhodes retired from first-class cricket in 1930, aged fifty-three he took a wicket with his last ball!

Schofield Haigh, though primarily a bowler, scored over 11,000 runs for his county between 1896 and 1912 and, in 1898, with George Hirst shared in a record partnership of 192 for the ninth wicket. 'Schofie' performed the hat-trick for Yorkshire three times and once took nine wickets in an innings. In 1900 when Yorkshire won the Championship, not only did Haigh and Rhodes top the bowling averages but, against Worcestershire, they bowled unchanged throughout an entire match. Huddersfield cricketers have much to live up to in the example of these four 'old timers'.

Looking at these men and the legends which have grown around them, and speculating, as one is apt to do, as to whether we shall ever see their like again, I must include one final George Herbert Hirst story; this I enjoyed reading in J. P. W. Mallalieu's *Sporting Days*.

'Just after the War, I was walking through Huddersfield's most attractive park where even under the eye of the Park Superintendent small boys are allowed to clout ball with bat. I stopped to watch; and, by and by, a shrunken old man with a cloth cap gently eased himself on to the grass and gently took a bat. "Lad," he said, "you hold it like this." I knew who was that shrunken old man. But the young boy did not; yet he took the bat, smiled and held it correctly!'

In recent years Huddersfield's sporting fame has been perpetuated not so much in football and cricket as in swimming and athletics by two great competitors Anita Lonsbrough and Derek Ibbotson.

In 1955 following successes in the three mile event in London and Manchester, Ibbotson played an important part in Chris Chataway's three-mile world record. He finished second to Chataway, who said afterwards 'I could never have broken the record without Derek Ibbotson's great unselfish help.' In August 1956 he became the ninth man to run the mile in under four minutes when he equalled the British national and English native records of three minutes and 59·4 seconds. In November of the same year he ran in the Olympic Games at Melbourne where he finished third to Vladimir Kuts and Gordon Pirie in the 5,000 metres.

In June 1957 Ibbotson ran the fastest mile to date by a British athlete when he did it in 3 minutes 58·4 seconds at Glasgow. A month later he beat this performance by setting up a new world record of 3 minutes 57·2 at the White City, London, against a field of the world's greatest milers.

Derek Ibbotson represented England many times after this including the Empire Games at Cardiff in 1958 and at Perth, Western Australia, in 1962. He still runs and works for his club, Longwood Harriers, where he trains and coaches the young athletes.

Huddersfield continued to be well represented in international sport when Anita Lonsbrough won the 220-yards breast stroke event in a match between Great Britain and Germany in June 1958. A month later she won the Empire Games Gold Medal for the same event in a record time of 2 minutes 53·5 seconds at Cardiff. In July 1959 she broke the world record for the 200 metres swimming against Holland.

Anita Lonsbrough's greatest triumph and the greatest individual sporting honour for the town came in August 1960 when she became Huddersfield's first ever Olympic Gold Medallist by winning the 200 metres breast stroke event in Rome in a time of 2 minutes 49·5 seconds.

In August 1962 Anita won her third individual gold medal when she won the 200 metres breast stroke in the European Championships at Leipzig. In September 1962 at Blackpool she reduced her world record for the 220 yards breast stroke to 2 minutes 52·2 seconds, and in the November at Perth, she broke the record yet again when she won the same event in 2 minutes 51·8 seconds; this gave Anita Lonsbrough yet another gold medal in the Empire Games. By winning the 110 yards and the 440 yards events she came away from Perth with two more gold medals.

On May 16th 1963 the Mayor, the late Alderman J. A. Bray, unveiled a commemorative plaque to Anita Lonsbrough in the Town Hall. Anita's final honour came in October 1964 when she carried the British flag at the Olympic Games in Tokyo and became the first woman ever to achieve this distinction. Up to the time of her marriage in 1965 Anita Lonsbrough worked as a clerk in the Borough Treasurer's Department.

The achievements of Derek and Anita alone do not of course justify a claim that amateur sport is booming in Huddersfield. Nevertheless, three local people have recently swum the channel, Miss K. Mayok in 1953, Frederick Oldman in August 1955 and Philip Kaye in August 1966. What is important is the fact that there are today over a hundred clubs in the Huddersfield and District Football League. This is a record number and shows that the interest in sport is still alive in the town even though the crowds at Leeds Road and Fartown are not what they were. Local sport must have its roots in village and social life, for, after all, this is where it all began.

As a postscript to this chapter it is fitting to mention the Huddersfield Amateur Swimming Club which was formed exactly one hundred years ago at Lockwood Baths. The first president Dr John Dow, himself winner of the River Thames Long Distance Championship, donated £25 for the purchase of medals to commemorate any individuals of outstanding service to the club. There are today 250 junior members and such is the interest in swimming that there are a further 100 children waiting to join the club.

Even as this book was being prepared for publication yet another noteworthy sporting feat was achieved by a Huddersfield man. On 30th July 1967, Malcolm Taylor, aged twenty-one completed the walk from John o'Groats to Land's End in 14 days 6 hours and 35 minutes to set up a new record for this 885-mile distance.

CHAPTER XVIII

Music and Entertainment

As we survey the popular entertainment and recreation of the last century we should bear in mind two important background features; first, the increasing prosperity of the town, reflected in the growth of activities of all kinds; and secondly, that religious tradition which either channelled recreation along certain lines or tended to restrict it altogether. Hobkirk noted with satisfaction the number of intellectual societies in the town in the 1860s but, when it came to musical or theatrical entertainment, Huddersfield had to improvise with existing buildings until the Town Hall and the Theatre Royal were completed, both in 1881.

The first theatre we know of, the New Theatre, flourished between 1816 and 1836 in a large barn at the bottom of Kirkgate. Choral singing used to take place variously at the old George Inn in the Market Place, a riding school in Albion Street and in an infants' school in Spring Street. The Horticultural Society frequently held its exhibitions in a warehouse, while the Commissioners of 1820 met at the Ramsden's Arms Inn. Perhaps typical of the informal intellectual meetings of the time were those held at 'Thornton's Temperance Hotel', New Street (now the site of Marks and Spencer), where Joseph Thornton[1] took the 'chair' at impromptu debates held in the coffee rooms. During the fifties Thornton's became well known for conversation, draughts and chess and, after 1868, we are told that members of the new Borough Council went there to discuss or 'explain away' their policies.

Huddersfield is renowned for choral singing. The Huddersfield Choral Society is today world-famous but is by no means

---

[1] Died 1887. Hotel continued until 1909.

the only local choir of national competition standard. First-class choirs of all types have flourished in our area for well over a hundred years, and we should consider why this has been so. Nonconformity brought with it two things, discipline and religious fervour. In Chapter V we spoke of the hesitancy with which they sang at Salendine Nook on receipt of their licence; but the singing soon became a very prominent feature of their worship. Wherever a new chapel was built a large choir followed, and by 1836 there were enthusiastic choirs at 'Nook', Highfield, Buxton Road, Pole Moor, Lockwood Baptist, Queen Street and Ramsden Street. Unlike the Parish Church choir, these were mixed, and participated in village 'sings' and social functions of all kinds; thus experience was gained and voices were developed. This, however, still does not answer the basic question: why did they sing so lustily in chapel? The Wesleyan doctrine of Salvation for all who repented was doubtless well worth celebrating in song, and certainly in Charles Wesley they had a prolific writer of hymns; and Methodists are still by tradition enthusiastic singers. But even more Calvinistic denominations, mainly Independents and Baptists, who would not appear to have the same cause for rejoicing burst into song. Perhaps they sang to appease the wrath of the Almighty, or was it as an expression of the independent spirit retaliating after an hour-long sermon on the subject of their sins and miseries? Here at any rate was a means of release for pent up feelings and a reaction against insignificance before the face of God and the drabness of a harsh way of life. The traditional reasons given for the rise of singing in Huddersfield have always mentioned the moorland air as being good for the lungs and so on: this may have been true at Pole Moor or Salendine Nook but hardly so in the town chapels. When the Anglican revival came, the Evangelical Movement also must have given rise to a missionary zeal which in turn inspired the congregation to 'sing to the Lord with cheerful voice'.

Yet another factor was the arrival of the German oratorios in eighteenth-century England—great works which completely overshadowed the traditional small anthems. Large numbers of performers were necessary for these works and the new industrial towns had the requisite population on which to draw. The inspiration of the new works, from Bach to Mendelssohn, was joy, praise or emancipation, and this must have appealed to many a Nonconformist temperament.

The Huddersfield Choral Society, though not the oldest of its kind,[1] was founded as far back as June 1836 following a meeting at the Plough Inn, Westgate. Sixteen founder-members decided to meet for practice in Spring Street Infants' School every month on or before the full moon. Once a quarter there would be a more polished performance to which guests might be invited. Members who arrived up to fifteen minutes late were to be fined threepence, and sixpence if they were absent altogether. The men paid a subscription of 2s. 6d. a half-year, ladies were admitted free but were liable to the fines. At the monthly meetings each member was allowed three gills of ale, bread and cheese, and something a little better for the quarterly concerts. Every member in turn was permitted to choose the next oratorio provided that the majority of members thought it possible to obtain the music. 'On the monthly nights any member shall be allowed to give his opinion after the perform-ance of any piece of music, provided he do so in a respectable manner, but no one shall be allowed to stop, interrupt or make any disturbance of the orchestra on pain of forfeiting the sum of 2s. 6d.' Good behaviour was enforced by a rule which ran: 'Any member being intoxicated or using obscene or abusive language or calling other members names shall forfeit sixpence for each offence.'

The Society's first conductor was Henry Horn, organist of St Paul's Church. In 1852 he was succeeded by James Battye, sexton at the Parish Church, a modest man—but perhaps second only to Sir Walter Parratt as the most accomplished musician the town ever produced. James Battye is still remem-bered for the anthems and part-songs he composed.

The first known performance of *Messiah* was on Good Friday 1844 at the Philosophical Hall when the entire work except for the 'Pastoral Symphony' was played, probably because the orchestra was short of violins. In those early days the soloists were chosen from among the Society's own members.

[1] Halifax 1818, Bradford 1821.

Music and Entertainment

One of the most famous was Susan Sykes from Brighouse who sang at all the concerts for twenty years and who was to become famous as Mrs Sunderland. Queen Victoria is alleged to have said to Mrs Sunderland: 'I am Queen of England but you are Queen of Song.' Indeed she often appeared at private recitals for the Royal Family and was privileged to sing the National Anthem before the Queen at the opening of Leeds Town Hall in 1858. When Mrs Sunderland retired in 1864 a two-day festival was held at the Philosophical Hall. 'On the second of those two summer nights, the streets surrounding the hall were packed by thousands unable to be accommodated within it; all traffic stopped and complete silence prevailed as from the open windows there floated forth upon the evening air the strains of the greatest, most popular and beloved artiste that Yorkshire ever knew.' The Society was paying its tribute to a real friend; and in 1888 on her golden wedding a special concert was given from the proceeds of which a fund for the annual Mrs Sunderland Musical Competition was inaugurated. She died in May 1905, aged eighty-six.

Stories abound of the early days of the Choral Society including that of the singer who dreamed he was in heaven supplying the bass part to the choir of angels singing the 'Hallelujah Chorus', and another concerning the bass player in the orchestra who was overheard to say, 'Pass me yon rosin and I'll show thee who t'King o' Glory is!'

Growing support and enthusiasm enabled the Choral Society to sing at the Crystal Palace in 1862 under Robert Burton, their new conductor from Leeds; but when the Philosophical Hall became a theatre in 1866 they soon felt the lack of a suitable place in which to perform. In 1872 they even gave a concert in Greenhead Park with the band of the Huddersfield Rifles. Joshua Marshall was conductor from 1876 to 1888 and, although support grew a little, it was the grand opening at the new Town Hall in 1881 which finally put the 'Choral' on its feet. The use of professional soloists and a wider range of works stem from this period. Charles Hallé and his orchestra accompanied 250 voices at the opening festival and, trained to perfection by Marshall, they sang *Elijah*, Berlioz' *Faust*, Spohr's *Last Judgment* and Rossini's *Stabat Mater*.

In 1887 the Huddersfield Choral Society, then 450 strong, became joint champions at the Welsh Eisteddfod in London, and the reception they got on their return was not unlike that of a football team triumphant from Wembley.

Huddersfield's fame as a musical town was also enhanced by the Glee and Madrigal Society, a band of singers who, under Joshua Marshall, won a competition in Manchester so decisively that they decided to stay together as a permanent choir. Thereafter they made their own tradition of competition successes and, during the First World War, sang *Elijah* in Westminster Abbey and then performed at No. 10 Downing Street at the invitation of Lloyd George.

Let us now follow the progress of the theatre. The Philosophical Hall was financed by the issue of Ten-Guinea Subscription Shares amongst the members of the Huddersfield Philosophical Society. The foundation stone was laid on 14th May 1836 on a site just below the chapel in Ramsden Street. The hall was opened on 24th May 1837 by Princess Victoria on the occasion of her eighteenth birthday and the event was commemorated by a dinner. The building consisted of a large hall with seats for 1,280, gallery and boxes; and there was a news room, reading room and a library. The front portion of the building was used as an auction room and an art gallery, and from 1859 to 1878 the Improvement Commissioners and later the Borough Council met there. In the Philosophical Hall political, religious and musical gatherings were held until 1866. Richard Oastler spoke there and the Choral Society performed there. In 1839 Robert Owen presided at a public debate on socialism, and when Johann Strauss the Elder came there with his Dance Orchestra, popular acclaim obliged him to make a repeat performance. In 1840 there was a great exhibition of science, art and invention. In 1846 Lord Shaftesbury addressed a rally for the Ten Hours Bill, and in the same year the stone laying of the new Railway Station was celebrated in the hall. Jenny Lind sang to a select audience in 1849 while Adelina Patti appeared there in 1862. In 1866 however, Huddersfield still lacked a permanent theatre until a Mr Morton Price purchased the Philosophical Hall at auction for £3,000 and turned it into the Theatre Royal.

Since the days of the New Theatre in Kirkgate there had been first the Circus Royal in Temple Street, now part of Westgate, from 1837 until 1846 when the street was demolished to build the new railway line; then from 1848 to 1862 the Riding School opposite St Paul's Church was the Theatre Royal (later, in turn, Hippodrome, Tudor and Essoldo), with stage, pit, gallery and boxes. In 1852 the Huddersfield Dramatic Institution gave two performances there for the relief of victims of the Holmfirth Flood and in 1856 a touring opera company played there for the first time in the town. In 1862 the premises were sold to the West Yorkshire Rifles for a drill hall, to be known as the 'Armoury' and Huddersfield was once more without a theatre.

From 1866 a wide range of productions was presented at the Philosophical Hall, from Shakespeare and grand opera to pantomime. In 1876 John le Blanc, well known as proprietor of the Gymnasium (later Ramsden Street Baths) became theatre manager under his real name of John White. White was a singer and showman who, typically, staged gymnastic turns which once included a death-defying leap from gallery to stage. In 1876 a Mr Shakespeare Hirst, 'Huddersfield's great and only amateur tragedian' appeared as Othello; on retirement from the stage, Hirst became—appropriately—licensee of the Shakespeare Inn, Northgate. 1877 saw a pantomime, *Robinson Crusoe* or *the Demon of Denby Dale and the Lily Lady of Linthwaite*! In 1878 *Uncle Tom's Cabin* was performed by a cast of genuine freed American slaves. In the same year the Town Council vacated their premises, and the old meeting chamber became a refreshment salon and lounge while the front of the theatre was lit by electricity. In 1879 the D'Oyly Carte Opera Company played *H.M.S. Pinafore* to full houses, and they were followed by Carl Rosa's English Opera Company conducted by Mr Rosa in person. Then, on 15th February 1880, on a Sunday morning, a constable on duty at the old police station in Bull and Mouth Street found the theatre was on fire. His discovery came too late to save the interior of the building from complete destruction.

The new Theatre Royal, which opened on 11th April 1881, was the first building in Huddersfield designed exclusively for theatrical productions. The stage was level with the street thus enabling large props, animals, and even a coach and horses to be driven on. The latter was a frequent feature of the Christmas pantomimes when I was a boy. The eighties and nineties witnessed many 'stupendous attractions' which featured brass bands, dogs, Maxim guns firing blank cartridges, and race horses steeplechasing over a real water jump. D'Oyly Carte continued to draw the crowds while *Lady Windermere's Fan, Charley's Aunt, The Geisha* and *The Belle of New York* made their first Huddersfield appearances at this period. In 1900 the Theatre Royal was closed for eleven months by order of the Corporation as it was necessary to improve the safety of the premises; better exits were made, and fireproof staircases, an asbestos curtain for the stage and a covered verandah outside were provided. The seating capacity was, in the interests of the audience, reduced to 1,160.

T. W. Rowley (1847–1925) performed at the Theatre Royal in 1882. He was Huddersfield's own comedian and, in his day, a music hall top liner. At the age of sixteen he once sang over a hundred songs from memory for a wager in a public house near Folly Hall; and he was earning thirty to forty pounds a week at the height of his stardom. In 1884 Rowley opened the Empire in St Peter's Street (now the site of the General Post Office) and tried every possible type of entertainment in his wooden theatre —opera, circus and variety.[1] Indeed Rowley literally stood on his head, but the audiences never came in sufficient numbers to make the venture pay. In 1900 there was talk of a new Grand Theatre on the site but it came to nothing. By 1902 Rowley's Empire had lost £25,000 and had swallowed up all his earnings and he had to sell out. Ironically when the Empire was taken over by new management, twice nightly variety shows were tried with great success; the Edwardian music-hall boom had reached Huddersfield and public transport had improved. Unfortunately for the Empire, the Magistrates in 1904 refused to renew the licence, but the proprietors were able to move to the Armoury when the Drill Hall in St Paul's Street had been

[1] In 1896 Rowley put on the 'theatrograph'—an early type of cinematograph which threw animated pictures onto a screen. Some were so realistic that the occupants of the front rows fled in terror!

opened. This they converted to the 'Hippodrome' which was opened by Vesta Tilley in July 1905.

The Choral Society was conducted by Sir Henry Coward from 1901 to 1932, and, under his direction, acquired new techniques and earned a national reputation. From this period onwards, the 'Choral' performed under the baton of many celebrated composers including Elgar, Parry, Walford Davies, Coleridge Taylor and Vaughan Williams. To commemorate his outstanding achievements there was instituted the Sir Henry Coward Memorial Fund to help local singers and musicians.

The Society was fortunate in securing the services of Dr (later Sir) Malcolm Sargent as its conductor in 1932;[1] and equally fortunate in the appointment at this time of Herbert Bardgett as chorus master. Under the direction of these two outstanding musicians of our time, the Huddersfield Choral Society has acquired international fame. The *Messiah*[2] at Christmas has become one of the great traditions of our town; both a social event and a religious experience, and criticism of one performance as against another has become purely academic.

There has, however, always been the desire to explore new horizons, and recordings and broadcasts have demanded an accuracy and expression never envisaged in the old days. Here we have been fortunate in the acoustic quality of the Town Hall a building large enough to take a big choir but not so vast that the performers cannot hear their own voices. The triumph of the Society in Vienna in 1958 was achieved in a hall very similar to the Town Hall, and this was followed in 1959 by a visit to Berlin, and in 1963 and 1965 by successful visits to Munich, Lisbon and Boston, U.S.A. In July 1949 they performed before the Queen (then Princess Elizabeth) and the Duke of Edinburgh. In October 1961 as a token of appreciation for his distinguished services to music in Huddersfield the Freedom of the Borough was presented to Sir Malcolm Sargent, and a Complimentary Resolution was passed by the Council to the Society to mark their outstanding contribution to the culture and prestige of the town over a period of 125 years.

[1] Sir Malcolm Sargent continued as conductor until his death in 1967.

[2] Records of the Choral Society performance of the *Messiah* have been sold all over the world.

Until comparatively recent times, the Society always had its own orchestra. 'The Choral Society Band' was usually composed of local musicians and there was seldom a lack of good musical talent. The Huddersfield Philharmonic Society, founded in 1884, owes its origins to Rev. John Thomas, Minister of Fitzwilliam Street Unitarian Church, himself a violinist. He taught his own string players and there were many who, in their day, owed all their musical education to 'Mr Thomas's Band'. Arthur W. Kaye was a celebrated teacher of the violin and many of our leading violinists today were once members of the A. W. Kaye String Orchestra. The Philharmonic Society flourished in the twenties under T. Fletcher Sykes as did the Huddersfield Permanent Orchestra under Wilfred Sizer. Many local musicians in those days found work in cinemas, until the arrival of the 'talkies'. Radio did not absorb all those who were then no longer needed in cinemas, and many left the profession altogether while some of the younger performers were deterred from entering it. Only the Philharmonic Orchestra has survived to us. The Choral Society had, moreover, found that for some of the newer concert works, the local orchestra needed reinforcement from outside. The Hallé, Northern Philharmonic and Yorkshire Symphony Orchestras were all later engaged to accompany the Society, and in recent years the Royal Liverpool Philharmonic Orchestra and the Huddersfield Choral Society have established a most happy relationship, performing and recording together.

A brief mention only can be made of other choirs which have brought renown to our area. The Huddersfield Vocal Union begun at Gledholt in 1913 under Fletcher Sykes, won First Prize at the Welsh National Eisteddfod in 1917 and again in 1925. In 1921 a similar honour was gained by the Holme Valley Male Voice Choir under Irving Silverwood.

There is a tradition of first-class organ playing in Huddersfield and this is probably due not only to the existence in the Town Hall of a fine Willis organ but also to the genius of Sir Walter Parratt[1] who was born in South Parade, and who at the age of eleven was organist at Armitage Bridge Parish Church.

[1] Sir Walter Parratt (1841–1924) lived in a house used by the Improvement Commissioners as offices from 1848 to 1859: it was eventually pulled down for road widening.

Music and Entertainment

From 1894 to 1924 Sir Walter was Master of the King's Musick at St George's Chapel, Windsor. There is the story that he once played Bach's Toccata and Fugue in D Minor on the organ of Brunswick Street Chapel while playing a game of chess with a friend at the same time. The game ended in checkmate to Sir Walter.

The Brass Band movement in Yorkshire is said to have originated in Leeds in 1836. Pre-eminently a working-class activity, we know of local bands playing in Richard Oastler's days and at most of the important outdoor events of the last century. In our area the standard of playing has traditionally been high. Bandsmen have contributed greatly to the musical life of the town and, in recent times, their musical standard has been considerably raised as a result of keen competition, in local and national contests, and by the execution of some difficult pieces composed especially for brass band.

The reputation of Huddersfield's musicians stands very high indeed. This I can attest from personal experience having sung and played with bands and orchestras first at home, then in other parts of the country, and finally overseas. I found the standard of musicianship I had left behind far superior to what I often found elsewhere, and other musicians were only too pleased to welcome me as an instrumentalist or as a singer from Huddersfield. I very soon discovered that I had a reputation to live up to, and whether in the pit of a theatre, concert hall, or dance hall, I remained convinced that standards of performance were usually higher in Huddersfield than elsewhere. This tradition is today well maintained by the Huddersfield Youth Orchestra, by the Department of Music at the College of Technology, the Philharmonic Society, and by the Amateur Operatic Society and the Light Opera Society.

From 1901 to 1918 the Theatre Royal introduced us to the musical comedies of Leslie Stuart, Lionel Monkton, Paul Rubens and many others, and Huddersfield saw *The Quaker Girl, The Arcadians, The Merry Widow, Floradora,* and *The Maid of the Mountains,* to name but a few. Nor was there a shortage of plays at this time; Sir Frank Benson with his Shakespearean Company came for the first time in 1905, and in 1908 the first Bernard Shaw play. In 1916 *Pygmalion* surprised the audiences with its strange adjectives. In 1912 four plays by Ibsen were presented; and Albert Chevalier, Matheson Lang, Gertrude Lawrence and Seymour Hicks all appeared at the Theatre Royal during this period. In 1916 a large audience saw the first performance in Huddersfield of *Madame Butterfly*.

In July 1918 the Theatre Royal opened under the management of Alfred Wareing, having been bought by a local company. Mr Wareing hoped to establish a Yorkshire Repertory Company and promised that the theatre would add a new dignity to the town. In fact repertory seasons were held from 1921 to 1930 but it was not until 1931 that Huddersfield's own resident company was formed.

During the twenties, however, despite appearances by Anna Pavlova, the world's greatest dancer, in Russian Ballet, a performance of the opera *La Bohème*, a season of international masterpieces by Tchekov, Pirandello and Ibsen, and many plays by Shakespeare and Shaw, the Theatre did not really pay its way. In 1919 James R. Gregson from Brighouse, a local playwright, became acting manager of the Theatre and was instrumental in the formation of the Huddersfield Thespians. Alfred Wareing offered them as encouragement the promise of one day performing at the Theatre Royal.

The Thespians won the British Drama League Competition in 1925 and this resulted in their performing in New York the following year, where they won a second prize. One of the founders of the society was Mr Montgomery of Hillhouse Higher Grade School; their secretary in 1926 was Philip Ahier. The activities of the Huddersfield Thespians were such that from their foundation in 1920 up to 1928 no fewer than sixty-four plays were put on.

For the Theatre Royal, the twenties were difficult times, and both the General Strike and the rival attractions at other places of entertainment were partly to blame for Wareing's announcement in 1928 that in only one year had box-office receipts exceeded expenditure. In fact the theatre had been kept alive only by profits from the sale of cigarettes and chocolates.

The occasion of this speech was the reopening of the Theatre Royal after redecoration in 1928, which included a striking mural painting over the proscenium arch by William O. Hutchinson. The scene depicted a fairground and included in the picture were many well-known personalities including Mr Wareing himself. I well remember sitting in the gallery, as a child, reading on the merry-go-round the words 'Life's a roundabout', though the philosophy was rather beyond my comprehension at the time.

Nineteen hundred and twenty-nine was for Alfred Wareing a stormy but memorable year. In the February there was the first performance anywhere of a British opera, *Bronwen* by Joseph Holbrooke, at the end of which the composer is said to have paid some uncomplimentary remarks to the orchestra. In the July the world premiere of a new Pirandello play *Lazzaro,* took place with a cast headed by Donald Wolfitt. In May 1930, poor support for Shaw's *Back to Methuselah* made the author remark that 'Huddersfield is plainly in a dark and pagan condition' and named the town 'Heathen Huddersfield'! This insult was followed by trouble over Alfred Wareing's production of Galsworthy's *Strife* during a textile dispute. Bernard Shaw was invited to intervene as Wareing believed the trade unions were boycotting the Theatre; but Shaw declined and advised Wareing to put on *East Lynne* and cut his losses!

In April 1931 the fiftieth anniversary of the Theatre Royal was celebrated by the inauguration of the Resident Company in *As You Like It,* thus fulfilling Alfred Wareing's original ambition. He said: 'Huddersfield which has often led the way in important movements, is about to have an opportunity of showing the rest of England what can be done with its theatre.' The company had over twenty-five artistes and there were to be distinguished guests from time to time. However, although twice-nightly performances were held in order to increase the revenue, the company was disbanded on 11th July, and the theatre closed for lack of support. Alfred Wareing resigned on 6th August; the experiment had failed, underlining the truth that good drama is not necessarily popular entertainment.

The Theatre Royal continued with plays by the Denville Stock Company, the Kennedy Players, and with musical comedy until 6th June 1936 when lack of support again caused the theatre to close down. James R. Gregson, then a member of the Borough Council, sought to have the Theatre Royal taken over by the Corporation, only to find that they had no powers to undertake such a step. The theatre was in fact saved when new proprietors came forward and improvements were made to the building.

During the war, the migration of many famous artistes from London to the provinces gave our theatre names such as Emlyn Williams, Beatrice Lillie and Tom Walls in quick succession. The D'Oyly Carte Opera Company, Sadler's Wells and the Old Vic companies came, as also did the Anglo-Polish Ballet. The audiences reacted to such fare and the theatre was well supported.

The Theatre Royal was demolished in 1961 to make way for a comprehensive redevelopment scheme in the town centre. Undeterred, the enthusiasts managed to convert a dance hall, once a billiard hall, near the Palace Theatre into the 'New Theatre'. This venture later became dependent for much of its financial support upon the Borough Council and, when it was decided in February 1967 not to continue this support, the New Theatre was wound up. For this, one can perhaps blame television, changing public taste and the economic situation among the factors; but for Miss Nita Valerie who had transferred her enthusiasm here, the closure was a big disappointment. She said: 'The town will not support anything second rate.' Experience suggests that only the most costly productions have, in the past, drawn the crowds. This was true during the war, as I well remember, and for such productions to pay, the theatre would have to be extremely large or the seats ridiculously expensive.

From 1905 onwards the Hippodrome was a success and in August 1909 the Palace Theatre opened in Kirkgate. Both theatres prospered with variety, revue and melodrama and both included silent films in their early programmes. In 1926 the Hippodrome was enlarged, and reopened with plays in the summer and musical shows in the winter, but in 1930 became the Tudor Cinema. The Palace continued its twice-nightly variety until 23rd January 1936 when fire broke out just before the start of a performance, and the interior of the building was badly damaged, though fortunately no one was hurt. Completely, modernised, it reopened on 1st March 1937 and variety shows continued until 1954. As in the case of the Theatre Royal, many top-line artistes came to the Palace during the war but again, with the arrival of television, live entertainment suffered a severe blow. The Palace reopened in 1955 but continuing lack of support made its closure in 1957 inevitable. In 1959 the Palace became the Palace Continental with dining, dancing and cabaret, but this too failed. Now Huddersfield is completely without a permanent theatre. The Amateur Operatic Society and the Light Opera Society use the ABC Cinema once a year while the Thespians use St Patrick's Parochial Hall, for periodic productions.

The cinema came to Huddersfield gradually. First Pringles showed films in the Victoria Hall in the Co-operative Buildings, Buxton Road; then in 1910, the Picturedrome was opened, also in Buxton Road. Nineteen hundred and eleven saw the Theatre de Luxe in the Old Post Office Skating Rink where silent films were also shown. The Picture House, Ramsden Street, opened in 1912 and was the first building to be put up specially for film shows; it stood next to the Theatre Royal and in its day had a fine organ. The Empire followed in 1915 and it, too, was designed exclusively for silent films, and there were cinemas in the suburbs by the early twenties. In those days there was no radio but, so long as films remained silent, the cinema was not an overwhelming competitor to the live theatre.

After the First World War, the Princess opened in 1923 and also showed silent films until April 1929 when *The Singing Fool*, starring Al Jolson, made its impact. This was the first talking picture; and a now departed relative of mine sobbed throughout the entire performance, saying 'Isn't it good!' By August 1929 half the local musicians employed in cinemas were out of work, and the Musicians' Union vainly tried to stem the tide by appealing to the public not to patronise 'canned music'. Cinemas from then onwards sprang up all over the town and eventually there were twenty-one of them, including the Ritz (now ABC) which seats over 2,000. Now in 1967 there are four.[1]

The world of the cinema has produced many stars and among

[1] The destruction of the Essoldo by fire on 9th December 1967 has, perhaps temporarily, reduced the number to three.

the great must surely be James Mason who was born in Huddersfield. He has been making films for thirty-four years; and although his home is in Beverley Hills, California, he still returns to Marsh to visit his relatives from time to time.

From what has been said so far about music and the stage the dictum that Huddersfield prefers the best is abundantly clear. After the disbandment of the Yorkshire Symphony Orchestra in 1955, the Corporation Arts Committee inaugurated an annual series of symphony concerts and recitals by some of the world's finest orchestras and artistes. These concerts have been supported with tremendous enthusiasm; I well remember as a boy, the thrill of sitting in the cheaper seats on the platform behind a first-class orchestra when the Town Hall was full to capacity.

Before the days of frequent outings to the coast and other modern types of entertainment, Huddersfield folk would take advantage of a tram ride to Honley; there a short walk led to Hope Bank Amusement Park advertised as: 'New Blackpool— Music for dancing on Saturdays, swings, donkey rides, aerial flights, boating, good stabling for horses, all kinds of temperance beverages—the favourite resort for enjoyment in summer, the most beautiful valley in the district'.

There were in addition brass band concerts and firework displays. Hope Bank was still thriving in the thirties when children fished in the lake, rode on the miniature railway, lost themselves in the maze or gazed at the hall of mirrors. After the war, popular taste grew away from purely local places of enter-tainment and today one of Brook Motors' factories stands where I once fished for minnows.

Many will look back with nostalgia to the days of 'Admission Saturdays 2*d.*: Other days 1*d.*!'

CHAPTER XIX

The Future

A B.B.C. PROGRAMME broadcast in February 1966, entitled 'By car to the shops', compared the rebuilding of Huddersfield with that of Plymouth. The plan for the reconstruction of Plymouth however was drawn up while the bombs were still falling and destroying the centre of the city. By comparison, Huddersfield came through the war unscathed and its plan for redevelopment follows that of Plymouth about twenty years later. Plymouth though now rebuilt, has its traffic problems unsolved because the estimates of future traffic were far too low. Huddersfield has learned from this and other experiences and a comprehensive plan has been evolved which will take us into a future where the motor car and the town will attempt to come to terms with each other. In order to achieve this happy state of affairs the town must be replanned on a massive scale.

Taylor Dyson, commenting on the 'thirties, remarked in his final chapter; 'Isn't Huddersfield changing!' To him the developments of those days must have seemed impressive, for the town centre had altered little since the last century save for a few cinemas and some new shop fronts. Taylor Dyson saw the Cloth Hall and the Kings Head Yard disappear and old property demolished between Northgate and the River Colne, the inhabitants being re-housed at Bracken Hall. A new public library was being built and there was the new Palace Theatre, while the old trams gave way to the trolley bus—the last word in modern transport. Huddersfield was indeed changing but only in detail leaving the town fundamentally unaltered.

Now the stage has been reached where a radical redevelopment of the town is vital if we are to avoid living in a perpetual traffic jam, asphyxiated by our own exhaust fumes. Nor is the traffic problem the only reason for a new plan. Some people must, of necessity, be brought back to live in the town if there is to be any real life there at all. At the same time shopping facilities must be brought up to date, for in our surrounding areas lies a very important source of custom which Huddersfield must continue to attract. Taylor Dyson was obviously impressed by the 'thirties; he would have been astounded had he lived in the 'seventies and seen what is, in fact, in store for us.

Eminent planning consultants, engaged by the Council, have produced a plan for the re-development of the Town Centre, and a photograph of the model of the new Huddersfield is shown facing page 234. Huddersfield lies on a splendid sloping site, the envy of many other towns, and this gives to many of our streets and their buildings wonderful vistas. If the car becomes the servant and not the master within a new Huddersfield central area, we can achieve convenience and comfort in unique surroundings. The key to the entire plan is the Inner Ring Road, due for completion in the early 'seventies. This new road will be a three-lane dual carriageway with the minimum number of access points in order to facilitate the flow of traffic. Ultimately,

An Artist's Impression of the St George's Square of the Future: by courtesy of Building Design Partnership

there will be parking available for about 14,000 cars, left of necessity in the off-street parking places and multi-storey car park, as the town's main streets are to be reserved for pedestrians only. Within the area bounded by the ring road, through traffic will be able to run from Trinity Street via Railway Street to St John's Road, and from Northumberland Street to Leeds Road, and along Lord Street and Zetland Street. Other roads in the town will be retained only for the servicing of the shops, at specified times of the day. Trees will grow along John William Street and New Street and shoppers will stroll under a continuous shelter or take refreshment at a kerbside cafe, similarly protected from the elements. We find recommended, sycamores for John William Street, ash trees for Westgate and Ramsden Street, and the flowering cherry for New Street.

It becomes increasingly apparent that access to Huddersfield by road is in need of improvement. Quite soon, the M.1. Motorway will reach Horbury on its way to Leeds from London, and the M.62 Lancashire-Yorkshire Motorway, will cut across from near Rastrick to Outlane on its way over the Pennines. Linking Huddersfield to the new motorway is proposed a new road, the Outlane Freeway, to join the Longroyd Freeway which will in turn link with Folly Hall and Wakefield Road, then on to the proposed new Leeds Road Freeway. An alternative route from M.62 will lead from near Bradley Bar where the Red Doles Freeway will run down to Leeds Road. Thus the freeway system will form an outer ring road following about half the perimeter at about three quarters of a mile from the town centre.

There are many who will appreciate the opportunity of living in the town and thus solving their problems of shopping and transport; and the atmosphere of the town centre will benefit from their presence. New housing can be used to attract skilled labour to Huddersfield while economy of space might be achieved by building new housing over the car parks. In the Spring Grove area, new blocks of flats will have open spaces between. There will be a new Spring Grove School and a subway for pedestrians, crossing the ring road. Grass, trees, paving and play areas will become features of the new site. Below the Parish Church there could be housing of a different type. To provide open spaces at ground level here would be difficult so the new accommodation envisaged would be for families, and there might be a subway under Venn Street.

Public transport has been surveyed and three bus stations are proposed as a result. A single terminus for all buses might, it is feared, overload the ring road at one point. Routes therefore from the south-east will terminate in the region of Zetland Street; those from the north-east will run to the Lord Street area, and all other services will use a new bus station to be located probably near the Railway Station. Through routes will skirt the fringe of the central pedestrian area.

Shopping facilities are to be modernised by large-scale schemes already started. The Murrayfield Scheme (Phase I) is, in fact, completed and comprises new shops and an office block, between New Street (Buxton Road prior to August 1966) and the Town Hall. On the other side of New Street, the Hammerson Development now building occupies the area between High Street, South Parade and the new Civic Centre (Phase I). The Murrayfield Scheme (Phase II) includes a new Market Hall stretching from Peel Street to Queensgate, facing the Public Library. Where the Theatre Royal stood will become an open space with trees and grass forming an oasis amongst the shops. Beneath the new market an underground service road will provide for delivery to the shops which replace the old Market Hall. A similar system will provide for the shops being built as part of the redevelopment of the Pack Horse Yard on which work commenced in late 1966. There are, however, limits to the number of shops which a town like Huddersfield can support, and careful consideration has been given not only to the shopping habits of the present population, but also to its future size, and anticipated spending power. Were the town to have too few shops, people would tend to look elsewhere; if there were too many, some would close while the service offered in those which remained would deteriorate as they struggled for survival, one against another.

Phase I of the Civic Centre Project, opened in October 1965, accommodates the Borough Treasurer's, Education, Health, Borough Architect's and Town Planning Departments. Phase II completed in 1967, comprises the central Police Headquarters, a suite of law courts, and the Weights and Measures Department. Phase III, when built, will provide a new Council Chamber, committee rooms and civic suite, and a tower block of offices for other Corporation departments. Then, for the first time, the Borough Council and its departments will have accommodation in keeping with a modern town.

Over a century ago John William Street was made and, in that scheme, buildings were erected which completely changed the character of the town. Then came the Charter of Incorporation in 1868, to be followed by a period of great municipal enterprise which gave Huddersfield the sound basis from which it has developed. In this century, comparatively few new buildings have gone up in the town, and the time has arrived to look the future firmly in the face, and re-plan boldly. In some other towns, where rapid development took place just before or after the last war, most of the buildings are still too new to scrap, thus it may be well nigh impossible to carry out a plan comparable with ours. Although Huddersfield was far from inactive in the earlier years of this century, there are many old buildings of the nineteenth century ready to be pulled down to make way for new, and this must be advantageous in the long run. The architecture of St George's Square, Westgate and Byram Street will survive, as will our magnificent Town Hall and the many churches and chapels still with us. The past is written in their stones and it is a history of which we should be all proud.

We may well ask ourselves who are the real heroes of our story—the part-time farmers, textile workers and 'clothiers' who lived in the countryside; the religious reformers; the master manufacturers who built up our industries by their enterprise; the generations of public-spirited men, and latterly women, who have served on the Borough Council, and its predecessors; or the thousands of men and women who have made the manufactures of Huddersfield synonymous with quality? Of course, there is no answer; but most of us share this common ancestry of hardworking, enterprising folk and the most fitting tribute we can pay is to remember them all as we celebrate this great Centenary.

APPENDIXES

Place Names of the Huddersfield Area

THE STUDY of place names is a science in itself and in this list of names it is possible only to give a general meaning to most. Some are still of uncertain origin and here space does not permit the various alternatives to be fully discussed.

Most names were determined before the Norman Conquest though few go back as far as our Celtic ancestors. Thus they are mainly Anglo-Saxon, Danish or Norse in origin. Generally speaking, the name of a place is a compound of two parts, the second part describing the area so named.

Thus we find *royd*, a clearing; *ley*, a meadow; *by*, a settlement; *ham*, a homestead; *ton*, a fenced farm; *field*, a piece of open country; *thwaite*, an 'assart' or land previously waste; *thorpe*, a hamlet; *thong*, a narrow strip of land; *worth*, a holding of land; *bury*, a fortified place.

There are two main types of the first part of a name—the personal and the descriptive. Personal names are found in *Skelman-thorpe*, the hamlet of Skelman; *Edger-ton*, the fenced farm of Eckhart; *Huddersfield*, the field of Huda (or Uther?); Descriptive names are found in *Stain-land*, the stony land; *Deigh-ton*, the fenced farm by the dyke; *Raw-thorpe*, an isolated hamlet.

Detailed derivations of names are to be found in: *The Place Names of the West Riding of Yorkshire*, Parts I, II and III,[1] English Place Name Society; *Angles, Danes and Norse in the District of Huddersfield*, W. J. Collingwood; *Place Names and Surnames*, Taylor Dyson; and *Place Names of South-West Yorkshire*, Armitage Goodall.

[1] Part I: Staincross Wapentake. Part II: Agbrigg Wapentake. Part III: Morley Wapentake.

Appendix II

Agbrigg: Aggi's bridge, traditional meeting place of the Wapentake near Wakefield.

Almondbury: The fortress of the Aelmann or Welsh, i.e. the last refuge of the Britons when the Angeles came; or the fortified place owned by all the men of the village. The fortress is almost certainly Castle Hill.

Armitage Bridge: Bridge of the Hermitage.

Aspley: Aspen tree meadow.

Austonley: Aelfstan's meadow.

Beaumont Park: The Beaumont family owned land round here from the fifteenth century.

Berry Brow: Fortified hillside; or hillside of barley; or wooded hillside.

Birchencliffe: Birch tree cliff.

Birkby: Settlement of the Britons or Birch farmstead.

Blackmoorfoot: Edge of the bleak moor.

Bradley: Broad meadow.

Brockholes: Badger holes.

Brighouse: Houses by the bridge.

Calder: Rapid stream.

Cawthorne: Cold thornbush.

Colne: Noisy river (origin obscure.)

Colne Bridge: The bridge which the monks built to join Bradley with Kirkheaton.

Cooper Bridge: A ford which cows could use.

Cowlersley: Coller's meadow; or charcoal burner's wood.

Cowcliffe: Bare cliff.

Crimble: A small plot of land.

Crosland: Land or estate where there is a cross.

Cumberworth: Estate of a Cumbrian or Briton.

Dalton: Enclosure in the dale.

Deighton: Enclosure by a ditch.

Denby; Denaby: The Danes' hamlet.

Edgerton: Eckhart's enclosure.

Elland: Land by the water.

Emley: Emma's meadow.

Farnley Tyas: Fern meadow of the Tyas (=German) family.
Fartown: A second hamlet within the Township of Huddersfield.
Fenay: Water meadow by the fen.
Fixby: Fegh's settlement.
Flockton: Floki's settlement.

Gledholt: Wood frequented by kites.
Golcar: Guthlaug's hillside pasture.
Grange Moor: Moor of an outlying farm of a religious settlement.

Helme: Farmstead or shelter.
Hepworth: Heppa's enclosure.
Holme: A piece of land surrounded by water.
Holmfirth: A wood in the low-lying land; or a ford across the swampy
  meadow.
Honley: Hana's clearing; or the glade of the woodcock.
Huddersfield: The open country of Huda, Hudraed.

Ingbirchworth: Farmstead by the birch trees in the meadow.

Kirkburton: Church of the enclosed farm (or cowshed)
Kirkheaton: Church of the high settlement.
Kirklees: Ecclesiastical lands.

Lepton: Enclosed strip of land; or a steep enclosure.
Leymoor: Clearing by the moor.
Linthwaite: Flax clearing.
Lindley: Flax meadow.
Lingards: Flax enclosure.
Lockwood: Enclosed wood.
Longley: Long clearing.
Longroyd Bridge: Bridge of the long clearing (boundary of Hudders-
  field Township).
Longwood: A village lying on a long narrow ledge, once wooded,
  below Longwood Edge.

Marsden: Boundary valley.
Meltham: Settlement for smelting; or for malting.
Milnsbridge: Bridge belonging to the mill.
Moldgreen: Green earth.

Netherthong: Lower narrow strip of land.
Netherton: Lower hamlet.
Newsome: New houses.

Outlane: Settlement on the Roman road 'out' and which formed the Wapentake boundary.

Paddock: An enclosure.
Pole Moor: Moorland about the marsh.
Pule Hill: Pool on the hill.

Quarmby: The settlement by the corn mill.

Rastrick: Isolated enclosure or place of rest (on the road from Brighouse to Rochdale).
Rawthorpe: Isolated hamlet.

Scammonden: Skambani's dale.
Scholes: Sheds or huts.
Scissett: Scissa's (Cecilia's) homestead.
Shelley: Meadow on a hillside.
Shepley: Sheep meadow.
Skelmanthorpe: Skelmar's settlement.
Slack: Hillside meadow.
Slaithwaite: Battlefield or a hillside; or a place where timber was felled.
Stainland: Stony land.
Standedge: Stone edge or escarpment.
Storthes (Hall) : Young plantations.

Thurstonland: domain of Thorsteinn.
'*Thwaite*': An assart=land previously waste.

Upper thong: Upper narrow strip of land.

Wessenden: Valley with rock suitable for whetstones.
Whitley: White meadow.
Wilberlee: Wild boar meadow.
Woodhouse; Woodsome: Wood house.
Wooldale: Ulf's dale.

Townships

THE EXTENT of the ancient parishes and townships in or near Huddersfield (The approximate area covered by this book):

Parish of Almondbury

ALMONDBURY[1] : Castle Hill, Longley, Newsome, Fenay Bridge, Taylor Hill, Austonley, S. Crosland, Armitage Bridge, Netherton.
FARNLEY TYAS : Woodsome Hall.
HOLME : Holme Moss.
HONLEY : Brockholes, Mytholm Bridge.
LINTHWAITE : Cowlersley, Milnsbridge (part), Blackmoorfoot.
LOCKWOOD : Beaumont Park, Crosland Moor, Dry Clough, Rashcliffe, Yews Hill, Thornton Lodge.
MARSDEN : Lingards, Pule Hill, Standedge, Wessenden.
MELTHAM : Helme, Thick Hollins, Harden Moss, Marten Nest, Shooters Nab.
NETHERTHONG : Holmfirth (part).
UPPERTHONG : Holmfirth (part).

Parish of Huddersfield

GOLCAR : Milnsbridge (part), Botham Hall, Scar Bottom, Leymoor, Scapegoat Hill.
HUDDERSFIELD : Bradley, Colne Bridge, Deighton, Edgerton, Gledholt, Birkby, Marsh (part), Sheepridge, Cowcliffe, Fartown, Paddock.
LINDLEY : Quarmby, Birchencliffe, Lindley Moor, Oakes, Salendine Nook, Marsh (part), Rein Wood, Royds Hall.

[1] Thus, Almondbury Township contained Cástle Hill, Longley etc.— smaller districts, villages or hamlets.

Appendix III

LONGWOOD: Outlane, Slack, Ball Royd, Snow Lea, Mount.
SCAMMONDEN: Deanhead, Pole Moor, West Carr.
SLAITHWAITE: Deer Hill, Hill Top, Merry Dale, Wilberlee.

Parish of Kirkheaton

DALTON: Bradley Mills, Dalton Bank, Moldgreen, Rawthorpe.
KIRKHEATON: Helme, Houses Hill, Upper Heaton.
LEPTON: Lascelles Hall, Rewley Hill, Gawthorpe, Tandem.
UPPER WHITLEY: Whitley Beaumont, Denby Grange, Grange Moor.

Parish of Kirkburton

CARTWORTH: Hinchcliffe Mill.
FULSTONE: Jackson Bridge.
HEPWORTH: Crow Edge.
KIRKBURTON: High Burton, Thorncliffe.
SCHOLES
SHELLEY
SHEPLEY
THURSTONLAND: Storthes Hall, Thunder Bridge.
WOOLDALE: Thongsbridge.

FIXBY, now in the County Borough, was formerly in the Parish of Halifax and in the Wapentake of Morley.

Population

THE HOLDING of a national census every ten years was instituted in 1801. From this date until 1861 the figures given below are for the Township of Huddersfield, the extent of which is shown in Appendix III.

1801	7,268	1841	25,068
1811	9,671	1851	30,880
1821	13,284	1861	34,874
1831	19,035		

From the acquisition of the Charter in 1868, the figures given for the Borough are:

1871	70,253	1881	81,841

In 1890 the district of Longwood became part of the County Borough.

1891	95,417	1921	119,725
1901	95,043	1931	123,048
1911	107,821		

In 1937 parts of the Colne Valley, Kirkheaton and Lepton were added. In 1938 part of South Crosland was added. There was no census in 1941.

1951	129,026	1961	130,652

1967 (Registrar General's Estimate) 132,210

Local Surnames

AN ANALYSIS of 3,519 families in the Colne Valley produced only 733 surnames.[1]

They fall into the four categories into which scholars have divided us; place names, fathers' names (patronymics), occupations and nicknames.

In very early days, baptismal names or Christian names were quite sufficient, but as village life grew more complicated so it became necessary to differentiate between the several persons who bore the same name.

In the Poll Tax Return for 1379 in Huddersfield we find:
John of the White field (Whytacre)
John by the Brook
John of the Greenwood
John from Mirfield
John the Cooper (maker of tubs)
John, son of little Ann (Annotson)

Of forty-six surnames contained in this document, Taylor Dyson[2] finds thirty are geographical, twelve patronymics, three occupations and one nickname. He also finds this pattern typical of West Riding surnames because our ancestors were strongly influenced by their environment; family and occupational ties were also strong in an area from which there was little shift of population. Perhaps the hard life they lived left them little time for nicknames or practical jokes.

The Colne Valley surnames of 1921 were classified as follows:

---

[1] Article by the Huddersfield Antiquarian Society in the *Huddersfield Examiner*, 30th December 1921.

[2] *Place Names and Surnames*, p. 109.

Appendix V

PLACE NAMES

Armitage: Hermitage, 42.[1]
Bamford: From Bamford, Lancashire, 135.[1]
Brook: By the brook, 34.[1]
Clegg: Clough; a hollow.
Firth: At the wide valley, 28.[1]
Garside: By the enclosure, 58.[1]
Haigh: An enclosure, 62.[1]
Hirst: At the wood, 110.[1]
Hoyle: A hollow, 33.[1]
Kay: At the quay.
Schofield: At the school field, 35.[1]
Shaw: At the wood, 120.[1]
Sykes: A small stream, 223.[1]
Wood: At the wood, 74.[1]

Lower down the list in order of numbers were: Crosland, Lockwood, Dalton, Denby, Helm, Lindley, Oakes, Newsome: these are all local places and are not those of any large towns because any migration would be from the countryside to the towns.

PATRONYMICS

Bates: Son of Bartholomew.
Batty: Son of Bartholomew.
Dixon: Son of Richard.
Dyson: Son of David.
Parkinson: Son of Peter.
Pearson: Son of Peter.
Perry: Son of Peter.
Pogson: Son of Margaret.
Richardson: Son of Richard.
Wadsworth: Son of Wade.
Wilkinson: Son of William.
Williamson: Son of William.
Wilson: Son of William.

OCCUPATIONAL

Bailey: Bailiff.

[1] Indicates actual number of families surveyed which bore this name.

303

Barker: Tannery worker.
Baxter: Baker.
Reeve: Land agent.
Ward: Guardian.

TEXTILE TRADES
Draper
Fuller
Lister: A dyer.
Taylor: A weaver, 57.[1]
Walker: Fuller, 55.[1] (comes from an old Norse word meaning 'to thicken' and is not derived from any concept of walking on the cloth).
Webb, Webster, Webber: Weaver.

NICKNAMES
Ambler
Brown: 8.[1]
Kaye: A jackdaw.
Luty: Loyal.
Russel: A fox.
Sharpe
Stott: A bull.
Swallow
Swift
Tyas: Teutonicus, a German.
White
Whitehead: 33.[1]
Wimpenny: Thrifty, 7.[1]

SOME OTHER NAMES FOUND IN OUR AREA

GEOGRAPHICAL (place names)
Ackroyd: Oak clearing.
Ainley: Isolated meadow.
Aspinall: By the well near the aspen trees.

Beaumont: Norman-French; beautiful mountain.

[1] Indicates actual number of families surveyed who bore this name.

Appendix V

Beverley: From Beverley.
Blackburn: From Blackburn or by the black stream.
Booth: At the cottage.
Boothroyd: At the cottage clearing.
Bradley: At the broad meadow.
Briggs: At the bridge.
Broadbent: At the wide expanse of coarse grass.

Charlesworth: Charles' estate.
Cliffe: By the slope or river bank.

Firth: At the wide valley or bay.

Greenhalgh: At the green hill.

Halstead: At the 'Hall stead'.
Hardcastle: Possibly from Harden Castle.
Hemingway: Derived from Low Countries; Hemming—a Dutch name.
Hepworth: From Hepworth.
Heywood: From Heywood, Lancashire; or occupational.
Hinchliffe: From Hinchcliffe Mill; at the steep cliff.
Holmes: Low lying land.
Holroyd: At the hollow in the clearing.
Horsfall: At the loud waterfall.

Ingham: Meadow settlement.

Lawton: From Lawton.
Learoyd: At the meadow clearing.
Lee, Leece, Legge: A lea (open land, grassland).
Littlewood: At the little wood.
Lodge: At the cottage.

Marsden: From Marsden.
Milnes: At the mill.
Moorhouse: At the house on the moor.
Murgatroyd: At Margaret's clearing.

Netherwood: At the lower wood.

Ogden: The oak valley.

Park: At the park (woodland reserved for hunting).
Pickles: At the meadows on the hilltops (peak leas).

Quarmby: From Quarmby.

Ramsden: Valley of rams.
Redfearn: From Redfearn.
Rhodes: At the cross roads; might be derived from 'Royd'—a clearing.
Rippon: From Ripon.
Robertshaw: At Robert's wood.
Rothery: The cattle corner.
Rothwell: The well in the clearing.

Schofield: At the school field.
Sheard: At the gap in the enclosure.
Shires: At the boundary.
Stancliffe: By the stone cliff.
Stead: At the farmstead.
Stocks: At the tree trunk.
Sugden: From Sugden, the pig valley.
Sutcliffe: From Sutcliffe, the south cliff.

Thackra: A corner for thatch.
Thornton: The settlement by the thorn trees.
Thorpe: At the village.

Wheelhouse: Place where wheels were made or kept.
Whiteley: At the white meadow.
Winterbottom: The valley with the wintry climate.
Woodhead: At the top end of the wood.
Wrigley: The ridge meadow.

PATRONYMICS
Addy: Son of Adam.

Appendix V

Atkinson: Son of Adam.
Alcock: From Alan.

Bateman: Son of Bartholomew.
Battye: Little Bartholomew.

Dawson, Dyson: Son of David.
Dobson: Son of Robert.

Edwards: Son of Edward.
Elliott: Son of Elias.

Hampson: Son of Hamo (Ham).
Hanson: Son of John (Johann).
Hodgson, Hodgkinson: Son of Roger.
Hopkinson: Son of little Robert.
Hughes: Son of Hugh.

Ibbotson, Ibberson: Son of Isabella.

Jones: Son of John.

Laycock: From Lawrence.
Lucas: Son of Luke.

Machen, Mason: Son of Matthew.
Mallinson: Son of little Mary.
Mitchell: Son of Michael.
Moxon: Son of Margaret.

Robertson, Robinson: Son of Robert.
Rogers: Son of Roger.

Stephenson: Son of Stephen.

OCCUPATIONAL
Cartwright: Maker of carts.
Clark: A clerk.
Crowther: A fiddler; musician.

Fletcher: Maker of arrows.

Hayward, Heywood: Hedge watcher, (kept cattle from straying.)

Jagger: One who works draught horses for hire.

Kilner: The lime burner.
King, Knight: From those who played such parts in mediaeval processions.

Mason: The stone mason.
Mellor, Milner: The Miller.
Mercer: The draper or dealer in clothes.

Oastler: The hostler; inn keeper.

Parker: The park keeper.

Smith: The smith, essential in every village.

Tinker: The pedlar (announced his coming with a bell).
Turner: One who works with a lathe.

Vickerman: The vicar's servant.

Wainwright: The repairer of carts.

NICKNAMES
Earnshaw: The young heron.
Fox: The sly one.
Jarmain: The German.
Middlemost: Baptised at Michaelmas.
Pollard: With the short hair; 'powled'.
Senior: The senior, to distinguish father and son.
Smailes: The small.

The Huddersfield Dialect

DESPITE THE pressures which have caused some other dialects to almost disappear, the local dialect of the Huddersfield area still survives. Indeed, within our area one can recognise variations in speech from village to village; even today there are dialectal differences between Marsden and Holmfirth, for example, or between Shepley and Golcar as representing localities to the east and west of the town.

There are two basic reasons for this. The original main routes for travel between Sheffield and Wakefield and from Halifax and the Calder Valley into Lancashire all avoided Huddersfield. Much of the independent spirit of our people has sprung from this relative isolation which even the coming of the railways never fully overcame.

Secondly there is the close connection between dialect and the woollen industry. Dialect terms, evolved in the early days of the cottage industry, survived the transition to the factory because the early mills were near the old homes of the clothiers, and later, when larger mills were established, they were worked almost entirely by local people who took with them their traditional modes of expression.

The vigour of the local dialect is seen in the work of the many writers who still use this medium. The *Huddersfield Examiner* has a notable record for publishing and encouraging dialect material and *Owd Joss* by F. A. Carter has been read with great interest over the years. The most famous of all dialect dramatists is James R. Gregson who came from our area; the poems of Fred Brown and George Allen North are regularly published by the Yorkshire Dialect Society. The glossary which follows is drawn mainly from Easther.[1]

[1] *A Glossary of the Dialect of Almondbury and Huddersfield*, Alfred Easther, 1883.

Appendix VI

Copies of this valuable book are now virtually unobtainable, and as it contains many expressions which were fast disappearing even in Easther's day, their inclusion in this commemorative volume may prove useful and interesting. Some of the textile terms used in this book have been especially included. Some items are not necessarily exclusive to Huddersfield but all of them are or have been used there.

The Reverend Alfred Easther, a southerner, found that Yorkshire folk claimed no 'foreigner' could ever speak their dialect and, furthermore, they alone spoke the purest form of English. The venerable headmaster would have been surprised to hear some immigrant children today at play in our streets and conversing in broad Yorkshire!

GLOSSARY OF SOME DIALECT TERMS

a (short sound): On; 'a Monda'—on Monday.

addle: To earn.

agate: At work; occupied with.

akkle: To dress up or tidy up; 'Aumun akkle misen'—I must tidy myself up.

avverbreead: Haverbread, made from oatmeal when wheat flour was dear.

baht: Without.

balk (bauk): A large beam or beam of scales for weighing.

band: String used for tying by weavers.

bat: Stroke; 'He's not struck a bat'—he's not done a stroke.

betty: A tidy-betty or guard placed in front of the fire to keep the ashes in.

billy: A machine for slubbing cardings.

bi-think (short i): To remember or to consider.

bobbin: A wooden spool or peg for winding yarn upon.

botch: To do a job carelessly.

brass: Money.

brat: A wool sorter's smock; a pinafore.

breastbeam: Part of a loom.

brokken: Broken.

brussen: Burst (applied to sacks); lucky (applied to a person).

buffet: Small stool.

Appendix VI

bunt: A bundle (of cloth).
burl: To pick small pieces of hair etc. from the cloth.
buzzer: Mill whistle or siren.

caird: A card or comb for dressing wool.
cal: To gossip.
capt: Surprised.
causey: A pavement, footpath.
chunter: To grumble.
clammed (or clemmed): Cold; hungry; kept short of food.
clicks: Hooks for moving packs of wool.
cockled: Uneven, applied to worsted cloth gone into lumps.
cop: Yarn spun on to a spindle.   'cop it'
crozzil: Hard cinder found in furnaces. - see chips
cropper: Cloth dresser.
cussen: Cast (adj.); cussen muck—slag heap.
cut: Canal; Huddersfield and Manchester Canal always known as
't' cut'.

din: Noise; 'Hod thi din'—be quiet!
do: A commotion; a lively time; 'A reight gooid do'—a most
successful party; to thrive; 'Au didn't do so well' can mean 'I
was ill'; to cheat 'Au've been dun'—I've been cheated.
donned up: Dressed in one's best clothes.
druft (or drufty): A drying wind.

fadge: Bundles of cloth or wool in a pack sheet skewered with
wooden pack pricks. The sheet held four or five pieces and was
placed across a horse and tied with a wanty or rope.
fast: Puzzled; 'Why don't you get on with your job?' 'Nay, Aum
fast!'
fearnaught: A wool mixing machine.
fent: A fag end of cloth, three-quarters of a yard beyond the length
of a piece. Weavers used to claim this to clothe their children.
fettle: To clean or set something in order.
fettler: A machine cleaner.
flit: To move, especially from one house to another.
fold: A collection of houses standing in a yard.
frame: To set about a task effectively; 'He frames well.'

311

Appendix VI

fruzzins: Hairs coming off the cloth when finished or from yarn when wound. Loose fluff, often under a bed.

gainest: Nearest.
gers: Grass; gers-drake—the corncrake.
gig: A kind of knife used to remove knots from the cloth.
going part: Part of a loom suspended before the cloth as it is woven. It has boxes to hold the shuttles and ledge before the sleigh in which the shuttle runs.
goit: Channel cut to carry water to the mill.
ginnil: A narrow passage between two buildings, or walls.
gok, gow, gum: Forms of 'God' used in mild oaths, e.g. 'by gum'.

hank: Thread wound on a large cylinder. A hank of wool or cotton is 840 yards; 560 yards in worsted. 6 hanks equals 1 bunch in cotton and worsted; 4 hanks equals 1 bunch in wool.

jacks: Part of a loom. Several pieces of wood are on a pivot which passes through their centres. At the end of each jack is a string leading eventually to the treadle.
jerry: A finishing machine which removed rough surface of cloth.
jip: Pain; punishment. 'Au'll gi thi jip if tha sez owt.'
joss: The master. 'He's nooan baan to be joss ovver me.'

knock on: To get on with a job.
koil oil: Coal place.
kop: To catch.

lake: To be idle. Men out of work are 'laking'.
lap: The end of a piece of cloth which in weaving laps (wraps) round the low beam.
lays: Term used in weaving when the warp threads are separated above and below a string called the lays band. 'Au cannot get the lays on it'—I do not understand it.
leck or weet: To wet as in wetting the cloth with stale urine to bring out the grease.
leet: To meet with. 'Au leet on 'im i't' street.'
lig: To lie down 'To lig i' bed.'
lithairse: Dye house; lister—dyer.

312

lozin: The dismissal or coming out, e.g. 'T'mill's lozin.'
lumb: Chimney (pronounced 'Chimley').
lurry: A waggon.

maister: Master.
middlin: Moderate; 'Aum just middlin.'
miln: A mill.
milner: Originally the one who put the cloth into the milling stocks.
moiting: To pick out motes (burs, etc.) from the cloth.
mongi: Idle; 'Th'art reight mongi.'
mule: Spinning machine.
mullek: A mess or muddle.
mungo: Old rags and woollen material, shredded to be rewoven.
muff: To make a small noise.

nogs: 'L'-shaped pieces of iron placed on the beam to hold the warp.
noils: Short fibres of wool removed by the combing machine.
noit: Business; 'What noit are ye at?'—'What are you doing?' In a bad way or in difficulty—I am at a noit!'
nope: To hit, especially on the head; hence, nuppit—a 'knocked' wit or half-wit.

okker: To hesitate.
olis: Always.
oss: To stir; move, to begin.
owt: Anything.

paand: Pound (£1).
perch: To examine cloth by putting it over a rod, pole or perch, in order to discover burls or motes.
pick: To throw the shuttle. Threads thus laid are called picks and they can be counted as so many picks to the inch. To pick a pick is to throw the shuttle across once.
piggin: A lading can or small vessel.
poise: To kick; 'Au poised 'im on t'shins.'
porty woof: Forty threads.
pund: Pound (lb.).

ravel coppin: When one thread catches another and rives many threads it is a ravel coppin.

Rordin: A Riding; a third part. Thus, Yorkshire has three Ridings.

roving: In wool spinning where the filaments are drawn out to a greater length.

Rush: A festival; originally when ruses were strewn on church floor, e.g. 'Ombri Rush' (Almondbury Fair).

saig: To saw.

saigins: Sawdust.

sam: To pick up or gather.

scribble: To give the first rough carding to wool or cotton.

shade or shed: The opening between two lines of warp through which the shuttle passes. Shed can be a parting of hair or as in watershed.

shale: When the weft is not driven up close enough it is said to shale.

shauve: A slice (of bread).

shiftless: Helpless.

shivvins: Small bits of wood in the wool or bits off the yarn (shavings).

shoddy: Waste material thrown off by machines, used for low priced cloth.

skep or skip: A willow basket.

skitter: To hurry one's work. A skittered piece of cloth is irregular in colour or texture.

slay or sleigh: Used in weaving to keep threads straight. It supports the shuttle as it runs and when pulled to the piece drives closer the wool threads.

sliver: A long carding of wool.

slub: To draw out cardings into greater length.

sluffed, sluffened: Disappointed; distressed; disheartened.

snicksnarl: When thread is so much twisted that on being slackened it runs into double twists, it is a snicksnarl.

stamperds: The four posts supporting a loom.

stapple (staple): Used to express the length of the woollen fibres.

stocks: Part of milling machinery.

strinkle: To scatter or sprinkle, e.g. oil or water on cloth.

sumpoil: Place to which surplus dye or other liquid flows.

taew: To strive. 'He taew'd with it long enough.'

tail goit: Channel from the mill.

temples: Two pieces of wood joined in the middle by a pin. At each end is a prod to fasten the cloth and to keep it stretched tight in the loom. Hence, Temple Street (?)—now part of Westgate.

tenter: Frame for stretching cloth to dry on tenter hooks.

thoil: To bear; endure; not begrudge; spare.

throng: Busy.

thrum: The ends of the warp cut off from a piece of cloth.

thump: Local name for a feast or fair, e.g. 'Longwood Thump'.

tig: To touch—as in children's games of 'tig' or 'tag'.

toit: To keep in toil; to keep in good order (as of a machine).

trap: A bad break in the thread, close to the cloth, or any bad place in a piece of cloth may be called a trap.

tum (vb.): The first process in carding when wool is worked between hand cards.

tuner: One who tunes or sets the looms for weaving.

Ummer: Local word for Hell; 'It's ez dark az Ummer ier!'

wanty: A girth for a pack-horse.

wappy: Quick, e.g. Wappy Nick (now Market Walk)—a short-cut between the two former Huddersfield market-places.

warpin woof: A frame about 10 ft long on which warps are prepared for the loom.

wartun: A quartern—about 24 lb of woollen warp.

waugh miln or *woff miln:* A fulling mill.

weigh balk: A beam for weighing; could also be the beam of an engine.

wind (short i): To wind bobbins.

wim wam: An impulse or fancy; also a toy or plaything.

winteredge: A winter hedge; a clothes horse.

wit: Commonsense; 'Muer brass ner wit'—more money than sense.

witch: A machine on top of the loom used to figure cloth; preceded the Jacquard Loom.

woarf or weave: A 10 ft measure applied to the warp.

wom: Home.

worsit: Worsted.

yark: To jerk; pull or snatch.

yeddin: A heading; portion of cloth at beginning and end of a piece, cut off when piece is removed from loom.

Climate and Weather

IN THE opinion of many, Huddersfield's climate is cold, windy, rainy, sunless and foggy. The fact that 1965 was the wettest for 106 years seems merely to confirm this gloomy view.

As one would expect, the rainfall in our area increases from east to west for it is the westerly winds which bring rain, and the figures for annual inches of rain fall show that the western end of our area receives twice as much as the other, thus:

Holme Moss has 60 inches, Slaithwaite 50, Golcar 40, Oakes 36, Huddersfield 30 and Bradley 27·5. Proceeding further eastwards, we find Heckmondwike 25 and Wakefield 22·5. In Lancashire, Bolton and Blackburn have 50 inches each. The national average for the British Isles as about 41 inches and for England 33, therefore the rainfall for the Borough is about average for the English Counties.

In an average year 1,132 hours of sunshine have been recorded at Ravensknowle compared with 1,247 hours at Oakes and the difference here can be accounted for by the comparatively clear atmosphere at the higher altitude. The mean average sunshine for Huddersfield is about three and a half hours per day as compared with four hours a day on the Lancashire coast.

Huddersfield endures its share of fog especially in the lower lying parts of the town. In 1962 Ravensknowle recorded thirty-eight foggy days as against twenty-five in Bradford and twenty-eight in Doncaster. On the other hand only twenty-three days of fog were recorded at Oakes, while London had twenty-two but the Clyde Valley in Scotland had fifty-six days. It will be interesting to see how the frequency of fog is affected by the Clean Air Act when it is fully implemented.

The Meteorological Station at Oakes is 772 feet above sea level and we would expect to lose about one degree fahrenheit for every

300 feet of altitude. Thus when we compare our average temperatures with those of London we find:

Huddersfield	January 39°	July 61°
London	41°	63°

The comparatively high winter figure of 39° is caused by the westerlies which not only bring rain but also keep the winters relatively mild. Average winter temperatures further east are much lower than ours.

In view of these facts and figures it may well be asked why it is that the Huddersfield climate can be so uncomfortable. The answer lies in the two interrelated factors of wind and altitude. Most of us live at between four and five hundred feet above sea level and some up to eight hundred feet or more; thus one expects the normal slight reduction in mean temperature which depends on altitude. In addition, we all experience high winds which make it feel colder than it really is, and when rain accompanies the wind the combined cooling effect is even greater. In 1962 Huddersfield recorded twenty-seven gale force winds, more than at Dungeness in the English Channel. By comparison only three such winds were recorded in London. These winds occasionally bring gusts of up to ninety miles per hour but even these are not regarded as abnormal. The normal pattern is that winds of up to twelve miles per hour are experienced on three days out of five and it is the frequency and persistence of strong winds which characterises the climate of our area.

These winds have not always been to our detriment however. During the Second World War it was said that enemy aircraft deliberately avoided the Pennines because of the gusts of high wind experienced flying over them.

In recent years the Meteorological Station at Oakes has encouraged parties of schoolchildren to make their own recordings. Some useful equipment to enable children to observe the weather has been made in school workshops and laboratories. Classes come to Oakes where they study wind and cloud by sending up balloons, observing their behaviour. Indeed, the amount of cloud, visible all the year round, is a feature of the eastern slopes of the Pennines.

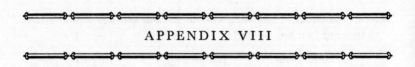

Honorary Freemen

<table>
<tr><td></td><td>Date when Honorary
Freedom conferred</td></tr>
<tr><td>Field-Marshal Viscount Montgomery,
   K.G., G.C.B., D.S.O.</td><td>26th October, 1945</td></tr>
<tr><td>Alderman Arthur Gardiner, O.B.E., J.P.</td><td>11th October, 1960</td></tr>
<tr><td>Alderman Harry Andrew Bennie Gray,
   C.B.E., J.P.</td><td>11th October, 1960</td></tr>
<tr><td>Rt. Hon. Harold Wilson, O.B.E., M.P.</td><td>1st March, 1968</td></tr>
</table>

On the 13th September, 1952, the Council conferred on The DUKE OF WELLINGTON'S REGIMENT the privilege, honour and distinction of marching through the streets of the County Borough of Huddersfield on all ceremonial occasions with bayonets fixed, colours flying and bands playing.

On the 13th October, 1961 the Council presented to the Huddersfield Choral Society a Complimentary Resolution recording their high appreciation of the glorious musical achievements of the Society since their formation in 1836 and paying tribute to the illustrious contribution of the Society to the art of music making, particularly choral singing, during the past 125 years and the fame which they have thereby brought to the Borough of Huddersfield.

PAST HONORARY FREEMEN

<table>
<tr><td></td><td>Date when Honorary
Freedom conferred</td></tr>
<tr><td>Alderman Wright Mellor, J.P., D.L. (Died
   17th May 1893)</td><td>25th September, 1889</td></tr>
<tr><td>Henry Frederick Beaumont, J.P., D.L.
   (Died 6th October, 1913)</td><td>28th August, 1894</td></tr>
</table>

Appendix VIII

	Date when Honorary Freedom conferred
Lt. Col. Sir Albert Kaye Rollit, LL.D., D.C.L., LITT.D., J.P., D.L. (Died 12th August, 1922)	28th August, 1894
James Nield Sykes, J.P. (Died 4th March, 1903)	12th March, 1895
Joseph Woodhead, J.P. (Died 21st May, 1913)	28th October, 1898
Sir Joseph Crosland, Kt., J.P., D.L. (Died 27th August, 1904)	28th October, 1898
Colonel Harold Wilson. (Died 11th December, 1930)	23rd May, 1901
Major Charles Brook. (Died 14th June, 1930)	23rd May, 1901
Sir Thomas Brooke, Bart., J.P., D.L. (Died 16th July, 1908)	25th July, 1906
The Rev. Robert Bruce, M.A., D.D. (Died 6th November, 1908)	25th July, 1906
William Brooke, J.P. (Died 16th February, 1920)	15th October, 1913
John Sykes, J.P. (Died 9th August, 1914)	15th October, 1913
Alderman William Henry Jessop, J.P. (Died 26th August, 1921)	18th September, 1918
George Thomson, J.P. (Died 10th October, 1921)	18th September, 1918
Sir John Arthur Brooke, Bart. M.A., J.P. (Died 10th July, 1920)	18th September, 1918
Benjamin Broadbent, C.B.E., M.A., J.P., LL.D. (Died 25th June, 1925)	18th September, 1918
James Edward Willans, LL.D., J.P. (Died 10th May, 1926)	18th September, 1918
Alderman Ernest Woodhead, M.A., J.P. (Died 10th June, 1944)	18th September, 1918
Earl Beatty, G.C.B., O.M., G.C.V.O., D.S.O. (Died 11th March, 1936)	24th July, 1920
The Earl of Oxford & Asquith, K.C., F.R.S. D.C.L., LL.D. (Died 15th February, 1928)	6th November, 1925
Sir William Pick Raynor, Kt., J.P. (Died 26th August, 1927)	17th December, 1926

319

Appendix VIII

	Date when Honorary Freedom Conferred
Alderman Wilfrid Dawson, J.P. (Died 11th August, 1936)	25th July, 1934
Alderman James Albert Woolven, J.P. (Died 14th March, 1941)	25th July, 1934
Alderman Rowland Mitchell, J.P. (Died 5th November, 1944)	25th July, 1934
Joseph Barlow, J.P. (Died 27th January, 1956)	23rd June, 1949
Sidney Kaye, O.B.E., LL.B. (Died 11th January, 1965)	19th November, 1957
Sir Malcolm Sargent, MUS.D. (Dunelm) D.MUS. (OXON.) (HON.) LL.D (Liverpool), HON. R.A.M., HON. F.R.C.O., F.R.C.M., F.R.S.A. (Died 3rd October, 1967)	13th October, 1961

LIST OF PAST MAYORS

Charles Henry Jones, J.P.	1868
Charles Henry Jones, J.P.	1868–69
Charles Henry Jones, J.P.	1869–70
Charles Henry Jones, J.P.	1870–71
Wright Mellor, J.P., D.L.	1871–72
Wright Mellor, J.P., D.L.	1872–73
Henry Brooke, J.P.	1873–74
David Sykes, J.P.	1874–75
John Fligg Brigg, J.P.	1875–76
Joseph Woodhead, J.P.	1876–77
Joseph Woodhead, J.P.	1877–78
Alfred Walker, J.P.	1878–79
Alfred Walker, J.P.	1879–80
Thomas Denham, J.P.	1880–81
John Fligg Brigg, J.P.	1881–82
John Fligg Brigg, J.P.	1882–83
Wright Mellor, J.P., D.L.	1883–84
John Varley, J.P.	1884–85
John Varley, J.P.	1885–86
Wright Mellor, J.P., D.L.	1886–87

Joseph Brooke, J.P.	1887–88
Joseph Brooke, J.P.	1888–89
Godfrey Sykes, J.P.	1889–90
Godfrey Sykes, J.P.	1890–91
Reuben Hirst, J.P.	1891–92
Reuben Hirst, J.P.	1892–93
John Joshua Brook, J.P.	1893–94
John Joshua Brook, J.P.	1894–95
John Lee Walker, J.P.	1895–96
John Lee Walker, J.P.	1896–97
William Henry Jessop, J.P.	1897–98
William Henry Jessop, J.P.	1898–99
George William Hellawell, J.P.	1899–1900
Robert MacShaw, J.P.	1900–01
Ernest Woodhead, M.A., J.P.	1901–02
Frederick Calvert	1902–03
Richard Henry Inman, J.P.	1903–04
Benjamin Broadbent, C.B.E., M.A., LL.D., J.P.	1904–05
Benjamin Broadbent, C.B.E., M.A., LL.D., J.P.	1905–06
Owen Balmforth, J.P.	1906–07
Owen Balmforth, J.P.	1907–08
John Holroyd, J.P.	1908–09
John Holroyd, J.P.	1909–10
George Thomson, J.P.	1910–11
George Thomson, J.P.	1911–12
Joseph Blamires, J.P.	1912–13
Joseph Blamires, J.P.	1913–14
Joseph Blamires, J.P.	1914–15
Joseph Blamires, J.P.	1915–16
William Henry Jessop, J.P.	1917–17
William Henry Jessop, J.P.	1917–18
Carmi Smith, J.P.	1918–19
James Albert Woolven, J.P.	1919–20
James Albert Woolven, J.P.	1920–21
Wilfrid Dawson, J.P.	1921–22
Wilfrid Dawson, J.P.	1922–23
Joseph Berry, J.P.	1923–24
Law Taylor, J.P.	1924–25
Law Taylor, J.P.	1925–26

Appendix VIII

Rowland Mitchell, J.P.	1926–27
Rowland Mitchell, J.P.	1927–28
Thomas Canby, J.P.	1928–29
Walker Thomas Priest, J.P.	1929–30
Walker Thomas Priest, J.P.	1930–31
Thomas Shires, J.P.	1931–32
Thomas Shires, J.P.	1932–33
Albert Hirst, J.P.	1933–34
Albert Hirst, J.P.	1934–35
Joseph Barlow, J.P.	1935–36
Joseph Barlow, J.P.	1936–37
Alfred Willis	1937–38
Fred Lawton	1938–39
Norman Crossley	1939–40
Arthur Edwin Sellers	1940–41
Arthur Gardiner, O.B.E., J.P.	1941–42
Walter Halstead 9th November, 1942–30th March, 1943	
John Ernest Lunn 5th May, 1943–9th November, 1943	
Arthur Samuel Moulton, M.B.E., J.P.	1943–44
Sidney Kaye, O.B.E., LL.B.	1944–45
Mary E. Sykes, B.A., LL.B.	1945–46
Thomas Smailes	1946–47
Oliver Smith, J.P.	1947–49
David James Cartwright, O.B.E.	1949–50
John L. Dawson, M.A., J.P.	1950–51
George B. Jones, M.B.E., J.P.	1951–52
James F. C. Cole,	1952–53
Wilfrid Mallinson	1953–54
John Armitage, J.P.	1954–55
John T. Gee, M.B.E.	1955–56
H. A. Bennie Gray, C.B.E., J.P.	1956–57
Reginald Wood	1957–58
R. H. Browne, J.P.	1958–59
J. Louis Brook	1959–26th March 1960
R. H. Browne, J.P.	21st April 1960–24th May, 1960
Norman Day	1960–61
Harry F. Brook	1961–62

Appendix VIII

John A. Bray	1962–63
M. L. Middlebrook-Haigh, M.B.E.	1963–64
Mary C. Gee	1964–65
Reginald Hartley, M.B.E., J.P.	1965–66
Douglas Graham, C.B.E.	1966–67

LIST OF FORMER TOWN CLERKS

Joseph Batley	1868–85
George Bellamy Nalder	1885–90
Henry Barber, LL.B.	1890–95
Frederick Charles Lloyd	1895–1903
Joseph Henry Field, O.B.E., LL.B.	1903–30
Samuel Proctor, O.B.E.	1930–45

IN CENTENARY YEAR

Mayors: Jack Sykes	1967–68
Thomas Painter Cliffe, T.D., LL.B.	1968–69
Town Clerk: Harry Bann	1945–

LIST OF CHAIRMEN OF THE HUDDERSFIELD BOARD OF IMPROVEMENT COMMISSIONERS

J. Sutcliffe	1848–49
Joseph Brook	1849–54
Charles Henry Jones	1854–55
Joseph Brierly	1855
Charles Henry Jones	1856 (3 months)
Joseph Brook	1856–58
John Freeman	1858–60
William Keighley	1860–62
John Sykes	1862–65
Joseph Turner	1856–67
Robert Skilbeck	1867–68

Clerks: T. W. Clough (1848–65); Joseph Batley (1865–68)

APPENDIX IX

Three Prime Ministers

IN PARTY politics the balance between the three major parties in Huddersfield is reflected, by coincidence, in the town's connection with three Prime Ministers, namely, H. H. Asquith (Liberal), Stanley Baldwin (Conservative), and Harold Wilson (Labour).

HENRY HERBERT ASQUITH (1852–1928) was a grandson of William Willans.[1] He attended Huddersfield College for a short period before continuing his education at Mirfield, Pudsey, Ripponden, London and Balliol College, Oxford. He entered Parliament in 1886 and was Prime Minister from 1908 to 1916. In 1925 he was created Earl of Oxford and Asquith, and in the same year he was made a Freeman of the Borough.

STANLEY BALDWIN (1867–1947) was a grandson of the Rev. G. B. Macdonald. He entered Parliament in 1908 and was Prime Minister three times—1923-4, 1924-9 and 1935-7. He was created Earl Baldwin of Bewdley in 1937. The following inscription is on the plaque which stands outside Queen Street Mission in commemoration of a most brilliant family.

This Tablet
was unveiled by Miss Florence Macdonald MBE (Granddaughter)
on the 25th May, 1938.
TO THE MEMORY OF
THE REV. GEORGE BROWNE MACDONALD
SUPERINTENDENT MINISTER AT THIS CHAPEL

[1] Mrs Asquith, daughter of William Willans, came to live in Trinity Street, a few doors above her father's house, in 1860.

Appendix IX

AND OF

HANNAH

HIS WIFE

WHO RESIDED AT NO. 16 QUEEN'S SQUARE FROM SEPTEMBER

1847 TO AUGUST 1850

WITH THEIR CHILDREN

HENRY JAMES

THE ELDEST CHILD

ALICE

WHO MARRIED JOHN L. KIPLING AND BECAME MOTHER OF

RUDYARD KIPLING

GEORGIANA

WHO MARRIED SIR EDWARD BURNE-JONES BART.

FREDERICK WILLIAM

WHO BECAME PRESIDENT OF THE WESLEYAN METHODIST CHURCH 1899

AND LAST SPOKE IN THIS CHAPEL AT THE CENTENARY CELEBRATIONS

4TH JULY 1919.

AGNES

WHO MARRIED SIR EDWARD POYNTER, BART, PRESIDENT OF THE

ROYAL ACADEMY.

LOUISA

WHO MARRIED ALFRED BALDWIN AND BECAME MOTHER OF

STANLEY, EARL BALDWIN OF BEWDLEY K.G.

A PRIME MINISTER OF ENGLAND.

JUDITH

YOUNGEST DAUGHTER, BORN HERE 14TH SEPTEMBER 1848. AUTHORESS.

JAMES HAROLD WILSON (b. 1916) was born in Milnsbridge where he attended New Street Council School. From there he won a scholarship to Royds Hall Secondary School. Following a brilliant career at Jesus College, Oxford, at the age of twenty-one he became a lecturer at New College, Oxford. Harold Wilson entered Parliament in 1945, becoming President of the Board of Trade in 1947. On the death of Hugh Gaitskell in 1963 he became Leader of the Opposition and Prime Minister in the following year.

325

Glossary of Heraldic Terms

Annulet: Small circle.

Argent: Silver.

Armed: Claws of a different colour or metal.

Azure: Blue.

Banded: Anything tied with a band.

Bar: Diminutive of the fess.

Barbed and Seeded Proper: Of a rose—having the seeds gold and the sepals green.

Bars Gemel: See Gemel.

Bend: A diagonal band drawn from dexter chief to sinister base.

Bendlet: Diminutive of the bend of the same shape.

Bezant: Gold coin.

Bezanty: Scattered with bezants.

Bordure or *Border:* A border round the edge of a shield.

Caboshed or *cabossed:* Beasts' heads borne without the neck and full faced.

Canton: Small square figure often placed in the dexter chief of the shield.

Charge: The symbol placed on the shield.

Chequy: The field covered with alternate squares of metal or colour and fur.

Chevron: Similar in shape to the rafters or gable of a house.

Chevronel: Diminutive of the chevron.

Chief: The upper part of the shield, or broad band covering this area.

Compony: A term applied to any ordinary made up of squares of alternate metal and colour or fur.

Conjoined: Joined together.

Counterchanged: The division of a shield into two parts, one of colour or fur and one metal, and so arranged that the charges placed upon the metal are of the colour and vice versa.

Counter Flory: An ordinary decorated with fleurs-de-lis, the points of the flowers running alternately in a contrary direction.

Couped: Cut off.

Courant: Running.

Crescent: Crescent moon with its horns up-turned.

Crozier: The pastoral staff of a bishop or abbot.

Debruised: Any charge with an ordinary placed upon it.

Demi or *Demy:* Signifies half.

Dexter: The heraldic right of an object, i.e. the side on the left of the spectator.

Displayed: Spread as a bird's wings.

Double Tressure: Two tressures, one within the other.

Endorsed: A charge raised above its normal position.

Engrailed: An object edged with small semi-circles, the points turning outwards.

Enhanced: Bearings placed above their usual position.

En Soleil: Placed on a sun.

Erased: Anything torn or plucked off with a ragged edge from its natural position.

Erect: Any naturally horizontal charge placed perpendicularly.

Ermine: A white fur with black spots.

Ermines: Fur represented by white spots on a black field.

Erminois: A fur, the field *or*, the spots *sable*.

Escallop: A cockleshell.

Fess: A broad band across the centre of the shield.

Field: The surface of the shield.

Fitchy: Having a pointed end; generally applied to crosses.

Fleur-de-lis: A conventional representation of the lily.

Flory: Flowered or adorned with fleurs-de-lis.

Fret: A saltire and mascle interlaced like a trellis.

Gemel: Bar; in pairs.

Gobony: Same as compony.

Gules: Red.

Guardant: Looking out of the field.

Guttee: Sprinkled with drops.

Hauriant: A fish rising to the surface to breathe.

Impaled: Two coats of arms placed side by side within one shield.
In bend: Lying in the same direction as a bend.
Indented: Having a toothed edge.
Inescutcheon: A small shield placed in the centre of another larger shield.
In saltire: Charges set in the form of a St Andrew's cross.

Label: The mark of cadency of an eldest son during his father's lifetime.
Langued: Tongued.
Lozenge: A diamond-shaped figure.
Lozengy: Covered with lozenges.
Lure: A device used in the training of hawks.

Martlet: A martin without legs.
Mascle: An open lozenge-shaped figure.
Maunche: A mediaeval sleeve.
Moline: Resembling the piece of iron attached to the millstone.
Mullett: A star with five points.

Or: Gold.
Ordinary: A simple device on a shield.
Orle: A band following the outline of a shield.

Pale: A broad band drawn vertically down the centre of the shield.
Paly: A number of pales.
Passant: Walking.
Per chevron: Lying or joined in the form of a chevron.
Per fess: Lying or joined in the form of a fess.
Per pale: Lying or joined vertically.
Pierced: Cut through the centre.
Pretence: A small shield borne in the centre of a larger shield.
Proper: In its natural colour.
Purpure: Purple.

Quatrefoil: A four-leaved flower.

Raguly: A conventional representation of a tree trunk having the branches lopped.

Rampant: Standing on one hind paw, the other three paws and tail raised, head looking to the dexter.

Respectant: Facing.

Sable: Black.

Saltire: A St Andrew's cross.

Sang: Blood.

Semee: Strewn or powdered.

Sinister: The heraldic left side of an object, i.e. the side on the right of the spectator.

Slipped: Torn from the main stem.

Sun in Splendour: The sun with rays, often with a human face.

Trefoil: Three-leaved plant.

Tressure: Double lines following the outline of the shield.

Trippant: The walking of a deer.

Vair: A kind of fur formed of bell-shaped squirrel skins, usually silver and blue.

Vert: Green.

Volant: Flying.

Vulning: Any creature in the act of wounding itself.

The Borough Coat of Arms

THE PRESENT Borough Arms was not the first heraldic device to be associated with the administration of Huddersfield. Prior to 1868 there were the Arms of the Ramsden family and the unauthorised device of the Improvement Commissioners.

On the front of the Corporation Estate Building, formerly the Ramsden Estate Building, in the centre of the town, is a series of carved shields heraldically showing the marriage alliances of the

The Ramsden Arms after 1689

Ramsdens. The first shield shows Ramsden with Wode in pretence; that is, the Wode Arms are placed in the centre of the Ramsden Arms. The Arms of Ramsden are argent, on a chevron sable, between three fleurs-de-lis also sable, three rams heads couped argent.[1] The Arms are also illustrated and tricked on a page of twelve drawings in the British Museum,[2] where the Ramsden Arms occupy the bottom left-hand corner of the recto and though the corner is torn away, sufficient remains of the drawing to show the Arms clearly.

The member of the Ramsden family who married into the Wode family was William who married Johanna Wode in 1531.[3] Johanna was regarded as a co-heir (there was however a son called George, but he was illegitimate) and therefore, had William been entitled to Arms, he would have marshalled the Wode Arms in pretence. The Arms used by the Wodes at the time of William's marriage were not those of the Wodes of Longley. Johanna's father, John, was using the Arms of Wood of Darington, Shropshire, to which he was not entitled.[4] Later, there was a Grant of Arms to Thomas Wode of Longley by William Harvey, Norroy, in 1550, the Arms granted being sable on a bend argent three fleurs-de-lis sable.[5] William did marshal the Arms, but he used his brother's Coat without authority. The Pedigree recorded in the 1612 Visitation of Yorkshire makes no mention of William as having any right to use the Arms.[6] The use of his brother's Arms was in keeping with William's character for he seems to have shown little sense of responsibility either towards his business interest, for he spent some time in the Fleet prison for debt, or towards his wife, for he was frequently absent and an unhappy marriage was indicated by a contemplated divorce in 1560. William's growing debts and unstable character would hardly make him an acceptable recipient of the honour of a Grant of Arms.

John, his brother, was of a more stable character, who thoroughly and slowly established himself as a landed gentleman. He had married Margaret Appleyard[7] and rented part of Longley Old Hall

[1] Granted to John Ramsden, April 1575, by Flower, Norroy, Harleian 1453 and Records of Grants in College of Arms.
[2] Harleian 1422. Eleven arms granted by Robert Cooke, Clarenceux, the twelfth, Ramsden, by Wm. Flower, Norroy.
[3] Marriage Settlement dated 19/7/1531. Ramsden MSS Box 1 Huddersfield Library and Isaac Horden Papers.
[4] College of Arms Records and 1664 Visitation of Shropshire.
[5] College of Arms Records.
[6] Checked in College of Arms.
[7] Photostat. Dodsworth MSS m 133, fol. 135v, Bodleian Library.

from William. By 1576 he commenced the building of Longley New Hall for his wife and six children. Having land, security and the prospect of a new house, all that was lacking was the hallmark of a Tudor gentleman—a Grant of Arms. The decade of 1570 shows one of the peaks in Grants of Arms, approximately 740 being granted.[1] Thus John was not alone in seeking the new status symbol. The decades preceeding 1570 had seen the dissolution of the monasteries and the passage of their lands into the ownership of other men, some avaricious like William, others careful like John. April 1575 brought John's social climb to its peak, and the Ramsden Arms were to be seen in Huddersfield. William's marriage proved childless and it was through John and his descendants that the Arms were borne by the family. As the fortunes of the Ramsdens were efficiently developed

and gradually extended, the family added to its social status by marriage into the Frechevilles, a knight; into the Lonsdales, a viscount; into the Ingrams, another viscount; into the Dundases, and so indirectly related to Edward III; and then in 1865 into the Somersets, a duke. One wonders what John, the Tudor gentleman, would have thought; how proud he would have been, for the Dukes of Somerset are descended from Jane Seymour's family, Henry VIII's

[1] E. Elmhirst, *Coat of Arms*, vol. iv, pp. 46–50: also A. R. Wagner, pp. 119-120.

third wife. From William, lying dying and about to be buried in St Sepulchre's without Newgate, would have come a cynical laugh, thinking what 'brass' he could have made from their lands.

In 1848 the Huddersfield Improvement Act was passed which placed local government in the hands of twenty-one Improvement Commissioners. The Huddersfield Improvement Commissioners did not become a corporate body in 1848 and therefore they were, at first, not entitled to a common seal or to a coat of arms of their own. This body wished to identify itself, and for this purpose employed a particular device but like William Ramsden, the Commissioners used another person's Arms. The device used by the Commissioners was argent a fess sable between three boars passant sable. The Commissioners had no right to these Arms.[1] The Arms belonged to the family of Hoghfourd where they occur as a quartering in the Arms of Carew of Ottery Mohun and of Bickleigh, Devon.[2] From 1848 to 1868 the Improvement Commissioners used these Arms as their own.[3] Debrett's *Titled Men* of 1870 shows the Arms as being the Coat of Arms of Huddersfield.[4] Papworth's *Ordinary of Arms* also quotes the device as belonging to Huddersfield.[5]

On the 30th September 1868 The Right Honourable Edward Fitzalan Howard, as deputy to the Duke of Norfolk, Earl Marshal, responding to a letter from the mayor, authorised Sir Charles Young, Garter, Robert Laurie, Clarenceux, and Walter Blount, Norroy, to grant and assign Armorial Bearings to the Mayor, Aldermen and Burgesses of the Borough of Huddersfield. By the 12th October the Letters Patent were signed and sealed and the Arms granted were to be: Or on a chevron between three rams passant sable as many towers argent, and for a Crest a ram's head couped argent armed or gorged with a collar sable in the mouth a sprig of cotton tree slipped and fructed proper.

These Arms bear some resemblance to the Ramsden family Arms in that the gold shield carried a black chevron with devices on it and also the chevron lies between symbols. This was a development of

---

[1] College of Arms Records.

[2] Visitation of Devon 1531. Checked at College of Arms.

[3] *History of Huddersfield*, p. 66, Taylor-Dyson 1951.

[4] Debrett's *Titled Men and List of Counties and Boroughs Returning Members to Parliament*, 1870–71, p. 127.

[5] Papworth's *Ordinary of British Armorials*, 1874, p. 723.

heraldic design in the sixteenth century when charges came to be set on and about chevrons and other ordinaries. The Ramsden Arms are silver and black and so a gold field produced a difference. The chevron is common to both but the fleurs-de-lis have gone, to be replaced by three rams alluding both to the Ramsdens and to the important woollen industry. The towers are a common feature in civic heraldry but they do not indicate that Huddersfield was once walled and the close proximity of Castle Hill is purely fortuitous. The black collar encircling the ram's neck is again only a difference and merely helps to distinguish Huddersfield's ram from other ram crests. It is interesting to note, however, that a ram's head crest occurs in the Arms of Barrow-in-Furness where the first mayor was Sir James Ramsden and the Arms were granted in 1867. In this case the ram's neck is encircled by a gold collar but there is no sprig of cotton.

In the case of Huddersfield there is in the ram's mouth a sprig of cotton alluding to the cotton textile industry. Huddersfield is so well known for its woollen textiles that people forget that cotton textiles have also had a place in Huddersfield's economy. John Varley started a cotton mill at the Waterside Mill in 1803.[1] At the Great Exhibition 1851 Jonas Brook & Bros. of Meltham Mills were exhibiting cotton thread.[2]

The motto, not part of the Grant of Arms, is *Juvat Impigros Deus*— God helps the diligent. This was the motto of the Improvement Commissioners, who, whatever else they showed, did not display heraldic diligence.

The great town of Huddersfield has a long and eventful history and its Arms neatly sum up part of this history from the Tudor farmer, King's woodward, landowner and gentleman called John Ramsden, through the transitional stage of local government under the Improvement Commissions to the year 1868 when the Mayor, Aldermen and Burgesses became 'ever hereafter one Body Politic and Corporate in deed, fact and name'—the Borough of Huddersfield.

---

[1] *History of Huddersfield Woollen Industry*, Crump and Ghorbal, p. 78.
[2] Catalogues of Great Exhibition 1851.

Heraldry in Huddersfield

ALDERSON: *Azure* a chevron engrailed ermine between three suns in splendour *or,* impaling *argent* three sheaves of three arrows proper, banded *gules,* and on a chief *azure* a bee volant *or.*

Georgiana Alderson, daughter of John Peel of Pastures House, Derby, was born 12th October 1801 and died 6th February 1850. She married the Reverend Christopher Alderson, rector of Kirkheaton for forty-four years, who was born on 30th August 1802 and died 11th September 1880.

(Memorial Kirkheaton Church)

ALSTON: *Azure* ten stars of six points (4, 3, 2, 1) *or,* impaling *argent* a chevron *gules* between three oxen *sable.*

A memorial in Kirkheaton Church records the death on 28th May 1841 of Charlotte Alston, wife of the Reverend Alston, and the daughter of Sir Henry Oxenden of Brome Park, Kent.
Arms were confirmed to the Oxenden family in 1445.

(Foster's Grantees of Arms)

APPLEYARDE: *Azure* a chevron *or* between three owls *argent.*
Among the Governors of the Grammar School of King James in Almondbury that 'wee have assigned nominated chosen and appointed' was Richarde Appleyarde of over Longley in the Parish of Almondbury. The Arms are emblazoned on the left hand side of the Letters Patent refounding the school in 1608.

ARMYTAGE: *Gules* a lion's head erased between three cross-crosslets *argent.*

John Armytage of Farnley Tyas bought Kirklees property in 1565.

335

John was the son of William, who, according to Henry St George, Norroy, in a pedigree of 1637, was descended from John Armytage of Wrigbowls living *circa* 1145 (who married Katherine, daughter of Henry Beaumont of Crosland).

Kirklees Priory, a Cistercian convent, was founded in 1155 by Reiner le Fleming, Lord of the Manor of Wath-upon-Dearne. The fee holder of the land was de Laci. There are references to the Priory between 1306 and 1315 when three nuns, Joan Heaton, Elizabeth Hopton and Alice Raggid were involved in a scandal and expelled. Kirklees like other convents was dissolved under the process of Dissolution, in 1539. Part of the property was, for a time, in the hands of William Ramsden (1513–1580).

Sir George Armytage, Fifth Baronet, married Elizabeth Radcliffe (1st June 1841). Elizabeth was the second daughter of Sir Joseph Radcliffe, Second Baronet, of Milnsbridge House, Huddersfield.

James Armytage of Deadmanstone (died 8th February 1811) son of Joseph Armytage of Alverthorpe Hall, Wakefield, married Ann, daughter of William Mountjoy (Arms *gules* three escutcheons *or*).

(*Victoria County History* (W.R.) Vol. 3; *History of Huddersfield Woollen Industry*—Crump and Ghorbal; Burkes *Peerage*; *Heraldry in Churches of West Riding*—Bloom 1894.)

AYLESFORD: *Argent* a chevron between three griffins passant *sable*.

William Walter Legge, 5th Earl of Dartmouth, married on 9th

June 1846, Augusta, a daughter of Heneage Finch, 5th Earl of Aylesford.

These Arms are to be seen impaled with the Legge Arms in the Dartmouth window of the Kaye Chapel in Almondbury Parish Church.

BATTYE: *Argent* a fess *sable* between three bats proper.

William Ramsden (died 1623) married as his second wife, Mary Battye, widow of Henry Battye of Birstall, in 1600. Mary died in December 1623. There was a pre-marital settlement of 'three score pounds per annum' by William on the 29th January 1600.

(Dugdale's *Visitation of Yorkshire:* 1666.)

BEAUMONT *of Whitley Beaumont: Gules* a lion rampant *argent* langued and armed *azure* within an orle of crescents *argent.*

William de Bellmonte, ancestor of the Beaumonts of Whitley Beaumont, received ten oxgangs of land in Huddersfield from Roger de Laci, Constable of Chester, *circa* 1206. William accompanied Roger and Richard I on the Third Crusade and was present at the siege of Acre. William's son, William is mentioned as an assign of John Muncebote in a Deed *circa* 1235 whereby John, son of Roger de Laci, granted the Whitley Lands, service and payment of one pair of white gloves per annum, and also the payment of ten shillings, to the

337

heirs of Peter Birkethwaite and one pound of cummin to William Dransfield ... (Cummin was cultivated for its medicinal property of relieving flatulence. The seed was also placed in the eyes of decapitated human heads to prevent birds pecking out the eyes).

Elizabeth, eldest daughter of Richard Beaumont, married 25th August 1501, John Wode of Longley Hall. John Wode was the father of Johanna Wode who married William Ramsden. John Wode's grandfather, Lawrence had married Jane, daughter of Adam Beaumont, and because of the canonical laws of consanguinity, a special licence was necessary for the marriage of Elizabeth and John.

Edward Beaumont married on 16th October 1571, Elizabeth Ramsden, daughter of John Ramsden, and niece to William.

Edward's son was Richard Beaumont on whom a baronetcy was conferred in 1628. Richard died unmarried, so the baronetcy ceased in 1631. The estates passed to another branch of the family, Major Thomas Beaumont, heir of Richard. Richard's great-great grandfather, also Richard, married as a second wife Elizabeth Stanley, the daughter of Sir John Harrington of Hornby Castle, thus bringing in the Arms of Harrington—*sable* a fret *argent* a label of three points *argent*.

Morvill: *Azure* semee de lis a fret *or*.

Moulton: *Argent* three bars *gules*.

Copley: *Argent* a cross moline *sable*.

English: *Sable* three lions passant *argent*.

Neville: *Gules* a saltire *argent*.

Clifton: *Sable* a bend *argent* thereon three mullets *gules*.

Wastley: *Argent* a cross raguly *gules*.

These Arms are marshalled on the Beaumont Tomb, but Richard was not entitled to quarter them.

(*Annals of the Church and Parish of Almondbury*—Hulbert 1882. Glover's *Visitation of Yorkshire*. G. W. T. mss. Huddersfield Reference Library. The Beaumont Tomb, Kirkheaton Church.)

BILL: *Ermine*, two woodbills *sable* with long handles in saltire proper, on a chief *azure* between two pelicans' heads erased *argent* vulning themselves proper, a pale *or* charged with a rose *gules*.

A Memorial in Kirkheaton Church records the death on 16th May 1792, of Dorothy Horsfall. She married Robert Bill. Dorothy was a

Appendix XII

Horsfall of Storthes Hall. Charles Horsfall Bill is found quartering the Arms of Bill with Horsfall.

BOWER: *Sable* a human leg coupled at the thigh, pierced bendwise by a broken spear, guttee de sang all proper, on a canton *argent* a tower *gules*.

The land of Stapleton in the North Riding of Yorkshire was conveyed by the family of Methams to George Pudsey. During the Civil War, George's son Thomas, had the land sequestered and leased to Marmaduke Pudsey of Cottingham. In 1708 the manor was conveyed as a settlement on Katherine Trotter who married William Bower. Elizabeth Bower, daughter of John Bower, married, as his second wife, on 10th August 1869, Sir John Lister Lister-Kaye of Denby Grange.

(*Victoria County History* (N.R.) Vol. 1; G. W. T. Papers and MSS Huddersfield Reference Library.)

BRIGG: Gules a bend vair between two roses *or,* all within a bordure indented *azure* and bezanty.

John Fligg Brigg was mayor of Huddersfield 1875–76, and 1881–83.

George Brigg, a volunteer in the Northern Army, was killed at the Battle of Goldsburgh in North Carolina on 16th December, 1862.

The Arms are to be seen in the West window of Almondbury Parish Church, where they form part of a memorial to Anne, mother of Fligg Brigg, who died at Fenay Lodge on 21st January 1867.

BROOKE *of Almondbury: Argent* a cross nebuly per pale *gules* and *sable* in the first and fourth quarters a boar's head erased *sable*.

These Arms are to be seen in a stained glass window in the entrance of the Ramsden Technical College. Thomas Brooke, F.S.A., was President of the Huddersfield Mechanics Institute 1879–84 and first President of the Technical School and Mechanics Institute January 1885.

A fourteenth century corn mill near Holmfirth was used as a fulling mill by John Brooke in 1591—hence the name New Mill. The family lived at Greenhill Bank, New Mill and had granted from

John Rowley, of Butterley, the use of nearby water in 1681. About 1738 the Brookes moved from New Mill to Honley, renting Neiley's Mill. Seeking more water power the business was moved in 1819 to Armitage Bridge.

(*History of Huddersfield Woollen Industry*—Crump and Ghorbal).

BROOKE OF NEWHOUSE: *Argent* on a bend *sable* a hawk's lure *or*, the line and ring *argent*.

These Arms are to be seen carved on a former warehouse in Upperhead Row.

The Brooke family were vigorously engaged in the Woollen textile trade in 1533. The family, though ceasing in the male line, continued by marriage into the Wilkinsons of Greenhead.

Huddersfield Parish Church has a number of grave stones recording the deaths of the family: Thomas the younger, 27th July 1537; Elizabeth wife of Thomas the elder, 1st February 1616; Thomas, 28th September 1624; Thomas, the elder, 17th November 1638.

The hall, Newhouse, was built *circa.* 1550; the last male heir, Joshua, dying there in 1652. In 1751 the Thornhills of Fixby purchased the property and in 1854 it passed by purchase to Sir John Ramsden.

(*History of Huddersfield Woollen Industry*: Crump and Ghorbal. *Brooke of Newhouse*: Philip Ahier.)

BUTLER: *Argent* on a chevron *azure* between three demi-lions passant guardant *gules* crowned *or*, three covered cups *or*.

On 22nd January 1670 a pre-marriage settlement was entered into relative to the future marriage of Sarah Butler, daughter of Charles Butler of Coates in Lincolnshire, and Sir John Ramsden (1648–90) first baronet, created 30th November 1689. The marriage took place on 7th March 1670 at Armthorpe. Sarah was born in 1649 and died the 14th January 1683, being buried at Brotherton on the 15th January.

(Arms to be seen on Market Cross, Huddersfield.)

Appendix XII

BYLAND ABBEY: *Gules* a lion rampant *argent* debruised by a crutch in bend *or*.

This Cistercian Abbey of St Mary was founded in 1134 by Roger de Mowbray. The Abbey had the fee of the house and manor of Denby Grange. This property was bought by Arthur Kaye in the middle of the sixteenth century.

DE BYRON: *Argent* three bendlets enhanced *gules*.

In the fourteenth century the family of de Byron held land in Lancashire at Byron and Clayton. A Coat of Arms in the Parish Church, Huddersfield, shows Robert de Byron quartering Cecilia, daughter of Richard Clayton—but marshalled the wrong way round.

The manor of Huddersfield came to the Byrons by purchase, in 1318, from John del Cloughes. Just as the Ramsdens bought former monastic lands so in 1540 Sir John Byron bought Newstead Abbey in Nottinghamshire. Sir John's son, John, having like William Ramsden (I) over-spent, mortgaged the manor of Huddersfield, on 2nd March 1573, to Gilbert Gerrard, Queen Elizabeth's Attorney, for £700.

(Brook MSS. Huddersfield Reference Library; Records Nottingham Public Library; *Victoria County History of Lancashire*, Vol. iv.)

CHARLES I: Arms as for James I.

The Arms of Charles I were erected 1625 in Almondbury Parish Church. In March of that year, Charles, Duke of York and Albany succeeded James I. The board bearing the emblazonment of the

Royal Arms carries the initials C (Carolus) R (Rex) but the Arms shown are Hanoverian, for the Stuart Arms were overpainted in 1714 on the accession of George I.

CLARKE: *Or a cross raguly between four trefoils vert.*

These are the Arms of William Chapel Clarke of Rushton Hall, Northamptonshire, who married Clara Thornhill, the only daughter of Thomas Thornhill and Clara (Peirse). The marriage took place on 20th November 1855. William Clarke assumed by Royal Licence the additional surname and Arms of Thornhill, adding to the chief a canton *gules* for difference to show that he was not a Thornhill by descent.

(Foster's *Yorkshire Pedigrees*.)

DE CLARE: *Or three chevrons gules.*

These Arms come into the district through the marriage of Richard de Clare, Earl of Gloucester, to Maud de Laci, daughter of John de Laci (died 1240).

CLITHEROE GRAMMAR SCHOOL: The School bears no Arms, but on its seal a tripple towered gate with portcullis, there being neither domes nor pennons on the towers. The Arms shown in the Chancel of Almondbury Parish Church are those of the town of Clitheroe. The School itself has used this device so long 'whereof the wit of man seemeth not to the contrary'.

The School held the advowson of Almondbury from 1636 to 1867 when Sir John Ramsden bought the advowson from the School.

'And we have given and granted, and by these presents do give and grant, to the governors aforesaid, all our whole Rectors of Almondbury in the County of York . . . with the advowson of the vicarage and all and singular messuages, burgages, lands etc. . . .'
Hampton Courte xxix day August, 1st and 2nd yeare of Our Reign Philip and Mary.

(*Portfolio of Fragments (Dutchy of Lancaster)*: M. Gregson, Third Edition 1869; *History of the Parish of Whalley*: Whitaker 1801.)

CLOTHWORKERS COMPANY: *Sable a chevron ermine between in chief two habicks argent and in base a teasel or.*

Appendix XII

The Company of Shearmen were incorporated by Henry VII and in 1528 they joined with the Fullers Company founded 1480 to form the Clothworkers.

In order to finish cloth, by levelling the nap, the shearmen stretched the cloth over a padded bench, securing the cloth with a havette or double-ended hook. The word havette comes from the French 'havet', a hook. Since the seventeenth century the word has been spelt habick.

The older part of the Technical College was built in 1884, to the cost of which the Clothworkers Company contributed. It is for this reason that the Company's Arms are to be seen in the entrance hall and above the outside entrance. The Arms were granted in 1530 by Thomas Benolt, Clarenceux.

(Records of the Clothworkers Company, London.)

CONYERS; *Azure* a maunch ermine, overall a bendlet *gules*.

These Arms are found in pretence with Ramsden. John Ramsden (1698–1769) the third baronet married a widow Margaret Bright, of Badsworth. Her father was William Norton of Sawley. The Visitation of Yorkshire 1564 records an Adam Conyers changing his name to Norton.

(*Visitation of Yorkshire* 1564; Ramsden MSS Huddersfield Reference Library.)

343

CROSLAND: Quarterly *argent* and *gules* a cross botonnee (cross crosslet) counterchanged.

These simple but effective Arms belonged to the Croslands of Almondbury. It was by a marriage that the family achieved heraldic fame. Thomas Crosland, who died 1587, had among others, daughters Alice and Grace. The records are in doubt as to which married into the Calvert family. A marriage with Leonard Calvert of Kipling certainly took place. A son George was born to the Crosland/Calvert alliance in 1578. George was eventually granted an Irish Peerage as Lord Baltimore. An attempt by George to found a Roman Catholic colony in America was not successful, and it fell to his son, Cecilius to bring this about by founding the state of Maryland in 1634 between the River Potomac and the 40th Parallel.

The Arms of Calvert quartering Crosland form the oldest and finest state banner in the U.S.A. and the Achievement of Arms is found on the State Seal.

(Dugdale, Glover, Tonge: *Visitations of Yorkshire*.)

CROSSLEY: Per chevron *or* and *vert* in chief a cross tau between two crosses moline fitchee *gules*, in base a hind trippant *argent* charged on the shoulder with a cross tau *gules*.

Owen Thomas Lloyd Crossley was appointed vicar of Almondbury Parish Church in 1901. His Arms are to be seen on the North wall of the Chancel. He was later appointed a Colonial Bishop.

DARTMOUTH: *Azure* a stag's head cabossed *argent*.

William Legge (1672–1750) was created Viscount Lewisham and Earl of Dartmouth on 5th September 1711. His son, George, married, 1726, Elizabeth Kaye, daughter and heiress of Sir Arthur Kaye of Woodsome. It was through this marriage that Woodsome and its estates passed to the Dartmouth family. George died during his father's lifetime and was known by the courtesy title of Viscount Lewisham. The Title passed to William's grandson, also called William. Woodsome was one of many properties owned by the Dartmouths and it was not until 1879 that the 6th Earl made Woodsome his country seat. After occupation by the Dartmouths until 1911 the house was let to Woodsome Golf Club, which club subsequently purchased the property. The Dartmouth Estate Book

(1805) is a valuable source of material for the early history of the woollen and cotton mills in the Huddersfield area.

(Burkes *Peerage* 1953; *History of Huddersfield*: Taylor-Dyson 1951.)

DAWTREY: *Azure* fusily of 5 pieces *argent*.

William Dawtrey was rector of Kirkheaton 1479–1511.

DOWKER: Per pale *gules* and *azure*, a lion rampant *argent* within a bordure lozengy *or* and *vert*.

George Lister Lister-Kaye, lieutenant-colonel in the 5th West Yorkshire Militia, born 14th November 1803, died 19th September 1871, married on 24th August 1847, Louisa Jessie, eldest daughter of Captain Dowker. Louisa died in October 1862.

(*Heraldry in the Church of the West Riding of Yorkshire*: Bloom, 1894. *Annals of the Church and Parish of Almondbury*: Hulbert, 1882.)

DUNDAS: *Argent* a lion rampant *gules* within a double tressure flory counter flory *gules*.

John Charles Ramsden (1788–1836), son of the fourth Baronet, married, in 1814, Isabella Dundas. She was the youngest daughter of Thomas, First Lord Dundas. Isabella had a brother, Lawrence, who was created Earl of Zetland, an honour later raised through another Lawrence to a marquisate. John died in the lifetime of his father and so did not inherit the title. The tressure is an honourable augmentation to the Dundas Arms. The Arms are well shown on the Ramsden Estate Building in Huddersfield where they are impaled with Ramsden. A single tressure is shown on the building, which is technically wrong, but has been permitted, and the Ramsden Arms lack the label of an eldest son.

(Records in the Office of the Lord Lyon.)

ELAND: *Gules* two bars between eight martlets three, two and three, *argent*.

This ancient family of the Township of Elland played a part in the history of Huddersfield in that Sir John Eland Sheriff of Yorkshire 1340–1, was the alleged murderer of Beaumont, Lockwood and Quarmby. Sir John was himself murdered in 1350 and his son and grandson were murdered in 1351. Sir John's granddaughter, Isobel, was the ward of Sir John Savile whom she married, and, as a result of the murders of the male heirs, Isobel became an heiress thus bringing the Arms and Eland estates to the Saviles.

(Flower's *Visitation of Yorkshire*, 1563.)

ELIZABETH II: Quarterly 1 and 4 England. 2 Scotland. 3 Ireland.

A very fine achievement of these Arms is to be seen in Holy Trinity Church. The Arms were placed in the Church in March 1966.

Appendix XII

At the restoration of Charles II in 1660 a Proclamation was issued requiring the display of Royal Arms in Churches. Prior to compliance with the Proclamation, an incumbent must obtain a Faculty.

The emblazonment is very fine and executed in a vigorous mediaeval style instead of the over-elaborate manner of many Victorian emblazonments.

FENAY: *Gules* a cross moline *or*.

These are the Arms of Nicholas Fenay, the builder of Fenay Hall in 1605. The name of the family makes frequent documentary appearances from the thirteenth century onwards. The family held land in Almondbury, Newsome, Lockwood and Cowlersley. The lands held by Nicholas Fenay were 'which said lands and tenements did belong to the late dissolved College of Jesus Rotherham'. Nicholas Fenay was a founder governor of the Free Grammar School at Almondbury and Deputy Steward of the Manor of Wakefield. He died in 1616. The Fenays occupied the Hall until 1766 when it passed first to the

Thornton family and then by purchase to the Norths. In 1800 the hall passed to the Battye family and then *circa* 1860 it was purchased by Sir John Brook.

(*History of the Church and Parish of Almondbury*: Hulbert 1882. *Survey of the Parish of Almondbury*, 1584. Records of Almondbury Grammar School.)

FENTON: *Argent* a cross between four fleurs-de-lis *sable*.

Greenhead House, now part of a school, was occupied by this family. Samuel Fenton died at Greenhead on 30th November 1763.

347

Appendix XII

James Crosland Fenton, who died on the 3rd April 1858 married Mary Jane Battye, sister of William Battye of Almondbury. For a time the Battyes occupied Fenay Hall. James's great grandfather was James Crosland, schoolmaster of Holme, who died 1763.

Captain Lewis Fenton, of Spring Grove House, stood as a Whig at the General Election of 1832, when he won with 263 votes, the Liberal candidate receiving 152 votes. On the 21st March 1873 an Indenture was entered into between Fenton Kenny and Sir John Ramsden concerning Spring Grove House.

(G.W.T. Papers and MSS. Huddersfield Reference Library. Ramsden MSS Huddersfield Reference Library.)

FINCHENDEN: *Argent* between two chevronels three finches *sable*.

Circa 1370 this family came into possession of the Woodsome Estates. Alice Finchenden, widow of Sir William, first holder of the land, granted, 1378, Woodsome to John Cay, freeholder, for a period of twenty years. Elizabeth Kaye, Alices's daughter, married John Kaye thus did the Woodsome Estate enter the Kaye Family.

On the right-hand side of Almondbury Parish Church South Porch can be seen Kaye quartering Finchenden.

(*Annals of the Church and Parish of Almondbury*: Hulbert, 1882.)

FITZWILLIAM: Lozengy *argent* and *gules*.

William Wentworth Fitzwilliam (1748–1833) was the second Earl. He succeeded to a substantial fortune on the death of his uncle Lord

348

Rockingham in 1782, and thus was able to live in splendour at Wentworth Woodhouse. In 1794 he was appointed, by Pitt, Lord Lieutenant of Ireland. On the dismissal of the Duke of Norfolk from office, Fitzwilliam was appointed Lord Lieutenant of the West Riding in 1798. It was in the latter capacity that Fitzwilliam played a part in suppressing the Luddite rebellion in Huddersfield. He also recommended Joseph Radcliffe, magistrate, in 1813, for his baronetcy as a reward for his fearless conduct during the period of unrest in 1812. Following the Peterloo massacre, a meeting was called at York to rebuke the Manchester magistrates for their conduct, and such was the violence of Fitzwilliam's language that he was dismissed from the Lord Lieutenancy of the West Riding.

(*Dictionary of National Biography*.)

FIXBY: *Azure* a saltire between four cross-crosslets *or*.

Sir Richard Thornhill of Thornhill (died 1287) married Matilda, daughter of Thomas de Fixby.

Apart from a quartering in Thornhill Arms there is no other reference to the Fixby Arms.

(Dugdale's *Visitation of Yorkshire*, 1666.)

FOUNTAINS ABBEY: *Azure* three horse shoes *or*.
The Abbey had the tithes of fallow land in the village of Bradley, while Huddersfield Parish Church had the tithes of the sheaves of the village. The monks worked the shales for brickmaking and bands of iron-stone at Colne Bridge, Denby, Emley and Flockton.

(Cottonian Vespasian E 19 Fol. 43. 1245; *Victoria County History* (N.R.) Vol. 1.)

FRECHEVILLE: *Azure* a bend between six escallops *argent*.

Sir John Ramsden Kt (1594–1646), married 1624, Margaret the daughter of Sir Peter Frecheville of Staveley in Derbyshire. The marriage settlement is dated 15th June 1624. Margaret was buried at Almondbury on 22nd December 1626. Sir Ralph Frecheville was called to Parliament in 1301. A barony was conferred on John Frecheville in 1664. The barony became extinct in 1682.

Appendix XII

(Dugdale's *Visitation of Derbyshire*, 1662–3. I. Horden MSS. Huddersfield Estate Office. Arms to be found on Market Cross.)

GAUNT *John of:* Quarterly France ancient and England, a label ermine (until *circa* 1393) Quarterly France ancient and England a label of France (after 1393).

John married, in 1359, as his first wife, Blanche heiress of Henry Duke of Lancaster. Through Blanche, John inherited the lands held by Lancaster which included Almondbury and Huddersfield. In 1362 John was created Duke of Lancaster.

(*Coat of Arms*, Vol. III, p. 25; Vol. VII, p. 83; Arms of Henry Duke of Lancaster in Chancel of Almondbury Parish Church).

GEORGE III (prior to 1816).
Quarterly 1 and 4 England, 2 Scotland, 3 Ireland with overall an inescutcheon of Hanover (*Gules* two lions passant guardant *or*: Brunswick; *Or* seme of hearts *gules*, a lion rampant *azure*: Luneburg; *gules* a horse courant *argent*: Westphalia: with overall an inescutcheon *gules* charged with Charlemagne's crown *or*). The larger inescutcheon is ensigned with the Electoral Bonnet which in 1816 was changed to the Hanoverian Royal Crown.

The Arms are to be seen on the balcony of Holmfirth Parish Church.

DE HETON: *Argent* two bars *sable*.

This family were associated with Kirkheaton, a sepulchral slab bearing their Arms being discovered in the Church in 1886.

Dodsworth says 'Holmeforth Water cometh to Kirk Heaton wher sometymes dwelt Sir John Heaton.' Dodsworth also records the Heton Arms in Dewsbury and Mirfield Churches.

Sir John Heton is said to have married Joan Heton, one of the five daughters of Alexander Nevile of Mirfield.

The Arms of de Heton are to be seen on a corbel in Almondbury Church. Their similarity to those of Quarmby can be misleading.

(Dodsworth's *Church Notes*, 1619–1631; *Yorkshire Archaeological Society*, Vol. XXXIV).

HOPTON: *Argent* two bars *sable* each charged with 3 mullets *or*.

Adam Hopton held two bovates of land in Kirkheaton 1306.
  (Charter dated at Gawkthorpe 1306).

HORSFALL *of Storthes Hall: Gules* three horses heads erased *argent* bridled *azure* impaling *argent* a chevron *gules* between three hinds heads erased *gules*.

William Horsfall (died 2nd August 1780) married Elizabeth Beckwith of Thurcroft, Yorkshire. She died 21st April 1793. William's eldest daughter, Dorothy, married Robert Bill: *ermine*, two woodbills *sable* with long handles in saltire proper, on a chief *azure* between two pelicans' heads erased *argent* vulning themselves a pale *or* charged with a rose *gules*.

  (Memorial Kirkburton Church).

HOSTE: *Azure* a bull's head cabossed *argent* winged and armed *or*.

Charles Dixon Hoste was appointed Vicar of Almondbury in 1905, in succession to the Reverend Crossley. After leaving Almondbury the Reverend Hoste became Vicar of Dewsbury and eventually a Canon of Salisbury Cathedral.

  His Arms are to be seen on the North wall of the Chancel in Almondbury Parish Church.

HUDDERSFIELD AND MANCHESTER RAILWAY AND CANAL COMPANY
The device is as follows:

1. A shield parted per pale bearing dexter a fleece and sinister a beehive.

2. A separate shield bearing *gules* three bendlets enhanced *or*.

The first shield is an armorial attempt to portray Huddersfield—the fleece for the woollen textiles and the beehive is allusive to industry in general. This is the only example of this device known to the author.

The second shield is the Arms of Grelley feudal lords of Manchester. These Arms form the basis of the Manchester Borough Arms granted 1842.

The Company was established by Act of Parliament in 1845. The Arms occur at the East end of the Railway Station façade.

HULBERT: Quarterly *argent* and *sable* in the first and fourth quarters a lion rampant *or*, overall a bend *gules* charged with three annulets *or*.

These Arms were granted in March 1639 by Borough, Garter. Charles Augustus Hulbert was appointed Vicar of Almondbury in 1867. He was the author of *The Annals of the Church and Parish of Almondbury*, published 1882. He was also a Canon of Ripon Cathedral.

His Arms are to be seen on the North wall of the Chancel in Almondbury Parish Church.

IRWIN: Ermine on a fess *gules* three escallops *or*.

Sir John Ramsden, 4th Baronet, married 1787, Louisa Susanna Ingram, fifth daughter and heiress of Charles, Viscount Irwin.

(Ramsden MSS. Huddersfield Reference Library.)

JAMES I: Quarterly 1 and 4 grand quarters: *Azure* three fleur-de-lis *or* (France Modern) quatering *gules* three lions passant guardant in pale *or* (England): 2 *or* a lion rampant within a double tressure flory counter-flory *gules* (Scotland): 3 *azure* a harp *or* stringed *argent* (Ireland).

In mediaeval times there had been a chantry school attached to Almondbury Church. On the suppression of the Chantries in 1547, the school was maintained by the Kaye family. By 1608 the inhabitants felt the need to refound their school as a free grammar school, and to this end petitioned James I for Letters Patent. Letters Patent of re-foundation were granted 'at Westminster the 24th day of November in the 6th year of the reign of His Majesty', being granted 'at the humble suit of the tenants and inhabitants of Almondbury to establish a free grammar school for the bringing up of children and youth in Grammar and all good learning, to consist of one master, one usher, and governed by six honest men of the most wise and discreet religious persons within the said Parish or dwelling within two miles thereof who shall be called Governors of the goods, possessions and revenues of the Free Grammar School of King James in Almondbury.'

(Arms to be seen on School Charter.)

KAYE: *Argent* two bendlets *sable*. A crest of a goldfinch proper was granted in 1564 to Arthur Kaye, by Flower, Norroy.

Alice Finchenden in 1378 granted her manor of Woodsome to John Cay, who married Alices's daughter Elizabeth. John Kaye (*circa* 1460) married Jane Laci of Cromwell Bottom (*argent, six roundels sable*); these Arms are to be seen impaled with Kaye in the Kaye Chapel window of Almondbury. John's grandson, George, married Margaret Radcliffe of Longley, Lancashire and their son Arthur married 25th May 1517, Beatrice Wentworth of Bretton (*sable* a chevron between three leopards faces *or*). Their son John, living *circa* 1585 married Dorothy Mauleverer (*sable* three greyhounds courant in pale *argent*). Their son Robert, living *circa* 1612, married Anne Flower of Whitewell, Rutland (*ermines* a cinquefoil *ermine*). The son John (died 1641) married 18th December 1603, Anne Ferne of Temple Belwood, Isle of Axholme. (Per bend *or* and *gules* two lions heads erased counterchanged). The son John (died 1662) married first Margaret Mosley of York (*sable* a fess *or* between three trefoils slipped *erminois*). Margaret's grandmother was Elizabeth Triggot (*argent* a chevron between three cross-crosslets fitchee *sable*). The son John (died 8th August 1706) married Anne Lister of Thornton in Craven (ermine on a fess *sable* three mullets *or*).

(Foster's *Yorkshire Pedigrees*: G.W.T. Papers Huddersfield Reference Library.)

KING JAMES'S GRAMMAR SCHOOL: Per fess *azure* and *gules* in chief three fleurs-de-lis and in base three lions passant guardant *or*.

These Arms are used by the School without authority or official record.

The charges in the unauthorised device are drawn from the Royal Arms of James I who granted a Charter of Government to the 'Fre Gramar Schole of Kinge James in Almondbury', dated at Westminster, 24th November 1608. This was not the foundation of the school, for a school and school house existed in 1547.

The first Governors were Robert Kaye, William Ramsden, George Crosland, Nicholas Fenay, Richard Appleyard and Robert Nettleton.

The school is sited on four acres of land granted by James I at a rent of four pence an acre.

(School Archives; *History of Huddersfield*: Taylor-Dyson 1951. Records College of Arms.)

Appendix XII

KIRKSTALL ABBEY: *Azure* three swords points in base *or*.

These are the Arms of William of Pictou. His Seal bears the device and the words SIGIL: WILLI: PICTAVESIS.

Henry de Laci, grandson of Ilbert, being, so he thought, about to die, vowed that he would found a Cistercian convent. As part of his lands he held the village of Barnoldswick. For this land, in commutation of service, Henry paid Hugh Bigod, Earl of Norfolk, five marks and a hawk each year. Henry made a grant of this land to the Abbot of Fountains Abbey for the founding of a daughter abbey. Unfortunately, Henry was 'behind with his payments' and so Hugh seized Barnoldswick. The monks who had settled found Barnoldswick bleak and open to robbers and so in 1152 they left and moved de Laci's foundation to Airedale settling on lands in the fee of William of Pictou.

(*Victoria County History* (W.R.), Vol 3. *An Historical Account of Kirkstall Abbey*: Wardell, 1882.)

LACI: *Or* a lion rampant *purpure* (first used by Henry, 3rd Earl of Lincoln).

This family came from Lassi in Northern France, not far from Dieppe, where their lands bordered upon those of de Warenne. The first holder of land in the Huddersfield area was Ilbert (*circa* 1070) who held the Honour of Pontefract. He and his descendants were land owners in the area until the mid-fourteenth century. The name and Arms did not pass directly through the family. Ilbert's grand-daughter married Robert de Lissours (1131) and, being an heiress the Arms passed out of the Laci line. However, her grandson John Fitz Eustace, Sixth Constable of Chester, assumed the name and Arms of Laci. There is a reference to Henry Laci, Tenth Constable of Chester, at the siege of Carlaverock:

> 'Henry, the good Earl of Lincoln, burning with valour and which is the chief feeling of his heart, leading the first squadron, had a banner of yellow silk with a purple lion rampant.'

Henry (died 1310) married twice. His first wife was Margaret Longespee, eldest daughter and co-heiress of William de Longespee, Second Earl of Salisbury, whose father was the illegitimate son of Henry II by Rosamund Clifford. Margaret had a son Edmund who was drowned in a well in Denbigh Castle and a daughter Alice, who was three times married. Representation of the House of Laci passed to the descendant of Maude Laci, daughter of John, Eighth Constable of Chester (died 1240), on her marriage to Richard de Clare, Earl of Gloucester.

(*Siege of Carlaverock*: Nicolas, 1828. Arms of de Laci in Chancel of Almondbury Parish Church. The Lacis held the advowson from 1231 to 1289.)

Appendix XII

Two separate shields:

1. Arms of Lancaster: Per fess *azure* and *gules* in chief a fleur-de-lis and in base a lion passant guardant *or*.

2. Arms of York: *Argent,* on a cross *gules* five lions passant guardant *or*.

These Arms occur at the West end of the railway station façade over the former booking office of this Company. The Company was established in 1836.

LEEDS, DUKE OF: Quarterly 1 and 4 ermine and *azure* overall a cross *or*. 2 : *gules* a double-headed eagle displayed between three fleurs-de-lis *argent*. 3 : *sable* a lion rampant *argent* on a canton *argent* a cross *gules*.

Parcels of land in the area of Holmfirth were held by the Lord of the Manor of Wakefield. By Indenture dated 10th July 1677 Sir Christopher Clapham conveyed the manor in trust to two others, Craven and Wiatt. By Indenture dated 4th June 1700 Clapham, Craven and Wiatt conveyed the manor to Thomas Osborne, 1st Duke of Leeds with descent to his heirs. George, 6th Duke (1775–1838), conveyed the manor to his son-in-law Sackville Lane Fox, of Bramham Park, who had married the Duke's daughter Charlotte Mary Anne Georgiana.

The dukedom of Leeds was conferred on Sir Thomas Osborne Bt., K.G. on 4th May 1694. The Duke was Lord High Treasurer of England 1673–9 and Lord President of the Council 1689–95.

LISTER: Ermine on a fess *sable* three mullets *or*.

Sir Arthur Kaye (3rd Baronet) who died 1726, had a brother George who married Dorothy Savile, daughter and heiress of Robert Savile of Elland. Their son John, nephew of Sir Arthur, inherited the Denby Grange estates and the title. Sir John Kay, 2nd baronet, had married Anne Lister of Thornton in Craven, and John, 4th baronet, took the surname Lister-Kaye. John (died 1752) married Ellen Wilkinson of Greenhead. The Wilkinsons lived at 'a good stone house called Greenhead', which had formerly been occupied by the Hirst family. On the ceiling was the date 1608 and above the fireplace the initials I.H.R.H. The fifth baronet died a bachelor in

357

1776, the title being extinguished. The estates were devised to John Lister Kaye who was created a baronet in his own right in 1812.

(Dugdale's *Visitation of Yorkshire,* 1666; Brooke MSS. Huddersfield Reference Library; Dodsworth's *Visit to Huddersfield Parish Church,* 1627.)

LONGFORD: Paly *or* and *gules,* a band ermine between two pairs of wings conjoined in lure points downwards ermine.

William Wingfield Longford was appointed Vicar of Almondbury in 1914. The wings on the field of the shield are a play on the Christian name Wingfield. After leaving Almondbury the Reverend Longford moved to Liverpool. His Arms are to be seen on the North wall of the Chancel of Almondbury Parish Church.

LOWTHER: *Or* six annulets 3, 2, 1 *sable.*

Sir William Ramsden, 2nd Baronet, married 1695, Elizabeth Lowther, who died 1764. She was the second daughter of John, 1st Viscount Londsdale.

(Ramsden MSS. Huddersfield Reference Library.)

LYNNE: *Gules* a demi lion rampant *argent,* a bordure *sable* bezantee.

Thomas Thornhill of Fixby (died 22nd March 1800) married at St George's, Hanover Square, London, on 9th October 1779, Eleanor Lynne of Horsley, Essex.

Eleanor died 30th December 1797.

(Foster's *Yorkshire Pedigrees.* Dugdale's *Visitation of Yorkshire* 1666. Arms carved on Oratory of Fixby Hall.)

MARSH: *Gules* a horse's head couped *argent,* a mullet for difference.

John Thornhill of Fixby and Toothill (born *circa* 1535, died 1607) married Jeneta Marsh, daughter and heiress of Edmund Marsh of The Knowles, Elland, at Elland Parish Church 17th December 1577.

'Jones Thonell et Janeta Marshe nupte 17.'

(Dugdale's *Visitation of Yorkshire,* 1666. *Parish Registers:* Elland, Vol. 1, 1559–1640.)

MARROW: *Azure* a fess engrailed between three maidens' heads *or*.

Sir Arthur Kaye, 3rd Baronet, who died 1726, married Anne Marrow (died 1740) one of the five daughters of Sir Samuel Marrow, created a baronet 1679. The Manor of Berkswell, Warwickshire, was granted in April 1557 to Thomas and Alice Marrow with remainder to their son Samuel and his heirs. Under a Settlement of 1674 the five co-heiresses of Sir Samuel were to hold court jointly and in 1705 and 1706 there is recorded a court held by Arthur and Anne Kaye.

(*Victoria and County History*: Warwick, Vol. IV; Court Rolls—Shire Hall, Warwick.)

MIRFIELD: *Vert* two lions passant guardant in pale *argent*.

Richard Beaumont (will proved 20th September 1472) married Cecilia Mirfield. By Licence dated 15th October 1468, the Archbishop of York granted permission for an Oratory at Whitley, for a period of three years.

(Dodsworth's *Church Notes*, 1619; Memorial Kirkheaton Church.)

NETTLETON: *Sable* two adders in pale entwined *or,* their heads respectant.

The allusion is to 'nettles entwisted'. The right to these Arms was investigated by Robert Glover and as proof was wanting there is the entry 'respited for proof'.

Appendix XII

Robert Nettleton of Almondbury and Siebel Ramsden were married on 26th February 1564.

One of the first Governors of the re-founded Almondbury Grammar School in 1609 was a Robert Nettleton. This same Robert set up a Charity (1613) for assisting the poor, preferring poor maids in marriage, preferring poor scholars in learning and repairing decayed bridges and ways.

The value of the 1613 estate was £20. 0s. 0d. Robert also lent William Ramsden (1558–1623) £40. 0s. 0d. to help repay the £975. 0s. 9d., the purchase price of the Manor of Huddersfield.

(Almondbury Parish Registers. Glover's *Visitation of Yorkshire.* *Annals of the Church and Parish of Almondbury*: Hulbert 1882.)

NEVILE (*of Liversedge*) : *Argent a saltire gules, a label of three points vert.*

Elizabeth, daughter of Robert Nevile of Hunslet and Liversedge, and his wife, daughter of Scargill, married 1456 Thomas Beaumont of Whytley.

Kateren, daughter of Sir Robert Nevile of Leversedge and Elenor, daughter of Sir John Towneley of Lancashire married, 1527, Richard Beaumont of Whytley.

(*Annals of the Church and Parish of Almondbury*: Hulbert. Tonge's *Visitation of Yorkshire.* Flower's *Visitation of Yorkshire.*)

NORRIS: Quarterly *or* and *gules,* in the second and third quarters a fret *or,* overall a fess *azure.*

William Foxley Norris was appointed Vicar of Almondbury in 1888. After leaving Almondbury he was appointed Dean of York and later appointed Dean of Westminster Abbey. His Arms are to be seen on the North wall of the Chancel of Almondbury Parish Church.

NORTH-BROWNLOW: Quarterly 1 and 4 *azure* a lion passant *or* between three fleurs-de-lis *argent* (North) 3 and 4—or within an orle of martlets an inescutcheon *sable* (Brownlow) and an inescutcheon of pretence bearing Kaye.

Appendix XII

Francis, 7th Baron North, married as his second wife, on 24th January 1736, Elizabeth, Dowager Viscountess Lewisham. Elizabeth was the daughter of Sir Arthur Kaye, 3rd Baronet, of Woodsome. Their eldest child was the Rt Rev Brownlow-North, Bishop of Winchester 1781. Brownlow's eldest son was the 6th Earl of Guildford.

Francis, 2nd Baron Guildford (1673–1729) married as his second wife Alice, daughter of Sir John Brownlow of Belton, Lincolnshire. Their son, Francis, was 1st Earl of Guildford. The Brownlow family had Arms recorded in 1593 by Robert Cooke, Clarenceux.

(Burkes *Peerage*, 1953. Archives City Library, Lincoln.)

NORTON: *Azure* a maunch ermine, overall a bend *gules*.

Sir John Ramsden, 3rd Baronet, married, 1748, Mrs Margaret Bright, widow of Thomas Liddell Bright of Badsworth. Her maiden name was Norton, the family having previously used the name Conyers.

NOSTELL PRIORY: *Gules* a cross between four lions rampant *or*.

This priory of Austin Canons was founded by Robert de Laci 1114. He held the fee of the land in the honour of Pontefract. Michael Wakefield was admitted to the vicarage of Huddersfield, 1216, on presentment to Walter, Archbishop of York, by the Prior and Convent of St Oswald, Nostell.

(Cottonian MSS. Vespasian E.19 Folio 182, 1216.)

PALMES: *Gules* three fleurs-de-lis *argent*, a chief vair.

William Ramsden (baptised 1625 died 1679), married *circa* 1648 Elizabeth, daughter of George Palmes of Naburn, which is a township in the parishes of Ancaster and St George near York. The 1564 *Visitation of Yorkshire* shows a marriage between Bryan Palmes of Naburn and Isobel, daughter and heiress of Thomas Lindley, of Lindley. Elizabeth died in 1691.

(Foster's *Yorkshire Pedigrees*. Ramsden MSS. Huddersfield Reference Library. Arms to be seen on Market Cross.)

Appendix XII

PILKINGTON: *Argent* a cross patence voided *gules*.

This family arose at Bury, Lancashire and moved firstly to Sowerby and then settled at Pilkington Hall, Wakefield. The Pilkingtons of Bradley were a family of substance. *Circa* Edward III Roger de Bellamont married Jane, daughter of Arthur Pilkington of Bradley. Frederick Pilkington of Nether Bradley married Grace, daughter of Edward Beaumont of Whitley *circa* 1565. In 1589 William Ramsden (II) married Rosamund, daughter of Thomas Pilkington of Bradley. One of their two daughters, Rosamund, married Ambrose Pudsey. Ambrose borrowed money from his father-in-law over a period of two years, reaching a total debt of nearly £300.

(Flower's *Visitation of Yorkshire. History of the Pilkington Family*: J. Pilkington, 1912. Brook MSS Huddersfield Reference Library. Ramsden MSS. Huddersfield Reference Library. Arms to be seen on Market Cross.)

PUDSEY: *Vert* a chevron between three mullets *or*.
(Crest: A cat regardant—pussy?)

A family bearing these Arms held the Manor of Barforth in the North Riding of Yorkshire from *circa* 1400 to the middle of the seventeenth century. The land came to the Pudseys via Elizabeth Layton who married John Pudsey of Bolton-in-Craven.

In 1616 a George Pudsey received a Royal Grant from the King in consideration of his having lent Mary Queen of Scots £1,000 that she had not repaid.

Thomas Pudsey of Bolton-in-Craven married Margaret, eldest daughter of Sir Roger Pilkington (died *circa* 1539).

In January 1615 Ambrose Pudsey of the Parish of Bolton, gentleman, and Rosamund daughter of William Ramsden of Longley Esquire, were married on the xxii between the hours of 8 and 9 before noon the same day.

(*Annals of the Church and Parish of Almondbury*: Hulbert, 1882. *Victoria County History* (N.R.), Vol. 1. Parish Registers—Almondbury Church.)

QUARMBY: *Argent* two bars and in chief a martlet *sable*.

This family forms one of the quartet of families influential locally in the thirteenth century. The other three being Beaumont, Lockwood and Eland. The Quarmbys lived at Quarmby Old Hall. Sir Robert de Bellmont married Agnes de Quarmby *circa* 1310.

The family is connected with the Legend of the Elland Feud where it is alleged that the Quarmbys murdered Sir John Eland.

(Glover's *Visitation of Yorkshire*.)

RADCLIFFE: *Argent* a bend engrailed *sable* charged with a crescent *argent* for difference.

Appendix XII

The local branch of this family arose from the marriage of William Radclyffe of Lancashire to Elizabeth Dawson of Milnsbridge, Huddersfield. William died in 1748. They had three children, William the heir, Charles and Mary. William died unmarried and devised his estates to his nephew Joseph Pickford, son of Mary and Joseph Pickford. The nephew assumed the name and Arms of Radcliffe in 1795 becoming Joseph Radcliffe of Milnsbridge House. Joseph's conduct in restoring order during a period of industrial unrest in Huddersfield arising from Luddite activities in 1812, resulted in the conferment of a Baronetcy on 2nd November 1813. As a special mark of favour no fee was required.

(Foster's *Pedigree of the Radcliffes*.)

RAWSON: Per fess wavy *sable* and *azure,* guttee d'*or* a quadrangular castle with four towers *argent,* on a chief or three ravens' heads erased *sable.*

These Arms were granted in 1895 to Christopher Rawson of Woolwich. Within the terms of the Grant the Arms passed among others to the descendants of an uncle, Stansfield Rawson, of Gledholt, Huddersfield.

(*Armorial Families*: Fox-Davies.)

RIPON–SEE OF: *Argent* on a saltire *gules* two keys in saltire wards upwards *or* on a chief *gules* a paschal lamb proper.

Prior to 1888 Huddersfield formed part of Diocese of Ripon and for this reason the Diocesan Arms can be seen in Huddersfield. In 1888, with the creation of the diocese of Wakefield, the Bishop of Ripon ceased to have authority in the area.

The See of Ripon was carved out of the See of York in 1836 when the Arms were granted. The keys are copied from those of the See of York and while in the Arms the wards of both keys are turned downwards and outwards, on a bench and dated 1494 the dexter key ward is turned upward and inward. When Sir Ninian Comper designed the present reredos to the High Altar he copied this mediaeval pattern on the shield beneath St Peter's feet.

On early seals the Paschal lamb faces the sinister whereas in the present Arms the lamb faces dexter.

Appendix XII

ROTHERHAM: Thomas: *Vert three stags trippant or.*

Thomas Scott, later known as Rotherham, Archbishop of York, founded the College of Jesus at Rotherham in 1483. The College survived until the Suppression. In 1485 the advowson of Almondbury Parish Church passed to the College. The Archbishop appointed a perpetual vicar to be paid £20 per annum. On the 12th July 1486 an indulgence was granted for the repair and restoration of the Church. During this collegiate period the Kaye and Beaumont Chapels were added to the Church. The last collegiate vicar was Richard Draper, instituted 1549. The Archbishop's Arms are to be seen in the Chancel.

(*Yorkshire Chantry Survey*: Surtees Society, p. 201. *Victoria County History* (W.R.), Vol. 3.)

SALUZZO: *Argent a chief azure.*

Edmund de Laci, 2nd Earl of Lincoln (died 1257) married Alicia daughter of Manfred III, Marquis de Saluzzo. The Marquis had two daughters Alasina and Beatrice.

Boniface of Saluzzo who was the absentee rector of Almondbury in 1289, was the legitimate son of Thomas of Saulzzo and Luisa of Ceva, and there was an illegitimate son also called Boniface. Boniface, although under twenty years old was not only rector of Almondbury but also a Papal Chamberlain. In 1313 his livings were sequestrated and he was excommunicated.

(*Enciclopedia storico–nobiliare–italiana*: Vol. VI, Milano, 1932. *Famiglie celebre d'Italia* by Litta. *Dizionario geografico storico statistico commerciale*, Vol. XVI, Turin, 1848.)

SAVILE: *Argent on a bend sable three owls argent.*

This family is mentioned at the time of Richard II when John Savile of Elland, Chevalier, paid twenty shillings tax. The house most closely associated with the family is Bradley Hall, Stainland: however they held property in Copley, Exley, Ovenden, and Batley.

Cecily Wode, eldest daughter of John Wode of Longley, married 1541, Thomas Savile of Exley. Through this marriage Longley Old Hall passed to Thomas, the Hall being subsequently purchased by William Ramsden (I).

(Whitley Beaumont MSS. D/1/63 1540; Poll Tax Returns 1379.)

Appendix XII

SEYMOUR (SOMERSET): Quarterly 1 and 4 *or* on a pile *gules* between six fleur-de-lis *azure,* three lions passant guardant *or.* 2 and 3 *gules* two wings conjoined in lure, tips downward, *or.*

Sir John William Ramsden, 5th Baronet, married 1865 Helen Seymour, daughter of Edward, 12th Duke of Somerset. The 2nd and 3rd quarters are the Arms of Seymour and the 1st and 4th quarters an honourable augmentation granted by Henry VIII to the family of his wife Jane Seymour.

SOOTHILL: *Gules* an eagle displayed *argent.*

John Soothill and his wife Alice Nevile had, among their nine daughters one Alice who on 20th June 1483 married John Beaumont of Lascelles Hall.

(Foster's *Yorkshire Pedigrees.*)

STRINGER: *Sable* three eagles displayed erminois.

Richard Beaumont of Whitley Beaumont married 11th June 1699 Katherine, heiress of Thomas Stringer of Sharleston. Richard was the son of Richard Beaumont (d. 1691) and Frances Lowther, daughter of Sir William Lowther of Swillington. Richard died without issue 27th June 1704.

(Memorial Kirkheaton Church.)

THORNHILL: *Gules,* two bars gemel and a chief *argent.*

366

Appendix XII

The Thornhills originally held land, by confirmation from de Warenne, in the area of Halifax, *circa* 1169. Sir Richard Thornhill (died 1287) married Matilda, daughter of Thomas de Ficksby. His great-grandson, Thomas Thornhill, (living *circa* 1374), (the second son of Sir Bryan Thornhill) married Margaret Lacy of Cromwell-botham, near Brighouse. The Arms are recorded as being borne *circa* 1560 and quarterings of Totehill, Ficksby, Marsh, Trigot, Byrton and Booth were confirmed in 1666.

(Dugdale's *Visitation of Yorkshire*, 1666.)

TOTEHILL of Rastrick: *or* on a chevron *sable* three crescents *argent*.

Early in the fifteenth century Richard Thornhill of Fixby married Margaret Totehill. She was the granddaughter of Thomas Totehill and his wife Modesta who herself was the daughter of Thomas Fixby of Fixby.

TYAS: *Argent* a fess *sable* and in chief three hammers each in bend sinisterwise *sable*.

This family has a tomb and inscription in the small Lede chapel near the Battle of Towton Memorial on the by-road from Wakefield to Tadcaster (shortly after the A.1 underpass). The inscription reads: HIS IACET NOBILIS MILES BALDVINUS TEUTONICUS.

Sir Baldwin married Marget Notton (nee Elland) and thus, from her deceased husband, inherited Woodsome Hall. In addition to Lede, Baldwin held land in Farnley—hence Farnley Tyas.

A Subsidy Roll of 1297 shows Francis Tyas, son of Baldwin, paying tax on ten sheep at sixpence each. *Circa* 1370 the Woodsome Estates were conveyed by the Tyases to the Finchenden family.

(Dodsworth *Church Notes,* 1619–1631. Yorkshire Archaelogical Society 1904.)

DE VERE: Quarterly *gules* and *or* in the first quarter a molet *argent.*

John Fitz Eustace, who assumed the surname de Laci, and was 6th Constable of Chester, married Alice de Vere.

VICTORIA: Quarterly 1 and 4 England, 2 Scotland, 3 Ireland.

These occur above the West door in the nave of Huddersfield Parish Church where they are unusually displayed on a lozenge.

A fine emblazonment may be seen on the Market Hall.

WAKEFIELD–SEE OF: *Or* a fleur-de-lis *azure* on a chief *azure* three celestial crowns *or.*

The gold shield with its blue fleur-de-lis is based on the former Arms of the Borough of Wakefield. The earlier Arms were a blue shield with a gold fleur-de-lis and were adopted in 1888 when the See of Wakefield was created. The basic Arms of the See being the colour reversal of the city's Arms. It was not until 1932 that the city obtained a grant of Arms when the royal character of the adopted city Arms was differenced by edging the fleur-de-lis with ermine.

The Arms of the See show their religious character by the celestial crowns.

The Arms of the See are to be found in many local churches and in the chancel of Almondbury where they form the last section of emblazonments of the holders of the advowson.

DE WARENNE: Chequy *or* and *azure*.

This famous mediaeval family comes from Bellencombre, near Dieppe, where they were neighbours of de Laci. Once settled in England the Warennes held, in addition to other lands, Elland, Brighouse, Halifax and Holmfirth. The de Warenne castle was at Sandal near Wakefield. These possessions cut through those of their Huddersfield neighbours, the de Lacis. The Conqueror's disposition of baronial land was very cunning.

John de Warenne (1286–1347) married Joanna Bar, whose mother was Eleanor, eldest daughter of Edward I. John had a mistress, Maude de Nerford, by whom he had some illegitimate children. John wished to divorce Joan and settle his estates on Maude's children. His neighbour, Thomas Laci disapproved and so John, knowing Thomas's wife Alice to be staying at the Laci's Canford Castle in Dorset, seized Alice and took her to live with him at John's castle at Reigate, in 1317. From this precipitate action arose the long lasting dispute between the local supporters of de Warenne and de Laci.

John de Warenne (1231– 1304) was at the Siege of Carlaverock: 'John the good Earl of Warren held the reins to regulate and govern the second squadron, as he who well knew how to lead noble and honourable men. His banner was handsomely chequered with gold and azure.'

(*Siege of Carlaverock*: Nicolas, 1828. *Reigate: Its Story Through the Ages*: Hooper, 1945. *Complete Peerage,* Vol. vii, 1896: G. E. C. Cockayne.)

Appendix XII

WEST RIDING COUNTY COUNCIL: *Ermine* a rose *argent* barbed and seeded proper, en soleil *or*, on a chief *gules* three roses *argent* barbed and seeded proper.

The rose, as a badge, was first used gold by Henry III. Edmund Crouchback, brother of Edward I bore a red rose. In opposition to the Lancastrians, the Yorkist Richard Plantagenet, claiming descent from the Mortimers, used their badge of a white rose. Edward IV placed the rose on a sun as a badge, the sun having been a badge of Richard II.

The Arms were granted on 2nd February 1927, together with a badge: 'A rose *argent*, barbed and seeded proper ensigned by a mural crown *or*.' The possession of a badge means that the County Council have a right to fly a standard.

The County Borough of Huddersfield is surrounded by the West Riding administrative area and so the Arms can be seen beyond the Borough boundaries.

WHALLEY ABBEY: *Gules/Azure* three whales haurient *or*, in the mouth of each a crozier *or*.

John Fitz Eustace, 6th Constable of Chester, who took the name and Arms of Laci, founded an Abbey at Stanlaw, in 1178. The site proved uncongenial and so the convent was moved to Whalley in 1296.

The rights of fishing were granted to the monks by Henry de Laci. They might fish in the rivers Ribble and Hodder on all days except Sundays, having, already, fishing rights in the River Calder.

In the reign of Edward II the monks had possession of parts of the rents of the lord's mill on the Colne.

The reason for the doubt over the tincture of the field arises from Whitaker stating it as gules, and the Abbey gates and Parish Church showing it as azure. While Edmonson and Moule term the fish Whales, there is a reference to the Arms being three silver fish (salmon?) on a blue ground.

(*History of the Parish of Whalley*: Whitaker, 1801.)

Appendix XII

WHITTINGTON: *Gules* a fess compony *or* and *azure,* in chief a martlet *or*.

Richard Piers Whittington was appointed Vicar of Almondbury in 1923, following the Reverend Longford. After leaving Almondbury in 1928 the Reverend Whittington was a Canon of Wakefield Cathedral and Rural Dean of Pontefract. His Arms are to be seen on the North wall of the Chancel in Almondbury Parish Church.

WIGGIN: Argent on a chevron *azure* between three quatrefoils each charged with four roundels per fess *gules* and *vert* three bezants.

Richard Henry Beaumont of Whitley Beaumont (born on 5th August 1805, died 1857) married on the 3rd December 1831, Catherine daughter of Timothy Wiggin of the U.S.A.

The principal device in the Arms, the red and green quatre foil is connected with the Huddersfield area. The word 'wiggin' is a dialect term for Mountain Ash. The berries were worn as a protection against witchcraft. A local witch was once heard to say 'I think I must give this Thomas Bromhall over, for they tye soe much Whighen about him'. A witch called Mashpot was foiled in her attempts because her selected victim carried three pieces of wiggin from three different lords' lands.

(Hatchment in Kirkheaton Church. Depositions from York Castle 1674.)

WILKINSON: *Azure* a fess erminois between three unicorns passant *argent*.

The Wilkinson family were associated with Greenhead. Matthew Wilkinson died on 21st November 1688 and his grave was in the second Huddersfield Parish Church. The third Parish Church contains the grave of John Wilkinson of Greenhead, magistrate, who married Ellen, daughter of John Townley of Newhouse. John Wilkinson died 29th February 1727. It is possible that the same John Wilkinson acquired Gledholt Hall in 1686 and re-modelled it. Over the doorway is a stone bearing the inscription I.W.E. 1720.

(Brooke MSS. Huddersfield Reference Library.)

WODE: *Argent* between two bendlets three fleurs-de-lis, a bordure engrailed *sable*.

These were the Arms used by the Wodes of Longley. In fact the Arms really belonged to a family of Wode of Darington, Shropshire. The first evidence of the Wodes is in 1342 when Marjorie Wode, a widow, stopped an action against Sir John Beaumont. John Wode (1475–1538) was the father of Johanna Wode (died 1565) who married William Ramsden in 1531. William Ramsden was about 18 years old and Johanna about 24 years old.

John Wode had a daughter Cecily who married 1541 Thomas Savile and Elizabeth who married Thomas Kay. John Wode himself had married, 25th August 1501, Elizabeth daughter of Richard Beaumont of Whitley Beaumont. John Wode had an illegitimate son George who for a while held property in Huddersfield. However, there is evidence of a 'Lease for 21 years at 14/– per annum by Richard Beaumont of Whitley, Esq., to Elizabeth Wodd, widow of John Wodd and Thomas Wodd her son.' Further, there is a Grant of Arms, 1550, by William Harvey, Norroy, to Thomas Wode of Longley, the Arms being '*sable* on a bend *argent* three fleurs-de-lis of the field'. William Harvey states that these Arms are based on those borne by Thomas's family. It is possible that John Wode, prior to 1538 became a member of the Church of England, but on his wife and son refusing to change from Roman Catholicism, he disowned them, thus such pedigrees as exist do not show Thomas.

Appendix XII

(*Whitley Beaumont Archives*: No. 228 November 8th 1554. Ramsden MSS. Huddersfield Reference Library.)

WORMALL: *Azure* a fess ermine between three boars couped *or*.

Opposite Almondbury Parish Church stands Wormall Hall, a stone building with a black and white timbered upper storey. The initials I.W.M. 1631 over the doorway refer to Isaac Wormall and his wife Mary. Isaac was born in 1600 and died 1642. Isaac was the first to establish a charitable connection with Almondbury Grammar School by charging a piece of land in 1633 with five shillings for the use of the school master. His great-grandson, Israel Wormall, devised his estates so that £5 should be paid to the schoolmaster, the income from the residue to go to charitable uses. In 1833 the Charity was reorganised giving an additional £10 to the schoolmaster on condition that four poor Almondbury boys should be educated at the school. In 1881, save for an annual £50 paid to the Technical College until 1905, the Charity was amalgamated with the endowment of the Grammar School.

(*History of the Church and Parish of Almondbury*: Hulbert, 1882.)

YORK–Archbishopric: *Gules* two keys in saltire endorsed *argent* in chief an Imperial Crown *or*.

Huddersfield lies in the archiepiscopal See of York.

The present Arms appear as early as 1397 on Archbishop Waldby's seal. Formerly the Crown was the Papal Tiara.

The Minster is dedicated to St Peter, whose symbol is the crossed keys . . . 'And I will give unto thee the keys of the Kingdom of Heaven and whatsoever thou shalt bind on earth shall be bound in Heaven and whatsoever thou shalt loose on earth shall be loosed in Heaven' (Matthew 16.v.19).

(*Ecclesiastical Heraldry*: Woodward 1894.)

BIBLIOGRAPHY AND SOURCE MATERIAL

GENERAL WORKS ON THE HISTORY OF HUDDERSFIELD

BALMFORTH, OWEN. *Jubilee History of the Corporation of Huddersfield.* Alfred Jubb, Huddersfield. 1918.

DYSON, TAYLOR. *The History of Huddersfield and District.* 2nd. ed. Alfred Jubb, Huddersfield. 1951.

HOBKIRK, CHARLES P. *Huddersfield: its History and Natural History.* 2nd. ed. Simpkin, Marshall & Co., London, 1868.

PARSONS, EDWARD. *The Miscellaneous History of Leeds, Halifax, Huddersfield, etc.* Simpkin, Marshall & Co., London, 1834.

SYKES, D. F. E. *The History of Huddersfield and its Vicinity.* Advertiser Press, Huddersfield. 1898.

Coronation Souvenir Handbook. Alfred Jubb, Huddersfield, 1937.

DIRECTORIES

Baines Directory of the County of York, Vol. I, The West Riding, 1822.

Huddersfield Directory and Year Book. George Harper, Chronicle Works, Huddersfield. 1873.

LAWTON, GEORGE. *Collection Relative to the Dioceses of York and Ripon.* Rivington, London. 1842.

Lewis's Topographical Directory of England. 1831.

Parkin's Almanack: 1863–73.

Pigot's Commercial Directory. 1819–20.

White's Directory. 1866 and 1870.

THE LOCAL COLLECTION OF THE HUDDERSFIELD PUBLIC LIBRARY CONTAINS:

Huddersfield Chronicle. 1850 to 1916.

Huddersfield Daily Chronicle. 1871 to 1916.

Huddersfield Daily Examiner. 1871 to the present day.

Huddersfield Observer. 1868 to 1871.

Bibliography

Huddersfield Weekly News. 1871 to 1879.
Huddersfield Weekly Examiner. 1855 to the present day.
Halifax and Huddersfield Express. 1831 to 1841.
Leeds Mercury. 1800 to 1849.
Yorkshire Factory Times. 1889 to 1913.

Of particular interest are:
BETJEMAN, JOHN, 'Huddersfield Discovered': *The Weekend Telegraph*, 2 October 1964.
HIRST, C. C. 'Woollen Manufacture': *The Huddersfield Examiner*, 17 & 24 September 1940.
'Huddersfield Past and Present': Supplement to *The Warehouseman & Draper*, 29 September 1900.
The Huddersfield Examiner. Supplement on the occasion of the paper's own jubilee 1851–1911, 9 September 1911.
The Huddersfield Examiner. On the occasion of Huddersfield's Diamond Jubilee: 22 September 1928.
The Huddersfield Examiner. 12 January to 29 March 1968: an excellent series of twelve weekly articles by Stanley Chadwick.
The Yorkshire Observer. On the occasion of Huddersfield's Diamond Jubilee, 6 July 1928.

REFERENCES

Some of these works have been used for more than one part of the book, in which case they are classified under the earliest chapter for which they have been of value. Items marked * are Ravensknowle Museum Publications.

CHAPTER I

AHIER, PHILIP. *The Story of Castle Hill.* Advertiser Press, Huddersfield. 1946.
COLLINGWOOD, W. G. *Angles, Danes and Norse in Huddersfield.** 2nd ed. Swindlehurst and Nicholson, Huddersfield. 1929.
PETCH, JAMES A. *Early Man.** Advertiser Press: Huddersfield. 1924.
RICHMOND, IAN A. *Huddersfield in Roman Times.** Huddersfield. 1925.
WOODHEAD, T. W. *Climate, Vegetation and Man.** Huddersfield. 1931.

Bibliography

CHAPTER II

AHIER, PHILIP. *The Story of the Three Parish Churches of St Peter in Huddersfield*, Part I. Advertiser Press, Huddersfield. 1948.

CHADWICK, S. J. 'Kirklees Priory': *Yorkshire Archaeological Journal.* Vol. XVI.

DARBY, H. C. and MAXWELL, I. S. *The Domesday Geography of Northern England.* Cambridge University Press. 1962.

CHAPTER III

'Almondbury in Feudal Times': *Yorkshire Archaeological Journal.* Vol. II.

CRUMP, W. B. *Huddersfield Highways Down the Ages.** Advertiser Press. Huddersfield. 1949.

Paterson's Roads 1829 (18th Edition).

CHAPTER IV

BENTLEY, PHYLLIS. *Colne Valley Cloth.* Huddersfield and District Woollen Export Group. 1947.

CRUMP, W. B. and GHORBAL, G. *History of the Huddersfield Woollen Industry.** Alfred Jubb, Huddersfield. 1935.

CRUMP, W. B. *The Leeds Woollen Industry, 1780–1820.*

HEATON, H. *The Yorkshire Woollen and Worsted Industries*, Oxford, 2nd ed. 1965.

WILSON, E. CARUS. 'The Woollen Industry': *Cambridge Economic History of Europe.* Vol. II. Chap, VI. Cambridge. 1952.

CHAPTER V

'Archbishop Herring's Visitation Returns 1743': *Yorkshire Archaeological Society.* 1929.

ENGLISH, B. A. (ed.) *West Riding Enclosure Awards.* National Register of Archives. 1965.

STOCK, PERCY. *Foundations* (History of Salendine Nook Baptist Church). Edward Mortimer, Halifax. 1933.

The Journal of John Wesley. Standard ed. 8 vols. London. 1909 to 1916.

VENN, HENRY, Rev. L. D. (ed.) *The Life of Rev. H. Venn, M.A.* 3rd ed. John Hatchard and Son: London. 1835.

Bibliography

CHAPTER VI

ATKINSON, F. (ed.) *Some aspects of the 18th Century Woollen and Worsted Industry in Halifax*, Bankfield Museum, Halifax, 1956.

LIPSON, E. *The History of the Woollen and Worsted Industries*. Frank Cass, London. 1965.

STOCKS, W. B. *Pennine Journey*. Advertiser Press, Huddersfield. 1958.

CHAPTER VII

BERRY, R. P. *History of the Volunteer Infantry of Huddersfield*. Simpkin Marshall, London. 1903.

COLE, G. D. H. *Chartist Portraits*. Macmillan. 1941.

CROFT, W. R. *History of the Factory Movement*. Whitehead and Sons, Huddersfield. 1888.

DRIVER, CECIL. *Tory Radical*, Oxford University Press, New York. 1946.

GARDINER, ARTHUR. *The Industrial Revolution and Child Slavery*. A. T. Green and Company, Slaithwaite. 1948.

LODGE, A. *Sad Times*. Joseph Woodhead: Huddersfield. 1870.

PEEL, F. *The Risings of the Luddites*, Heckmondwike 1880.

Radical Papers. A collection of the pamphlets of Joshua Hobson and others held at Ravensknowle Museum.

Report of Select Committee appointed to consider the state of the Woollen Manufacture in England, 1806. *Reports* 1806 Vol. III.

SYKES, D. F. E. *Ben O'Bills, the Luddite*. Worker Press, Huddersfield.

The Radcliffe Papers, 126/26, 27 and 46. Copies of the correspondence of Sir Joseph Radcliffe about the year 1812, held by Sheepscar Library, Leeds.

THOMPSON, E. P. *The Making of the English Working Class*. Gollancz. 1963.

WHITE, R. J. *Waterloo to Peterloo*. Heinemann. 1957.

CHAPTER VIII

A *Historical Record of St Patrick's Church Huddersfield 1832 to 1932*. Swindlehurst and Nicholson, Huddersfield.

AHIER, PHILIP. *The Story of the Three Parish Churches of St Peter in Huddersfield*: Parts II and III. Advertiser Press, Huddersfield. 1948 to 1950.

Bibliography

Banking in Huddersfield. Miscellaneous papers with some original bank notes held at Ravensknowle Museum.

GOODWIN, A. 'How the Ancient Parish of Halifax was Divided': *Halifax Antiquarian Society Papers*. 1961.

HARTLEY, W. C. E. *Notes on Huddersfield Banks*: MSS held by Huddersfield Public Library. 1951.

Jubilee Year Book of New North Road Baptist Chapel. J. E. Wheatley, Huddersfield. 1896.

SYKES, A. W. *Ramsden Street Chapel 1825 to 1925*. Advertiser Press: Huddersfield. 1925.

WEATHERHEAD, A. S. *Holy Trinity Huddersfield 1819 to 1904*. J. Broadbent, Huddersfield. 1913.

WOODHEAD, T. W. *History of the Huddersfield Water Supplies.** Wheatley Dyson, Huddersfield. 1939.

CHAPTER IX

CLAPHAM, J. H. 'Transference of the Worsted Industry from East Anglia to the West Riding': *Economic Journal*. Vol. XX. 1910.

DAWBARN, WILLIAM. *Market Days in Manufacturing Towns—Huddersfield*. Essays, tales, etc. Virtue and Company, London. 1862.

Read Hollidays—a History of the Rise and Development of the Firm. Published privately. November. 1914.

UNWIN, G. *The Transition to the Factory System*. English Historical Review Vol. XXXVI 1922.

CHAPTER X

BATEMAN, JOSIAH. *The Holmfirth Flood*. Seeley, London. 1852.

DYSON, TAYLOR, *Almondbury and its Ancient School*. Advertiser Press, Huddersfield, 1926.

Huddersfield Improvement Bill. Minutes of Evidence Select Committee of House of Lords 19th June 1848, House of Commons 24th July 1848.

Huddersfield Tenant Right Question. A Memorial of Deputation. 1858. Copy held by Huddersfield Public Library.

NORMINGTON, T. *The Lancashire and Yorkshire Railway*. John Heywood: London and Manchester. 1898.

Bibliography

CHAPTER XI

AHIER, PHILIP. *Studies in Local Topography*. Advertiser Press, Huddersfield. 1933 to 1935.

Borough of Huddersfield, Charter of Incorporation (copy). S. Brown, Huddersfield. 1868.

Minutes of Evidence. Select Committee of the House of Commons— House of Lords Record Office Reports Vol. XIII 1852–3.

Privy Council Papers P.C. 8/142 (dated Dec. 1867–May 1868).

CHAPTER XII

BROOK, ROY. *The Tramways of Huddersfield*. Advertiser Press, Huddersfield. 1959.

History of the Library Movement in Huddersfield. Public Library Handbook.

'The Corporation Electricity Supply: Huddersfield'. *Lighting:* 1 February 1894.

The Rise of the British Gas Industry. The Gas Council.

WARRILOW, W. E. 'In Old Huddersfield'. *The Electrical Times*. 25 October 1928.

CHAPTER XIII

CROWTHER, A. *A History of Huddersfield College 1839 to 1937*. Thesis. University of Leeds. 1959.

CURTIS, S. J. *History of Education in Great Britain*. University Tutorial Press. 1965.

DARWELL. *A History of Elementary Education*. Thesis. 1951. Copy held in Huddersfield Public Library.

HINCHCLIFFE, G. *A History of King James's Grammar School in Almondbury*. Advertiser Press, Huddersfield. 1963.

CHAPTER XIV

'A Century of Wool Machinery Making': *The Textile Manufacturer*. December 1935.

Alternating Current Electric Motors. Brook Motors Limited. 1954.

Broadbent Complete One Hundred Years 1864 to 1964. Published for Thomas Broadbent and Sons Limited, Huddersfield.

379

Bibliography

DONELLY, DESMOND. *David Brown's.* Collins, London. 1960.

Hexagon Courier: Supplement to the magazine of I.C.I. Limited. December 1965.

Hopkinsons. Booklet 5100. Published for Hopkinsons Limited, Huddersfield.

John Taylors Limited 1856 to 1956. Published for John Taylors Limited, Huddersfield.

One Hundred Years of Service 1850 to 1950. Published for W. C. Holmes and Company, Huddersfield.

SADLER, M. E. Report on Secondary and Technical Education in Huddersfield (1904).

The Engineer's Practical Guide and the Working of the Steam Engine Explained by the Use of the Indicator. 7th ed. Hopkinson and Company, Huddersfield. 1875.

CHAPTER XV

BURGIN, T. and EDSON, P. *Spring Grove.* Oxford University Press, London. 1967.

DRIFFIELD, L. V. *Huddersfield Incorporated Chamber of Commerce History 1853 to 1953.*

Huddersfield and District Trades and Industrial Council. Jubilee Souvenir. Alfred Jubb, Huddersfield. 1935.

Huddersfield and District Trades and Industrial Council. 75th Anniversary. Huddersfield Examiner. 1960.

Huddersfield and District Trades and Industrial Council. 80th Anniversary. Huddersfield Examiner. 1965.

Huddersfield Sells Textiles. Published for Huddersfield Junior Chamber of Commerce. 1966.

CHAPTER XVI

Local Government and the Public services: all material supplied by Corporation Departments and the Public Utility services.

CHAPTER XVII

CHADWICK, STANLEY. *Northern Union.* Venturers' Press, Huddersfield. 1946.

Bibliography

Huddersfield and District Cricket League. Jubilee Handbook. 1891 to 1951.

Huddersfield Town A.F.C. Photographs, History and Year Book. 1925 to 1926.

MALLALIEU, J. P. W. *Sporting Days.* Phoenix Books, London. 1955.

Stanley Chadwick's Rugby League Almanac 1952. Rugby League Review.

THOMSON, A. A. *Hirst and Rhodes.* Epworth Press. 1959.

CHAPTER XVIII

CHADWICK, STANLEY. *Theatre Royal.* Advertiser Press, Huddersfield. 1941.

'Hope Bank Pleasure Gardens': *The Brook, July/August* 1965. Brook Motors Works newspaper.

WILMHURST, W. L. and CROWTHER, S. H. *The Huddersfield Choral Society.* Huddersfield Examiner. 1961.

CHAPTER XIX

Huddersfield Town Centre Map. Final Draft. Building Design Partnership. December 1965.

APPENDICES

ARMITAGE GOODALL, *Place Names of South West Yorkshire.* Cambridge University Press. 1914.

Climatological Atlas of the British Isles. (M.O. 488) H.M.S.O. 1952.

DYSON, TAYLOR. *Place Names and Surnames.* Simpkin Marshall, London. 1944.

EASTHER, A. Rev. *Glossary of the Dialect of Almondbury and Huddersfield.* English Dialect Society. 1883.

HAIGH, W. E. *A New Glossary of the Dialect of the Huddersfield District.* Oxford University Press: London. 1928.

Huddersfield Meterological Survey 1965. Thunderstorm Census Organization Publication. No. 66/60. February 1966.

Rainfall Map–National Average 1881 to 1915. H.M.S.O. 1949.

REANEY, P. H. *Dictionary of British Surnames.* Routledge and Kegan Paul: London. 1958.

SMITH, A. H. *The Place Names of the West Riding of Yorkshire.* Cambridge University Press. 1961.

Bibliography

ITEMS OF GENERAL INTEREST

BENTLEY, PHYLLIS. *O Dreams, O Destinations.* Gollancz: London 1962.

CULLEY, NORMAN. *A Sketch Book :* Part I. Wheatley Dyson, Huddersfield. 1938.

CULLEY, NORMAN. *The Second Book of Huddersfield.* Wheatley Dyson, Huddersfield. 1939.

DAVIES, STELLA. *North Country Bred.* Routledge and Kegan Paul. 1963.

FLETCHER, J. S. *The Making of Modern Yorkshire.* G. Allen and Unwin, London. 1918.

JACKSON, BRIAN, AND MARSDEN, DENNIS. *Education and the Working Class.* Penguin Books, 1966.

LOCKWOOD, ERNEST. *Colne Valley Folk.* Heath Cranton, London. 1936.

MAYHALL, JOHN. *Annals of Yorkshire.* C. H. Johnson, Leeds. 1861.

MITCHELL and DEANE. *Abstract of British Historical Statistics.* Cambridge University Press. 1962.

MORRIS, JAMES. 'A Ticket to Huddersfield': *Encounter.* May 1963.

PARSONS, E. *History and Description of the Manufacturing Districts of the West Riding* (2 Vols.). 1834.

SPENCER, NOËL. *A Scrap Book of Huddersfield.* 2 vols. Vol. I printed by Wheatley Dyson, Huddersfield. Vol. II printed by S. P. Laud, Norwich. 1948.

TATE, W. E. *The Parish Chest.* Cambridge 1961.

TATE, W. E. and SINGLETON, E. B. *A History of Yorkshire.* Darwen Finlayson, London. 1960.

ACKNOWLEDGEMENTS

THE AUTHOR acknowledges with thanks the assistance given to him by the following: the Rt Hon Alice Bacon, M.P., of the Home Office, for access to material in the Public Record Office: John Goodchild, M.A., of the County Hall, Wakefield, for access to the County Archives: J. M. Collinson, M.A., of the Sheepscar Library, Leeds, for granting access to transcripts of the Radcliffe MSS. and maps of Huddersfield in 1844–50: Miss A. G. Foster, B.A., of the Yorkshire Archaeological Society, for use of its library: Joseph Turner of Blackpool for material relating to his father, Sir Joseph Turner: the Rev. J. C. Bowmer, M.A., B.D., for access to records in the Methodist archives: the House of Lords Record Office for granting access to Parliamentary Papers: E. W. Aubrook, F.M.A., of the Tolson Memorial Museum, Huddersfield, for granting research facilities and assistance from members of the museum staff: A. R. Bielby, M.A., of Huddersfield New College, for access to research material: F. S. Hudson, M.A. and J. P. Toomey, M.A., both of King James's Grammar School, for information relating to Castle Hill: H. S. Bell, F.T.I., of the Huddersfield College of Technology, for advice and assistance from members of the Department of Textile Industries: and W. E. Tate, B.Litt., F.S.A., late of the Department of Education, University of Leeds, for advice on research materials.

Interviews have been granted by: Harry Armitage, B.Sc., formerly Headmaster of Hillhouse Central School: W. B. Stocks and Neil Fraser, both of the Huddersfield Railway Circle: Rev. Canon Anthony Hunter, B.A., Vicar of Huddersfield: Rev. Harold Hammond of the Queen Street Mission: Rev. Fr. P. E. McGee of St Patrick's Church: S. Morris Bower of the Huddersfield Meteorological Station, Oakes: Donald R. Sykes, M.A., on Yorkshire dialect material: G. H. Grattan-Guinness, B.A., B.Sc., A.K.C., Deputy Chief Education officer, Huddersfield: George Richardson of Huddersfield Town AFC, player from 1914 to 1923: the late Donald M. Sharp, J.P., of Huddersfield & District Associated Trades & Industrial Council: Arthur Sunley of the Huddersfield Amateur Swimming Club: D. G. Duke-Evans of the Huddersfield Incorporated

Acknowledgements

Chamber of Commerce: Richard Greenhalgh of Standard Fireworks Ltd: Wilfred Slater of Huddersfield C. & A.C.: the late Norman Clegg for material on Methodism in Huddersfield: Harold Blackburn of L. B. Holliday & Co. Ltd: Anthony Galvin of Huddersfield Town A.F.C.: Colin Garthwaite of Huddersfield & District Cricket League: Clifford Thorpe of the Ministry of Labour Employment Exchange, Huddersfield: Mrs Evelyn Bray of the Huddersfield Brass Band Association: John O'Connell, B.A., of the Oastler College of Education.

Information, material and assistance have been received from: C. & J. Hirst & Sons Ltd: Brook Motors Ltd: John Haigh & Sons Ltd: J. L. Brierley Ltd: John Taylors Ltd: Taylor & Lodge Ltd: Yorkshire Electricity Board: Huddersfield Choral Society: Huddersfield Amateur Swimming Club: North Eastern Gas Board: Thomas Broadbent & Sons Ltd: W. C. Holmes Ltd: I.C.I. Ltd, Huddersfield: David Brown Gear Industries Ltd: John Brooke & Sons Ltd, Armitage Bridge: Hopkinsons Ltd: Yorkshire County Cricket Club: Huddersfield Conservative Association: Huddersfield Liberal Association: Huddersfield & Kirkburton Central Labour Party: Salendine Nook Baptist Church: Milton Congregational Church: Birkby Baptist Church: Almondbury Parish Church: Holy Trinity Church: and the Society of Friends.

The following Departments of the Huddersfield Corporation were also consulted: Chief Constable: Estate and Property Management: Welfare: Health: Borough Engineer: Work Study: Education: Chief Fire Officer: Road Safety: Civil Defence: Borough Treasurer: Passenger Transport: Waterworks: Weights and Measures: Architecture and Town Planning: Markets: and Public Cleansing and Haulage.

All the items on heraldry and genealogy are by L. E. Rothwell, Heraldic Adviser to the County Borough of Huddersfield.

Illustrations in this book have been contributed by Noël Spencer, Headmaster of the Huddersfield School of Art from 1934 to 1946: Leslie Taylor, a student at the school of art from 1964 to 1967: the book jacket and heraldic illustrations were drawn by Paul Hampson, student at the Huddersfield School of Art from 1965 to 1968: and finally, maps and other heraldic illustrations were drawn by Arthur Boughey.

384

INDEX

Index

Index

Index

Index

Index

Index

Index

Stainland, 10, 55, 142, 221, 365
Stamp duty, 172
Standedge, 51, 147, 149
Standedge Tunnel, 149
Stannard, Rev. J. T., 126
Stansfield, W. R. C., M.P., 123, 124, 168
Starkey Family, 97, 130, 169
Starkey, Joseph, 169
Starkey, Thomas, 154
Station, Railway, 148, 174, 241, 276
Stephen, King, 16, 17
Stephenson, Clem, footballer, 260
Steam Engine, 73-5
Stocks, William, constable, 122, 152
Storthes (Hall), 339, 351
Street lamps, 114, 249
Summers, William, M.P., 191-2
Sunderland, Mrs (Susan Sykes), 274
Swinden, Arthur, footballer, 265
Sykes, Sir Charles, M.P., 219-20, 267
Sykes, D. F. E., 85, 122, 187, 207
Sykes, T. Fletcher, 280

Taunton Commissioners 1868, 200
Taxable land, 13
Taxation, 83
Taylor, Enoch and James, 78, 89
Taylor, Jeffrey, 263
Taylor, John, manufacturer, 141
Taylor, Ken, 267
Taylor, Law, Mayor, 243
Taylor, Malcolm, 271
Taylor Hill, 52, 75, 92
Technical College, 203, 205, 232-3,
  241, 255, 339, 343
Tenant Right Dispute 1858, 156-8, 173
Ten Hours Bill, 97-105, 111, 206, 276
Tentering, 41
Terrington, Lord, of Huddersfield, 192
Thornhill, 9, 15
Thornhill, Thomas, Squire of Fixby,
  99, 107-10
Town Hall, Huddersfield, 151-2, 176,
  185, 275, 279

Upperhead Row, 49, 52, 55, 113, 117,
  133, 141, 340

Wakefield, 14, 17, 24, 32, 36, 46-7, 52,
  65, 76, 117, 124, 149, 190, 193,
  198, 240, 264, 316, 336, 362, 364,
  368
Waterloo, 182, 222-4, 226, 234, 266
Waterworks (1743), 55. *See also* Acts
Watson, Willie, 268
Weaving, 35, 40-1, 135-8, 141
Welfare Department, 250

Wellington Mills; bombed 1940, 236
Wesley, John, 61-65, 80, 128
Wessenden Moor, 2, 224
Wessenden Reservoir, 73, 159, 178
Westgate, 117, 118, 142, 152, 181, 207,
  274, 277, 289, 291
West Nab, 2
West Riding County Council, 193, 256,
  370
Whiteacre, John, 122, 129
White, John, 152, 277
Whitefield, George, 64
Whiteley, William, engineer, 213
Whitley Beaumont, 337, 359-60, 371-2
Wholesale Market, 184
Wilberforce, William, 129
Willans, J. E., J.P., 168, 233
Willans, William, 125, 168, 324
Willeying, 39
William I, King, 11, 13, 14
Wilson, Benjamin, brewer and banker,
  118-19
Wilson, Harold, Freeman, 249, 318,
  324-5
Wilson, Ray, footballer, 262
Wiltshire, 35
Windy Hill, 2
Witch machine, 138
Wodes of Longley, 20, 27, 338, 372
Wood, John (Cropper), 41, 90, 103
Wood, Joseph, 120-2
Woodhead, Ernest, 187, 219, 221, 233
Woodhead, Joseph, 170, 172-3, 192,
  235
Woodhead Road, 52
Woodhouse, 54, 129-30, 245
Woodhouse, Sir James (Lord Terring-
  ton of Huddersfield), 192-3, 218
Woodsome, 21, 195-6, 344-5, 348, 353,
  361, 368
Wool, 29-46, 69-73, 135-9
'Wooldriver', 36-7
Woolven, Alderman J. A., 221
Workhouse, 105
Worsted, 45, 139-41
Wrigley, Ernest, footballer, 265

Yeomanry, 84, 95, 96
York, 3, 5, 6, 8, 31, 32, 37, 43, 46, 47,
  76, 81, 92, 94-5, 97, 103, 108, 117,
  125, 132, 146, 193, 196, 373
Yorkshire, 8, 11, 31, 33-4, 38, 45, 61,
  65, 73, 75, 97-8, 101, 117, 129,
  134-5, 140, 156, 190, 200, 218,
  251, 258, 265, 267-9, 275, 281, 286
Young Men's Mental Improvement
  Society, 203
Youth Orchestra, 281

394